PHP Programming Solutions

Vikram Vaswani

New York   Chicago   San Francisco
Lisbon   London   Madrid   Mexico City   Milan
New Delhi   San Juan   Seoul   Singapore   Sydney   Toronto

The **McGraw·Hill** Companies

Library of Congress Cataloging-in-Publication Data

Vaswani, Vikram.
 PHP programming solutions / Vikram Vaswani.
   p. cm.
 ISBN 0-07-148745-X (alk. paper)
 1. PHP (Computer program language) 2. Web sites—Design. I. Title.
QA76.73.P224V38 2007
005.13'3—dc22
                           2007017013

PHP Programming Solutions

1234567890 DOC DOC 01987

ISBN-13: 978-0-07-148745-0
ISBN-10:   0-07-148745-X

Sponsoring Editor Wendy Rinaldi	**Technical Editor** Chris Cornutt	**Composition** International Typesetting and Composition
Editorial Supervisor Patty Mon	**Copy Editor** Lauren Kennedy	**Illustration** International Typesetting and Composition
Project Manager Rasika Mathur (International Typesetting and Composition)	**Proofreader** Megha Ghai **Indexer** Steve Ingle	**Art Director, Cover** Jeff Weeks
Acquisitions Coordinator Mandy Canales	**Production Supervisor** Jean Bodeaux	**Cover Designer** Pattie Lee

For the baby:
how lucky are we?

About the Author

Vikram Vaswani is the founder and CEO of Melonfire (http://www.melonfire.com/), a consulting services firm with special expertise in open-source tools and technologies. He is a passionate proponent of the open-source movement and frequently contributes articles and tutorials on open-source technologies—including Perl, Python, PHP, MySQL, and Linux—to the community at large. His previous books include *MySQL: The Complete Reference* (McGraw-Hill, 2003; http://www.mysql-tcr.com/) and *How to Do Everything with PHP and MySQL* (McGraw-Hill, 2005; http://www.everythingphpmysql.com/).

Vikram has more than eight years of experience working with PHP and MySQL as an application developer. He is the author of Zend Technologies' *PHP 101* series for PHP beginners, and has extensive experience deploying PHP in a variety of different environments (including corporate intranets, high-traffic Internet Web sites, and mission-critical thin client applications).

A Felix Scholar at the University of Oxford, England, Vikram combines his interest in Web application development with various other activities. When not dreaming up plans for world domination, he amuses himself by reading crime fiction, watching old movies, playing squash, blogging, and keeping an eye out for unfriendly Agents. Read more about him and *PHP Programming Solutions* at http://www.php-programming-solutions.com.

About the Technical Reviewer

Chris has been involved in the PHP community for about eight or nine years now. Soon after discovering the language, he started up his new Web site, PHPDeveloper .org, to share the latest happenings and opinions from other PHPers all around the Web. Chris has written for PHP publications such as *php|architect* and the *International PHP Magazine* on topics ranging from geocoding to trackbacks. He also was a coauthor of *PHP String Handling* (Wrox Press, 2003).

Chris lives in Dallas, Texas, with his wife and works for a large natural gas distributor maintaining their Web site and developing Web applications in PHP.

Contents

Acknowledgments

This book was written over the course of a (long!) two years, under some fairly tight deadlines. Fortunately, I was aided immeasurably in the process by a diverse group of people, all of whom played an important role in getting this book into your hands.

First and foremost, I'd like to thank my wife, the most important person in my life. Putting up with me can't be easy, yet she does it with grace, intelligence, and humor—something for which I will always be grateful. This book is dedicated to her.

The editorial and marketing team at McGraw-Hill has been wonderful to work with, as usual. This is my third book with them, and they seem to get better and better with each one. Acquisitions coordinator Mandy Canales, technical editor Chris Cornutt, and editorial director Wendy Rinaldi all guided this book through the development process. I'd like to thank them for their expertise, dedication, and efforts on my behalf.

Finally, for making the entire book-writing process more enjoyable than it usually is, thanks to: Patrick Quinlan, Ian Fleming, Bryan Adams, the Stones, *MAD Magazine*, Scott Adams, FHM, Gary Larson, VH1, George Michael, Kylie Minogue, *Buffy*, Farah Malegam, FM 107.9, Stephen King, Shakira, Anahita Marker, Park End, John le Carre, Barry White, Robert Crais, Robert B. Parker, Baz Luhrmann, Stefy, Anna Kournikova, Swatch, Gaim, Ling's Pavilion, Tonka, HBO, Ferrari, Mark Twain, Tim Burton, Harish Kamath, John Sandford, the Tube, Dido, Google.com, *The Matrix*, Lee Child, Quentin Tarantino, Alfred Hitchcock, Woody Allen, the St. Hugh's College bops, Michael Schumacher, Mambo's and Tito's, Easyjet, Humphrey Bogart, the Library Bar, Brix, Urvashi Singh, 24, Amazon.com, U2, The Three Stooges, Pacha, Oscar Wilde, Punch, Daniel Craig, Kelly Clarkson, Scott Turow, Slackware Linux, Calvin and Hobbes, Blizzard Entertainment, Otto, Pablo Picasso, Popeye and Olive, *The West Wing*, Santana, Rod Stewart, and all my friends, at home and elsewhere.

Introduction

If you're reading this book, you probably already know what PHP is—one of the world's most popular programming languages for Web application development. Widely available and backed by the support of a vociferous and enthusiastic user community, the language was in use on more than *20 million* Web sites at the end of 2006…and that number is only expected to grow!

Personally, I've always believed the reason for PHP's popularity to be fairly simple: It has the unique distinction of being the only open-source server-side scripting language that's both easy to learn and extremely powerful to use. Unlike most modern server-side languages, PHP uses clear, simple syntax and delights in non-obfuscated code; this makes it easy to read and understand, and encourages rapid application development. And then of course, there's cost and availability—PHP is available free of charge on the Internet, for a variety of platforms and architectures, including UNIX, Microsoft Windows, and Mac OS, as well as for most Web servers.

For these reasons, and many more, developers are flocking to PHP in droves. Their managers aren't complaining either—using the PHP platform helps organizations benefit from the cost savings that accompany community-driven software, and simultaneously deliver high-quality products by using community-generated, well-tested PHP widgets to reduce development and deployment time.

Where does this book come in? Well, PHP has hundreds of built-in functions, classes, and extensions; filtering and analyzing these to identify the most appropriate strategy to deal a particular problem is often beyond developers new to the language, especially those working under tight project deadlines. With this book in hand, developers no longer need to worry about this; *PHP Programming Solutions* offers ready-made solutions to 250+ commonly encountered problems, making use of both native and external libraries to teach developers the most effective way to use PHP in their development projects.

Overview

PHP Programming Solutions is a full-fledged developer guide with two primary goals: to deliver solutions to commonly encountered problems, and to educate developers about the wide array of built-in functions and ready-made PHP widgets available to them. Task-based categorization makes it easy to locate solutions, and each section comes with working code, a detailed explanation, and applicable usage tips and guidelines. The solutions described use both PHP's native functions and off-the-shelf PEAR classes.

   PHP Programming Solutions includes coverage of a wide variety of categories, including string and number manipulation, input validation and security, authentication, caching, XML parsing, database abstraction, and more. The solutions are intended to (1) simplify and shorten the application development cycle; (2) reduce test time; (3) improve quality; and (4) provide you, the developer, with the tools you need to quickly solve real PHP problems with minimal time and fuss.

A Word About PHP, PEAR, and PECL

One of the nice things about a community-supported language such as PHP is the access it offers to hundreds of creative and imaginative developers across the world. Within the PHP community, the fruits of this creativity may be found in PEAR, the PHP Extension and Application Repository (`http://pear.php.net/`), and PECL, the PHP Extension Community Library (`http://pecl.php.net/`), which contains hundreds of ready-made widgets and extensions that developers can use to painlessly add new functionality to PHP.

   Using these widgets is often a more efficient alternative to rolling your own code, which is why every chapter in *PHP Programming Solutions* includes between four and ten listings that use PEAR/PECL widgets to solve the defined problem, be it creating an HTML progress bar to track uploads or recursively scanning a directory tree for files matching a particular regular expression. Many of these problems can be solved "by hand," but often that's an inefficient approach when a ready-made PEAR class already exists. This book attempts to make such classes more accessible/visible to developers and educate them about some of the hidden jewels in the PEAR and PECL repositories.

Audience

PHP Programming Solutions is intended for both novice and intermediate developers. To this end, chapters are structured such that they start out by solving fairly easy problems, and then proceed to more difficult/complex ones. This is deliberately done to give inexperienced PHP developers the fundamental knowledge needed to understand the more complex code listings further along in the chapter.

If you're an experienced PHP developer—say, if you've been using PHP for two years or more—it's quite likely that you'll find this book much less useful (than the reader segments described previously). Nevertheless, you will certainly find some listings that will intrigue you. Here's a teaser:

▶ Using a CAPTCHA to protect form submissions (8.18).

▶ Working with the Standard PHP Library (4.3).

▶ Charting task status with a dynamically-updating HTML progress bar (7.10).

▶ Finding out how much resource each line of your PHP script consumes (12.11).

▶ Extracting thumbnails from digital photos (11.18).

▶ Using SOAP to manually generate blog trackbacks (10.16).

▶ Localizing your PHP applications (12.16).

▶ And lots more!

Pre-requisites and Assumptions

In order to use the listings in this book, you will need a functioning PHP 5.x installation, ideally with an Apache 2.x Web server and a MySQL 5.x database server. Many of the listings in this book make use of external (free!) classes and extensions; you will almost certainly need to download these classes, or recompile your PHP build to activate the necessary extensions.

This book also assumes you have some prior knowledge of PHP, as well as familiarity with Hypertext Markup Language (HTML), Cascading Style Sheets (CSS), Structured Query Language (SQL), Extensible Markup Language (XML), and client-side scripting. If you're completely new to PHP, this is probably not the first book you should read—instead, consider working your way through the introductory PHP tutorials at `http://www.php.net/tut.php` and `http://www.melonfire.com/community/columns/trog/archives.php?category=PHP`, or purchasing a beginner guide such as *How to Do Everything with PHP and MySQL* (McGraw-Hill, 2005; `http://www.everythingphpmysql.com/`), and then return to this title.

Organization

This book is organized as both a tutorial and a reference guide, so you can read it any way you like.

▶   If you're not very experienced with PHP, you might find it easier to read the problems and their solutions sequentially, so that you learn basic techniques in a structured manner. This approach is recommended for users new to the language.

▶   If you've already used PHP, or if you're experienced in another programming language and are switching to PHP, you might prefer to use this book as a desktop reference, flipping it open on an as-needed basis to read about specific problems and their solutions. (The extensive index at the back of this book is designed specifically for this sort of quick lookup.)

Here's a quick preview of what each chapter in *PHP Programming Solutions* contains:

Chapter 1, "Working with Strings" discusses common problems when working with strings in PHP. Some of the problems discussed include removing unnecessary whitespace, finding and replacing string patterns, counting and extracting string segments, identifying duplicate words, encrypting text, and generating string passwords.

Chapter 2, "Working with Numbers" discusses number manipulation in PHP. Some of the problems discussed include converting number bases; calculating trigonometric values; working with complex numbers and fractions; generating prime numbers; and translating numbers into words in different languages.

Chapter 3, "Working with Dates and Times" discusses common issues when working with temporal values in PHP. Some of the problems discussed include converting between time zones; calculating the number of days in a month or year; performing date arithmetic; and working with arbitrarily large date values.

Chapter 4, "Working with Arrays" discusses PHP arrays. It includes listings for recursively traversing and searching a series of nested arrays, sorting arrays by more than one key, filtering array elements by user-defined criteria, and swapping array keys and values.

Chapter 5, "Working with Functions and Classes" discusses problems encountered when defining and using functions and classes in PHP. Some of the problems solved include using variable-length argument lists and default arguments; checking class ancestry; overloading class methods; cloning and comparing objects; using abstract classes; and adjusting class member visibility.

Chapter 6, "Working with Files and Directories" is all about PHP's interaction with the file system. Solutions are included for tasks such as searching and replacing patterns within files; comparing file contents; extracting specific lines or bytes from files; recursively processing directories; and converting files between UNIX and MS-DOS formats.

Chapter 7, "Working with HTML and Web Pages" discusses common tasks related to using PHP in a Web application. It includes listings for finding and turning text URLs into HTML hyperlinks; generating Dynamic HTML (DHTML) menu trees from a database; visually displaying the progress of server tasks; and caching and paginating content.

Chapter 8, "Working with Forms, Sessions, and Cookies" discusses common problems of input validation, security, and data persistence. Listings are included for storing and retrieving session variables; authenticating users and protecting pages from unauthorized access; building a session-based shopping cart; and creating persistent objects.

Chapter 9, "Working with Databases" discusses solutions for common problems involving PHP and databases. It includes listings for retrieving a subset of an SQL result set; writing portable database code; performing transactions; protecting special characters in query strings; and storing binary data in a table.

Chapter 10, "Working with XML" discusses common problems related to using PHP with XML. It includes listings for processing node and attribute values; validating XML against Document Type Definitions (DTDs) or Schemas; transforming XML with XSLT style sheets; parsing RSS feeds; and interfacing with Simple Object Access Protocol (SOAP) services.

Chapter 11, "Working with Different File Formats and Network Protocols" is all about interfacing the language with as many servers, protocols, and formats as possible. It includes listings for connecting to FTP servers; reading mail in online mailboxes; querying DNS and WHOIS servers; extracting thumbnails from digital photographs; dynamically generating PDF files; and creating e-mail messages with attachments.

Chapter 12, "Working with Exceptions and Other Miscellanea" discusses common problems related to exception handling and error processing. It also includes solutions for profiling and benchmarking your PHP scripts; executing external programs from within PHP; altering the PHP configuration at run time; creating compiled PHP bytecode; and localizing PHP applications.

Companion Web Site

You can find the PHP code for every single solution in this book on the companion Web site, at `http://www.php-programming-solutions.com`. Code listings are organized by chapter and problem number, and may be directly downloaded and installed to your development environment.

Working with Strings

IN THIS CHAPTER:

I f you're like most novice PHP developers, you probably have only a passing acquaintance with PHP's string functions. Sure, you know how to print output to a Web page, and you can probably split strings apart and glue them back together again. But there's a lot more to PHP's string toolkit than this: PHP has more than 175 string manipulation functions, and new ones are added on a regular basis. Ever wondered what they were all for?

If you have, you're going to be thrilled with the listings in this chapter. In addition to offering you a broad overview of PHP's string manipulation capabilities, this chapter discusses many other tasks commonly associated with strings in PHP— removing unnecessary whitespace, finding and replacing string patterns, counting and extracting string segments, identifying duplicate words, encrypting text and generating string passwords. Along the way, you'll find out a little more about those mysterious string functions, and also learn a few tricks to help you write more efficient code.

1.1 Controlling String Case

Problem

You want to force a string value to upper- or lowercase.

Solution

Use the strtoupper() or strtolower() functions:

```php
<?php
// define string
$rhyme = "And all the king's men couldn't put him together again";

// uppercase entire string
// result: "AND ALL THE KING'S MEN COULDN'T PUT HIM TOGETHER AGAIN"
$ucstr = strtoupper($rhyme);
echo $ucstr;

// lowercase entire string
// result: "and all the king's men couldn't put him together again"
$lcstr = strtolower($rhyme);
echo $lcstr;
?>
```

Comments

When it comes to altering the case of a string, PHP makes it easy with four built-in functions. Two of them are illustrated previously: the `strtoupper()` function uppercases all the characters in a string, while the `strtolower()` function lowercases all the characters in a string.

For more precise control, consider the `ucfirst()` function, which capitalizes the first character of a string (good for sentences), and the `ucwords()` function, which capitalizes the first character of every word in the string (good for titles). Here's an example:

```php
<?php
// define string
$rhyme = "and all the king's men couldn't put him together again";

// uppercase first character of string
// result: "And all the king's men couldn't put him together again"
$ucfstr = ucfirst($rhyme);
echo $ucfstr;

// uppercase first character of every word of string
// result: "And All The King's Men Couldn't Put Him Together Again"
$ucwstr = ucwords($rhyme);
echo $ucwstr;
?>
```

1.2 Checking for Empty String Values

Problem

You want to check if a string value contains valid characters.

Solution

Use a combination of PHP's `isset()` and `trim()` functions:

```php
<?php
// define string
$str = "   ";
```

```
// check if string is empty
// result: "Empty"
echo (!isset($str) || trim($str) == "") ? "Empty" : "Not empty";
?>
```

Comments

You'll use this often when working with form data, to see if a required form field contains valid data or not. The basic technique is simple: use `isset()` to verify that the string variable exists, then use the `trim()` function to trim whitespace from the edges and equate it to an empty string. If the test returns true, it's confirmation that the string contains no value.

> ### NOTE
> It's instructive to note that many developers use PHP's `empty()` function for this purpose. This isn't usually a good idea, because `empty()` will return true even if the string passed to it contains the number 0 (PHP treats 0 as Boolean `false`). So, in the following illustration, the script will produce the result `"Empty"` even though the string variable actually contains data.

```
<?php
// define string
$str = "0";

// check if string is empty
// result: "Empty"
echo (empty($str)) ? "Empty" : "Not empty";
?>
```

1.3 Removing Characters from the Ends of a String

Problem

You want to remove the first/last *n* characters from a string.

Solution

Use the `substr()` function to slice off the required number of characters from the beginning or end of the string:

```
<?php
// define string
$str = "serendipity";
```

```php
// remove first 6 characters
// result: "ipity"
$newStr = substr($str, 6);
echo $newStr;

// remove last 6 characters
// result: "seren"
$newStr = substr($str, 0, -6);
echo $newStr;
?>
```

Comments

The `substr()` function enables you to slice and dice strings into smaller strings. It typically accepts three arguments, of which the last is optional: the string to act on, the position to begin slicing at, and the number of characters to return from its start position. A negative value for the third argument tells PHP to remove characters from the end of the string.

1.4 Removing Whitespace from Strings

Problem

You want to remove all or some whitespace from a string, or compress multiple spaces in a string.

Solution

Use a regular expression to find and replace multiple whitespace characters with a single one:

```php
<?php
// define string
$str = "   this is a string with  lots of    emb e dd   ↵
ed whitespace    ";

// trim the whitespace at the ends of the string
// compress the whitespace in the middle of the string
// result: "this is a string with lots of emb e dd ed whitespace"
$newStr = ereg_replace('[[:space:]]+', ' ', trim($str));
echo $newStr;
?>
```

Comments

There are two steps involved in performing this task. First, use the `trim()` function to delete the unnecessary whitespace from the ends of the string. Next, use the `ereg_replace()` function to find multiple whitespace characters in the string and replace them with a single space. The end result is a string with all extra whitespace removed.

Alternatively, remove all the whitespace from a string, by altering the replacement string used by `ereg_replace()`. The following variant illustrates this:

```php
<?php
// define string
$str = "   this is a string with   lots of    emb e dd  ↵
ed whitespace     ";

// remove all whitespace from the string
// result: "thisisastringwithlotsofembeddedwhitespace"
$newStr = ereg_replace('[[:space:]]+', '', trim($str));
echo $newStr;
?>
```

1.5 Reversing Strings

Problem

You want to reverse a string.

Solution

Use the strrev() function:

```php
<?php
// define string
$cards = "Visa, MasterCard and American Express accepted";

// reverse string
// result: "detpecca sserpxE naciremA dna draCretsaM ,asiV"
$sdrac = strrev($cards);
echo $sdrac;
?>
```

Comments

It's extremely simple, this "give it a string, and `strrev()` gives it back to you in reverse" task. But despite the fact that it's nothing to write home about, `strrev()` is often used to perform some advanced tasks. See the listing in "1.20: Extracting Sentences from a Paragraph" for an example.

1.6 Repeating Strings

Problem

You want to repeat a string *n* times.

Solution

Use the `str_repeat()` function:

```php
<?php
// define string
$laugh = "ha ";

// repeat string
// result: "ha ha ha ha ha ha ha ha ha ha "
$rlaugh = str_repeat($laugh, 10);
echo $rlaugh;
?>
```

Comments

PHP's `str_repeat()` function is equivalent to Perl's x operator: it repeats a string a fixed number of times. The first argument to `str_repeat()` is the string to be replicated; the second is the number of times to replicate it.

The `str_repeat()` function can come in quite handy if you need to print a boundary line of special characters across your output page—for example, an unbroken line of dashes or spaces. To see this in action, view the output of the following code snippet in your browser—it displays a line of ø characters across the page by continuously printing the HTML character code `&Oslash`:

```php
<?php
// define string
$special = "&Oslash;";
```

```
// repeat string
$rspecial = str_repeat($special, 62);
echo $rspecial;
?>
```

1.7 Truncating Strings

Problem

You want to truncate a long string to a particular length, and replace the truncated characters with a custom placeholder—for example, with ellipses.

Solution

Use the substr() function to truncate the string to a specified length, and append the custom placeholder to the truncated string:

```php
<?php
function truncateString($str, $maxChars=40, $holder="...") {
    // check string length
    // truncate if necessary
    if (strlen($str) > $maxChars) {
        return trim(substr($str, 0, $maxChars)) . $holder;
    } else {
        return $str;
    }
}

// define long string
$str = "Just as there are different flavors of client-side scripting,⏎
there are different languages that can be used on
the server as well.";

// truncate and print string
// result: "Just as there are different flavours of..."
echo truncateString($str);

// truncate and print string
// result: "Just as there are di >>>"
echo truncateString($str, 20, " >>>");
?>
```

Comments

The user-defined function `truncateString()` accepts three arguments: the string to truncate, the length at which to truncate it (default 40 characters), and the custom character sequence to use at the point of termination (default ...). Within the function, the `strlen()` function first checks if the string is over or under the permissible limit. If it's over the limit, the `substr()` function slices off the bottom end of the string, and the placeholder is appended to the top end.

1.8 Converting Between ASCII Characters and Codes

Problem

You want to retrieve the American Standard Code for Information Interchange (ASCII) code corresponding to a particular character, or vice versa.

Solution

Use the `ord()` function to get the ASCII code for a character:

```php
<?php
// define character
$char = "\r";

// retrieve ASCII code
// result: 13
$asc = ord($char);
echo $asc;
?>
```

Use the `chr()` function to get the character corresponding to an ASCII code:

```php
<?php
// define ASCII code
$asc = 65;

// retrieve character
// result: "A"
$char = chr($asc);
echo $char;
?>
```

Comments

PHP's `ord()` function retrieves the ASCII code corresponding to a particular character (or the first character, if the argument to `ord()` contains more than one character). The `chr()` function does the reverse, returning the character corresponding to a specific ASCII code.

You can use `chr()` to generate the entire alphabet, if you like:

```php
<?php
// result: "abcd...xyz"
for ($a=97; $a<(97+26); $a++) {
    echo chr($a);
}
?>
```

> **NOTE**
>
> *You can find a list of ASCII characters and codes at* `http://www.lookuptables`
> `.com/,` *and a Unicode table at* `http://www.unicode.org/Public/UNIDATA/`
> `NamesList.txt.`

1.9 Splitting Strings into Smaller Chunks

Problem

You want to break up a long string into smaller segments, each of a fixed size.

Solution

Use the `str_split()` function to break the string into fixed-length "chunks":

```php
<?php
// define string
$str = "The mice jumped over the cat, giggling madly ↵
as the moon exploded into green and purple confetti";

// define chunk size
$chunkSize = 11;

// split string into chunks
// result: [0] = The mice ju [1] = mped over t [2] = he cat, gig
// [3] = gling madly ...
```

```
$chunkedArr = str_split($str, $chunkSize);
print_r($chunkedArr);
?>
```

Comments

The `str_split()` function splits a string into fixed-length blocks and returns them as elements of an array. By default, each "chunk" is one character long, but you can alter this by passing the `str_split()` function a second argument defining the chunk size (as in the previous snippet).

1.10 Comparing Strings for Similarity

Problem

You want to compare two strings to see if they sound similar.

Solution

Use the `metaphone()` function to test if the strings sound alike:

```php
<?php
// compare strings
// result: "Strings are similar"
echo (metaphone("rest") == metaphone("reset")) ? ↵
"Strings are similar" : "Strings are not similar";

// result: "Strings are similar"
echo (metaphone("deep") == metaphone("dip")) ? ↵
"Strings are similar" : "Strings are not similar";

// result: "Strings are not similar"
echo (metaphone("fire") == metaphone("higher")) ? ↵
"Strings are similar" : "Strings are not similar";
?>
```

Comments

PHP's `metaphone()` function—a more accurate version of its `soundex()` function—is one of the more unique ones in the PHP string toolkit. Essentially, this function produces a signature for the way a string sounds; similar-sounding strings produce the same signature. You can use this property to test two strings to see if they're similar—simply calculate the `metaphone()` keys of each string and see if they're the same.

> **TIP**
>
> The `metaphone()` function comes in handy in search queries, to find words similar to the search string the user provides. Also consider the `levenshtein()` and `similar_text()` functions to compare strings by character instead of pronunciation.

1.11 Parsing Comma-Separated Lists

Problem

You want to extract the individual elements of a comma-separated list.

Solution

Decompose the string into an array using the comma as the delimiter:

```php
<?php
// define comma-separated list
$ingredientsStr = "butter, milk, sugar, salt, flour, caramel";

// decompose string into array
// using comma as delimiter
$ingredientsArr = explode(", ", $ingredientsStr);

// iterate over array
// print individual elements
foreach ($ingredientsArr as $i) {
    print $i . "\r\n";
}
?>
```

Comments

PHP's `explode()` function makes it a single-step process to split a comma-separated string list into an array of individual list elements. The previous listing clearly illustrates this: the `explode()` function scans the string for the delimiter and cuts out the pieces around it, placing them in an array. Once the list items have been extracted, a `foreach()` loop is a good way to process the resulting array.

TIP

You can combine the elements of an array into a comma-separated string list — the reverse of the listing above — with PHP's `implode()` *function.*

1.12 Parsing URLs

Problem

You want to extract the protocol, domain name, path, or other significant component of a URL.

Solution

Use the `parse_url()` function to automatically split the URL into its constituent parts:

```php
<?php
// define URL
$url = "http://www.melonfire.com:80/community/columns/trog/ ⏎
article.php?id=79 &page=2";

// parse URL into associative array
$data = parse_url($url);

// print URL components
foreach ($data as $k=>$v) {
    echo "$k: $v \n";
}
?>
```

Comments

The `parse_url()` function is one of PHP's more useful URL manipulation functions. Pass it a Uniform Resource Locator (URL), and `parse_url()` will go to work splitting it into its individual components. The resulting associative array contains separate keys for the protocol, host name, port number, remote path, and GET arguments. You can then easily access and use these keys for further processing—for example, the variable `$data['host']` will return the value www.melonfire.com.

Consider the output of the previous script, which illustrates this:

```
scheme: http
host: www.melonfire.com
port: 80
path: /community/columns/trog/article.php
query: id=79&page=2
```

1.13 Counting Words in a String

Problem

You want to count the number of words in a sentence or paragraph.

Solution

Use a pattern to identify the individual words in the string, and then count how many times that pattern recurs:

```php
<?php
// define string
$text = "Fans of the 1980 group will have little trouble recognizing ↵
the group's distinctive synthesized sounds and hypnotic dance beats,↵
since these two elements are present in almost every song on the ↵
album; however, the lack of diversity and range is troubling, and I'm ↵
hoping we see some new influences in the next album. More
intelligent lyrics might also help.";

// decompose the string into an array of "words"
$words  = preg_split('/[^0-9A-Za-z\']+/', $text, -1, ↵
PREG_SPLIT_NO_EMPTY);

// count number of words (elements) in array
// result: "59 words"
echo count($words) . " words";
?>
```

Comments

The preg_split() function is probably one of PHP's most underappreciated functions. This function accepts a Perl-compliant regular expression and a subject string, and returns an array containing substrings matching the pattern. It's a great way of finding the matches in a string and placing them in a separate array for further processing. Read more about the function and its arguments at `http://www.php .net/preg_split`.

In this listing, the regular expression `[^0-9A-Za-z\']+` is a generic pattern that will match any word. All the words thus matched are fed into the $words array. Counting the number of words in the string is then simply a matter of obtaining the size of the $words array.

An alternative is to use the new str_word_count() function to perform this task. Here's an example:

```php
<?php
// define string
$text = "Fans of the 1980 group will have little trouble recognizing ↵
the group's distinctive synthesized sounds and hypnotic dance beats,↵
since these two elements are present in almost every song on the ↵
album; however, the lack of diversity and range is troubling, and I'm
↵
hoping we see some new influences in the next album. More intelligent
lyrics might also help.";

// count number of words
// result: "58 words"
$numWords = str_word_count($text);
echo $numWords . " words";
?>
```

NOTE

Wondering about the discrepancy in the results above? The str_word_count() *function ignores numeric strings when calculating the number of words.*

1.14 Spell-Checking Words in a String

Problem

You want to check if one or more words are spelled correctly.

Solution

Use PHP's `ext/pspell` extension to check words against an internal dictionary:

```php
<?php
// define string to be spell-checked
$str = "someun pleez helpp me i canot spel";

// check spelling
// open dictionary link
$dict = pspell_new("en", "british");

// decompose string into individual words
// check spelling of each word
$str = preg_replace('/[0-9]+/', '', $str);
$words = preg_split('/[^0-9A-Za-z\']+/', $str, -1, ↵
PREG_SPLIT_NO_EMPTY);
foreach ($words as $w) {
    if (!pspell_check($dict, $w)) {
        $errors[] = $w;
    }
}

// if errors exist
// print error list
if (sizeof($errors) > 0) {
    echo "The following words were wrongly spelt: " . ↵
implode(" ", $errors);
}
?>
```

> **NOTE**
>
> In order for this listing to work, PHP must be compiled with support for the `pspell` extension. (You can obtain instructions from the PHP manual at `http://www.php.net/pspell`.)

Comments

The first task here is to identify the individual words in the sentence or paragraph. You accomplish this using the `preg_split()` function and regular expression previously discussed in the listing in the "1.13: Counting Words in a String" section. The `pspell_new()` function is used to open a link to the appropriate language dictionary, and the `pspell_check()` function iterates over the word list, checking each word against the dictionary. For words that are incorrectly spelled, `pspell_check()` returns false; these words are flagged, placed in an array and displayed in a list once the process is complete.

   With a little modification, you can have the previous listing check a file (rather than a variable) for misspelled words, and even offer suggestions when it encounters errors. Consider this variant, which illustrates the process and incorporates a call to `pspell_suggest()` to recommend alternatives for each wrongly-spelled word:

```php
<?php
// define file to be spell-checked
$file = "badspelling.txt";

// check spelling
// open dictionary link
$dict = pspell_new("en", "british", "", "", PSPELL_FAST);

// open file
$fp = fopen ($file, 'r') or die ("Cannot open file $file");

// read file line by line
$lineCount = 1;
while ($line = fgets($fp, 2048)) {
    // clean up trailing whitespace
    $line = trim($line);

    // decompose line into individual words
    // check spelling of each word
    $line = preg_replace('/[0-9]+/', '', $line);
    $words = preg_split('/[^0-9A-Za-z\']+/', $line, -1, ⏎
PREG_SPLIT_NO_EMPTY);

    foreach ($words as $w) {
        if (!pspell_check($dict, $w)) {
            if (!is_array($errors[$lineCount])) {
                $errors[$lineCount] = array();
            }
            array_push($errors[$lineCount], $w);
        }
    }
    $lineCount++;
}
```

```
// close file
fclose($fp);

// if errors exist
if (sizeof($errors) > 0) {
    // print error list, with suggested alternatives
    echo "The following words were wrongly spelt: \n";
    foreach ($errors as $k => $v) {
        echo "Line $k: \n";
        foreach ($v as $word) {
            $opts = pspell_suggest($dict, $word);
            echo "\t$word (" . implode(', ', $opts) . ")\n";
        }
    }
}
?>
```

NOTE

It's important to remember that pspell_check() *returns false on numeric strings. This can result in numerous false positives if your string contains numbers by themselves. The previous listing works around this problem by removing all the number sequences from the string/file before passing it to* pspell_check().

1.15 Identifying Duplicate Words in a String

Problem

You want to identify words that appear more than once in a string.

Solution

Decompose the string into individual words, and then count the occurrences of each word:

```php
<?php
// define string
$str = "baa baa black sheep";

// trim the whitespace at the ends of the string
$str = trim($str);
```

```
// compress the whitespace in the middle of the string
$str = ereg_replace('[[:space:]]+', ' ', $str);

// decompose the string into an array of "words"
$words = explode(' ', $str);

// iterate over the array
// count occurrences of each word
// save stats to another array
foreach ($words as $w) {
    $wordStats[strtolower($w)]++;
}

// print all duplicate words
// result: "baa"
foreach ($wordStats as $k=>$v) {
    if ($v >= 2) { print "$k \r\n"; }
}
?>
```

Comments

The first task here is to identify the individual words in the sentence or paragraph. You accomplish this by compressing multiple spaces in the string, and then decomposing the sentence into words with explode(), using a single space as [the] delimiter. Next, a new associative array, $wordStats, is initialized and a key is created within it for every word in the original string. If a word occurs more than once, the value corresponding to that word's key in the $wordStats array is incremented by 1.

Once all the words in the string have been processed, the $wordStats array will contain a list of unique words from the original string, together with a number indicating each word's frequency. It is now a simple matter to isolate those keys with values greater than 1, and print the corresponding words as a list of duplicates.

1.16 Searching Strings

Problem

You want to search a string for a particular pattern or substring.

Solution

Use a regular expression with PHP's `ereg()` function:

```php
<?php
// define string
$html = "I'm <b>tired</b> and so I <b>must</b> go
<a href='http://domain'>home</a> now";

// check for match
// result: "Match"
echo ereg("<b>(.*)+</b>", $html) ? "Match" : "No match";
?>
```

Use a regular expression with PHP's `preg_match()` function:

```php
<?php
// define string
$html = "I'm <b>tired</b> and so I <b>must</b> go
<a href='http://domain'>home</a> now";

// check for match
// result: "Match"
echo preg_match("/<b>(.*?)<\/b>/i", $html) ? "Match" : "No match";
?>
```

Comments

When it comes to searching for matches within a string, PHP offers the `ereg()` and `preg_match()` functions, which are equivalent: both functions accept a regular expression and a string, and return true if the string contains one or more matches to the regular expression. Readers familiar with Perl will usually prefer the `preg_match()` function, as it enables them to use Perl-compliant regular expressions and, in some cases, is faster than the `ereg()` function.

> **TIP**
>
> *For case-insensitive matching, use the `eregi()` function instead of the `ereg()` function.*

> **TIP**
>
> *Read more about regular expressions at `http://www.melonfire.com/community/columns/trog/article.php?id=2`.*

1.17 Counting Matches in a String

Problem

You want to find out how many times a particular pattern occurs in a string.

Solution

Use PHP's `preg_match_all()` function:

```php
<?php
// define string
$html = "I'm <b>tired</b> and so I <b>must</b> go
<a href='http://domain'>home</a> now";

// count occurrences of bold text in string
// result: "2 occurrence(s)"
preg_match_all("/<b>(.*?)<\/b>/i", $html, &$matches);
echo sizeof($matches[0]) . " occurrence(s)";
?>
```

Comments

The `preg_match_all()` function tests a string for matches to a particular pattern, and returns an array containing all the matches. If you need the total number of matches, simply check the size of the array with the `sizeof()` function.

For simpler applications, also consider the `substr_count()` function, which counts the total number of occurrences of a substring within a larger string. Here's a brief example:

```php
<?php
// define string
$text = "ha ha ho hee hee ha ho hee hee ho ho ho ha hee";

// count occurrences of "hee " in string
// result: "5 occurrence(s)"
echo substr_count($text, "hee") . " occurrence(s)";
?>
```

1.18 Replacing Patterns in a String

Problem

You want to replace all/some occurrences of a pattern or substring within a string with something else.

Solution

Use a regular expression in combination with PHP's `str_replace()` function (for simple patters):

```php
<?php
// define string
$str = "Michael says hello to Frank";

// replace all instances of "Frank" with "Crazy Dan"
// result: "Michael says hello to Crazy Dan"
$newStr = str_replace("Frank", "Crazy Dan", $str);
echo $newStr;
?>
```

For more complex patters, use a regular expression in combination with PHP's `preg_replace()` function:

```php
<?php
// define string
$html = "I'm <b>tired</b> and so I <b>must</b> go ↵
<a href='http://domain'>home</a> now";

// replace all bold text with italics
// result: "I'm <i>tired</i> and so I <i>must</i> go
<a href='http://domain'>home</a> now"
$newStr = preg_replace("/<b>(.*?)<\/b>/i", "<i>\\1</i>", $html);
echo $newStr;
?>
```

Comments

For simple applications that don't need complex pattern matching or regular expressions, consider PHP's `str_replace()` function. You can't use regular expressions with this function—all it enables you to do is replace one (or more) substrings with one (or more) replacement strings. Although it's limited, it can be faster than either `ereg_replace()` or `preg_replace()` in situations which don't call for advanced expression processing.

PHP's `preg_replace()` function takes the `preg_match()` function a step forward—in addition to searching for regular expression matches in the target string, it can also replace each match with something else. The `preg_replace()` function accepts a Perl-compliant regular expression, and its return value is the original string after all substitutions have been made. If no matches could be found, the original string is returned. Note also the use of a *back-reference* (\\1) in the `preg_replace()` version of the listing; this back-reference serves as a placeholder for text enclosed within the pattern to be matched.

By default, both functions replace all occurrences of the search string with the replacement string. With `preg_replace()`, however, you can control the number of matches that are replaced by passing the function an optional fourth parameter. Consider the following snippet, which limits the number of replacements to 1 (even though there are two valid matches):

```php
<?php
// define string
$html = "I'm <b>tired</b> and so I <b>must</b> go
        <a href='http://domain'>home</a> now";

// replace all bold text with italics
// result: "I'm <i>tired</i> and so I <b>must</b> go
        <a href='http://domain'>home</a> now"
$newStr = preg_replace("/<b>(.*?)<\/b>/i", "<i>\\1</i>", $html, 1);
echo $newStr;
?>
```

As an interesting aside, you can find out the number of substrings replaced by `str_replace()` by passing the function an optional fourth parameter, which counts the number of replacements. Here's an illustration:

```php
<?php
// define string
$str = "Michael says hello to Frank. Frank growls at Michael. Michael ↵
feeds Frank a bone.";

// replace all instances of "Frank" with "Crazy Dan"
$newStr = str_replace("Frank", "Crazy Dan", $str, &$counter);
```

```
// print number of replacements
// result: "3 replacement(s)"
echo "$counter replacement(s)";
?>
```

> ### TIP
> You can perform multiple search-replace operations at once with `str_replace()`, by using arrays for both the search and replacement strings.

1.19 Extracting Substrings

Problem

You want to extract the substring preceding or following a particular match.

Solution

Use the `preg_split()` function to split the original string into an array delimited by the match term, and then extract the appropriate array element(s):

```php
<?php
// define string
$html = "Just when you begin to think the wagon of ↵
<a name='#war'>Vietnam</a>-grounded movies is grinding to a slow halt, ↵
you're hit squarely in the <a name='#photo'>face</a> with another ↵
one. However, while other movies depict the gory and glory of war ↵
and its effects, this centers on the ↵
<a name='#subject'>psychology</a> of troopers before ↵
they're led to battle.";

// split on <a> element
$matches = preg_split("/<a(.*?)>(.*?)<\/a>/i", $html);

// extract substring preceding first match
// result: "Just when...of"
echo $matches[0];

// extract substring following last match
// result: "of troopers...battle."
echo $matches[sizeof($matches)-1];
?>
```

Comments

The `preg_split()` function accepts a regular expression and a search string, and uses the regular expression as a delimiter to split the string into segments. Each of these segments is placed in an array. Extracting the appropriate segment is then simply a matter of retrieving the corresponding array element.

This is clearly illustrated in the previous listing. To extract the segment preceding the first match, retrieve the first array element (index 0); to extract the segment following the last match, retrieve the last array element.

If your match term is one or more regular words, rather than a regular expression, you can accomplish the same task more easily by `explode()`-ing the string into an array against the match term and extracting the appropriate array elements. The next listing illustrates this:

```php
<?php
// define string
$str = "apples and bananas and oranges and pineapples and lemons";

// define search pattern
$search = " and ";

// split string into array
$matches = explode($search, $str);

// count number of segments
$numMatches = sizeof($matches);

// extract substring preceding first match
// result: "apples"
echo $matches[0];

// extract substring between first and fourth matches
// result: "bananas and oranges and pineapples"
echo implode($search, array_slice($matches, 1, 3));

// extract substring following last match
// result: "lemons"
echo $matches[$numMatches-1];
?>
```

1.20 Extracting Sentences from a Paragraph

Problem

You want to extract the first or last sentence from a paragraph.

Solution

Use the strtok() function to break the paragraph into sentences, and then extract the appropriate sentence:

```php
<?php
// define string
$text = "This e-mail message was sent from a notification-only address! ⏎
It cannot accept incoming e-mail. Please do not reply to this message. ⏎
Do you understand?";

// extract first sentence
// result: "This e-mail message was sent from a notification-only ⏎
address"
$firstSentence = strtok($text, ".?!");
echo $firstSentence;

// extract last sentence
// result: "Do you understand"
$lastSentence = strrev(strtok(strrev(trim($text)), ".?!"));
echo $lastSentence;
?>
```

Comments

To extract the first or last sentence of a paragraph, it is necessary to first break the string into individual sentences, using the common sentence terminators—a period, a question mark, and an exclamation mark—as delimiters. PHP's strtok() function is ideal for this: it splits a string into smaller segments, or tokens, based on a list of user-supplied delimiters. The first token obtained in this manner will be the first sentence of the paragraph.

Extracting the last sentence is a little more involved, and there are quite a few ways to do it. The previous listing uses one of the simplest: it reverses the paragraph and extracts the last sentence as though it were the first, again using strtok(). The extracted segment is then re-reversed using the strrev() function.

1.21 Generating String Checksums

Problem

You want to obtain a hash signature for a string

Solution

Use PHP's md5() or sha1() functions:

```php
<?php
// define string
$str = "two meters north, five meters west";

// obtain MD5 hash of string
// result: "7c00dcc2a1e4e89133b849a003448788"
$md5 = md5($str);
echo $md5;

// obtain SHA1 hash of string
// result: "d5db0063b0e2d4d7d33514e2da3743ce8daa44bf"
$sha1 = sha1($str);
echo $sha1;
?>
```

Comments

A hash signature is a lot like a fingerprint—it uniquely identifies the source that was used to compute it. Typically, a hash signature is used to verify if two copies of a string or file are identical in all respects; if both produce the same hash signature, they can be assumed to be identical. A hash function, like PHP's md5() or sha1() function, accepts string input and produces a fixed-length signature (sometimes called a checksum) that can be used for comparison or encryption. The md5() function produces a 128-bit hash, while the sha1() function produces a 160-bit hash. Read more at http://www.faqs.org/rfcs/rfc1321.html.

1.22 Encrypting Strings (One-Way Encryption)

Problem

You want to encrypt a string using one-way encryption.

Solution

Use PHP's `crypt()` function:

```php
<?php
// define cleartext string
$password = "guessme";

// define salt
$salt = "rosebud";

// encrypt string
// result: "rouuR6YmPKTOE"
$cipher = crypt($password, $salt);
echo $cipher;
?>
```

Comments

PHP's `crypt()` function accepts two parameters: the string to encrypt and a key (or salt) to use for encryption. It then encrypts the string using the provided salt and returns the encrypted string (or ciphertext). A particular combination of cleartext and salt is unique—the ciphertext generated by `crypt()`-ing a particular string with a particular salt remains the same over multiple `crypt()` invocations.

Because the `crypt()` function uses one-way encryption, there is no way to recover the original string from the ciphertext. You're probably wondering what use this is—after all, what's the point of encrypting something so that it can never be decrypted? Well, one-way encryption does have its uses, most notably for password verification: it's possible to validate a previously-encrypted password against a user's input by re-encrypting the input with the same salt and checking to see if the two pieces of ciphertext match. The next example illustrates this process:

```php
<?php
// define cleartext string
$password = "guessme";
```

```
// define salt
$salt = "rosebud";

// encrypt string
$cipher = crypt($password, $salt);

// assume the user inputs this
$input = "randomguess";

// encrypt the input
// test it against the encrypted password
// result: "Passwords don't match"
echo ($cipher == crypt($input, $salt)) ? ↵
"Passwords match" : "Passwords don't match";

// now assume the user inputs this
$input = "guessme";

// encrypt the input
// test it against the encrypted password
// result: "Passwords match"
echo ($cipher == crypt($input, $salt)) ? ↵
"Passwords match" : "Passwords don't match";
?>
```

Here, the cleartext password is encrypted with PHP's crypt() function and the defined salt, with the result checked against the (encrypted) original password. If the two match, it indicates that the supplied password was correct; if they don't, it indicates that the password was wrong.

1.23 Encrypting Strings (Two-Way Encryption)

Problem

You want to encrypt a string using two-way encryption.

Solution

Use PHP's ext/mcrypt extension to perform two-way encryption or decryption:

```
<?php
// function to encrypt data
```

```php
function encryptString($plaintext, $key) {
    // seed random number generator
    srand((double) microtime() * 1000000);

    // encrypt string
    $iv = mcrypt_create_iv( ↵
mcrypt_get_iv_size(MCRYPT_BLOWFISH, MCRYPT_MODE_CFB), ↵
MCRYPT_RAND);
    $cipher = mcrypt_encrypt(MCRYPT_BLOWFISH, $key, ↵
$plaintext, MCRYPT_MODE_CFB, $iv);

    // add IV to ciphertext
    return $iv . $cipher;
}

// function to decrypt data
function decryptString($ciphertext, $key) {
    // extract IV
    $iv = substr($ciphertext, 0,↵
mcrypt_get_iv_size(MCRYPT_BLOWFISH, MCRYPT_MODE_CFB));
    $cipher = substr($ciphertext, ↵
mcrypt_get_iv_size(MCRYPT_BLOWFISH, MCRYPT_MODE_CFB));

    // decrypt string
    return mcrypt_decrypt(MCRYPT_BLOWFISH, $key, $cipher,↵
MCRYPT_MODE_CFB, $iv);
}

// define cleartext string
$input = "three paces west, up the hill, turn nor-nor-west ↵
and fire through the left eye socket";

// define key
$key = "rosebud";

// returns encrypted string
$ciphertext = encryptString($input, $key);
echo $ciphertext;

// returns decrypted string
$cleartext = decryptString($ciphertext, $key);
echo $cleartext;
?>
```

> **NOTE**
>
> *In order for this listing to work, PHP must be compiled with support for the* `mcrypt` *extension (you can obtain instructions from the PHP manual at* `http://www.php.net/mcrypt`*).*

Comments

The previous listing uses two user-defined functions: `encryptString()` and `decryptString()`. Internally, both use functions provided by PHP's `ext/mcrypt` extension, which supports a wide variety of encryption algorithms (Blowfish, DES, TripleDES, IDEA, Rijndael, Serpent, and others) and cipher modes (CBC, CFB, OFB, and ECB). Both functions accept a string and a key, and use the latter to encrypt or decrypt the former.

The `encryptString()` function begins by seeding the random number generator and then generating an initialization vector (IV) with the `mcrypt_create_iv()` function. Once an IV has been generated, the `mcrypt_encrypt()` function performs the encryption using the supplied key. The encryption in this example uses the Blowfish algorithm in CFB mode. The IV is prepended to the encrypted string; this is normal and does not affect the security of the encryption.

The `decryptString()` function words in reverse, obtaining the IV size for the selected encryption algorithm and mode with the `mcrypt_get_iv_size()` function and then extracting the IV from the beginning of the encrypted string with the `substr()` function. The IV, encrypted string, and key are then used by the `mcrypt_decrypt()` function to retrieve the original cleartext string.

Read more about encryption algorithms and modes at `http://en.wikipedia.org/wiki/Encryption_algorithm`.

1.24 Generating Pronounceable Passwords

Problem

You want to generate a pronounceable password.

Solution

Use PEAR's `Text_Password` class:

```php
<?php
// include Text_Password class
include "Text/Password.php";
```

```
// create object
$tp = new Text_Password();

// generate pronounceable password
// result: "sawralaeje" (example)
$password = $tp->create();
echo $password;
?>
```

Comments

If you're looking for a quick way to generate pronounceable passwords—perhaps for a Web site authentication system—look no further than the PEAR Text_Password class (available from http://pear.php.net/package/Text_Password). By default, the class method create() generates a ten-character pronounceable password using only vowels and consonants.

You can define a custom length for the password by passing an optional size argument to the create() method, as follows:

```
<?php
// include Text_Password class
include "Text/Password.php";

// create object
$tp = new Text_Password();

// generate 5-character pronounceable password
// result: "ookel" (example)
$password = $tp->create(5);
echo $password;
?>
```

1.25 Generating Unpronounceable Passwords

Problem

You want to generate an unpronounceable password.

Solution

Use PEAR's `Text_Password` class with some additional parameters:

```php
<?php
// include Text_Password class
include "Text/Password.php";

// create object
$tp = new Text_Password();

// generate 7-character unpronounceable password
// result: "_nCx&h#" (example)
$password = $tp->create(7, 'unpronounceable');
echo $password;
?>
```

Comments

The PEAR `Text_Password` class (available from `http://pear.php.net/package/Text_Password`) is designed specifically to generate both pronounceable and unpronounceable passwords of varying lengths. To generate an unpronounceable password made up of alphabets, numbers, and special characters, call the class method `create()` with two additional flags: the desired password size and the keyword `unpronounceable` (the default behavior is to generate pronounceable passwords ten characters long).

   If you'd like to restrict the characters that can appear in the password, you can pass the `create()` method a third argument: either of the keywords `'numeric'` or `'alphanumeric'`, or a comma-separated list of allowed characters. The following code snippets illustrate this:

```php
<?php
// include Text_Password class
include "Text/Password.php";

// create object
$tp = new Text_Password();

// generate 7-character unpronounceable password
// using only numbers
// result: "0010287" (example)
$password = $tp->create(7, 'unpronounceable', 'numeric');
echo $password;

?>
```

```php
<?php
// include Text_Password class
include "Text/Password.php";

// create object
$tp = new Text_Password();

// generate 12-character unpronounceable password
// using only letters and numbers
// result: "P44g62gk6YIp" (example)
$password = $tp->create(12, 'unpronounceable', 'alphanumeric');
echo $password;
?>
```

```php
<?php
// include Text_Password class
include "Text/Password.php";

// create object
$tp = new Text_Password();

// generate 5-character unpronounceable password
// using a pre-defined character list
// result: "okjnn" (example)
$password = $tp->create(5, 'unpronounceable', 'i,j,k,l,m,n,o,p');
echo $password;
?>
```

CHAPTER 2

Working with Numbers

IN THIS CHAPTER:

Numbers. You can't get away from them. They're always there, crawling around in your application, needing constant care and attention. And the more sophisticated the application is, the more demanding the numbers become. Addition and subtraction isn't good enough any more—now you have to perform trigonometric operations on the numbers, draw graphs with them, make them more readable with commas and padding, and yield to their logarithmic limits. It's almost enough to make you weep.

That's where this chapter comes in. The solutions on the following pages range from the simple to the complex, but all of them address common number manipulation tasks. In the former category are listings for converting number bases; calculating trigonometric values; checking whether numeric values are odd or even; and formatting numbers for greater readability. In the latter category are listings to work with complex numbers and fractions; calculate standard deviation, skewness, and frequency; generate prime numbers using a technique invented by the ancient Greeks; and spell numbers as words in different languages.

2.1 Generating a Number Range

Problem

You have two endpoints and want to generate a list of all the numbers between them.

Solution

Use PHP's `range()` function:

```php
<?php
// define range limits
$x = 10;
$y = 36;

// generate range as array
// result: (10, 11, 12...35, 36)
$range = range($x, $y);
print_r($range);
?>
```

Comments

The `range()` function accepts two arguments—a lower limit and an upper limit—and returns an array containing all the integers between, and including, those limits. You can also create a number range that steps over particular numbers, by passing the step value to the function as a third, optional argument. The following example illustrates this:

```php
<?php
// define range limits
$x = 10;
$y = 30;

// generate range as array
// contains every third number
// result: (10, 13, 16, 19, 22, 25, 28)
$range = range($x, $y, 3);
print_r($range);
?>
```

A simple application of the `range()` function is to print a multiplication table. The following listing illustrates how to do this, by generating all the numbers between 1 and 10 and then using the list to print a multiplication table for the number 5:

```php
<?php
// print multiplication table
foreach (range(1, 10) as $num) {
    echo "5 x $num = " . (5 * $num) . "\n";
}
?>
```

TIP

You can also use `range()` to generate an array of sequential alphabetic characters, by passing it letters as limits instead of numbers. See listing 6.26 for an example.

2.2 Rounding a Floating Point Number

Problem

You want to round off a floating-point number.

Solution

Use the round() function:

```php
<?php
// define floating point number
$num = (2/3);

// round to integer
// result: 1
$roundNum = round($num);
echo $roundNum . "\n";

// round to 1 decimal place
// result: 0.7
$roundNum = round($num, 1);
echo $roundNum . "\n";

// round to 3 decimal places
// result: 0.667
$roundNum = round($num, 3);
echo $roundNum;
?>
```

Comments

The round() function rounds a number to a specified number of decimal places. Calling round() without the optional second argument makes it round to an integer value (0 decimal places). When rounding to an integer, the round() function will return the closest integer value. To force rounding to a lower or higher integer value, use the ceil() or floor() functions instead, as follows:

```php
<?php
// define floating point numbers
$num = (1/3);

$r = round($num);
$c = ceil($num);
$f = floor($num);

// result: "0 1 0"
echo "$r $c $f"
?>
```

2.3 Finding the Smallest or Largest Number in an Unordered Series

Problem

You want to find the maximum or minimum value of a series of unordered numbers.

Solution

Arrange the numbers in sequence and then extract the endpoints of the sequence:

```php
<?php
// define number series
$series = array(76, 7348, 56, 2.6, 189, 67.59, 17594, 2648, 1929.79,⏎
54, 329, 820, -1.10, -1.101);

// sort array
sort($series);

// extract maximum/minimum value from sorted array
// result: "Minimum is -1.101 "
$min = $series[0];
echo "Minimum is $min ";

// result: "Maximum is 17594"
$max = $series[sizeof($series)-1];
echo "Maximum is $max";
?>
```

Comments

There are many different ways to find the smallest or largest value in a number series. The previous listing demonstrates one of the simplest. The numbers are placed in an array, and the `sort()` function is used to sort the array so that the numbers line up sequentially. The smallest value will end up at the beginning of the list—the first element of the array—while the largest will end up at the end of the list—the last element of the array.

2.4 Testing for Odd or Even Numbers

Problem

You want to find out if a number is odd or even.

Solution

Use PHP's bitwise & operator:

```php
<?php
// define number
$num = 31;

// see if number is odd or even
// result: "Number is odd"
echo (1&$num) ? "Number is odd" : "Number is even";↵
?>
```

Comments

For odd numbers expressed in binary format, the least significant digit is always 1, whereas for even numbers, it is always 0. PHP's bitwise & operator returns 1 if both of its operands are equal to 1. Using these two principles, it's easy to create a conditional test for odd and even numbers.

If you don't fully understand the listing above, take a look at http://www .gamedev.net/reference/articles/article1563.asp for a tutorial on bitwise manipulation. Alternatively, you can consider a different test, which involves dividing the number by 2 and checking the remainder (with even numbers, the remainder will be zero). This alternative is illustrated as follows:

```php
<?php
// define number
$num = 10;

// see if number mod 2 returns a remainder
// result: "Number is even"
echo ($num % 2) ? "Number is odd" : "Number is even";
?>
```

2.5 Formatting Numbers with Commas

Problem

You want to make a large number more readable by using commas between groups of thousands.

Solution

Use PHP's `number_format()` function:

```php
<?php
// define number
$amount = 3957459.7398;

// round and format number with commas
// result: "3,957,460"
$formattedAmount = number_format($amount);
echo $formattedAmount;
?>
```

Comments

The `number_format()` function is a great tool to use when formatting large integer or floating-point numbers. When invoked with a single argument, it rounds up the number if necessary and then inserts commas between every group of thousands. Note that the output of the function is a string, not a number, and so it cannot be used for further numeric manipulation.

If you have a floating-point number and don't necessarily want to round it up to an integer, you can pass `number_format()` a second argument, which will control the number of decimals the formatted number should contain. Here's an example:

```php
<?php
// define number
$amount = 3957459.7398;

// format number with commas and 2 decimal places
// result: "3,957,459.74"
$formattedAmount = number_format($amount, 2);
echo $formattedAmount;
?>
```

For certain numbers, you might also want to use a custom decimal and/or thousands separator. You can accomplish this by passing number_format() two additional arguments, the first for the decimal separator and the second for the thousands separator. The next example illustrates this:

```
<?php
// define number
$amount = 3957459.7398;

// format number with custom separator
// result: "3'957'459,74"
$formattedAmount = number_format($amount, 2, ',', '\'');
echo $formattedAmount;
?>
```

2.6 Formatting Numbers as Currency Values

Problem

You want to format a number as per local or international currency conventions.

Solution

Define the target locale and then apply the appropriate monetary format via PHP's money_format() function:

```
<?php
// define currency amount (in INR)
$amount = 10000;

// display in INR
// result:  "INR 10000"
setlocale(LC_MONETARY, 'en_IN');
$inr = money_format('%i', $amount);
echo $inr;

// display in US dollars (convert using 1 USD = 45 INR)
// result:  "$ 222.22"
setlocale(LC_MONETARY, 'en_US');
$usd = money_format('%n', $amount/45);
echo $usd;
```

```
// display in euros (convert using 1 EUR = 52 INR)
// result:
setlocale(LC_MONETARY, 'fr_FR');
$eur = money_format('%i', $amount/52);
echo $eur;
?>
```

Comments

The previous listing takes a number and formats it so it conforms to Indian (INR), American (US) and European (EUR) currency conventions. The `setlocale()` function sets the locale, and hence the local conventions for currency display—notice that the Indian and American locales differ in their placement of thousand separators, while the European locale uses commas instead of decimals.

You can make further adjustments to the display using `money_format()`'s wide array of format specifiers, listed at `http://www.php.net/money_format`. This example uses the `%n` and `%i` specifiers, which represent the national currency symbol and the three-letter international currency code respectively.

> **NOTE**
>
> The `money_format()` function is not available in the Windows version of PHP.

2.7 Padding Numbers with Zeroes

Problem

You want to format a number with leading or trailing zeroes.

Solution

Use the `printf()` or `sprintf()` function with appropriate format specifiers:

```
<?php
// result: 00012
printf("%05d", 12);

// result: 00169.000
printf("%09.3f", 169);
```

```
// result: 00003475.986000
printf("%015.6f", 3475.986);

// result: 74390.99
printf("%02.2f", 74390.98647);
?>
```

Comments

PHP's `printf()` and `sprintf()` functions are very similar to the `printf()` and `sprintf()` functions that C programmers are used to, and they're incredibly versatile when it comes to formatting both string and numeric output. Both functions accept two arguments, a series of *format specifiers* and the raw string or number to be formatted. The input is then formatted according to the format specifiers and the output is either displayed with `printf()` or assigned to a variable with `sprintf()`.

Some common field templates are:

Specifier	What It Means
%s	String
%d	Decimal number
%x	Hexadecimal number
%o	Octal number
%f	Float number

You can also combine these field templates with numbers that indicate the number of digits to display—for example, `%1.2f` implies that only two digits should be displayed after the decimal point. Adding 0 as the padding specifier tells the function to zero-pad the numbers to the specified length. You can use an alternative padding character by prefixing it with a single quote (`'`). Read more at `http://www.php.net/sprintf`.

2.8 Converting Between Bases

Problem

You want to convert a number to a different base—binary, octal, hexadecimal, or custom.

Solution

Use PHP's `decbin()`, `decoct()`, `dexhec()`, or `base_convert()` functions:

```php
<?php
// define number
$num = 100;

// convert to binary
// result: "Binary: 1100100 "
$bin = decbin($num);
echo "Binary: $bin ";

// convert to octal
// result: "Octal: 144 "
$oct = decoct($num);
echo "Octal: $oct ";

// convert to hexadecimal
// result: "Hexadecimal: 64 "
$hex = dechex($num);
echo "Hexadecimal: $hex ";

// convert to base 6;
// result: "Base6: 244"
$base6 = base_convert($num, 10, 6);
echo "Base6: $base6";
?>
```

Comments

PHP comes with a number of functions to convert a number from one base to another. The previous listing takes a base-10 (decimal) number and converts it to binary, octal, and hexadecimal with the `decbin()`, `decoct()`, and `dechex()` functions respectively. To convert in the opposite direction, use the `bindec()`, `octdec()`, and `hexdec()` functions.

If you need to convert a number to or from a custom base, use the `base_convert()` function, which accepts three arguments: the number, the base it's currently in, and the base it's to be converted to.

A common application of base conversion routines like this involves obtaining hexadecimal values for RGB (red, green, blue) color codes, suitable for use in

Hypertext Markup Language (HTML) Web pages. The following snippet illustrates a function that does just this with the dechex() function:

```php
<?php
// function to convert RGB colors to their hex values
function rgb2hex($r, $g, $b) {
    return sprintf("#%02s%02s%02s", dechex($r), dechex($g), ↵
dechex($b));
}

// result: "#00ff40"
$hex = rgb2hex(0,255,64);
echo $hex;
?>
```

2.9 Converting Between Degrees and Radians

Problem

You want to convert an angle measurement from degrees to radians, or vice versa.

Solution

Use PHP's rad2deg() and deg2rad() functions:

```php
<?php
// result: "90 degrees = 1.57079632679 radians "
$degrees = 90;
$radians = deg2rad($degrees);
echo "$degrees degrees = $radians radians ";

// result: "1.57079632679491 radians = 90 degrees"
$radians = 1.57079632679491;
$degrees = rad2deg($radians);
echo "$radians radians = $degrees degrees";
?>
```

Comments

The formula to convert an angle measurement in degrees (D) to radians (R) is $D = R * 180/pi$. Fortunately, PHP comes with a function to do it for you automatically:

the `deg2rad()` function. Or, if you have a value that's already in radians, you can convert it to degrees with the `rad2deg()` function.

2.10 Converting Numbers into Words

Problem

You want to print a number as one or more literal words.

Solution

Use PEAR's Numbers_Words class:

```php
<?php
// include Numbers_Words class
include "Numbers/Words.php";

// create object
$nw = new Numbers_Words();

// print numbers in words

// result: "190000000 in words is one hundred ninety million."
echo "190000000 in words is " . $nw->toWords(190000000) . ".\n";

// result: "637 in words is six hundred thirty-seven."
echo "637 in words is " . $nw->toWords(637) . ".\n";

// result: "-8730 in words is minus eight thousand seven hundred ⌐
thirty."
echo "-8730 in words is " . $nw->toWords(-8730) . ".";
?>
```

Comments

The PEAR Numbers_Words class, available from `http://pear.php.net/package/Numbers_Words`, is designed specifically for the purpose of spelling out a number as one or more words. The class' `toWords()` method accepts a positive or negative integer and outputs the corresponding string. As the previous listing illustrates, it can handle both extremely large values and negative integers.

You aren't limited to English-language strings either—the Numbers_Words class can translate your number into a variety of different languages, including German, French, Hungarian, Italian, Spanish, Russian, and Polish. The following listing illustrates this:

```php
<?php
// include Numbers_Words class
include "Numbers/Words.php";

// create object
$nw = new Numbers_Words();

// print numbers in words in different languages

// French - result: "78 in French is soixante-dix-huit."
echo "78 in French is " . $nw->toWords(78, 'fr') . ".\n";

// Spanish - result:  "499 in Spanish is cuatrocientos noventa ↵
y nueve." echo "499 in Spanish is " . $nw->toWords(499, 'es') . ".\n";

// German - result: "-1850000 in German is minus en million ↵
// otte hundrede halvtreds tusinde."
echo "-1850000 in German is " . $nw->toWords(-1850000, 'dk') . ".";
?>
```

You can obtain a complete list of supported languages from the package archive, and it's fairly easy to create a translation table for your own language as well.

> **NOTE**
>
> The `toWords()` method does not support decimal values. To convert decimal values and fractions, consider the `toCurrency()` method instead.

2.11 Converting Numbers into Roman Numerals

Problem

You want to print a number as a Roman numeral.

Solution

Use PEAR's Numbers_Roman class:

```php
<?php
// include Numbers_Roman class
include "Numbers/Roman.php";

// create object
$nr = new Numbers_Roman();

// result: "5 in Roman is V."
echo "5 in Roman is " . $nr->toNumeral(5) . ".\n";

// result: "318 in Roman is CCCXVIII".
echo "318 in Roman is " . $nr->toNumeral(318) . ".";
?>
```

Comments

The PEAR Numbers_Roman class, available from `http://pear.php.net/ package/Numbers_Roman`, translates regular numbers into their Roman equivalents. The class' `toNumeral()` method accepts an integer and outputs the corresponding Roman numeral.

You can print a series of Roman numerals by combining the `toNumeral()` method with a loop, as shown here:

```php
<?php
// include Numbers_Roman class
include "Numbers/Roman.php";

// create object
$nr = new Numbers_Roman();

// print numbers 1 to 100 as Roman numerals
// result: "I II III IV...XCVIII XCIX C"
foreach (range(1, 100) as $x) {
    print $nr->toNumeral($x) . " ";
}
?>
```

You can also reverse the process with the `toNumber()` method, illustrated in the following code snippet:

```php
<?php
// include Numbers_Roman class
include "Numbers/Roman.php";

// create object
$nr = new Numbers_Roman();

// print CVII as an Arabic number
// result: "CVII = 107"
echo "CVII = " . $nr->toNumber('CVII');
?>
```

> **NOTE**
>
> The `toNumeral()` method does not support decimal or negative values.

2.12 Calculating Factorials

Problem

You want to find the factorial of a number.

Solution

Use a loop to count down and multiply the number by all the numbers between itself and 1:

```php
<?php
// define number
$num = 5;

// initialize variable
$factorial = 1;

// calculate factorial
// by multiplying the number by all the
// numbers between itself and 1
```

```
// result: "Factorial of 5 is 120"
for ($x=$num; $x>=1; $x--) {
    $factorial = $factorial * $x;
}
echo "Factorial of $num is $factorial";
?>
```

Comments

A factorial of a number *n* is the product of all the numbers between *n* and 1. The easiest way to calculate it is with a `for()` loop, one that starts at *n* and counts down to 1. Each time the loop runs, the previously calculated product is multiplied by the current value of the loop counter. The end result is the factorial of the number *n*.

2.13 Calculating Logarithms

Problem

You want to find the logarithm of a number.

Solution

Use PHP's `log()` or `log10()` function:

```
<?php
// find natural log of 6
// result: "Natural log of 6 is 1.79175946923. "
$logBaseE = log(6);
echo "Natural log of 6 is $logBaseE. ";

// find base-10 log of 5
// result: "Base10 log of 5 is 0.698970004336."
$logBase10 = log10(5);
echo "Base10 log of 5 is $logBase10.";
?>
```

Comments

Logarithms come in handy when you are solving differential equations, and most scientific calculators enable you to easily calculate the natural and base-10 logarithm of any number. PHP is no different—its `log()` and `log10()` functions return the natural and base-10 logarithm of their input argument.

To calculate the logarithm for any other base, you would normally use the logarithmic property $\log_y X = \log_b X / \log_b Y$. In PHP, you can instead simply specify the base as a second parameter to `log()`, as shown here:

```php
<?php
// find binary (base-2) log of 10
// result: "Binary log of 10 is 3.32192809489"
$logBase2 = log(10, 2);
echo "Binary log of 10 is $logBase2";
?>
```

The exponential function does the reverse of the natural logarithmic function, and is expressed in PHP through the `exp()` function. The following listing illustrates its usage:

```php
<?php
// find e ^ $num
// result: "Exponent of 0.69315 is 2"
$exponentE = exp(0.69315);
echo "Exponent of 0.69315 is " . round($exponentE, 2);
?>
```

2.14 Calculating Trigonometric Values

Problem

You want to perform a trigonometric calculation, such as finding the sine or cosine of an angle.

Solution

Use one of PHP's numerous trigonometric functions:

```php
<?php
// define angle
$angle = 45;

// calculate sine
// result: "Sine: 0.850903524534 "
```

```
$sine = sin($angle);
echo "Sine: $sine \n";

// calculate cosine
// result: "Cosine: 0.525321988818 "
$csine = cos($angle);
echo "Cosine: $csine \n";

// calculate tangent
// result: "Tangent: 1.61977519054 "
$tangent = tan($angle);
echo "Tangent: $tangent \n";

// calculate arc sine
// result: "Arc sine: -1.#IND "
$arcSine = asin($angle);
echo "Arc sine: $arcSine \n";

// calculate arc cosine
// result: "Arc cosine: -1.#IND "
$arcCsine = acos($angle);
echo "Arc cosine: $arcCsine \n";

// calculate arc tangent
// result: "Arc tangent: 1.54857776147 "
$arcTangent = atan($angle);
echo "Arc tangent: $arcTangent \n";

// calculate hyperbolic sine
// result: "Hyperbolic sine: 1.74671355287E+019 "
$hypSine = sinh($angle);
echo "Hyperbolic sine: $hypSine \n";

// calculate hyperbolic cosine
// result: "Hyperbolic cosine: 1.74671355287E+019 "
$hypCsine = cosh($angle);
echo "Hyperbolic cosine: $hypCsine \n";

// calculate hyperbolic tangent
// result: "Hyperbolic tangent: 1 "
$hypTangent = tanh($angle);
echo "Hyperbolic tangent: $hypTangent \n";
?>
```

Comments

PHP comes with a rich toolkit of functions designed specifically to assist in trigonometry. With these functions, you can calculate sines, cosines, and tangents for any angle. While there aren't yet built-in functions to calculate secants, cosecants, and cotangents, it's still fairly easy to calculate these inversions with the functions that *are* available. PHP also includes functions to calculate hyperbolic and inverse hyperbolic sines, cosines, and tangents; read more about these at http://www.php .net/math.

2.15 Calculating Future Value

Problem

You want to find the future value of a sum of money, given a fixed interest rate.

Solution

Calculate the future value by compounding the sum over various periods using the supplied interest rate:

```php
<?php
// define present value
$presentValue = 100000;

// define interest rate per compounding period
$intRate = 8;

// define number of compounding periods
$numPeriods = 6;

// calculate future value assuming compound interest
// result: "100000 @ 8 % over 6 periods becomes 158687.43"
$futureValue = round($presentValue * pow(1 + ($intRate/100),
$numPeriods), 2);
echo "$presentValue @ $intRate % over $numPeriods periods becomes
$futureValue";
?>
```

Comments

The formula to calculate the future value (F) of a particular amount (P), given a fixed interest rate (r) and a fixed number of years (n) is $F = P(1 + r/100)^n$. Performing the calculation in PHP is a simple matter of turning this formula into executable code. Nevertheless, you'd be surprised how many novice programmers forget all about PHP's operator precedence rules and, as a result, generate incorrect results. The previous listing uses braces to correctly define the order in which the variables are processed.

2.16 Calculating Statistical Values

Problem

You want to calculate statistical measures, such as variance or skewness, for a number set.

Solution

Use PEAR's Math_Stats class:

```php
<?php
// include Math_Stats class
include "Math/Stats.php";

// initialize object
$stats = new Math_Stats();

// define number series
$series = array(76, 7348, 56, 2.6, 189, 67.59, 17594, 2648, 1929.79,↵
54, 329, 820);

// connect object to series
$stats->setData($series);

// calculate complete statistics
$data = $stats->calcFull();
print_r($data);
?>
```

Comments

PEAR's Math_Stats class, available from `http://pear.php.net/package/Math_Stats`, is designed specifically to calculate statistical measures for a set of numbers. This number set must be expressed as an array, and passed to the class' `setData()` method. The `calcFull()` method can then be used to generate a basic or expanded set of statistics about the number set. The return value of this method is an associative array, with keys for each statistical measure calculated. For example, the variable `$data['median']` would return the median of the number set.

To get a better idea of the kind of analysis performed, consider the following output of the `calcFull()` method:

```
Array
(
    [min] => 2.6
    [max] => 17594
    [sum] => 31113.98
    [sum2] => 375110698.612
    [count] => 12
    [mean] => 2592.83166667
    [median] => 259
    [mode] => Array
        (
            [0] => 1929.79
            [1] => 820
            [2] => 2648
            [3] => 7348
            [4] => 17594
            [5] => 329
            [6] => 189
            [7] => 54
            [8] => 56
            [9] => 67.59
            [10] => 76
            [11] => 2.6
        )

    [midrange] => 8798.3
    [geometric_mean] => 324.444468821
    [harmonic_mean] => 26.1106363977
    [stdev] => 5173.68679862
    [absdev] => 3301.9175
    [variance] => 26767035.0902
    [range] => 17591.4
```

```
[std_error_of_mean] => 1493.51473294
[skewness] => 2.02781206173
[kurtosis] => 2.98190358339
[coeff_of_variation] => 1.99538090541
[sample_central_moments] => Array
    (
        [1] => 0
        [2] => 24536448.8327
        [3] => 280820044848
        [4] => 4.2858793901E+015
        [5] => 6.34511539688E+019
    )

[sample_raw_moments] => Array
    (
        [1] => 2592.83166667
        [2] => 31259224.8844
        [3] => 489107716046
        [4] => 8.23326983124E+015
        [5] => 1.42287015523E+020
    )

[frequency] => Array
    (
        [2.6] => 1
        [54] => 1
        [56] => 1
        [67.59] => 1
        [76] => 1
        [189] => 1
        [329] => 1
        [820] => 1
        [1929.79] => 1
        [2648] => 1
        [7348] => 1
        [17594] => 1
    )

[quartiles] => Array
    (
        [25] => 61.795
        [50] => 259
        [75] => 2288.895
    )
```

```
[interquartile_range] => 2227.1
[interquartile_mean] => 568.563333333
[quartile_deviation] => 1113.55
[quartile_variation_coefficient] => 94.7423947862
[quartile_skewness_coefficient] => 0.822904225226
)
```

As the previous listing illustrates, calcFull() generates a complete set of statistics about the data, including its mean, median, mode, and range; its variance and standard deviation; its skewness, kurtosis, and moments; and its quartiles, inter-quartile range, and quartile deviation. Normally, you'd need a fair bit of time with a calculator to calculate these values; the Math_Stats class generates them for you quickly and accurately.

It's also possible to generate a histogram and plot the frequency distribution of a data set, with PEAR's Math_Histogram package at http://pear.php.net/package/Math_Histogram. The following listing illustrates this:

```php
<?php
// include Math_Histogram class
include "Math/Histogram.php",

// define number series
$series = array(10,73,27,11,92,97,49,86,92,4,32,61,2,13,48,81,94,17,8);

// initialize an object
$hist = new Math_Histogram();

// connect class to data series
$hist->setData($series);

// define number of bins and upper/lower limits
$hist->setBinOptions(10,0,100);

// calculate frequencies
$hist->calculate();

// print as ASCII bar chart
echo $hist->printHistogram();
?>
```

Here, too, a number series is expressed as an array and passed to the setData() and calculate() methods for processing. The number and size of the histogram bins can be controlled with the setBinOptions() method. The printHistogram() method displays an ASCII representation of the histogram, as shown here:

```
Histogram
    Number of bins: 10
    Plot range: [0, 100]
    Data range: [2, 97]
    Original data range: [2, 97]
BIN (FREQUENCY) ASCII_BAR (%)
10.000    (4    ) |**** (21.1%)
20.000    (3    ) |*** (15.8%)
30.000    (1    ) |* (5.3%)
40.000    (1    ) |* (5.3%)
50.000    (2    ) |** (10.5%)
60.000    (0    ) | (0.0%)
70.000    (1    ) |* (5.3%)
80.000    (1    ) |* (5.3%)
90.000    (2    ) |** (10.5%)
100.000   (4    ) |**** (21.1%)
```

NOTE

The Math_Histogram package supports both simple and cumulative histograms, as well as histograms in three and four dimensions.

2.17 Generating Unique Identifiers

Problem

You want to generate a unique, random numeric identifier that cannot be easily guessed.

Solution

Use a combination of PHP's uniqid(), md5(), and rand() functions:

```php
<?php
// generate a random, unique ID
// result: "5542ec0a1928b99ef90cb87503094fe4" (example)
$id = md5(uniqid(rand(), true));
echo $id;
?>
```

Comments

PHP's uniqid() function returns an alphanumeric string based on the current time in microseconds, suitable for use in any operation or transaction that is keyed on a unique alphanumeric string. Because the identifier is based on a time value, there is a very slight possibility of two identical identifiers being generated at the same instant; to reduce this possibility, add a random element to the procedure by combining the call to uniqid() with a call to rand() and md5().

2.18 Generating Random Numbers

Problem

You want to generate one or more random numbers.

Solution

Use PHP's rand() function:

```php
<?php
// generate a random number
// result: 18785 (example)
echo rand();

// generate a random number between 0 and 100
// result: 4 (example)
echo rand(0, 100);
?>
```

Comments

Generating a random number in PHP is as simple as calling the rand() function. If you'd optionally like to limit the random number to a specific range, you can pass rand() the upper and lower limits of the range.

To obtain a random floating-point number, divide the random number produced by a very large value. The getrandmax() function is a good choice here—it returns the maximum value that rand() could possibly generate on your system. Here's an illustration:

```php
<?php
// generate a random floating-point number
// result: 0.721182897427 (example)
echo rand()/getrandmax();
?>
```

If you need more than one random number, use `rand()` in combination with a loop and array. Here's an example:

```php
<?php
// generate a series of 10 random numbers between 0 and 100
// result: "12 95 88 87 61 49 61 4 99 75" (example)
for ($x=0; $x<10; $x++) {
    echo rand(0, 100) . " ";
}
?>
```

2.19 Generating Prime Numbers

Problem

You want to generate a series of prime numbers, or find out if a particular number is prime.

Solution

Use the Sieve of Eratosthenes to filter out all the numbers that are not prime and display the rest:

```php
<?php
// list all primes between 2 and some integer ⏎
// using the Sieve of Erastothenes
function listPrimes($end) {
    // generate an array of all possible integers
    // between the first prime and the supplied limit
    $sieve = range(2, $end);

    // retrieve the size of the array
    $size = sizeof($sieve);
```

```
        // reset internal array pointer to beginning of array
        reset($sieve);

        // iterate over the array
        while (list($key, $val) = each($sieve)) {
            // for each element
            // check if subsequent elements are divisible by it
            // remove them from the array if so
            for ($x=$key+1; $x<$size; $x++) {
                if ($sieve[$x] % $val == 0) {
                    unset($sieve[$x]);
                }
            }
        }

        // at the end, elements left in array are primes
        return $sieve;
}

// list all the primes between 2 and 100
// result: "2 3 5 7...83 89 97"
echo implode(" ", listPrimes(100));
?>
```

Comments

A prime number is a number that has only two divisors: itself and 1. There are quite a few ways to generate a sequence of prime numbers, but the method listed previously is one of the oldest (and also one of the most efficient). Known as the Sieve of Eratosthenes, after the Greek scholar of the same name, it essentially requires you to perform three steps:

▶ List all the integers between 2 and some number n.

▶ Begin with the first number in the list. Remove all the numbers from the list that are (a) greater than it, and (b) multiples of it.

▶ Move to the next available number and repeat the process.

The numbers left behind after this filtering, or *sieving*, process will be prime numbers—that is, numbers that cannot be divided by any other number except themselves and 1.

NOTE

To get a clearer idea of how the Sieve of Eratosthenes works, list all the numbers between 2 and 50 on a sheet of paper and follow the steps described previously. Or visit `http://en.wikipedia.org/wiki/Sieve_of_Eratosthenes` *for a more detailed explanation and analysis. For alternative ways of generating prime numbers, visit* `http://www.olympus.net/personal/7seas/primes.html`.

A variant of this listing involves checking if a particular number is prime. You can accomplish this by dividing the number by all the numbers smaller than it (excluding 1) and checking the remainder. If the remainder is 0 at any stage, it means that the number was fully divisible and, hence, cannot be prime. Here's a function that encapsulates this logic:

```php
<?php
// check if a number is a prime number
function testPrime($num) {
    // divide each number
    // by all numbers lower than it (excluding 1)

    // if even one such operation returns no remainder
    // the number is not a prime
    for ($x=($num-1); $x>1; $x--) {
        if (($num % $x) == 0) {
            return false;
        }
    }
    return true;
}


// test if 9 is prime
// result: "Number is not prime"
echo testPrime(9) ? "Number is prime" : "Number is not prime";
?>
```

Using the `testPrime()` function described previously, it's easy to write a function that satisfies another common requirement: listing the first *n* primes. Take a look:

```php
<?php
// list first N primes
function getFirstNPrimes($n) {
    // define an empty array to store primes
    $primesArray = array();
```

```php
    // start with the first prime
    $count = 2;

    // sequentially test numbers
    // until the required number of primes is obtained
    while (sizeof($primesArray) < $n)     {
        if (testPrime($count)) {
            $primesArray[] = $count;
        }
        $count++;
    }

    return $primesArray;
}


// list the first 90 primes
echo implode(" ", getFirstNPrimes(90));
?>
```

NOTE

The previous method can also be used as an alternative to the Sieve of Eratosthenes to generate a list of prime numbers; however, it will be nowhere near as efficient. With the Sieve of Eratosthenes, the pool of numbers under consideration continually diminishes in size as multiples are eliminated; this speeds things up considerably. With the previous method, every number in the given range has to be actively tested for "prime-ness" by dividing it by all the numbers before it; as the numbers increase in value, so does the time it takes to test them.

2.20 Generating Fibonacci Numbers

Problem

You want to generate a series of Fibonacci numbers, or find out if a particular number belongs to the Fibonacci sequence.

Solution

Define the first two numbers, and use a loop to calculate the rest:

```php
<?php
// generate the first N Fibonacci numbers
function generateFibonacciNumbers($size) {
```

```
    // define array to hold Fibonacci numbers
    $fibonacciArray = array();

    $fibonacciArray[0] = 0; // by definition
    $fibonacciArray[1] = 1; // by definition

    // generate numbers
    for ($x=2; $x<=$size; $x++) {
        $fibonacciArray[$x] = $fibonacciArray[$x-2] + ↵
$fibonacciArray[$x-1];
    }

    // return array
    return $fibonacciArray;
}

// list the first 20 Fibonacci numbers
// result: "0 1 1 2 3 5 8...2584 4181 6765"
echo implode(" ", generateFibonacciNumbers(20));
?>
```

Comments

In the Fibonacci number sequence, every number is formed from the sum of the previous two numbers. The first few numbers in this sequence are 1, 1, 2, 3, 5, and 8. As the previous listing illustrates, it's fairly easy to convert this rule into working PHP code.

If you'd prefer, you can save yourself some time with PEAR's Math_Fibonacci class, from `http://pear.php.net/package/Math_Fibonacci`. This class comes with a `series()` method that generates the first *n* numbers of the Fibonacci sequence, and a `term()` method, which lets you find the *n*th term of the sequence. Both methods return an object, which must be decoded with the `toString()` method. The following listing illustrates this:

```
<?php
// include Math_Fibonacci class
include "Math/Fibonacci.php";

// list the first 20 Fibonacci numbers
// result: "0 1 1 2 3 5 8...4181 6765"
$series = Math_Fibonacci::series(20);
foreach ($series as $k=>$v) {
    print $v->toString() . " ";
}
```

```
// calculate the 5th Fibonacci number
// result: 5
$fib5 = Math_Fibonacci::term(5);
print $fib5->toString();
?>
```

You can also test if a particular number belongs to the Fibonacci sequence, with the `isFibonacci()` class method. The next listing illustrates:

```
<?php
// include Math_Fibonacci class
include "Math/Fibonacci.php";

// define number
$num = 21;

// check if number belongs to the Fibonacci sequence
// result: "Is a Fibonacci number"
echo Math_Fibonacci::isFibonacci(new Math_Integer($num)) ↵
? "Is a Fibonacci number" : "Is not a Fibonacci number";
?>
```

2.21 Working with Fractions

Problem

You want to perform a mathematical operation involving fractions.

Solution

Use PEAR's Math_Fraction class:

```
<?php
// include Math_Fraction class
include "Math/Fraction.php";

// define a new fraction
$fract = new Math_Fraction(1,2);
```

```
// print as string
// result: "1/2 "
echo $fract->toString() . " \n";

// print as float
// result: 0.5
echo $fract->toFloat()
?>
```

Comments

A fraction is a number in the form a/b. In this form, a is called the *numerator* and b is called the *denominator*. The denominator of a fraction can never be 0. Examples of fractions include 1/3, 19/7, and 1.5/3.5.

PHP's math toolkit doesn't include functions for dealing with values represented in fraction notation, so if you need to work with that type of notation, you'll have to rely entirely on PEAR's Math_Fraction class at `http://pear.php.net/package/Math_Fraction`. A fraction here is expressed as an object, generated by passing the fraction's numerator and denominator as arguments to the class constructor. Two methods, `toString()` and `toFloat()`, take care of displaying the fraction, either as a fraction or a floating-point value.

Of course, representing a fraction is only the tip of the iceberg—most of the time, you're going to want to perform mathematical operations on it. The accompanying Math_FractionOp class provides a number of methods to support this requirement. Take a look at the next listing, which creates two fraction objects and then performs a variety of operations on them:

```
<?php
// include Math_Fraction class
include "Math/Fraction.php";

// include Math_FractionOp class
include "Math/FractionOp.php";

// define two fractions
$fract1 = new Math_Fraction(1,2);
$fract2 = new Math_Fraction(1,3);

// add the fractions
// result: "Sum: 5/6"
$obj = Math_FractionOp::add($fract1, $fract2);
echo "Sum: " . $obj->toString() . "\n";
```

```
// subtract the fractions
// result: "Difference: 1/6"
$obj = Math_FractionOp::sub($fract1, $fract2);
echo "Difference: " . $obj->toString() . "\n";

// multiply the fractions
// result: "Product: 1/6"
$obj = Math_FractionOp::mult($fract1, $fract2);
echo "Product: " . $obj->toString() . "\n";

// divide the fractions
// result: "Quotient: 3/2"
$obj = Math_FractionOp::div($fract1, $fract2);
echo "Quotient: " . $obj->toString() . "\n";

// invert (reciprocal) a fraction
// result: "Reciprocal: 2/1"
$obj = Math_FractionOp::reciprocal($fract1);
echo "Reciprocal: " . $obj->toString() . "\n";

// compare the fractions
// returns -1 if LHS < RHS, 0 if LHS = RHS, 1 otherwise
// result: 1
echo Math_FractionOp::compare($fract1, $fract2);
?>
```

The add(), sub(), mult(), and div() methods take care of fraction addition, subtraction, multiplication, and division respectively. The reciprocal() method produces a new fraction by swapping the numerator and denominator of the original one. Finally, the compare() method makes it possible to compare two fractions and decide which one is larger. Each of these methods returns a new Math_Fraction object; the actual value of this object must be retrieved using either the toString() or toFloat() method discussed previously.

2.22 Working with Complex Numbers

Problem

You want to perform a mathematical operation involving complex numbers.

Solution

Use the PEAR Math_Complex class:

```php
<?php
// include Math_Complex class
include "Math/Complex.php";

// define a new complex number
$complex = new Math_Complex(3,-5);

// as string
// result: "3-5i"
echo $complex->toString() . "\n";

// retrieve real part of complex number
// result: "Real part: 3"
echo "Real part: " . $complex->getReal() . "\n";

// retrieve imaginary part of complex number
// result: "Imaginary part: -5"
echo "Imaginary part: " . $complex->getIm() . "\n";

// retrieve norm of complex number
// result: "Norm: 5.83095189485"
echo "Norm: " . $complex->norm();
?>
```

Comments

A complex number is a number made up of two components: a real part and an imaginary part. It is usually written as a + bi, where a and b are real numbers and i is an imaginary number equal to the square root of −1. Examples of complex numbers are 3+5i, 6−81i and 9−3i.

PHP's math toolkit doesn't include built-in functions for dealing with complex numbers, so you'll have to turn to PEAR's add-on Math_Complex class, at http://pear.php.net/package/Math_Complex. Here, a complex number object is first generated by passing the number's real and imaginary parts to the object constructor. The object's toString() method combines these two components and returns a suitable-for-display string.

You can also do the reverse—given a complex number object, you can break it up into its components with the getReal() and getIm() methods, which retrieve the real and imaginary components respectively. You can calculate the *norm* of the number with the norm() method.

Once you've got a complex number object, the next step is usually to perform mathematical operations with it. The accompanying Math_ComplexOp class provides numerous methods to help you with this. The next listing illustrates these methods by generating two complex number objects and performing mathematical operations on them:

```php
<?php
// include Math_Complex class
include "Math/Complex.php";

// include Math_ComplexOp class
include "Math/ComplexOp.php";

// define two complex numbers
$complex1 = new Math_Complex(3,2);
$complex2 = new Math_Complex(1,4);

// add the complex numbers
// result: "Sum: 4+6i"
$obj = Math_ComplexOp::add($complex1, $complex2);
echo "Sum: " . $obj->toString() . "\n";

// subtract the complex numbers
// result: "Difference: 2-2i"
$obj = Math_ComplexOp::sub($complex1, $complex2);
echo "Difference: " . $obj->toString() . "\n";

// multiply the complex numbers
// result: "Product: -5+14i"
$obj = Math_ComplexOp::mult($complex1, $complex2);
echo "Product: " . $obj->toString() . "\n";

// divide the complex numbers
// result: "Quotient: 0.647058823529 - 0.588235294118i"
$obj = Math_ComplexOp::div($complex1, $complex2);
echo "Quotient: " . $obj->toString() . "\n";
```

```php
// invert a complex number
// result: "Inverted value: 0.230769230769 - 0.153846153846i"
$obj = Math_ComplexOp::inverse($complex1);
echo "Inverted value: " . $obj->toString() . "\n";

// conjugate a complex number
// result: "Conjugated value: 3-2i"
$obj = Math_ComplexOp::conjugate($complex1);
echo "Conjugated value: " . $obj->toString() . "\n";

// multiply a complex number and its conjugate
// product is always a real number (imaginary part = 0)
// result: "Multiplied value: 17 + 0i"
$obj = Math_ComplexOp::mult($complex2, Math_ComplexOp::
conjugate($complex2));
echo "Multiplied value: " . $obj->toString();
?>
```

The add(), sub(), mult(), and div() methods take care of complex number addition, subtraction, multiplication, and division respectively. The inverse() method returns the inverse of the number, while the conjugate() method returns its conjugate. The return value of all these methods is a new Math_Complex object; the actual value of this object can be retrieved using the toString() method.

CHAPTER 3

Working with Dates and Times

IN THIS CHAPTER:

L ike most programming languages, PHP comes with a fairly full-featured set of functions for date and time manipulation. Two of these functions are probably familiar to you from your daily work as a developer— the date() function for formatting dates and times and the mktime() function for generating timestamps. But it's unlikely that you've had as much contact with the other members of the collection—the strtotime() function, the gmdate() function, or the microtime() function.

These functions, together with many more, make it easy to solve some fairly vexing date/time manipulation problems. Over the course of this chapter, I'll show you how to solve such problems, with listings for converting between time zones; checking the validity of a date; calculating the number of days in a month or year; displaying a monthly calendar; performing date arithmetic; and working with date values outside PHP's limits.

NOTE

PHP's date and time functions were rewritten in PHP 5.1, with the result that every date or time function expects the default time zone to be set (and generates a notice if this is not the case). The listings in this chapter assume that this default time zone has previously been set, either via the $TZ environment variable or the date.timezone setting in the php.ini configuration file. In the rare cases when it is necessary to over-ride the system-wide time zone setting, PHP offers the date_default_timezone_set() function, which can be invoked to set the time zone on a per-script basis, as may be seen in the listing in "3.12: Converting Between Different Time Zones."

3.1 Getting the Current Date and Time

Problem

You want to display the current date and/or time.

Solution

Use PHP's getdate() function:

```php
<?php
// get current date and time
$now = getdate();
```

```
// turn it into strings
$currentTime = $now["hours"] . ":" . $now["minutes"] .↵
":" . $now["seconds"];
$currentDate = $now["mday"] . "." . $now["mon"] . "." . $now["year"];

// result: "It is now 12:37:47 on 30.10.2006" (example)
echo "It is now $currentTime on $currentDate";
?>
```

Comments

PHP's getdate() function returns an array of values representing different
components of the current date and time. Here's an example of what the array might
look like:

```
Array
(
    [seconds] => 34
    [minutes] => 14
    [hours] => 9
    [mday] => 23
    [wday] => 2
    [mon] => 5
    [year] => 2006
    [yday] => 137
    [weekday] => Monday
    [month] => February
    [0] => 1107752144
)
```

As the previous listing illustrates, it's easy enough to use this array to generate a
human-readable date and time value. However, formatting options with getdate()
are limited, so if you need to customize your date/time display extensively, look at
the listing in "3.2: Formatting Timestamps" for an alternative way of accomplishing
the same thing.

NOTE

Notice that the 0th element of the array returned by getdate() *contains a UNIX timestamp
representation of the date returned—the same one that* mktime() *would generate.*

3.2 Formatting Timestamps

Problem

You want to turn a UNIX timestamp into a human-readable string.

Solution

Use PHP's date() function to alter the appearance of the timestamp with various formatting codes:

```php
<?php
// get date
// result: "30 Oct 2006" (example)
echo date("d M Y", mktime()) . " \n";

// get time
// result: "12:38:26 PM" (example)
echo date("h:i:s A", mktime()) . " \n";

// get date and time
// result: "Monday, 30 October 2006, 12:38:26 PM" (example)
echo date ("l, d F Y, h:i:s A", mktime()) . " \n";

// get time with timezone
// result: "12:38:26 PM UTC"
echo date ("h:i:s A T", mktime()) . " \n";

// get date and time in ISO8601 format
// result: "2006-10-30T12:38:26+00:00"
echo date ("c", mktime());
?>
```

Comments

PHP's date() function is great for massaging UNIX timestamps into different formats. It accepts two arguments—a format string and a timestamp—and uses the format string to turn the timestamp into a human-readable value. Each character in the format string has a special meaning, and you can review the complete list at http://www.php.net/date.

The `date()` function is usually found in combination with the `mktime()` function, which produces a UNIX timestamp for a particular instant in time. This timestamp is represented as the number of seconds since January 1 1970 00:00:00 Greenwich Mean Time (GMT). Called without any arguments, `mktime()` returns a timestamp for the current instant in time; called with arguments, it returns a timestamp for the instant represented by its input. The following snippets illustrate this:

```php
<?php
// get current timestamp
// result: 1162218979 (example)
echo mktime() . " \n";

// get timestamp for 01:00 AM 31 Jan 2007
// result: 1170205200
echo mktime(1,0,0,1,31,2007);
?>
```

> **NOTE**
>
> *An alternative to the* `mktime()` *function is the* `time()` *function, which returns a UNIX timestamp for the current instant in time. Unlike* `mktime()`, *however,* `time()` *cannot be used to produce timestamps for arbitrary date values.*

3.3 Checking Date Validity

Problem

You want to check if a particular date is valid.

Solution

Use PHP's `checkdate()` function:

```php
<?php
// check date 31-Apr-2006
// result: "Invalid date"
echo checkdate(31,4,2006) ? "Valid date" : "Invalid date";
?>
```

Comments

Applications that accept date input from a user must validate this input before using it for calculations or date operations. The `checkdate()` function simplifies this task considerably. It accepts a series of three arguments, representing day, month and year, and returns a Boolean value indicating whether the combination make up a legal date.

An alternative way of accomplishing the same thing can be found in the PEAR Calendar class, available from `http://pear.php.net/package/Calendar`. This class offers an `isValid()` method to test the validity of a particular date value. The following listing illustrates this:

```php
<?php
// include Calendar class
include "Calendar/Day.php";

// initialize Day object to 31-Apr-2006
$day = & new Calendar_Day(2006, 4, 31);

// check date
// result: "Invalid date"
echo $day->isValid() ? "Valid date" : "Invalid date";
?>
```

3.4 Converting Strings to Timestamps

Problem

You want to convert a string, encapsulating a date or time value, into the corresponding UNIX timestamp.

Solution

Use PHP's `strtotime()` function:

```php
<?php
// define string
$str = "20030607";

// convert string to timestamp
$ts = strtotime($str);
```

```
// format as readable date/time value
// result: "Saturday, 07 June 2003 12:00:00 AM" (example)
echo ($ts === -1) ? "Invalid string" : date("l, d F Y h:i:s A", $ts);
?>
```

Comments

PHP's `strtotime()` function performs the very important function of converting a human-readable date value into a UNIX timestamp, with minimal calculation required on the part of the application. The date value can be any English-language date descriptor; `strtotime()` will attempt to identify it and return the corresponding timestamp. If `strtotime()` cannot convert the description to a timestamp, it will return –1.

In addition to date strings, the `strtotime()` function also accepts English-language time descriptors like "now," "next Wednesday," or "last Friday," and you can use it to perform rudimentary date arithmetic. The following listing illustrates this:

```
<?php
// assume now is "Monday, 30 October 2006 02:56:34 PM"

// define string
$str = "next Friday";

// convert string to timestamp
$ts = strtotime($str);

// format as readable date/time value
// result: "Friday, 03 November 2006 12:00:00 AM"
echo ($ts === false) ? "Invalid string" : date("l, d F Y h:i:s A", $ts);

// define string
$str = "2 weeks 6 hours ago";

// convert string to timestamp
$ts = strtotime($str);

// format as readable date/time value
// result: "Monday, 16 October 2006 08:56:34 AM"
echo ($ts === false) ? "Invalid string" : date("l, d F Y h:i:s A", $ts);
?>
```

TIP

For more sophisticated date arithmetic, take a look at the listing in "3.16: Performing Date Arithmetic." Read more `strtotime()` *examples in the PHP manual at* `http://www .php.net/strtotime`.

3.5 Checking for Leap Years

Problem

You want to check if a particular year is a leap year.

Solution

Write a function to see if the year number is divisible by 4 or 400, but not 100:

```php
<?php
// function to test if leap year
function testLeapYear($year) {
    $ret = (($year%400 == 0) || ($year%4 == 0 && $year%100 != 0)) ⏎
? true : false;
    return $ret;
}

// result: "Is a leap year"
echo testLeapYear(2004) ? "Is a leap year" : "Is not a leap year";

// result: "Is not a leap year"
echo testLeapYear(2001) ? "Is a leap year" : "Is not a leap year";
?>
```

Comments

A year is a leap year if it is fully divisible by 400, or by 4 but not 100. The function `testLeapYear()` in the previous listing encapsulates this logic, using PHP's `%` operator to check for divisibility, and returns a Boolean value indicating the result.

An alternative way to do this is to use the `checkdate()` function to test for the presence of an extra day in February of that year. The following listing illustrates this:

```php
<?php
// function to test if leap year
function testLeapYear($year) {
    return checkdate(2, 29, $year);
}

// result: "Is a leap year"
echo testLeapYear(2004) ? "Is a leap year" : "Is not a leap year";

// result: "Is not a leap year"
echo testLeapYear(2001) ? "Is a leap year" : "Is not a leap year";↵
?>
```

3.6 Finding the Number of Days in a Month

Problem

You want to find the number of days in a particular month.

Solution

Use PHP's `date()` function with the "`t`" modifier:

```php
<?php
// get timestamp for month and year Mar 2005
$ts = mktime(0,0,0,3,1,2005);

// find number of days in month
// result: 31
echo date("t", $ts);
?>
```

Comments

Given a UNIX timestamp, the date() function's "t" modifier returns the number of days in the corresponding month. The return value will range from 28 to 31.

An alternative way of accomplishing the same thing is to use the PEAR Date class, available at http://pear.php.net/package/Date. Here, a Date() object is first initialized to a specific day, month, and year combination, and then the class' getDaysInMonth() method is used to retrieve the number of days in that month. The next listing illustrates this:

```php
<?php
// include Date class
include "Date.php";

// initialize Date object to 1-Mar-2005
$dt = new Date();
$dt->setYear(2005);
$dt->setMonth(3);
$dt->setDay(1);

// get number of days in month
// result: 31
echo $dt->getDaysInMonth();
?>
```

3.7 Finding the Day-in-Year or Week-in-Year Number for a Date

Problem

You want to find the day-in-year or week-in-year number for a particular date.

Solution

Use PHP's date() function with the "z" or "W" modifier:

```php
<?php
// get day of year for 01-Mar-2008
// result: 61
echo date("z", mktime(0,0,0,3,1,2008))+1;
```

```php
// get week of year for 01-Mar-2008
// result: 09
echo date("W", mktime(0,0,0,3,1,2008));
?>
```

Comments

Given a UNIX timestamp, the `date()` function's `"z"` modifier returns the day number in the year, while the `"W"` modifier returns the week number. Note that day numbers are indexed from 0, so it is necessary to add 1 to the final result to obtain the actual day number in the year. Also look at the listing in "3.8: Finding the Number of Days or Weeks in a Year" for another application of this technique.

Alternatively, you can use PEAR's Date class, available from `http://pear` `.php.net/package/Date`, to obtain the week number. Here, a `Date()` object is first initialized to a specific day, month, and year combination, and then the class' `getWeekOfYear()` method is used to retrieve the week number for that date.

```php
<?php
// include Date class
include "Date.php";

// initialize Date object to 1-Mar-2008
$dt = new Date();
$dt->setYear(2008);
$dt->setMonth(3);
$dt->setDay(1);

// get week number in year
// result: 9
echo $dt->getWeekOfYear();
?>
```

3.8 Finding the Number of Days or Weeks in a Year

Problem

You want to find the number of days or weeks in a particular year.

Solution

Use PHP's date() function with the "z" or "W" modifiers:

```php
<?php
// get total number of days in the year 2001
$numDays = date("z", mktime(0,0,0,12,31,2001))+1;

// get total number of weeks in the year 2001
$numWeeks = date("W", mktime(0,0,0,12,28,2001));

// result: "There are 365 days and 52 weeks in 2001."
echo "There are $numDays days and $numWeeks weeks in 2001.\n";
?>
```

Comments

Given a UNIX timestamp, the date() function's "z" modifier returns the day number in the year, while the "W" modifier returns the week number. By passing a timestamp representation of the last day or last week of the year, it's possible to quickly find the total number of days or weeks in the year. Also look at the listing in "3.7: Finding the Day-in-Year or Week-in-Year Number for a Date" for another application of this technique.

Note that the value returned by the "z" modifier is indexed from 0, so it is necessary to add 1 to the final result to obtain the actual number of days in the year.

3.9 Finding the Day Name for a Date

Problem

You want to find which day of the week a particular date falls on.

Solution

Use PHP's date() function with the "l" modifier:

```php
<?php
// get timestamp for date 04-Jun-2008
$ts = mktime(0,0,0,6,4,2008);
```

```
// get day of week
// result: "Wednesday"
echo date("l", $ts);
?>
```

Comments

Given a timestamp representing a particular date, the date() function's "l" modifier returns the weekday name corresponding to that date. If you need a numeric value (0 = Sunday, 1 = Monday, …) rather than a string, use the "w" modifier instead.

3.10 Finding the Year Quarter for a Date

Problem

You want to find which quarter of the year a particular date falls in.

Solution

Use PHP's date() function with the "m" modifier:

```
<?php
// get timestamp for date 04-Jun-2008
$ts = mktime(0,0,0,6,4,2008);

// get quarter
// result: 2
echo ceil(date("m", $ts)/3);
?>
```

Comments

Given a timestamp representing a particular date, the date() function's 'm' modifier returns the month number (range 1–12) corresponding to that date. To obtain the corresponding year quarter, divide the month number by 3 and round it up to the nearest integer with the ceil() function.

An alternative way of accomplishing the same thing is to use the PEAR Date class, available from http://pear.php.net/package/Date. Here, a Date() object is first initialized to a specific day, month, and year combination, and then the class' `getQuarterOfYear()` method is used to retrieve the year quarter for that month. The next listing illustrates this:

```php
<?php
// include Date class
include "Date.php";

// initialize Date object
$dt = new Date();
$dt->setYear(2008);
$dt->setMonth(6);
$dt->setDay(6);

// get quarter
// result: 2
echo $dt->getQuarterOfYear();
?>
```

3.11 Converting Local Time to GMT

Problem

You want to convert local time to Greenwich Mean Time (GMT).

Solution

Use PHP's `gmdate()` function:

```php
<?php
// convert current local time (IST) to GMT
// result: "15:06:25 30-Oct-06 GMT" (example)
echo gmdate("H:i:s d-M-y T") . "\n";

// convert specified local time (IST) to GMT
// result: "23:00:00 01-Feb-05 GMT" (example)
$ts = mktime(4,30,0,2,2,2005);
echo gmdate("H:i:s d-M-y T", $ts);
?>
```

Comments

The `gmdate()` function formats and displays a timestamp in GMT. Like the `date()` function, it accepts a format string that can be used to control the final appearance of the date and time value. Conversion to GMT is performed automatically based on the time zone information returned by the operating system.

An alternative way of finding GMT time is to find the local time zone offset from GMT, and subtract that from the local time. This offset can be found by using the `date()` function's `"Z"` modifier, which returns, in seconds, the time difference between the current location and Greenwich. A negative sign attached to the offset indicates that the location is west of Greenwich.

The next listing illustrates this:

```php
<?php
// convert current local time (IST) to GMT
// result: "15:07:56 30-Oct-06 GMT" (example)
echo date("H:i:s d-M-y", time()-date("Z")) . " GMT \n";

// convert specified local time (IST) to GMT
// result: "23:00:00 01-Feb-05 GMT"
$ts = mktime(4,30,0,2,2,2005);
echo date("H:i:s d-M-y", $ts-date("Z", $ts)) . " GMT";
?>
```

3.12 Converting Between Different Time Zones

Problem

You want to obtain the local time in another time zone, given its GMT offset.

Solution

Write a PHP function to calculate the time in the specified zone:

```php
<?php
// function to get time
// for another time zone
// given a specific timestamp and hour offset from GMT
```

```
function getLocalTime($ts, $offset) {
    // performs conversion
    // returns UNIX timestamp
    return ($ts - date("Z", $ts)) + (3600 * $offset);
}

// get current local time in Singapore
// result: "00:11:26 31-10-06 SST"
echo date("H:i:s d-m-y", getLocalTime(mktime(), 8)) . " SST \n";

// get current local time in India
// result: "21:41:26 30-10-06 IST"
echo date("H:i:s d-m-y", getLocalTime(mktime(), +5.5)) . " IST \n";

// get current local time in USA (Eastern)
// result: "11:11:26 30-10-06 EST"
echo date("H:i:s d-m-y", getLocalTime(mktime(), -5)) . " EST \n";

// get current local time in USA (Pacific)
// result: "08:11:26 30-10-06 PST"
echo date("H:i:s d-m-y", getLocalTime(mktime(), -8)) . " PST \n";

// get time in GMT
// when it is 04:30 AM in India
// result: "23:00:00 01-02-05 GMT "
echo date("H:i:s d-m-y", getLocalTime(mktime(4,30,0,2,2,2005), 0)) .↵
" GMT \n";
?>
```

Comments

Assume here that you're dealing with two time zones: Zone 1 and Zone 2. The user-defined function getLocalTime() accepts two arguments: a UNIX timestamp for Zone 1 and the time zone offset, in hours from GMT, for Zone 2. Because it's simpler to perform time zone calculations from GMT, the Zone 1 UNIX timestamp is first converted to GMT (see the listing in "3.12: Converting Between Different Time Zones" for more on this step) and then the stated hour offset is added to it to obtain a new UNIX timestamp for Zone 2 time. This timestamp can then be formatted for display with the date() function.

Note that given UNIX timestamps are represented in seconds, the hour offset passed to getLocalTime() must be multiplied by 3600 (the number of seconds in 1 hour) before the offset calculation can be performed. Note also that if the hour offset passed to getLocalTime() is 0, GMT time will be returned.

If this is too complicated for you, you can also perform time zone conversions with the PEAR Date class, available from http://pear.php.net/package/ Date. Here, a Date() object is initialized and its current time zone is set with the setTZ() method. The corresponding time in any other region of the world can then be obtained by invoking the convertTZ() method with the name of the region. Take a look:

```php
<?php
// include Date class
include "Date.php";

// initialize Date object
$d = new Date("2005-02-01 16:29:00");

// set time zone
$d->setTZ('Asia/Calcutta');

// convert to UTC
// result: "2005-02-01 10:59:00"
$d->toUTC();
echo $d->getDate() . " \n";

// convert to American time (EST)
// result: "2005-02-01 05:59:00"
$d->convertTZ(new Date_TimeZone('EST'));
echo $d->getDate() . " \n";

// convert to Singapore time
// result: "2005-02-01 18:59:00"
$d->convertTZ(new Date_TimeZone('Asia/Singapore'));
echo $d->getDate() . " \n";
?>
```

A complete list of valid region names for time zone conversion can be obtained from the package documentation.

TIP

There's also a third "shortcut" solution to this problem: simply use the `date_default_timezone_set()` *function to set the default time zone to the target city or time zone, and use the* `date()` *function to return the local time in that zone. Here's an example:*

```php
<?php
// set default time zone to destination
// result: "00:11:26 31-10-06 SST"
date_default_timezone_set('Asia/Singapore');
echo date("H:i:s d-m-y") . " SST \n";

// set default time zone to destination
// result: "08:11:26 30-10-06 PST"
date_default_timezone_set('US/Pacific');
echo date("H:i:s d-m-y") . " PST \n";
?>
```

3.13 Converting Minutes to Hours

Problem

You want to convert between mm and hh:mm formats.

Solution

Divide or multiply by 60 and add the remainder:

```php
<?php
// define number of minutes
$mm = 156;

// convert to hh:mm format
// result: "02h 36m"
echo sprintf("%02dh %02dm", floor($mm/60), $mm%60);
?>

<?php
// define hours and minutes
$hhmm = "02:36";
```

```
// convert to minutes
// result: "156 minutes"
$arr = explode(":", $hhmm);
echo $arr[0]*60 + $arr[1] . " minutes";
?>
```

Comments

Which is more easily understood: "105 minutes" or "1 hour, 45 minutes"? The previous listing takes care of performing this conversion between formats.

Given the total number of minutes, the number of hours can be obtained by dividing by 60, with the remainder representing the number of minutes. The sprintf() function takes care of sticking the two pieces together.

Given a string in hh:mm format, the explode() function splits it on the colon (:) separator, converts the first element from hours to minutes by multiplying it by 60, and then adds the second element to get the total number of minutes.

3.14 Converting Between PHP and MySQL Date Formats

Problem

You want to convert a MySQL DATETIME/TIMESTAMP value to a UNIX timestamp suitable for use with PHP's date() function, or vice versa.

Solution

To convert a MySQL TIMESTAMP/DATETIME type to a UNIX timestamp, use PHP's strtotime() function or MySQL's UNIX_TIMESTAMP() function:

```php
<?php
// run database query, retrieve MySQL timestamp
$connection = mysql_connect("localhost", "user", "pass") ↵
or die ("Unable to connect!");
$query = "SELECT NOW() AS tsField";
$result = mysql_query($query) ↵
or die ("Error in query: $query. " . mysql_error());
$row = mysql_fetch_object($result);
mysql_close($connection);
```

```php
// convert MySQL TIMESTAMP/DATETIME field
// to UNIX timestamp with PHP strtotime() function
// format for display with date()
echo date("d M Y H:i:s", strtotime($row->tsField));
?>


<?php
// run database query, retrieve MySQL timestamp
// convert to UNIX timestamp using MySQL UNIX_TIMESTAMP() function
$connection = mysql_connect("localhost", "user", "pass") ↵
or die ("Unable to connect!");
$query = "SELECT UNIX_TIMESTAMP(NOW()) as tsField";
$result = mysql_query($query) or die ("Error in query: $query. " .
mysql_error());
$row = mysql_fetch_object($result);
mysql_close($connection);

// timestamp is already in UNIX format
// so format for display with date()
echo date("d M Y H:i:s", $row->tsField);
?>
```

To convert a UNIX timestamp to MySQL's TIMESTAMP/DATETIME format, use the date() function with a custom format strong, or use MySQL's FROM_UNIXTIME() function:

```php
<?php
// create UNIX timestamp with mktime()
$ts = mktime(22,4,32,7,2,2007);

// turn UNIX timestamp into MYSQL TIMESTAMP/DATETIME format (string)
// result: "2007-07-02 22:04:32"
echo date("Y-m-d H:i:s", $ts);

// turn UNIX timestamp into MYSQL TIMESTAMP/DATETIME format (numeric)
// result: 20070702220432
echo date("YmdHis", $ts);
?>
<?php
// create UNIX timestamp with PHP mktime() function
$ts = mktime(22,4,32,7,2,2007);

// turn UNIX timestamp into MYSQL TIMESTAMP/DATETIME format
// using MySQL's FROM_UNIXTIME() function
$connection = mysql_connect("localhost", "user", "pass") ↵
or die ("Unable to connect!");
```

```
$query = "SELECT FROM_UNIXTIME('$ts') AS tsField";
$result = mysql_query($query) or die ("Error in query: $query. " . ↵
mysql_error());
$row = mysql_fetch_object($result);
mysql_close($connection);
// result: "2007-07-02 22:04:32"
echo $row->tsField;
?>
```

Comments

A common grouse of PHP/MySQL developers is the incompatibility between the date formats used by the two applications. Most of PHP's date/time functions use a UNIX timestamp; MySQL's DATETIME and TIMESTAMP fields only accept values in either YYYYMMDDHHMMSS or "YYYY-MM-DD HH:MM:SS" format. PHP's date() function will not correctly read a native DATETIME or TIMESTAMP value, and MySQL will simply zero out native UNIX timestamps. Consequently, converting between the two formats is a fairly important task for a PHP/MySQL developer.

Fortunately, there are a couple of ways to go about this, depending on whether you'd prefer to do the conversion at the PHP application layer or the MySQL database layer.

▶ At the PHP layer, you can convert a MySQL DATETIME or TIMESTAMP value into a UNIX timestamp by passing it to the PHP strtotime() function, which is designed specifically to parse and attempt to convert English-readable date values into UNIX timestamps (see the listing in "3.4: Converting Strings to Timestamps"). Going the other way, you can insert a UNIX timestamp into a MySQL DATETIME or TIMESTAMP field by first formatting it with the PHP date() function.

▶ At the MySQL layer, you can convert a MySQL DATETIME or TIMESTAMP value into a UNIX timestamp with the MySQL UNIX_TIMESTAMP() function. Or, you can save a UNIX timestamp directly to a MySQL DATETIME or TIMESTAMP field by using MySQL's built-in FROM_UNIXTIME() function to convert the timestamp into MySQL-compliant format.

3.15 Comparing Dates

Problem

You want to compare two dates to see which is more recent.

Solution

Use PHP's comparison operators to compare the timestamps corresponding to the two dates:

```php
<?php
// create timestamps for two dates
$date1 = mktime(0,0,0,2,1,2007);
$date2 = mktime(1,0,0,2,1,2007);

// compare timestamps
// to see which represents an earlier date
if ($date1 > $date2) {
    $str = date ("d-M-Y H:i:s", $date2) . " comes before " .↵
date ("d-M-Y H:i:s", $date1);
} else if ($date2 > $date1) {
    $str = date ("d-M-Y H:i:s", $date1) . " comes before " .↵
date ("d-M-Y H:i:s", $date2);
} else {
    $str = "Dates are equal";
}
// result: "01-Feb-2007 00:00:00 comes before 01-Feb-2007 01:00:00"
echo $str;
?>
```

Comments

PHP's comparison operators work just as well on temporal values as they do on numbers and strings. This is illustrated in the previous listing, which compares two dates to see which one precedes the other.

An alternative is the PEAR Date class, available from `http://pear.php.net/package/Date`. Comparing dates with this class is fairly simple: initialize two `Date()` objects, and then call the `compare()` method to see which one comes first. The `compare()` method returns 0 if both dates are equal, −1 if the first date is before the second, and 1 if the second date is before the first. Here's an illustration:

```php
<?php
// include Date class
include "Date.php";

// initialize two Date objects
$date1 = new Date("2007-02-01 00:00:00");
$date2 = new Date("2007-02-01 01:00:00");
```

```
// compare dates
// returns 0 if the dates are equal
//         -1 if $date1 is before $date2
//          1 if $date1 is after $date2
// result: -1
echo Date::compare($date1, $date2);
?>
```

You could also use either one of the Date() objects' before() and after() methods on the other. The next listing illustrates this:

```php
<?php
// include Date class
include "Date.php";

// initialize two Date objects
$date1 = new Date("2007-02-01 00:00:00");
$date2 = new Date("2006-02-01 00:00:00");

// check if $date1 is before $date2
// result: "false"
echo $date1->before($date2) ? "true" : "false";

// check if $date2 is before $date1
// result: "true"
echo $date1->after($date2) ? "true" : "false";
?>
```

TIP

You can compare a date relative to "today" with the isPast() *and* isFuture() *methods. Look in the package documentation for examples.*

3.16 Performing Date Arithmetic

Problem

You want to add (subtract) time intervals to (from) a date.

Solution

Convert the date to a UNIX timestamp, express the time interval in seconds, and add (subtract) the interval to (from) the timestamp:

```php
<?php
// set base date
$dateStr = "2008-09-01 00:00:00";

// convert base date to UNIX timestamp
// expressed in seconds
$timestamp = strtotime($dateStr);

// express "28 days, 5 hours, 25 minutes and 11 seconds"
// in seconds
$intSecs = 11 + (25*60) + (5*60*60) + (28*24*60*60);

// add interval (in seconds)
// to timestamp (in seconds)
// format result for display
// returns "2008-09-29 05:25:11"
$newDateStr = date("Y-m-d h:i:s", $timestamp + $intSecs);
echo $newDateStr;
?>
```

Comments

When you're dealing with temporal data, one of the more common (and complex) tasks involves performing addition and subtraction operations on date and time values. Consider, for example, the simple task of calculating a date 91 days hence. Usually, in order to do this with any degree of precision, you need to factor in a number of different variables: the month you're in, the number of days in that month, the number of days in the months following, whether or not the current year is a leap year, and so on.

PHP doesn't provide built-in functions for this type of arithmetic, but it's nevertheless fairly easy to do. The previous listing illustrates one approach to the problem, wherein the time interval is converted to seconds and added to (or subtracted from) the base timestamp, also expressed in seconds.

Another option is to use PEAR's Date class, available from http://pear .php.net/package/Date. This class comes with two methods to perform date and time arithmetic: addSpan() and subtractSpan(). The "span" in both cases is a DateSpan() object, created from a delimited string containing day, hour, minute, and second intervals. This span is added to (or subtracted from) a previously initialized `Date()` object, and a new date and time is calculated and returned as another `Date()` object. Here's an example:

```php
<?php
// include Date class
include "Date.php";

// initialize Date object
$d = new Date("2007-02-01 00:00:00");

// add 28 days, 5 hours, 25 minutes and 11 seconds
// result: "2007-03-01 05:25:11"
$d->addSpan(new Date_Span("28:05:25:11"));
echo $d->getDate() . " \n";

// now subtract 1 day, 30 minutes
// result: "2007-02-28 04:55:11"
$d->subtractSpan(new Date_Span("01:00:30:00"));
echo $d->getDate();
?>
```

3.17 Displaying a Monthly Calendar

Problem

You want to print a calendar for a particular month.

Solution

Use PEAR's Calendar class:

```php
<?php
// include Calendar class
include "Calendar/Month/Weekdays.php";
include "Calendar/Day.php";

// initialize calendar object
$month = new Calendar_Month_Weekdays(2008, 1);

// build child objects (days of the month)
$month->build();
```

```
// format as table
echo "<pre>";

// print month and year on first line
echo "            " . sprintf("%02d", $month->thisMonth()) . "/" .↵
$month->thisYear() . "\n";

// print day names on second line
echo "  M   T   W   T   F   S   S\n";

// iterate over day collection
while ($day = $month->fetch()) {
    if ($day->isEmpty()) {
        echo "    ";
    } else {
        echo sprintf("%3d", $day->thisDay()) . " ";
    }

    if ($day->isLast()) {
        echo "\n";
    }
}
echo "</pre>";
?>
```

Comments

Displaying a dynamic calendar on a Web page might seem trivial, but if you've ever tried coding it firsthand, you'll know the reality is somewhat different. Better than working your way through the numerous calculations and adjustments, then, is using the PEAR Calendar class, available from `http://pear.php.net/package/Calendar`. This class is designed specifically to generate a monthly or yearly calendar that you can massage into whatever format you desire.

The Calendar package includes a number of different classes, each for a specific purpose. The previous listing uses the `Calendar_Month_Weekdays()` class, which provides the methods needed to generate a monthly calendar sorted into weeks. (This is the same type you probably have hanging on your wall.) The class is initialized with a month and year, and its `build()` method is invoked to build the calendar data structure. A `while()` loop is then used in combination with the `fetch()` method to iterate over the Calendar data structure and print each day. Four utility method—`isFirst()`, `isLast()`, `isEmpty()` and `isSelected()`—enable you to customize the appearance of particular dates in the month.

Figure 3-1 illustrates the output of the listing above.

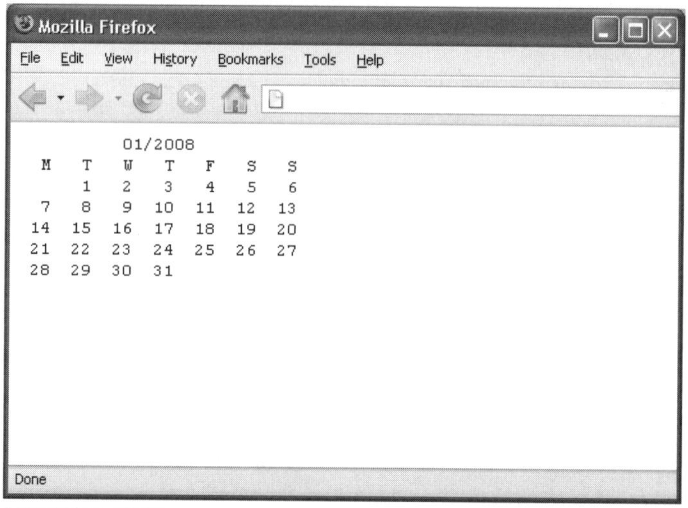

Figure 3-1   *A calendar generated with the PEAR Calendar class*

The Calendar package is fairly sophisticated, and enables a developer to create and customize a variety of different calendar types. There isn't enough space here to discuss it in detail, so you should take a look at the examples provided with the package to understand what you can do with it.

3.18 Working with Extreme Date Values

Problem

You want to work with dates outside the range 01-01-1970 to 19-01-2038.

Solution

Use the ADOdb Date Library:

```php
<?php
// include ADODB date library
include "adodb-time.inc.php";
```

```
// get date representation for 01-Mar-1890
// returns "01-Mar-1890"
echo adodb_date("d-M-Y", adodb_mktime(4,31,56,3,1,1890)) . " \n";

// get date representation for 11-Jul-3690 10:31 AM
// result: "11-Jul-3690 10:31:09 AM"
echo adodb_gmdate("d-M-Y h:i:s A", adodb_mktime(16,1,9,07,11,3690)) . "
\n";

// get date representation for 11-Jul-3690 04:01 PM
// result: "11-Jul-3690 04:01:09 PM"
echo adodb_gmdate("d-M-Y h:i:s A", adodb_gmmktime(16,1,9,07,11,3690));
?>
```

Comments

Because PHP uses 32-bit signed integers to represent timestamps, the valid range of a PHP timestamp is usually 1901–2038 on UNIX, and 1970–2038 on Windows. None of the built-in PHP date functions will work with dates outside this range. Needless to say, this is a Bad Thing.

You can work around this problem with the Active Data Objects Data Base (ADOdb) Date Library, a free PHP library that uses 64-bit floating-point numbers instead of 32-bit integers to represent timestamps, thus significantly increasing the valid range. This library is freely available from `http://phplens.com/ phpeverywhere/adodb_date_library`, and it provides 64-bit substitutes for PHP's native date and time functions, enabling you to work with dates from "100 A.D. to 3000 A.D. and later."

As the previous listing illustrates, input and output parameters for the ADOdb functions are identical to those of the native PHP ones, enabling them to serve as drop-in replacements.

CHAPTER
4

Working with Arrays

IN THIS CHAPTER:

PHP's array manipulation API was redesigned in PHP 4.x to simplify common array manipulation tasks. New objects designed specifically for array iteration were introduced in PHP 5.x as part of the Standard PHP Library (SPL) to make array manipulation even more extensible and customizable.

The result is a sophisticated toolkit that enables you to easily perform complex tasks, including recursively traversing and searching a series of nested arrays, sorting arrays by more than one key, filtering array elements by user-defined criteria, and swapping array keys and values. In this chapter, I'll discuss all of these tasks, and many more ... so keep reading!

4.1 Printing Arrays

Problem

You want to print the contents of an array.

Solution

Use PHP's `print_r()` or `var_dump()` functions:

```php
<?php
// define array
$data = array(
    "UK" => array(
        "longname" => "United Kingdom", "currency" => "GBP"),
    "US" => array(
        "longname" => "United States of America", "currency" => ↵
"USD"),       "IN" => array(
        "longname" => "India", "currency" => "INR"));

// print array contents
print_r($data);
var_dump($data);
?>
```

Comments

The `print_r()` and `var_dump()` functions are great ways to X-ray the contents of an array variable, and print a hierarchical listing of its internals. The previous listing demonstrates them both in action. Note that `var_dump()` produces more verbose output (including information on data types and lengths) than `print_r()`.

4.2 Processing Arrays

Problem

You want to iteratively process the elements in an array.

Solution

Use a `foreach()` loop and appropriate temporary variables, depending on whether the array has numeric indices or string keys:

```php
<?php
// define indexed array
$idxArr = array("John", "Joe", "Harry", "Sally", "Mona");

// process and print array elements one by one
// result: "John | Joe | Harry | Sally | Mona | "
foreach ($idxArr as $i) {
    print "$i | ";
}
?>
<?php
// define associative array
$assocArr = array("UK" => "London", "US" => "Washington",↵
"FR" => "Paris", "IN" => "Delhi");

// process and print array elements one by one
// result: "UK: London US: Washington FR: Paris IN: Delhi "
foreach ($assocArr as $key=>$value) {
    print "$key: $value";
    print "<br />";
}
?>
```

Comments

PHP's `foreach()` loop is the simplest way to iterate over an array. At each iteration, the current array element is assigned to a temporary variable, which can then be used for further processing. For associative arrays, two temporary variables may be used, one each for the key and value.

Alternatively, you may prefer to use the Iterators available as part of the SPL. *Iterators* are ready-made, extensible constructs designed specifically to loop over item collections—directories, files, class methods, and (naturally!) array elements. To process an array, use an ArrayIterator, as illustrated here:

```php
<?php
// define associative array
$assocArr = array("UK" => "London", "US" => "Washington",↵
"FR" => "Paris", "IN" => "Delhi");

// create an ArrayIterator object
$iterator = new ArrayIterator($assocArr);

// rewind to beginning of array
$iterator->rewind();

// process and print array elements one by one
// result: "UK: London US: Washington FR: Paris IN: Delhi "
while($iterator->valid()) {
    print $iterator->key() . ": " . $iterator->current() . "\n";
    $iterator->next();
}
?>
```

Here, an ArrayIterator object is initialized with an array variable, and the object's `rewind()` method is used to reset the internal array pointer to the first element of the array. A `while()` loop, which runs so long as a `valid()` element exists, can then be used to iterate over the array. Individual array keys are retrieved with the `key()` method, and their corresponding values are retrieved with the `current()` method. The `next()` method moves the internal array pointer forward to the next array element.

You can read more about the ArrayIterator at `http://www.php.net/~helly/php/ext/spl/`.

4.3 Processing Nested Arrays

Problem

You want to process all the elements in a series of nested arrays.

Solution

Write a recursive function to traverse the array:

```php
<?php
// function to recursively traverse nested arrays
function arrayTraverse($arr) {
    // check if input is array
    if (!is_array($arr)) { die ("Argument is not array!"); }

    // iterate over array
    foreach($arr as $value) {
        // if a nested array
        // recursively traverse
        if (is_array($value)) {
            arrayTraverse($value);
        } else {
            // process the element
            print strtoupper($value) . " \n";
        }
    }
}

// define nested array
$data = array(
    "United States",
    array("Texas", "Philadelphia"),
    array("California",
    array ("Los Angeles", "San Francisco")));

// result: "UNITED STATES TEXAS PHILADELPHIA CALIFORNIA LOS ANGELES SAN
FRANCISCO"
arrayTraverse($data);
?>
```

Comments

It's fairly easy to iterate over a single array, processing each and every element in turn. Dealing with a series of nested arrays requires a little more effort. The previous listing illustrates the standard technique, a recursive function that calls itself to travel ever deeper into a layered array.

The inner workings of the arrayTraverse() function are fairly simple. Every time the function encounters an array value, it checks to see if that value is an array or a scalar. If it's an array, the function calls itself and repeats the process until it reaches a scalar value. If it's a scalar, the value is processed—the previous listing calls `strtoupper()`, but you can obviously replace this with your own custom routine—and then the entire performance is repeated for the next value.

You could also use an Iterator from the SPL. *Iterators* are ready-made, extensible constructs designed specifically to loop over item collection—directories, files, class methods, and array elements. A predefined RecursiveArrayIterator already exists and it's not difficult to use this for recursive array processing. Here's how:

```php
<?php
// define nested array
$data = array(
    "United States",
    array("Texas", "Philadelphia"),
    array("California",
    array ("Los Angeles", "San Francisco")));

// initialize an Iterator
// pass it the array to be processed
$iterator - new RecursiveIteratorIterator(new RecursiveArrayIterator
($data));

// iterate over the array
// result: "UNITED STATES TEXAS PHILADELPHIA CALIFORNIA LOS ANGELES SAN
FRANCISCO"
foreach ($iterator as $value) {
    print strtoupper($value) . " \n";
}
?>
```

To recursively process an array, initialize a RecursiveIteratorIterator object (this is an Iterator designed solely for the purpose of iterating over other recursive Iterators) and pass it a newly minted RecursiveArrayIterator. You can now process all the elements of the nested array(s) with a `foreach()` loop.

You can read more about the RecursiveArrayIterator, the RecursiveIteratorIterator, and the RecursiveIterator interfaces at `http://www.php.net/~helly/php/ext/spl/`.

4.4 Counting the Number of Elements in an Array

Problem

You want to find out how many elements an array contains.

Solution

Use PHP's count () function:

```php
<?php
// define indexed array
$animals = array("turtle", "iguana", "wolf", "anteater", "donkey");

// get array size (number of elements)
// result: 5
echo count($animals);
?>
```

Comments

The count () function returns the number of elements in the array. An alternative is to use the sizeof () function, which does the same thing.

4.5 Converting Strings to Arrays

Problem

You want to decompose a string into individual elements and store them in an array, or combine the elements of an array into a single string.

Solution

Use PHP's explode () function to split a string by delimiter and store the separate segments in a numerically indexed array:

```php
<?php
// define string
$alphabetStr = "a b c d e f g h i j k";

// break string into array
// using whitespace as the separator
// result: ("a","b","c","d","e","f","g","h","i","j","k")
print_r(explode(" ", $alphabetStr));
?>
```

Use PHP's `implode()` function to combine array elements into a single string, with an optional delimiter as "glue":

```php
<?php
// define array
$names = array("John", "Joe", "Harry", "Sally", "Mona");

// combine array elements into string
// using "and" as the separator
// result: "John and Joe and Harry and Sally and Mona"
echo implode(" and ", $names);
?>
```

Comments

PHP's `explode()` function makes it a single-step process to split a delimiter-separated string list into an array of individual list elements. The previous listing clearly illustrates this: the `explode()` function scans the string for the delimiter and cuts out the pieces around it, placing them in an array. Once the list items have been extracted, a `foreach()` loop is a good way to process the resulting array.

PHP's `implode()` function does the reverse. It iterates over an array, joining the elements into a single string. An optional delimiter, typically a comma (,) or colon (:), can be used to separate the array elements from each other in the final string. The previous listing illustrates this by using the word `"and"` to join the various array elements into a readable sentence.

4.6 Swapping Array Keys and Values

Problem

You want to interchange the keys and values of an associative array.

Solution

Use PHP's `array_flip()` function:

```php
<?php
// define associative array
$opposites = array("white" => "black", "day" => "night", "open" =>
"close");
```

```
// exchange keys and values
// returns ("black" => "white", "night" => "day", "close" => "open")
print_r(array_flip($opposites));
?>
```

Comments

PHP's `array_flip()` function performs a very specialized task. It reverses the key-value relationship for all the elements of an associative array, returning a new array that is the mirror image of the original. This function should not be confused with the `array_reverse()` function, discussed in the listing in "4.12: Reversing Arrays."

4.7 Adding and Removing Array Elements

Problem

You want to add or remove elements from an array.

Solution

Use PHP's `array_pop()`, `array_push()`, `array_shift()`, and `array_unshift()` functions to attach or detach elements from the beginning or ends of a numerically indexed array:

```
<?php
// define indexed array
$superheroes = array("spiderman", "superman");

// add an element to the end of the array
// result: ("spiderman", "superman", "the incredible hulk")
array_push($superheroes, "the incredible hulk");
print_r($superheroes);

// take an element off the beginning of the array
// result: ("superman", "the incredible hulk")
array_shift($superheroes);
print_r($superheroes);
```

```
// add an element to the beginning of the array
// result: ("the human torch", "superman", "the incredible hulk")
array_unshift($superheroes, "the human torch");
print_r($superheroes);

// take an element off the end of the array
// result: ("the human torch", "superman")
array_pop($superheroes);
print_r($superheroes);
?>
```

Use PHP's `array_splice()` function to add or remove elements from the middle of an array:

```
<?php
// define array
$colors = array("violet", "indigo", "blue", "green", "yellow",↵
"orange", "red", "purple", "black", "white");

// remove middle 4 elements
// result: ("violet", "indigo", "blue", "purple", "black", "white")
array_splice($colors, 3, 4);
print_r($colors);

// add 2 elements between "black" and "white"
// result: ("violet", "indigo", "blue", "purple", "black",↵
"silver", "brown", "white")
array_splice($colors, 5, 0, array("silver", "brown"));
print_r($colors);
?>
```

Comments

PHP comes with four functions to add and remove elements from the ends of an array. The `array_unshift()` function adds an element to the beginning of an array, while the `array_shift()` function removes the first element of an array. The `array_push()` and `array_pop()` functions work in a similar manner, but operate on the end of an array instead. Note that the array is automatically re-indexed after each operation.

TIP

You can add multiple elements with `array_unshift()` *and* `array_push()` —*simply specify them as additional arguments in the function call.*

NOTE

It is not usually appropriate to use the `array_unshift()` *and* `array_push()` *functions with associative arrays. Elements added in this manner will have numeric, rather than string, indices.*

To add or remove elements from the middle of an array, use the `array_splice()` function. This function packs a lot of power under an unassuming exterior—it can be used to "splice in" new array elements, optionally replacing existing elements in the process.

The `array_splice()` function accepts four arguments: the array to operate on, the index to begin splicing at, the number of elements to return from the start position, and an array of replacement values. Omitting the final argument causes `array_splice()` to remove elements without replacing them; this comes in handy for removing elements from the middle of an array. Note that the array is automatically re-indexed after `array_splice()` has finished.

TIP

You can actually use `array_splice()` *to perform all the functions of* `array_pop()`, `array_push()`, `array_shift()`, *and* `array_unshift()`. *The PHP manual page at* `http://www.php.net/array-splice` *has more information.*

NOTE

The `array_unshift()`, `array_shift()`, `array_pop()`, *and* `array_push()` *functions only work with previously initialized arrays. You'll get an error if you attempt to use them on uninitialized array variables.*

4.8 Extracting Contiguous Segments of an Array

Problem

You want to retrieve two or more successive elements from an array.

Solution

Use PHP's `array_slice()` function:

```php
<?php
// define array
$colors = array("violet", "indigo", "blue", "green", "yellow",⏎
"orange", "red", "purple", "black", "white");

// extract middle 4 elements
// result: ("green", "yellow", "orange", "red");
$slice = array_slice($colors, 3, 4);
print_r($slice);
?>
```

Comments

PHP enables you to extract a subsection of an array with the `array_slice()` function, in much the same way that the `substr()` function enables you to extract a section of a string. The function takes three arguments: the array variable to operate on, the index to begin slicing at, and the number of elements to return from the start position.

It's important to note that `array_slice()` is less intrusive than the `array_splice()` function discussed in the listing in "4.7: Adding and Removing Array Elements"—`array_splice()` alters the original array, while `array_slice()` merely returns a subset, leaving the original array unchanged.

4.9 Removing Duplicate Array Elements

Problem

You want to strip an array of all duplicate elements to obtain a unique set.

Solution

Use PHP's `array_unique()` function:

```php
<?php
// define an array containing duplicates
$numbers = array(10,20,10,40,35,80,35,50,55,10,55,30,40,70,50,10,35,⏎
85,40,90,30);
```

```
// extracts all unique elements into a new array
// result: "10, 20, 40, 35, 80, 50, 55, 30, 70, 85, 90"
echo join(", ", array_unique($numbers));
?>
```

Comments

The `array_unique()` function is an easy way to produce a list of the unique elements of an array. This function finds all the unique elements of an array (either associative or numerically indexed) and places them into a new array. The original array remains unchanged.

To filter array elements by other criteria, take a look at the listing in "4.15: Filtering Array Elements."

4.10 Re-indexing Arrays

Problem

You want to re-index a numerically indexed array after removing elements from it, to close up the "gaps" in the indexing sequence.

Solution

Use PHP's `array_values()` function:

```
<?php
// define indexed array
$superheroes = array(0 => "spiderman", 1 => "superman",↵
2 => "captain marvel", 3 => "green lantern");

// remove an element from the middle of the array
// result: (0 => "spiderman", 1 => "superman", 3 => "green lantern")
unset ($superheroes[2]);

// rearrange array elements to remove gap
// result: (0 => "spiderman", 1 => "superman", 2 => "green lantern")
$superheroes = array_values($superheroes);
print_r($superheroes);
?>
```

Comments

If you remove one or more elements from the middle of an integer-indexed array with the unset() function, PHP doesn't automatically re-index the array for you. As a result, you end up with an array containing nonsequential index numbers.

It's generally a good idea to close up these "holes" in the array indexing sequence, to eliminate the possibility of them skewing your array calculations. The simplest way to do this is to retrieve the list of array values with the array_values() function, and then reassign this list back to the original array variable. This re-indexes the array and closes up the gaps.

NOTE

Because associative arrays use string indices, you don't need to re-index them in this manner after unset() -*ting their elements.*

4.11 Randomizing Arrays

Problem

You want to shuffle an array randomly, or retrieve one or more random elements from an array.

Solution

Use PHP's shuffle() and array_rand() functions:

```php
<?php
// define array of numbers from 1 to 5
$numbers = range(1,5);

// shuffle array elements randomly
// result: "3, 5, 1, 2, 4" (example)
shuffle($numbers);
echo join (", ", $numbers);
?>
<?php
// define array of numbers from 1 to 12
$numbers = range(1,12);

// pick 5 random keys from the array
$randKeys = array_rand($numbers, 5);
```

```
// print the chosen elements
// result: "3, 5, 1, 2, 4" (example)
echo join (", ", $randKeys);
?>
```

Comments

PHP's `shuffle()` function randomly re-arranges the elements of the array
passed to it. Key-value associations are retained for associative arrays, but not for
numerically indexed arrays.

 If you'd prefer to leave the array order untouched and just pull out some elements
at random instead, the `array_rand()` function is a better bet. This function
returns an array of randomly extracted keys, which you can then use to retrieve the
corresponding array values.

4.12 Reversing Arrays

Problem

You want to reverse the order of elements in an array.

Solution

Use PHP's `array_reverse()` function:

```
<?php
// define array of numbers
$numbers = array("one", "two", "three", "four", "five");

// return an array with elements reversed
// result: ("five", "four", "three", "two", "one")
print_r(array_reverse($numbers));
?>
```

Comments

PHP's `array_reverse()` function is pretty simple—give it an array and it returns
a new array containing the elements of the original array, but in reverse order. Key-
value association is retained for associative arrays, but numerically indexed arrays
are re-indexed.

4.13 Searching Arrays

Problem

You want to search an array for a particular key or value.

Solution

Use PHP's `array_key_exists()` or `in_array()` functions:

```php
<?php
// define associative array
$data = array(
    "UK" => "United Kingdom",
    "US" => "United States of America",
    "IN" => "India",
    "AU" => "Australia");

// search for key
// result: "Key exists"
echo array_key_exists("UK", $data) ? "Key exists" : ↵
"Key does not exist";

// search for value
// result: "Value exists"
echo in_array("Australia", $data) ? "Value exists" : ↵
"Value does not exist";
?>
```

Comments

PHP comes with two functions that let you search both array keys and values: the `array_key_exists()` function scans an array's keys for matches to your search term, while the `in_array()` function checks its values.

It should be noted, though, that the search capability here is fairly primitive; both functions will return false unless they find an exact match for your search term. If you need more sophisticated search capabilities—for example, support for regular expression or partial matches—consider writing your own search function, as in the script that follows:

```php
<?php
// function to search array keys and values
function arraySearch($needle, $haystack) {
    // check if input is array
    if (!is_array($haystack)) { die ("Second argument is not array!"); }

    // iterate over array
    foreach ($haystack as $key=>$value) {
        // check keys and values for match
        // return true if match
        if (preg_match("/$needle/i", $value) || preg_match("/$needle/↵
i", $key)) {                   return true;
            break;
        }
    }
}


// define associative array
$data = array(
    "UK" => "United Kingdom",
    "US" => "United States of America",
    "IN" => "India",
    "AU" => "Australia");

// search array
// returns "Match"
echo arraySearch("us", $data) ? "Match" : "No match";

// returns "No match"
echo arraySearch("xz", $data) ? "Match" : "No match";
?>
```

Here, the preg_match() function is used to search both keys and values of an array for a match. You can, of course, modify this to suit your own requirements.

> **NOTE**
>
> *The* arraySearch() *function described here will not work correctly with multidimensional arrays. To recursively search a multidimensional array, flip forward to the listing in "4.14: Searching Nested Arrays."*

4.14 Searching Nested Arrays

Problem

You want to search a series of nested arrays for a particular key or value.

Solution

Write a recursive function to traverse the arrays and run a custom search function on each element:

```php
<?php
// function to recursively traverse nested arrays
// and search for values matching a pattern
function arraySearchRecursive($needle, $haystack, $path="") {
    // check if input is array
    if (!is_array($haystack)) { die ("Second argument is not array!"); }

    // declare a variable to hold matches
    global $matches;

    // iterate over array
    foreach($haystack as $key=>$value) {

        if (preg_match("/$needle/i", $key)) {
            $matches[] = array($path . "$key/", "KEY: $key");
        }

        if (is_array($value)) {
            // if a nested array
            // recursively search
            // unset the path once the end of the tree is reached
            $path .= "$key/";
            arraySearchRecursive($needle, $value, $path);
            unset($path);
        } else {
            // if not an array
            // check for match
            // save path if match exists
            if (preg_match("/$needle/i", $value)) {
                $matches[] = array($path . "$key/", "VALUE: $value");
            }
        }
    }
}
```

```
            // return the list of matches to the caller
            return $matches;
}


// define nested array
$data = array (
    "United States" => array (
        "Texas",
        "Philadelphia",
        "California" => array (
            "Los Angeles",
            "San Francisco" => array(
                "Silicon Valley"))));


// search for string "in"
// result: an array of 2 occurrences with path
print_r(arraySearchRecursive("co", $data));
?>
```

Comments

This listing is actually a combination of techniques discussed in the listing in "4.3: Processing Nested Arrays" and the listing in "4.13: Searching Arrays." Here, the custom `arraySearchRecursive()` function traverses the nested array, checking each key and value for matches to the search string with the `preg_match()` function. Matches, if any, are placed in a separate `$matches` array. At each stage of recursion, the "path" to the element—the sequence of array keys leading to the element—is tracked; this path is also stored in the `$matches` array as an aid to identifying the matching elements post search.

An alternative way to recursively search an array is to use the RecursiveIterat orIterator and RecursiveArrayIterator objects, two of the new Iterators available in PHP 5.0 and better. To do this, initialize a RecursiveIteratorIterator object (this is an Iterator designed solely for the purpose of iterating over other recursive Iterators) and pass it a newly minted RecursiveArrayIterator. You can now search all the elements of the nested array(s) with a `foreach()` loop and a call to `preg_match()`. Here's an example:

```
<?php
// define associative array
$data = array (
    "United States" => array (
        "Texas",
        "Philadelphia",
        "California" => array (
```

```
            "Los Angeles",
            "San Francisco" => array(
                "Silicon Valley"))));

// define search string
$needle = "il";
$matches = array();

// recursively search array
$iterator = new RecursiveIteratorIterator(new RecursiveArrayIterator ↵
($data));
foreach ($iterator as $value) {
    if(preg_match("/$needle/i", $value)) {
        $matches[] = $value;
    }
}

// print matching values
// result: ("Philadelphia", "Silicon Valley")
print_r($matches);
?>
```

You can read more about the RecursiveArrayIterator, the RecursiveIteratorIterat
or, and the RecursiveIterator interfaces at `http://www.php.net/~helly/php/`
`ext/spl/`.

4.15 Filtering Array Elements

Problem

You want to eliminate those elements of an array that don't match certain criteria.

Solution

Create a custom filter for the array with PHP's `array_filter()` function:

```php
<?php
// function to test if a number is positive
function isPositive($value) {
    return ($value > 0) ? true : false;
}
```

```
// define array of numbers
$series = array(-10,21,43,-6,5,1,84,1,-32);

// filter out positive values
// result: (21, 43, 5, 1, 84, 1)
print_r(array_filter($series, 'isPositive'));
?>
```

Comments

PHP's `array_filter()` function is great for identifying those array elements that match specific, user-defined criteria. It works by running each array member through a user-defined function and checking the return value. Those array members associated with a true return are flagged as "special," and placed in a separate array.

This is clearly illustrated in the previous listing. Here, the user-defined `isPositive()` function returns true if its input argument is greater than 0. The `array_filter()` function runs `isPositive()` on every member of the `$series` array, and checks to see which members generate a true value. The true return serves as a flag to filter out positive values, which are then placed in a separate `$positives` array.

4.16 Sorting Arrays

Problem

You want to sort an array by key or value.

Solution

Use PHP's `sort()` function on numerically indexed arrays:

```
<?php
// define indexed array
$animals = array("wolf", "lion", "tiger", "iguana", "bear",⏎
"zebra", "leopard");

// sort alphabetically by value
// result: ("bear", "iguana", "leopard", "lion", "tiger", "wolf",
"zebra")
sort($animals);
print_r($animals);
?>
```

Use PHP's `asort()` or `ksort()` function on string-indexed arrays:

```php
<?php
// define associative array
$animals = array("wolf" => "Rex", "tiger" => "William",↵
"bear" => "Leo",  "zebra" => "Adam", "leopard" => "Ian");

// sort alphabetically by value, retaining keys
// result: ("zebra" => "Adam", ..., "tiger" => "William")
asort($animals);
print_r($animals);

// sort alphabetically by keys, retaining values
// result: ("bear" => "Leo", ..., "zebra" => "Adam")
ksort($animals);
print_r($animals);
?>
```

Comments

PHP's array manipulation API comes with a number of functions to sort array elements. The most commonly used one is the `sort()` function, which sorts numerically indexed arrays in alphanumeric order. This function is not suitable for associative arrays, as it destroys the key-value association of those arrays. If you need to sort an associative array, consider using the `asort()` or `ksort()` functions, which sort these arrays by value and key respectively while simultaneously maintaining the key-value relationship. The previous listing illustrates all three of these functions.

An interesting entrant in the sort sweepstakes is the `natsort()` function, which sorts array elements using a natural-language algorithm. This comes in handy to sort array values "the way a human being would." Key-value associations are maintained throughout the sorting process. The next listing illustrates this:

```php
<?php
// define array
$userList = array("user1","user10","user20","user2");

// normal sort
// result: ("user1", "user10", "user2", "user20")
sort($userList);
print_r($userList);
```

```
// natural-language sort
// result: ("user1", "user2", "user10", "user20")
natsort($userList);
print_r($userList);
?>
```

> ### *TIP*
>
> *You can reverse the sort order of the* `sort()`*,* `asort()`*, and* `ksort()` *functions by replacing them with calls to* `rsort()`*,* `arsort()`*, and* `krsort()` *respectively.*

4.17 Sorting Multidimensional Arrays

Problem

You want to sort a multidimensional array using multiple keys.

Solution

Use PHP's `array_multisort()` function:

```php
<?php
// create a multidimensional array
$data = array();
$data[0] = array("title" => "Net Force", "author" => "Clancy, Tom",
"rating" => 4);
$data[1] = array("title" => "Every Dead Thing", "author" => "Connolly,
John", "rating"=> 5);
$data[2] = array("title" => "Driven To Extremes", "author" => "Allen,
James", "rating" => 4);
$data[3] = array("title" => "Dark Hollow", "author" => "Connolly,
John", "rating" => 4);
$data[4] = array("title" => "Bombay Ice", "author" => "Forbes,
Leslie", "rating" => 5);

// separate all the elements with the same key
// into individual arrays
foreach ($data as $key=>$value) {
   $author[$key]  = $value['author'];
   $title[$key]  = $value['title'];
   $rating[$key]  = $value['rating'];
}
```

```
// sort by rating and then author
array_multisort($rating, $author, $data);
print_r($data);
?>
```

Comments

If you're familiar with Structured Query Language (SQL), you already know how the ORDER BY clause enables you to sort a resultset by more than one field. That's essentially what the `array_multisort()` function was designed to do: it accepts a series of input arrays and uses them as sort criteria. Sorting begins with the first array; values in that array that evaluate as equal are sorted by the next array, and so on.

This function comes in handy when dealing with symmetrical multidimensional arrays, like the one in the previous listing. Such an array is typically created from an SQL resultset. To sort such an array, first break it into individual single arrays, one for each unique key, and then use `array_multisort()` to sort the arrays in the priority you desire. In such a situation, the last argument to `array_multisort()` must be the original multidimensional array.

4.18 Sorting Arrays Using a Custom Sort Function

Problem

You want to sort an array using a custom sorting algorithm.

Solution

Define your sorting algorithm and use the `usort()` function to process an array with it:

```
<?php
// function to compare length of two values
function sortByLength($a, $b) {
    if (is_scalar($a) && is_scalar($b)) {
        if (strlen($a) == strlen($b)) {
          return 0;
        } else {
          return (strlen($a) > strlen($b)) ? 1 : -1;
        }
    }
}
```

```
// define array
$data = array("abracadabra", "goo", "indefinitely",⏎
"hail to the chief", "aloha");

// sort array using custom sorting function
// result: ("goo", "aloha", ..., "hail to the chief")
usort($data, 'sortByLength');
print_r($data);
?>
```

Comments

Often, PHP's built-in sorting functions may be insufficient for your needs. For such situations, PHP offers the `usort()` function, which enables you to sort an array using a custom sorting algorithm. This sorting algorithm is nothing more than a comparison function, which accepts two arguments and decides whether one is larger or smaller than the other. The comparison must return a number less than 0 if the first argument is to be considered less than the second, and a number greater than 0 if the first argument is to be considered greater than the second.

The previous listing illustrates this, presenting a comparison function that can be used to sort array elements by their length, with the shortest items first. The `strlen()` function is used to calculate the number of characters in each element; this then serves as the basis for re-sorting the array.

4.19 Sorting Nested Arrays

Problem

You want to sort a series of nested arrays.

Solution

Write a recursive function to traverse the arrays and sort each one:

```
<?php
// function to compare length of two values
function sortByLength($a, $b) {
    if (is_scalar($a) && is_scalar($b)) {
        if (strlen($a) == strlen($b)) {
          return 0;
```

```
        } else {
            return (strlen($a) > strlen($b)) ? 1 : -1;
        }
    }
}


// function to recursively sort
// a series of nested arrays
function sortRecursive(&$arr, $sortFunc, $sortFuncParams = null) {

    // check if input is array
    if (!is_array($arr)) { die ("Argument is not array!"); }

    // sort the array using the named function
    $sortFunc($arr, $sortFuncParams);

    // check to see if further arrays exist
    // recurse if so
    foreach (array_keys($arr) as $k) {
        if (is_array($arr[$k])) {
            sortRecursive($arr[$k], $sortFunc, $sortFuncParams);
        }
    }
}


// define nested array
$data = array (
    "United States" => array (
        "West Virginia",
        "Texas" => array(
            "Dallas", "Austin"),
        "Philadelphia", "Vermont", "Kentucky",
        "California" => array (
            "San Francisco", "Los Angeles", "Cupertino", "Mountain
View")));

// sort $data recursively using asort()
sortRecursive($data, 'asort');
print_r($data);

// sort $data recursively using custom function()
sortRecursive($data, 'usort', 'sortByLength');
print_r($data);
?>
```

Comments

This listing builds on the technique discussed in the listing in "4.3: Processing Nested Arrays" to recursively traverse a series of nested arrays. The `sortRecursive()` function accepts three arguments: an array, the name of an array sorting function (either built-in or user-defined), and optional arguments to said function. It then traverses the array and all the arrays internal to it, sorting each by the specified function.

Note that the array input to `sortRecursive()` is passed by reference, so any changes take place to the array variable itself and not a copy.

4.20 Merging Arrays

Problem

You want to merge two or more arrays into a single array.

Solution

Use PHP's `array_merge()` or `array_merge_recursive()` functions:

```php
<?php
// define arrays
$statesUS = array("Maine", "New York", "Florida", "California");
$statesIN = array("Maharashtra", "Tamil Nadu", "Kerala");

// merge into a single array
// result: ("Maine", "New York", ..., "Tamil Nadu", "Kerala")
$states = array_merge($statesUS, $statesIN);
print_r($states);
?>
```

```php
<?php
// define arrays
$ab = array("a" => "apple", "b" => "baby");
$ac = array("a" => "anteater", "c" => "cauliflower");
$bcd = array("b" => "ball", "c" => array("car", "caterpillar"),↵
"d" => "demon");

// recursively merge into a single array
$abcd = array_merge_recursive($ab, $ac, $bcd);
print_r($abcd);
?>
```

Comments

PHP's `array_merge()` function accepts two or more arrays as arguments, and combines them to create a single array. The behavior of this function is fairly straightforward when dealing with numerically indexed arrays, but can trip you up when you're working with associative arrays: If you try merging associative arrays that have some key names in common, only the last such key-value pair will appear in the merged array.

To work around this problem, use the `array_merge_recursive()` function when merging associative arrays. This function ensures that common keys are recursively merged into a single sub-array and no data is lost during the merge process. You see this in the output of the second listing in the previous code.

You can also create an associative array by merging two numerically indexed arrays, using the `array_combine()` function. Elements of the first array are converted into keys of the combined array, while elements of the second array become the corresponding values. Here's an example:

```php
<?php
// define array for keys
$keys = array("UK", "US", "FR", "IN");

// define array for values
$values = array("London", "Washington", "Paris", "Delhi");

// combine into single associative array
// returns ("UK" => "London", "US" => "Washington", ...)
$capitals = array_combine($keys, $values)↵
or die ("Unable to match keys and values");
print_r($capitals);
?>
```

4.21 Comparing Arrays

Problem

You want to compare two arrays to find the common or different elements.

Solution

Use PHP's `array_intersect()` function to find the elements common to two arrays:

```php
<?php
// define arrays
$salt = array("sodium", "chlorine");
$acid = array("hydrogen", "chlorine", "nitrogen");

// get all elements from $acid
// that also exist in $salt
// result: ("chlorine")
$intersection = array_intersect($acid, $salt);
print_r($intersection);
?>
```

Use PHP's `array_diff()` function to find the elements that exist in either one of the two arrays, but not both simultaneously:

```php
<?php
// define arrays
$salt = array("sodium", "chlorine");
$acid = array("hydrogen", "chlorine", "nitrogen");

// get all elements that do not exist
// in both arrays simultaneously
// result: ("hydrogen", "nitrogen", "sodium")
$diff = array_unique(array_merge(↵
  array_diff($acid, $salt), array_diff($salt, $acid)
));
print_r($diff);
?>
```

Comments

Consider a Venn diagram (Figure 4-1) illustrating the intersection of two sets. Assuming these sets are represented as arrays, most developers find themselves having to deal with one of two tasks: finding the elements common to both arrays (C), or finding the elements that exist in either one of the two arrays, but not both simultaneously (A+B).

Obtaining the common set elements (C) is simple—the `array_intersect()` function is designed to do just this. Finding the elements that exist in either one of the two arrays, but not both simultaneously, is a little more complex, and requires knowledge of the `array_diff()` function.

Given two arrays, this `array_diff()` function returns all the elements from the second array that do not exist in the first. This means that you can obtain the required

Figure 4-1   *A Venn Diagram*

(A+B) set by running `array_diff()` twice, swapping the order of comparison each time, and then merging the resulting arrays. You should also run the `array_unique()` function on the merged array to eliminate any duplicates. This process is illustrated in the second listing.

Note that the `array_diff()` and `array_intersect()` functions only compare array values; they ignore the corresponding keys when calculating the array intersection or difference. You can improve on this situation by providing the `array_diff_assoc()` and `array_intersect_assoc()` functions, which take keys into account as well. The following listing illustrates the difference:

```php
<?php
// define arrays
$a = array("sodium", "chlorine", "hydrogen");
$b = array("chlorine", "sodium", "hydrogen");

// insensitive to keys
// result: ()
print_r(array_diff($a, $b));

// sensitive to keys
// result: ("sodium", "chlorine")
print_r(array_diff_assoc($a, $b));

// insensitive to keys
// result: ("sodium", "chlorine", "hydrogen")
print_r(array_intersect($a, $b));

// sensitive to keys
// result: ("hydrogen")
print_r(array_intersect_assoc($a, $b));
?>
```

CHAPTER
5

Working with Functions and Classes

IN THIS CHAPTER:

A s with any programming language worth its salt, PHP supports functions and classes, which you can use to make your code more modular, maintainable, and reusable. Functions, in particular, have been well-supported in PHP for a long time, and so most of the new developments in PHP have focused on the object model, which has been completely redesigned to bring PHP in closer compliance with OOP standards.

The solutions in this chapter are therefore a mix of old and new techniques. Among the golden oldies: dealing with variable scope; using variable-length argument lists and default arguments; extending classes; using class constructors; and checking class ancestry. Among the brash newcomers: overloading methods; cloning and comparing objects; using abstract classes; and protecting class members from outside access. Together, they add up to a fairly interesting collection. See for yourself!

5.1 Defining Custom Functions

Problem

You want to define your own functions.

Solution

Use PHP's `function` keyword to name and define custom functions, and invoke them as required:

```php
<?php
// define function
// to calculate circle area
function getCircleArea($radius) {
    return pi() * $radius * $radius;
}

// invoke function
// for circle of radius 10
// result: "The area of a circle with radius 10 is 314.159265359"
echo "The area of a circle with radius 10 is " . getCircleArea(10);
?>
```

Comments

A *function* is an independent block of code that performs a specific task, and can be use more than once at different points within the main program. Every programming language comes with built-in functions and typically also allows developers to define their own custom functions. PHP is no exception to this rule.

Function definitions in PHP begin with the `function` keyword, followed by the function name (this can be any string that conforms to PHP's naming rules), a list of arguments in parentheses, and the function's code within curly braces. *Function arguments* make it possible to supply variable input to the function at run time. Within the function itself, the `return` keyword is used to return the result of the function's operations to the calling program. In the previous example the function is named `getCircleArea()`, accepts a single argument (the circle radius, represented by `$radius`), and uses this argument to calculate the area of the circle.

Once a named function has been defined in the manner described previously, using it is as simple as calling (or *invoking*) it by its name, in much the same way one would call built-in functions such as `implode()` or `exists()`. An example of such function invocation can be seen in the previous listing, which demonstrates the newly-minted `getCircleArea()` function being invoked with an argument of 10 units (the circle radius) and returning a value of 314.16 units (the corresponding circle area).

5.2 Avoiding Function Duplication

Problem

You want to test if a function has already been defined.

Solution

Use PHP's `function_exists()` function:

```php
<?php
// sample function
function doThis() {
    return false;
}
```

```
// test if function exists
// result: "Function exists"
echo function_exists("doThis") ? "Function exists" :↵
"Function does not exist";

// result: "Function does not exist"
echo function_exists("doThat") ? "Function exists" :↵
"Function does not exist";
?>
```

Comments

It's a good idea to check for the prior existence of a function before declaring it, because PHP generates an error on any attempt to re-declare a previously defined function. The function_exists() function provides an easy solution to the problem, as illustrated in the previous example.

5.3 Accessing External Variables from Within a Function

Problem

You want to access a variable from the main program within a function definition.

Solution

Use the global keyword within the function definition to import the variable from the global scope:

```
<?php
// define variable outside function
$name = "Susan";

// access variable from within function
function whoAmI() {
    global $name;
    return $name;
}
```

```
// call function
// result: "Susan"
echo whoAmI();
?>
```

Comments

By default, variables within a function are isolated from variables outside it in PHP. The values assigned to them, and the changes made to them, are thus "local" and restricted to the function space alone. Often, however, there arises a need to share a variable from the main program with the code inside a function definition. You can accomplish this by making the variable "global," so that it can be manipulated both inside and outside the function. PHP's global keyword, when prefixed to a variable name within a function definition, takes care of making the variable global. This is illustrated in the previous listing.

An alternative way of accomplishing the same thing is to access the variable by name from the special $_GLOBALS associative array, as demonstrated in the next listing:

```
<?php
// define variable outside function
$name = "Susan";

// access variable from within function
function whoAmI() {
    return $GLOBALS['name'];
}

// call function
// result: "Susan"
echo whoAmI();
?>
```

For a more detailed demonstration of variable scope inside and outside a function, consider the following listing:

```
<?php
// define a variable outside the function
$name = "Joe";
```

```php
// define a function to alter the variable
function whoAmI() {
    // access the variable from inside the function
    global $name;

    // check the variable
    // result: "I am Joe at the beginning of the function."
    echo "I am $name at the beginning of the function.\n";

    // redefine the variable inside the function
    $name = "Jane";

    // check the variable
    // result: "I am Jane at the end of the function."
    echo "I am $name at the end of the function.\n";
}

// check the variable
// result: "I am Joe before running the function."
print "I am $name before running the function.\n";

// call the function
echo whoAmI();

// check the variable
// result: "I am Jane after running the function."
print "I am $name after running the function.\n";
?>
```

NOTE

PHP also comes with so-called supergglobal variables (or superglobals) — variables that are always available, regardless of whether you're inside a function or outside it. The $_SERVER, $_POST, *and* $_GET *variables are examples of superglobals, which is why you can access things like the currently executing script's name or form values even inside a function. The good news about superglobals is that they're always there when you need them, and you don't need to jump through any hoops to use the data stored inside them. The bad news is that the superglobal club is a very exclusive one, and you can't turn any of your own variables into superglobals. Read more about superglobals and variable scope at* http://www.php.net/variables.predefined *and* http://www.php.net/variables.scope.

5.4 Setting Default Values for Function Arguments

Problem

You want to set default values for one or more function arguments, thereby making them optional.

Solution

Assign default values to those arguments in the function signature:

```php
<?php
// define function
// with default arguments
function orderPizza($crust, $toppings, $size="12") {
    return "You asked for a $size-inch pizza with a $crust crust ⏎
and these toppings: " . implode(', ', $toppings);
}

// call function without optional third argument
// result: "You asked for a 12-inch pizza with a ⏎
// thin crust and these toppings: cheese, anchovies"
echo orderPizza("thin", array("cheese", "anchovies"));
?>
```

Comments

Normally, PHP expects the number of arguments in a function invocation to match that in the corresponding function definition, and it will generate an error in case of a smaller argument list. However, you might want to make some arguments optional, using default values if no data is provided by the user. You can do this by assigning values to the appropriate arguments in the function definition.

> **TIP**
>
> *Place optional arguments after mandatory arguments in the function's argument list.*

5.5 Processing Variable-Length Argument Lists

Problem

You want your function to support a variable number of arguments.

Solution

Use PHP's `func_get_args()` function to read a variable-length argument list:

```php
<?php
// define a function
function someFunc() {
    // get the number of arguments passed
    $numArgs = func_num_args();

     // get the arguments
    $args = func_get_args();

    // print the arguments
    print "You sent me the following arguments: ";
    for ($x=0; $x<sizeof($args); $x++) {
        print "\nArgument $x: ";
        // check if an array was passed
        // iterate and print contents if so
        if (is_array($args[$x])) {
            print " ARRAY ";
            foreach ($args[$x] as $index=>$element) {
                print " $index => $element ";
            }
        } else {
            print " $args[$x] ";
        }
    }
}

// call the function with different arguments
// returns: "You sent me the following arguments:
// Argument 0: red
// Argument 1: green
// Argument 2: blue
```

```
// Argument 3: ARRAY 0 => 4 1 => 5
// Argument 4: yellow"
someFunc("red", "green", "blue", array(4,5), "yellow");
?>
```

Comments

PHP's func_get_args() function is designed specifically for functions that receive argument lists of varying length. When used inside a function definition, func_get_args() returns an array of all the arguments passed to the function; the individual arguments can then be extracted and processed with a for() loop. Remember that the argument list can contain a mixture of scalar variables and arrays, so if you're unsure what input to expect, make it a point to check the type of each argument before deciding how to process it.

Here's another example of this in action:

```
<?php
// define function that accepts
// a dynamic number of arguments
function calcSum() {
    $sum = 0;

    // get argument list as array
    $args = func_get_args();

    // process argument list
    // add each argument to previous total
    // if any of the arguments is an array
    // use a loop to process it
    for ($x=0; $x<sizeof($args); $x++) {
        if (is_array($args[$x])) {
            foreach ($args[$x] as $a) {
                $sum += $a;
            }
        } else {
            $sum += $args[$x];
        }
    }
    return $sum;
}
```

```php
// call function with 2 scalar arguments
// result: "The sum of 1 and 10 is 11."
echo "The sum of 1 and 10 is " . calcSum(1,10) . ".\n";

// call function with mixture
// of 3 scalar and array arguments
// result: " The sum of 1, 2, 5 and 1 is 9."
echo "The sum of 1, 2, 5 and 1 is " . calcSum(1, 2, array(5,1)) . ".\n";
?>
```

5.6 Returning Multiple Values from a Function

Problem

You want to return more than one value from a function.

Solution

Place the set of desired return values in an array, and return that instead:

```php
<?php
// define function
// that returns more than one value
function getUserInfo() {
    return array("Simon Doe", "London", "simon@some.domain.edu");
}

// extract returned list into separate variables
// result: "My name is Simon Doe from London.
// Get in touch at simon@some.domain.edu"
list ($name, $place, $email) = getUserInfo();
echo "My name is $name from $place. Get in touch at $email";
?>
```

Comments

A PHP function can only return a single value to the caller; however, this value may be of any supported type (scalar, array, object, and so on). So, if you'd like a function to return multiple values, the simplest way to do this is to add them all to an array and return that instead.

5.7 Manipulating Function Inputs and Outputs by Reference

Problem

You want to pass input arguments to, or receive return values from, a function by reference (instead of by value).

Solution

To pass an argument by reference, prefix the argument with the & symbol in the function definition:

```php
<?php
// define a function
// that changes a variable by reference
function changeDay(&$day) {
    $day = "Thursday";
    return $day;
}

// define a variable outside the function
$day = "Sunday";

// check variable
// result: "Before running changeDay(), it is Sunday."
echo "Before running changeDay(), it is $day.\n";

// pass variable by reference
changeDay($day);

// check variable
// result: "After running changeDay(), it is Thursday."
echo "After running changeDay(), it is $day.";
?>
```

To return a value by reference, prefix both the function name and the function invocation with the & symbol:

```php
<?php
// define a function
// that returns a value by reference
function &incrementNum() {
    global $num;
    $num++;
    return $num;
}

// define a variable outside the function
$num = 0;

// invoke function
// get return value of function as reference
// result: "Number is 1."
$retVal =& incrementNum();
echo "Number is $retVal.\n";

// invoke function again
incrementNum();

// check reference
// result: "Number is 2."
echo "Number is $retVal.\n";
?>
```

Comments

By default, arguments to PHP functions are passed "by value"—that is, a copy of the variable is passed to the function, with the original variable remaining untouched. However, PHP also allows you to pass "by reference"—that is, instead of passing a value to a function, you pass a reference to the original variable and have the function act on that instead of a copy.

In the first example, because the argument to changeDay() is passed by reference, the change occurs in the original variable rather than in a copy. That's the reason why, when you re-access the variable $day after running the function on it, it returns the modified value "Thursday" instead of the original value "Sunday."

It's also possible to get a reference to a function's return value, as in the second example. There, $retVal is a reference to (not a copy of) a global variable.

So, every time the global variable changes, the value of `$retVal` changes as well. If, instead, you set things up to get a copy of (not a reference to) the function's return value, the value of `$retVal` would remain 1.

> **NOTE**
>
> *References make it possible to manipulate variables outside the scope of a function, in much the same way as the global keyword did in the listing in "5.3: Accessing External Variables From Within a Function." The PHP manual makes the relationship clear when it says "...when you declare [a] variable as global $var, you are in fact creating reference to a global variable." Read more about references at* `http://www.php.net/references`.

5.8 Dynamically Generating Function Invocations

Problem

You want to dynamically generate a function invocation from a PHP variable.

Solution

Use parentheses to interpolate the variable name with the function invocation:

```php
<?php
// sample function
function playTrack($id) {
    echo "Playing track $id";
}

// define variable for operation
$op = "play";

// build function name from variable
$func = $op . "Track";

// call function
// result: "Playing track 45"
$func(45);
?>
```

Comments

PHP supports the use of *variable functions*, wherein a function name is dynamically generated by combining one or more variables. When PHP encounters such a variable function, it first evaluates the variable(s) and then looks for a function matching the result of the evaluation. The previous listing illustrates this, creating a function invocation from a variable.

5.9 Dynamically Defining Functions

Problem

You want to define a function dynamically when another function is invoked.

Solution

Nest one function inside the other:

```php
<?php
// define function
function findOil() {
    // define nested function
    // this function only becomes available
    // once the outer function has been invoked
    function startDrilling() {
        echo "Started drilling. We're gonna be rich!\n";
    }
    echo "Found an oil well. Thar she blows!\n";
}

// run functions
// returns: "Found an oil well. Thar she blows!"
findOil();
// returns: "Started drilling. We're gonna be rich!"
startDrilling();
?>
```

Comments

PHP supports nested functions, wherein the inner function is defined only when the outer one is invoked. In the previous listing, the startDrilling() function does not exist until after the `findOil()` function is called. You can verify this by invoking `startDrilling()` before and after invoking `findOil()`; PHP will return an "undefined function" fatal error in the first instance, but not in the second.

5.10 Creating Recursive Functions

Problem

You want to recursively perform a task.

Solution

Write a recursive function that runs repeatedly until a particular condition is met:

```php
<?php
// recursive function
// to calculate factorial
function calcFactorial($num) {
    // define variable to hold product
    static $product = 1;

    // recurse until $num becomes 1
    if ($num > 1) {
        $product = $product * $num;
        $num--;
        calcFactorial($num);
    }
    return $product;
}

// result: "Factorial of 5 is 120"
echo "Factorial of 5 is " . calcFactorial(5);
?>
```

Comments

PHP supports *recursive functions*, which are essentially functions that call themselves repeatedly until a particular condition is met. Recursive functions are commonly used to process nested data collections—for example, multidimensional arrays, nested file collections, XML trees, and so on. The previous listing illustrates a simple example of recursion—a function that calculates the factorial of a number by repeatedly calling itself with the number, reducing it by 1 on each invocation. Recursion stops only once the number becomes equal to 1.

Here's another example of recursion; this one processes a directory collection and prints a list of the files found:

```php
<?php
// define recursive function
// to display directory contents
function recurseDir($dir) {
    // check for valid argument
    if (!is_dir($dir)) { die("Argument '$dir' is not a directory!"); }

    // open directory handle
    $dh = opendir($dir) or die ("Cannot open directory '$dir'!");

    // iterate over files
    while (($file = readdir($dh)) !== false)  {
        // ignore . and .. items
        if ($file != "." && $file != "..") {
            if (is_dir("$dir/$file")) {
                // if this is a subdirectory
                // recursively process it
                recurseDir("$dir/$file");
            } else {
                // if this is a file
                    // print file name and path
                echo "$dir/$file \n";
            }
        }
    }
}

// recursively process directory
recurseDir('/tmp');
?>
```

Here, every time the function encounters a directory entry, it first checks to see if that value is a file or a directory. If it's a directory, the function calls itself again to process the directory; if it's a file, the file name is printed. The process continues until the end of the directory tree is reached.

5.11 Defining Custom Classes

Problem

You want to define your own class.

Solution

Define a class with the `class` keyword, populate it with properties and methods, and spawn objects from it with the `new` keyword:

```php
<?php
// define class
// for a generic computer
class Generic {
    // properties
    public $cpu;
    public $mem;

    // method to set memory specification
    public function setMemory($val) {
        $this->mem = $val;
        echo "Setting memory to $val MB...\n";
    }

    // method to set processor specification
    public function setCpu($val) {
        $this->cpu = $val;
        echo "Setting processor to \"$val\"...\n";
    }

    // method to print current configuration
    public function getConfig() {
        echo "Current configuration: $this->cpu CPU, $this->mem MB RAM\
n";
    }
}

// create an object of the class
$myPC = new Generic;
```

```
// set processor and memory
$myPC->setCpu("Pentium IV");
$myPC->setMemory(1024);

// display configuration
// result: "Current configuration: Pentium IV CPU, 1024 MB RAM"
$myPC->getConfig();
?>
```

Comments

In PHP, a *class* is simply a group of related functions and variables. It can be used to as a template to spawn specific instances, referred to as *objects*. Every object has certain characteristics, or *properties*, and certain predefined functions, or *methods*. These properties and methods of the object correspond directly with the variables and functions within the class definition.

Once a class has been defined, PHP allows you to spawn as many instances as you like from it. Each of these instances is a completely independent object, with its own properties and methods, and can thus be manipulated independently of other objects. This comes in handy in situations where you need to spawn more than one instance of an object—for example, two simultaneous database links for two simultaneous queries, or two shopping carts.

In PHP, class definitions begin with the `class` keyword, followed by the class name (any string that conforms to PHP's variable naming rules) and the class members—methods and properties—within curly braces. Class methods and properties are defined in the normal way, with an optional visibility declaration preceding each. Three levels of visibility exist, ranging from most visible to least visible: "public," "protected," and "private" (learn more about visibility in the listing in "5.20: Copying Object Instances").

NOTE

In case you need to access functions or variables within the class definition itself, PHP offers the `$this` keyword, which is used to access class methods and properties that are "local" to the class.

Defining a class is only half the puzzle—the other half consists of creating and using an instance of the class. You use the `new` keyword to create a new instance of the class, which you can then assign to a PHP variable in the usual manner. Class methods and properties can then be accessed via this variable, using `->` notation to connect the two. In the previous listing, the class is named Generic and it contains two properties ($cpu and $mem) and three methods (setMemory(), setCpu(), and getConfig()). The $myPC variable represents an instance of this class, with specific values set for the $cpu and $mem properties.

5.12 Automatically Executing Class Initialization and Deinitialization Commands

Problem

You want to automatically execute certain statements when an instance of a class is created or destroyed.

Solution

Use a class constructor and/or destructor:

```php
<?php
// define class
class testClass {

    // PHP 5 constructor
    function __construct() {
        echo "Running the constructor...\n";
    }

    // PHP 5 destructor
    function __destruct() {
        echo "Running the destructor...\n";
    }
}

// create an object
// result: "Running the constructor..."
$test = new testClass();

// then destroy it
// result: "Running the destructor..."
unset($test);
?>
```

Comments

PHP makes it possible to automatically execute code when a new instance of a class is created, using a special class method called a *constructor*. You can also run code when a class instance ends using a so-called *destructor*. Constructors and destructors can be implemented by defining functions named __construct() and __destruct() within the class, and placing object (de)initialization code within them. The previous listing illustrates how this might work, while the following listing contains a more concrete example of it in action:

```php
<?php
// define class
// to manually implement file locking
class fileLock {
    // define properties
    private $file;

    // constructor
    public function __construct($file) {
        $this->file = $file;
        $this->lock();
    }

    // method to create lock file
    public function lock() {
        // clear file cache
        clearstatcache();

        // check if a lock file already exists
        // if not, create one
        // if it does, retry after a few seconds
        echo "Attempting to lock file...\n";
        if (!file_exists($this->file . ".lock")) {
            touch ($this->file . ".lock", time()) ↵
or die("ERROR: Could not create lock file!\n");
            echo "File locked!\n";
        } else {
            echo "Lock exists, retrying after 2 seconds...\n";
            sleep(2);
            $this->lock();
        }
    }
}
```

```php
        // method to write data to locked file
        public function write($data) {
                // try to write to file
                // display error and return if unsuccessful
                echo "Attempting file write...\n";
                if (!$fp = fopen($this->file, "a+")) {
                    echo "ERROR: Cannot open file for writing!\n";
                    return false;
                }
                if (!fwrite($fp, $data)) {
                    echo "ERROR: Cannot write to file!\n";
                    return false;
                }
                if (!fclose($fp)) {
                    echo "ERROR: Cannot close file!\n";
                }
                echo "Data written to file!\n";
        }

        // destructor
        public function __destruct() {
            $this->unlock();
        }

        // method to remove lock file
        public function unlock() {
            // delete lock file
            echo "Unlocking file...\n";
            unlink ($this->file . ".lock") ↵
or die("ERROR: Cannot remove lock file!");
            echo "File unlocked!\n";
        }
}

// create object
// set file lock
$fl = new fileLock("/tmp/data.txt");

// write data to file
$fl->write("I can see you!");

// remove lock
unset($fl);
?>
```

In this example, a new instance of the fileLock class is instantiated and passed the name of the target file. Internally, the class constructor assigns this name to a class property, and then runs the `lock()` method to place a lock on the file. After the file has been successfully locked, the `write()` method is used to write data to the file. Following a successful write operation, the object instance is destroyed with `unset()`; internally, this activates the object destructor, which takes care of calling the `unlock()` method to remove the lock placed on the file.

It's worth noting that important differences exist between PHP 4.x and PHP 5.x with regard to constructors and destructors. As you've seen, in PHP 5.x, constructor and destructor methods must be named `__construct()` and `__destruct()`, respectively. However, PHP 4.x does not support destructors, and constructor methods must have the same name as the class.

To keep your class code portable between PHP 4.x and 5.x, therefore, it's a good idea to define an older PHP 4.x-style constructor to serve as a pointer to the newer PHP 5.x constructor. Here's an example of one such portable class definition:

```php
<?php
// define class
class testClass {

    // PHP 5 constructor
    function __construct() {
        echo "Running the constructor...\n";
    }

    // PHP 4 constructor
    function testClass() {
        $this->__construct();
    }
}

// create an instance of the class
// result: "Running the constructor..."
$obj = new testClass();
?>
```

It's important to remember, also, that the three levels of visibility introduced in PHP 5.x are also not supported in PHP 4.x, and so the keywords `public`, `private`, and `protected` in a PHP 4.x class definition will produce fatal errors.

5.13 Deriving New Classes from Existing Ones

Problem

You want to derive a new class from an existing class.

Solution

Use the `extends` keyword to create a derived class that inherits all the methods and properties of the base class:

```php
<?php
// define base class
class Generic {
    // properties
    protected $cpu;
    protected $mem;

    // constructor
    function __construct() {
        echo "Initializing system configuration...\n";
    }

    // method to set memory specification
    public function setMemory($val) {
        $this->mem = $val;
        echo "Setting memory to $val MB...\n";
    }

    // method to set processor specification
    public function setCpu($val) {
        $this->cpu = $val;
        echo "Setting processor to \"$val\"...\n";
    }

    // method to print current configuration
    public function getConfig() {
        echo "Current configuration: $this->cpu CPU, $this->mem MB RAM\n";
    }
```

```php
        // destructor
        public function __destruct() {
            echo "De-initializing system configuration...\n";
        }
    }

    // define extended class
    class Server extends Generic {
        // define some more properties
        protected $disk;

        // define some more methods
        function __construct() {
            // run parent constructor
            parent::__construct();
        }

        // method to set disk drive specification
        function setDisk($val) {
            $this->disk = $val;
            echo "Setting disk storage to $val GB...\n";
        }

        // method to add memory
        function addMemory($val) {
            $this->mem += $val;
            echo "Adding $val MB of memory\n";
        }

        // override parent method to print current configuration
        public function getConfig() {
            echo "Current configuration: " . $this->cpu . ↵
    " CPU, $this->mem MB RAM, " . $this->disk . " GB disk storage\n";
        }
    }

    // create an object of the derived class
    $webServer = new Server;

    // use methods inherited from base class
    $webServer->setMemory(2048);
    $webServer->setCpu("Intel Pentium IV");
    $webServer->setDisk(450);
```

```
// use method defined in derived class
$webServer->addMemory(2048);

// display configuration
// result: "Current configuration: Intel Pentium IV CPU, 4096 MB RAM, ⏎
// 450 GB disk storage"
$webServer->getConfig();
?>
```

Comments

Two important features of object-oriented programming are extensibility and inheritance. Very simply, this means that you can create a new class based on an existing class, add new features (read: properties and methods) to it, and then create objects based on this new class. These objects will contain all the features of the original parent class, together with the new features of the child class.

The `extends` keyword is used to extend a parent class to a child class. All the functions and variables of the parent class immediately become available to the child class. This is clearly visible in the previous listing, where the `$webServer` object, which is an instance of the derived Server class, uses methods and properties originally defined in the base Generic class.

In this example, it is worthwhile noting that the parent class' constructor has been explicitly called in the child class' constructor. This ensures that all necessary initialization of the parent class is carried out when a child class is instantiated. Child-specific initialization can then be done in the child class' constructor.

> **NOTE**
>
> If a child class does not have a constructor, the parent class' constructor is automatically called.

5.14 Checking If Classes and Methods Have Been Defined

Problem

You want to check if a particular class or class method has been defined.

Solution

Use PHP's `class_exists()` function to test for the existence of a class:

```php
<?php
// sample class
class alphaClass {
    public function __construct() {
        return false;
    }
}

// test if class exists
// result: "Class exists"
echo class_exists("alphaClass") ? "Class exists" : ↵
"Class does not exist";

// result: "Class does not exist"
echo class_exists("betaClass") ? "Class exists" : ↵
"Class does not exist";
?>
```

Use PHP's `method_exists()` function to test for the existence of a class method:

```php
<?php
// sample class
class Dog {
    public function bark() {
        echo "Bow wow wow!";
    }
}

// create instance of class
$spaniel = new Dog;

// test if method exists
// using object instance
// result: "Method exists"
echo method_exists($spaniel, "bark") ? "Method exists" : ↵
"Method does not exist";

// result: "Method does not exist"
echo method_exists($spaniel, "growl") ? "Method exists" : ↵
"Method does not exist";
?>
```

Comments

The class_exists() function accepts a class name and checks the list of declared classes to see if it exists, while the method_exists() function accepts an object instance and a method name, and checks the instance to see if it contains a matching method.

   You can also use the is_callable() function to test for the existence of a class method using the class name (instead of an object instance). Here's an example:

```php
<?php
// sample class
class Dog {
    public function bark() {
        echo "Bow wow wow!";
    }
}

// test if method exists
// using class name
// result: "Method exists"
echo is_callable(array("Dog", "bark")) ? "Method exists" : ↵
"Method does not exist";
?>
```

   To check for the existence of a method within a class from within the class definition itself, use the $this construct in combination with either method_exists() or is_callable(). Here's an example:

```php
<?php
// sample class
class Cat {
    // check if a method exists
    // within the class itself
    public function canBark() {
        return method_exists($this, "bark");
    }
}

// create instance of class
$tomcat = new Cat;
```

```
// returns false as Cat::bark() is undefined
// result: "Obviously I can't bark, I'm a cat!"
echo $tomcat->canBark() ? "Look, I can bark like a dog" : ↵
"Obviously I can't bark, I'm a cat!";
?>
```

5.15 Retrieving Information on Class Members

Problem

You want to obtain information about a specific class or instance, including information on class members and instance properties.

Solution

Use PHP's get_class(), get_parent_class(), get_class_methods(), get_class_vars(), and get_object_vars() methods:

```php
<?php
// define base class
class Dog {
    // define some properties
    public $name;
    public $age;

    // define some methods
    public function __construct() {
        echo "Constructing a Dog.\n";
    }

    public function wagTail() {
        echo "Hmmm...this is a happy Dog.\n";
    }
}

// extend class
class Bloodhound extends Dog {
    // define some extra properties
    public $color;
```

```php
    // define some extra methods
    public function sniff() {
        echo "This Dog can smell food a mile away\n";
    }

    public function __destruct() {
        echo "Destroying a Dog.\n";
    }
}

// create an instance of the extended class
$myDog = new Bloodhound();
$myDog->name = "Barry";
$myDog->age = 5;
$myDog->color = "black";

// retrieve class name from instance
echo "Class: " . get_class($myDog) . "\n";

// retrieve parent class name from instance
echo "Parent class: " . get_parent_class(get_class($myDog)) . "\n";

// get and print list of class properties
$vars = get_class_vars(get_class($myDog));
echo "Class properties: ";
foreach ($vars as $key => $value) {
    if (!isset($value)) { $value = "<undef>"; }
    echo "$key=$value ";
}
echo "\n";

// get and print list of object methods
$methods = get_class_methods(get_class($myDog));
echo "Class methods: ";
foreach ($methods as $m) {
    echo "$m ";
}
echo "\n";

// get and print list of instance properties
$vars = get_object_vars($myDog);
echo "Instance properties: ";
```

```
foreach ($vars as $key => $value) {
    if (!isset($value)) { $value = "<undef>"; }
    echo "$key=$value ";
}
echo "\n";
?>
```

Comments

As the previous listing illustrates, PHP comes with quite a few functions to retrieve detailed information on a class or instance. The get_class() function returns the name of the class that spawned a specific object instance, while the get_parent_class() function provides the name of its parent class. The get_class_methods() function lists the methods defined for a specific class, while the get_class_vars() methods lists the corresponding class properties. Similar, but not identical, to the get_class_vars() method is the get_object_vars() method, which works on an instance instead of a class; this function lists defined instance properties together with their current values.

> **TIP**
>
> To test whether an object is an instance of a specific class, use the `instanceof` operator. See the listing in "5.17: Checking Class Antecedents" for an example.

An alternative way of obtaining the same information is to use *reflection*, one of the new features in PHP. Reflection makes it simple to look inside a class and obtain detailed information on its constants, methods, properties, and interfaces.

The easiest way to obtain class information with reflection is to initialize an object of the ReflectionClass class with the name of the class to be inspected. Here's how:

```php
<?php
// define base class
class Dog {
    // define some properties
    public $name;
    public $age;

    // define some methods
    public function __construct() {
        echo "Constructing a Dog.\n";
    }
```

```php
    public function wagTail() {
        echo "Hmmm...this is a happy Dog.\n";
    }
}

// use reflection to inspect the class
Reflection::export(new ReflectionClass('Dog'));
?>
```

Or, you can use the ReflectionClass' getConstants(), getMethods(), and getProperties() methods to obtain information on class constants, methods, and properties, respectively:

```php
<?php
// define base class
class Dog {
    // define some properties
    public $name;
    public $age;

    // define some methods
    public function __construct() {
        echo "Constructing a Dog.\n";
    }

    public function wagTail() {
        echo "Hmmm...this is a happy Dog.\n";
    }
}

// use reflection to inspect the class
$reflector = new ReflectionClass('Dog');

// list constants
echo "Constants: ";
foreach ($reflector->getConstants() as $key => $value) {
    echo "$key=$value  ";
}
echo "\n";

// list properties
echo "Properties: ";
$vars = $reflector->getProperties();
```

```php
foreach ($vars as $obj) {
    echo $obj->getName() . "   ";
}
echo "\n";

// list methods
echo "Methods: ";
$methods = $reflector->getMethods();
foreach ($methods as $obj) {
    echo $obj->getName() . "   ";
}
echo "\n";
?>
```

5.16 Printing Instance Properties

Problem

You want to print the current values of an object's properties.

Solution

Use a `foreach()` loop to iterate over the instance's properties, and display their contents with `echo`:

```php
<?php
// define class
class Dog {
    // define some properties
    public $breed;
    public $name;
    public $age;

    // define some methods
    public function __construct() {
        echo "Constructing a Dog.\n";
    }
}
```

```
// create object
$doggy = new Dog();
$doggy->name = "Tipsy";
$doggy->breed = "Bloodhound";
$doggy->age = 7;

// iterate over object properties
// print properties and current values
foreach ($doggy as $key => $value) {
    echo "$key: $value\n";
}
?>
```

Comments

PHP now offers simplified access to the properties and corresponding values of a class instance. It is now possible to iterate over an object's properties as though they were an associative array, with a `foreach()` loop and appropriate temporary variables. The process is illustrated in the previous listing.

5.17 Checking Class Antecedents

Problem

You want to find out if an object is an instance of a particular class, or has a particular class in its parentage.

Solution

Use PHP's `instanceof` operator and `is_subclass_of()` functions:

```
<?php
// define base class
class Dog {
    // some code
}

// extend class
class Bloodhound extends Dog {
    // some code
}
```

```
// create object instance
$spike = new Bloodhound;

// returns true
// result: "$spike is an instance of Bloodhound"
echo ($spike instanceof Bloodhound) ? "\$spike is an instance ↵
of Bloodhound" : "\$spike is not an instance of Bloodhound";

// returns true
// result: "$spike is a subclass of Dog"
echo is_subclass_of($spike, "Dog") ? "\$spike is a subclass of ↵
Dog" : "\$spike is not a subclass of Dog";
?>
```

Comments

PHP's `instanceof` operator and `is_subclass_of()` function accept two
arguments—an object and the name of a class—and check whether the object
is descended from the named class. The difference between `instanceof` and
`is_subclass_of()` is subtle but important: Both return true if the object has the
named class in its parent tree, but `instanceof` also returns true if the object itself is
an instance of the named class while `is_subclass_of()` returns false in this case.

5.18 Loading Class Definitions on Demand

Problem

You want to have PHP find and read class definition files dynamically whenever it
encounters a request for new object creation.

Solution

Use the `__autoload()` function to define how PHP locates and loads class
definitions:

```
<?php
// function to automatically look for
// and load class definitions as needed
function __autoload($class) {
    require("defs/" . $class . ".php");
}
```

```
// create an instance of the FormHandler class
$obj = new FormHandler();
?>
```

Comments

PHP classes are usually stored in independent files, which must be read into a script with include() or require() before objects can be spawned from them. For program code that uses objects heavily, this results in numerous calls to include() or require() at the top of every script, adding to clutter and making maintenance difficult.

Earlier, developers would work around this problem by writing a single initialization function that located and loaded all the necessary class definition files. This is no longer necessary, because the PHP engine now supports a special __autoload() function designed specifically for this task. If the __autoload() function is defined, PHP will use the code within the function to find and load class definitions automatically. This is illustrated in the previous listing, where the __autoload() function automatically searches the defs/ directory for a file matching the requested class and loads it if available.

Needless to say, you can customize the behavior of this function to load definitions from other sources as well—for example, from a database or a different file system. Another interesting possibility involves using *namespaces* (similar to those in XML) to name PHP classes; these namespaces can then be translated into actual disk locations, allowing simple and efficient categorization of your code. Consider the following simple example, which illustrates how this might work:

```php
<?php
// function to automatically look for
// and load class definitions as needed
// using namespaces
function __autoload($class) {
    $filePath = implode("/", explode("_", $class)) . ".php";
    require("defs/$filePath");
}

// look in the Page/Form sub-directory for the class definition
$obj = new Page_Form_TextBox();
?>
```

Here, the name of the class provides a clue to its location on disk. The name is split into segments on the basis of a separator (here, an underscore), and these segments are used to generate the directory location of the class definition file. The contents of this file are then read into memory by the __autoload() function, providing a system for on-demand loading of class definitions.

5.19 Comparing Objects for Similarity

Problem

You want to compare two objects to see if they belong to the same class and have the same properties and values.

Solution

Use PHP's == operator:

```php
<?php
// sample class
class Session {
    public $id;
    function __construct($id) {
        $this->id = $id;
    }
}

// create two object instances
$clientA = new Session(100);
$clientB = new Session(100);
$clientC = new Session(200);

// compare independent, identical instances with ==
// result: "true"
echo ($clientA == $clientB) ? "true" : "false";

// compare independent, different instances with ==
// result: "false"
echo ($clientA == $clientC) ? "true" : "false";
?>
```

Comments

PHP's `==` operator returns true if the objects being compared are instances of the same class and have the same set of property-value pairs.

To test if two PHP variables actually refer to the same object instance, use the `===` operator instead. Here's an example:

```php
<?php
// sample class
class Session {
    public $id;
    function __construct($id) {
        $this->id = $id;
    }
}

// create two object instances
$clientA = new Session(100);
$clientARef =& $clientA;
$clientB = new Session(100);

// compare independent, identical instances with ===
// result: "false"
echo ($clientA === $clientB) ? "true" : "false";

// compare an instance and its reference with ===
// result: "true"
echo ($clientA === $clientARef) ? "true" : "false";
?>
```

5.20 Copying Object Instances

Problem

You want to create an exact copy of a class instance.

Solution

Clone the primary class instance and transfer its properties to the copy with PHP's `clone` keyword:

```php
<?php
// sample class
class Dog {
    // properties
    public $name;
    public $age;

    // methods
    public function getInfo() {
        echo "I am $this->name, $this->age years old\n";
    }
}

// create instance of class
$spaniel = new Dog;

// set properties
$spaniel->name = "Sam Spade";
$spaniel->age = 6;

// clone object
$terrier = clone $spaniel;

// get properties (clone)
// result: "I am Sam Spade, 6 years old"
$terrier->getInfo();
?>
```

Comments

The `clone` keyword makes it possible to easily create an exact copy of a class instance. All the properties of the original object are transferred to the clone.

By defining a special `__clone()` method in the class, you can automatically execute certain program statements when an object of that class is cloned. This is useful to do clone-specific initialization, or to make adjustments to specific properties of the clone. Here's an extension of the previous example, which appends the word "clone" to the `name` property of all clones:

```php
<?php
// sample class
class Dog {
    // properties
    public $name;
    public $age;

    // methods
    public function getInfo() {
        echo "I am $this->name, $this->age years old\n";
    }

    // method to run on clone operations
    // alter a property of the clone
    public function __clone() {
        $this->name .= " (clone)";
    }
}

// create instance of class
$spaniel = new Dog;

// set properties
$spaniel->name = "Sam Spade";
$spaniel->age = 6;

// get properties (original)
// result: "I am Sam Spade, 6 years old"
$spaniel->getInfo();

// clone object
$terrier = clone $spaniel;

// get properties (clone)
// result: "I am Sam Spade (clone), 6 years old"
$terrier->getInfo();
?>
```

NOTE

Comparing an object and its clone with the == operator will return true (unless the __ clone() method previously altered a property of the clone), while the same comparison performed with the === operator will always return false. For more information on comparing objects, see the listing in "5.19: Comparing Objects for Similarity."

5.21 Creating Statically-Accessible Class Members

Problem

You want to create a class property or method that can be used without first instantiating an object of the class.

Solution

Use PHP's `static` keyword on the corresponding property or method:

```php
<?php
// sample class
class Instance {
    // define static property
    static $instanceCounter = 0;

    // constructor
    // increments ID every time a
    // new instance is created
    public function __construct() {
        echo "Creating new Instance...\n";
        self::$instanceCounter++;
    }

    // method to return current instance ID
    public function getInstanceCounter() {
        return self::$instanceCounter;
    }
}

// create instances
$a = new Instance;
$b = new Instance;

// retrieve counter value
// correct result: "There have been 2 Instances created"
echo "There have been " . $a->getInstanceCounter() . " Instances ⏎
created\n";
// incorrect result: "There have been Instances created"
echo "There have been " . $a->instanceCounter . " Instances created\n";
?>
```

```php
<?php
// sample class
class Baby {
    // define static method
    public static function factory() {
        return new Baby;
    }

    // constructor
    // private, so that it cannot be
    // called directly
    private function __construct() {
        echo "Creating a Baby...\n";
    }
}

// create an instance of the class
$boy = Baby::factory(); // correct
$boy = new Baby();      // wrong, will generate fatal error
?>
```

Comments

PHP supports the static keyword for class methods and properties. Essentially, this keyword lets you create properties or methods that are independent of class instances. You use a *static* property or method from outside the class, without first initializing an object of the class.

The first listing demonstrates the use of the static keyword with class properties, by building a simple instance counter. Here, because the `$instanceID` variable is a static class property, only one copy of it will exist at any time (regardless of how many instances of the class are created). Each time a new instance is created, the class constructor increments the `$instanceID` variable by 1. In this manner, the static `$instanceID` property serves as a counter, making it easy to find out how many instances of the class have been created. Note that because the `$instanceID` variable is static, it cannot be accessed from a class instance with `instance->property` notation.

The second listing demonstrates object creation using a static class method. Here, the only way to create a new object is via the static method `factory()` which, being static, can only be accessed from outside the class with `class::method` notation. Any attempt to create an object instance with the `new` keyword will be rejected and cause a fatal error, because the class constructor is marked private.

5.22 Altering Visibility of Class Members

Problem

You want to restrict certain methods and/or properties from being accessed through an object instance or a derived class.

Solution

Use the `public`, `private`, and `protected` keywords to define the level of accessibility (*visibility*) of class methods and properties:

```php
<?php
// sample class
class testClass {
    // define some properties
    public $publicVar;
    private $privateVar;
    protected $protectedVar;

    // define some methods
    public function publicMethod() { return; }
    private function privateMethod() { return; }
    protected function protectedMethod() { return; }
}

// create instance of class
$dummy = new testClass;

// attempt to set properties
$dummy->publicVar = 255;                  // works
$dummy->privateVar = false;               // generates error
$dummy->protectedVar = "Email address";   // generates error

// attempt to run methods
$dummy->publicMethod();      // works
$dummy->privateMethod();     // generates error
$dummy->protectedMethod();   // generates error
?>
```

Method or Property Marked as	Accessible from Class Definition	Accessible from Class Instance	Accessible from Extended Class Definition	Accessible from Extended Class Instance
Public	Yes	Yes	Yes	Yes
Protected	Yes	No	Yes	No
Private	Yes	No	No	No

Table 5-1   *Differences in PHP visibility levels*

Comments

PHP supports the concept of visibility in the object model. *Visibility* controls the extent to which object properties and methods can be manipulated by the caller, and plays an important role in defining how open or closed a class is. Three levels of visibility exist, ranging from most visible to least visible; these correspond to the `public`, `protected`, and `private` keywords.

By default, class methods and properties are "public"; this allows the calling script to reach inside your object instances and manipulate them directly. If you don't like the thought of this intrusion, you can mark a particular property or method as private or protected, depending on how much control you want to cede over the object's internals. "Private" methods and properties are only accessible within the base class definition, while "protected" methods and properties are accessible within both base and inherited class definitions. Attempts to access these properties or methods outside their visible area produces a fatal error that stops script execution.

Table 5-1 explains the differences in the three levels of visibility in greater detail.

5.23 Restricting Class Extensibility

Problem

You want to place restrictions on class inheritance and extensibility—for example, you want to force certain methods to always be defined in child classes, or prevent particular classes or methods from being extended at all.

Solution

Use the `final` keyword to prevent methods (or classes) from being extended:

```php
<?php
// define class
final class Generic {
    public function __construct() {
        echo "Initializing system configuration...\n";
    }
}

// extend class
// generates fatal error
// because class Generic cannot be extended
class Server extends Generic {
    public function __construct() {
        parent::__construct();
    }
}
?>
```

Use an abstract class to mark methods as mandatory:

```php
<?php
// define abstract class
abstract class addingMachine {
    // define abstract methods
    abstract public function add();
    abstract public function subtract();
}

// implement abstract class
// generates fatal error
// because definition does not include
// mandatory methods add() and subtract()
class Calculator extends addingMachine {
    // constructor
    public function __construct ($a, $b) {
        $this->a = $a;
        $this->b = $b;
    }
}
?>
```

Comments

PHP enables developers to impose strict control over the manner in which classes are extended. For example, it's now possible to prevent a class or class method from being extended in a derived class, by prefixing the class name or method name with the `final` keyword. Any attempt to extend the class or override the method, as the case may be, will produce a fatal error. An example of this can be seen in the first listing.

PHP also allows developers to mark certain class methods as mandatory, and require that they be defined in derived classes. This is done by declaring the mandatory method(s), as well as the class encapsulating them, as `abstract`. Classes extending an *abstract class* must implement those methods marked as abstract; failure to do so will produce a fatal error when the class definition is loaded. The second listing demonstrates this.

NOTE

PHP will generate an error if a class definition contains abstract methods, but is not itself marked abstract. As the PHP manual puts it, "any class that contains at least one abstract method must also be abstract."

5.24 Overloading Class Methods

Problem

You want to "overload" a class method so that it behaves differently based on the number of arguments or data types passed to it.

Solution

Define the special `__call()` method in the class and use a `switch/case` statement within it to execute different code depending on the arguments and/or data types received:

```php
<?php
// define class
class XYCoordinate {
    public $data;
```

```php
        public function __construct($x, $y) {
            $this->data = array($x, $y);
        }
    }

    // define class
    class Renderer {
        // define overloaded method
        public function __call($method, $args) {
            // check for allowed method names
            if ($method == "render") {
                $numArgs = count($args);
                // execute different code
                // depending on number of arguments passed
                if ($numArgs == 1) {
                    echo "Rendering a Point...\n";
                } else if ($numArgs == 2) {
                    echo "Rendering a Line...\n";
                } else if ($numArgs >= 3) {
                    echo "Rendering a Polygon...\n";
                } else {
                    die("ERROR: Insufficient data\n");
                }
            } else {
                die ("ERROR: Unknown method '$method'\n");
            }
        }
    }

    // create instance
    $r = new Renderer();

    // call method with one argument
    // result: "Rendering a Point..."
    $r->render(new XYCoordinate(1,2));

    // call same method with two arguments
    // result: "Rendering a Line..."
    $r->render(new XYCoordinate(1,2), new XYCoordinate(20,6));

    // call same method with three arguments
    // result: "Rendering a Polygon..."
    $r->render(new XYCoordinate(1,2), new XYCoordinate(20,6),
    new XYCoordinate(4,4), new XYCoordinate(18,4));
    ?>
```

Comments

PHP enables you to "overload" a class method so that it behaves differently under different circumstances. The previous listing illustrates, defining a special __call() method that executes different code depending on whether it is called with one, two, or more than two arguments (for information on the special __call() method, see the listing in "5.26: Auto-Generating Class API Documentation").

It's also possible to overload a method so it responds differently to different data types. The next listing illustrates this, defining a virtual invert() method via __call() that inverts the supplied argument and returns it to the caller. Depending on whether the supplied argument is a Boolean, string, number, or array, a different technique is used to create the inverted value.

```php
<?php
// define class
class overloadedClass {
    // define overloaded method
    public static function __call($method, $args) {
        // check method name
        if ($method == "invert") {
            // check number of arguments
            if (sizeof($args) == 1) {
                $arg = $args[0];
                // check argument type
                // and perform appropriate task
                if (is_string($arg)) {
                    return strrev($arg);
                } else if (is_numeric($arg)) {
                    return 1/$arg;            // reciprocal of number
                } else if (is_array($arg)) {
                    return array_reverse($arg);
                } else if (is_bool($arg)) {
                    return ($arg === FALSE) ? true : false;
                } else if (is_null($arg)) {
                    return null;
                }
            } else {
                die ("ERROR: Incorrect number of arguments\n");
            }
```

```
        } else {
            die ("ERROR: Unknown method '$method'\n");
        }
    }
}

// create instance
$o = new overloadedClass;

// execute overloaded method with different datatypes
echo $o->invert("egg") . "\n";      // result: "gge"
echo $o->invert(true) . "\n";       // result: false
echo $o->invert(2) . "\n";          // result: 0.5
// result: ('t', 'a', 'c')
print_r($o->invert(array("c", "a", "t"))) . "\n";
?>
```

NOTE

PHP's version of overloading is not, in actual fact, "true" overloading. As understood by other, stronger, object-oriented implementations (Java springs to mind), overloading refers to a situation where the same method behaves differently depending on the scope in which it is called, or the arguments passed to it. So, an overloaded add() *method might perform concatenation when called with string arguments, but mathematical addition when called with numeric arguments. PHP's version of overloading does not currently conform to this other, more widely-accepted meaning of the term. True overloading may, however, still be simulated in PHP through creative use of the* __call() *function and a series of* switch/case *statements and conditional tests, as demonstrated in this listing—look at* http://www.php.net/oop5 .overloading *for some more examples.*

5.25 Creating "Catch-All" Class Methods

Problem

You want to create a "catch-all" method that intercepts and handles all method calls for a class.

Solution

Define the special __call() method in the class and use it to intercept requests for nonexistent methods:

```php
<?php
// define class
class virtualMethodClass {
    // define method
    // to intercept all calls for ⏎
    // methods that are not already defined
    function __call($method, $args) {
        echo "You called method [$method] with arguments [" . ⏎
implode(", ", $args) . "]\n";
    }
}

// create object instance
$obj = new virtualMethodClass();

// call a method that does not exist
// result: "You called method [calculateArea] with arguments []"
$obj->calculateArea();

// call another method that does not exist
// with arguments
// result: "You called method [jump] with arguments [10, inches]"
$obj->jump("10", "inches");
?>
```

Comments

Normally, PHP generates an error if you attempt to call a class method that does not exist. However, PHP 5.x introduced the ability to "overload" class methods, by enabling you to define a special __call() method that dynamically handles requests for nonexistent class methods.

One use of this new capability might be to add sophisticated error handling to your class, to deal gracefully with bad method calls; another might be to create "virtual" methods that don't actually exist in the class definition. Because __call() receives two pieces of information—the name of the method, and the arguments supplied to it—it's fairly easy to write conditional tests to deal with a variety of different situations within __call() itself.

The next listing provides a concrete example of how __call() can serve as a provider of an entire family of "virtual" methods to a class. In this example, __call() intercepts get*(Property)*() and set*(Property)*() method calls and internally manipulates the corresponding object property, either retrieving its current value for the caller or setting it to a new value. Thus, a call to the nonexistent class method getAge() is intercepted by __call() and internally translated into a request for the current value of the class property age.

```php
<?php
// define class
class Dog {
    // define properties
    private $breed;
    private $name;
    private $age;

    // define a method
    // to handle all set() and get() requests
    function __call($method, $args) {
        // if get()
        // check if the property exists
        // return its value
        if (substr($method, 0, 3) == "get") {
            $property = substr($method, 3);
            foreach ($this as $key => $value) {
                if (strtolower($property) == strtolower($key)) {
                    return $value;
                }
            }
        // if set()
        // check if the property exists
        // alter its value
        } else if (substr($method, 0, 3) == "set") {
            $property = substr($method, 3);
            foreach ($this as $key => $value) {
                if (strtolower($property) == strtolower($key)) {
                    $this->{$key} = $args[0];
                }
            }
        }
```

```
          // for all other calls
          // generate an error
          } else {
              trigger_error ("Could not find method $method", E_USER_
ERROR);
          }
      }
}

// create an instance of the class
$doggy = new Dog();

// set some properties
// using methods that do not actually exist
// all these method calls are handled by __call()
$doggy->setName("Ronald");
$doggy->setAge(3);
$doggy->setBreed("sheepdog");

// check if the properties have been set
print_r($doggy);

// this will generate an error
// because it is not a set() or get() call
$doggy->walk();
?>
```

Calls for methods other than get *(Property)* () and set *(Property)* () are diverted to the PHP error-handling mechanism. This behavior is by no means set in stone—as the previous listing illustrates, __call() makes it possible to completely customize how a class responds to calls for nonexistent methods.

NOTE

PHP also supports property overloading with the __set () and __get () methods, which are triggered on requests to set and get nonexistent class properties. Read more about this at http://www.php.net/oop5.overloading.

5.26 Auto-Generating Class API Documentation

Problem

You want to automatically generate API class documentation from code comments.

Solution

Use phpDocumentor-style comments to mark up your code, and then use the phpDocumentor engine to parse the comments and generate documentation from them:

```php
<?php
/**
 * generic Pet class
 *
 * @package Animals
 * @access public
 * @copyright GPL
 * @version 1.1
 * @author K-9
 * @todo add run() and walk() methods
 * @todo add default values for all properties
 */
class Pet {
    /**
     * pet's name
     *
     * @access private
     * @var string
     */
    private $name;

    /**
     * sets pet's name
     *
     * @access public
     * @param string $name input value
     * @version 1.0
```

```
    */
    public function setName($name) {
        $this->name = $name;
        return true;
    }

    /**
     * makes pet sleep
     *
     * @access public
     * @return string $sleepStr snoring sounds
     * @see wake()
     * @version 2.3
     */
    public function sleep() {
        $sleepStr = "Zz zzz zz\n";
        return $sleepStr;
    }
}
?>
```

Comments

If you're like most developers, you probably hate the thought of writing formal API documentation for your code. Fortunately, there is a solution—with the addition of a few simple tags to your code (which you can add as code comments during the development process), you can automate the generation of API documentation.

This is accomplished with the help of phpDocumentor (http://www.phpdoc .org/), an auto-documentation tool that uses special comment tags embedded within program code to create and cross-reference API documents. As the previous example illustrates, these comment tags provide information on a diverse range of items: method arguments and return values, property data types and descriptions, copyright and version information, to-do items, author information, and links to reference sources.

Once the code has been marked up, the phpDocumentor application reads the comment tags and generates API documentation from the information found in them. phpDocumentor can also detect extended classes and generate cross-referenced class trees depicting parent-child relationships. For more information and a detailed tutorial, visit http://www.phpdoc.org/.

CHAPTER
6

Working with Files and Directories

IN THIS CHAPTER:

You've probably used PHP many times to read data from, and write data to, files on the system. But that's just the tip of the iceberg—PHP's file manipulation API is powerful and full-featured enough to perform almost any file manipulation task, from deleting directories to counting the number of characters in a file.

These two tasks, along with many others, form the subject matter of this chapter, which takes you on a tour of PHP's file API and delivers solutions to common file system interaction problems. Solutions are included for tasks such as viewing file attributes; copying, renaming and deleting files; searching and replacing patterns within files; comparing files; extracting specific lines or bytes from files; recursively processing directories; converting files between UNIX and MS-DOS formats; and calculating disk usage. Enjoy!

6.1 Testing Files and Directories

Problem

You want to check if a particular file (or directory) exists on the file system.

Solution

Use PHP's `file_exists()` function:

```php
<?php
// check to see if file exists
// result: "File exists"
echo file_exists('dummy.txt') ? "File exists" : "File does not exist";
?>
```

Comments

Before performing any operation on a file (or directory), especially when the file path and name come through user input, it's a good idea to see if that file (or directory) actually exists on the file system. Attempting to move, copy, or read a file that doesn't exist is a quick way to make PHP barf warnings all over your screen.

The solution to the problem is the `file_exists()` function, which accepts a file path and name as an argument and returns a Boolean value indicating whether or not that path and name is valid.

6.2 Retrieving File Information

Problem

You want to obtain detailed information about a particular file, such as its size or type.

Solution

Use one or more of PHP's numerous file information functions, such as `stat()`, `filesize()`, or `filetype()`:

```php
<?php
// set the file name
$file = "dummy.txt";

// get file statistics
$info = stat($file);
print_r($info);

// get file type
$type = filetype($file);
echo "File type is $type\n";

// get file size
$size = filesize($file);
echo "File size is $size bytes\n";

// is file readable?
echo is_readable($file) ? "File is readable\n" : ↵
"File is not readable\n";

// is file writable?
echo is_writable($file) ? "File is writable\n" : ↵
"File is not writable\n";

// is file executable?
echo is_executable($file) ? "File is executable\n" : ↵
"File is not executable\n";
?>
```

Comments

PHP comes with a number of different functions to obtain detailed information on file attributes such as size, type, owner, permissions, and creation/modification times. The `stat()` function retrieves file statistics such as the owner and group ID, the file system block size, the device and inode number, and the file's creation, access, and modification times. The `filesize()` function returns the size of the file in bytes; the `filetype()` function returns the type of the file (whether file, directory, link, device, or pipe); and the `is_readable()`, `is_writable()`, and `is_executable()` functions return Boolean values indicating the current status of the file.

> ### TIP
> If PHP's file functions don't appear to be working as advertised, try using the absolute file path to get to the file, instead of a relative path.

> ### NOTE
> Some of the information returned by the `stat()` and `filetype()` functions, such as inode numbers and UNIX permission bits, may not be relevant to the Windows version of PHP.

> ### NOTE
> The results of a call to `stat()` are cached. You should use the `clearstatcache()` function to reset the cache before your next `stat()` call to ensure that you always get the most recent file information.

6.3 Reading Files

Problem

You want to read the contents of a local or remote file into a string or an array.

Solution

Use PHP's `file_get_contents()` or `file()` function:

```php
<?php
// set the file name
$file = "dummy.txt";
```

```php
// read file contents into an array
$dataArr = file($file);
print_r($dataArr);

// read file contents into a string
$dataStr = file_get_contents($file);
echo $dataStr;
?>
```

Comments

The `file_get_contents()` function is a fast and efficient way to read an entire file into a single string variable, whereupon it can be further processed. The `file()` function is similar, except that it reads a file into an array, with each line of the file corresponding to an element of the array.

If you're using an older PHP build that lacks the `file_get_contents()` function, you can instead use the `fread()` function to read a file into a string. Here's how:

```php
<?php
// define file to read
$file = "dummy.txt";

// open file
$fp = fopen($file, "rb") or die ("Cannot open file");

// read file contents into string
$dataStr = fread($fp, filesize($file));
echo $dataStr;

// close file
fclose($fp) or die("Cannot close file");
?>
```

> **NOTE**
>
> *In case you were wondering, the options passed to* `fopen()` *in the previous listing are used to open the file in read-only mode (* `"r"` *) and binary mode (* `"b"` *).*

If you're trying to read a file over a network link, it may not always be a good idea to slurp up a file in a single chunk due to network bandwidth considerations. In such situations, the recommended way to read a file is in "chunks" with the fgets() function, and then combine the chunks to create a complete string. Here's an illustration:

```php
<?php
// open file
$fp = fopen("/mnt/net/machine2/hda1/dummy.txt", "rb")↵
or die ("Cannot open file");

// read contents into a string
while (!feof($fp)) {
    $dataStr .= fgets($fp, 1024);
}

// close file
fclose($fp) or die ("Cannot close file");

// display contents
echo $dataStr;
?>
```

6.4 Reading Line Ranges from a File

Problem

You want to read a particular line or line range from a file.

Solution

Read the file into an array with PHP's file() function, and then extract the required lines:

```php
<?php
// read file into array
$data = file('fortunes.txt') or die("Cannot read file");

// get first line
echo $data[0] . "\n";

// get last line
echo end($data) . "\n";
```

```php
// get line 5
echo $data[4] . "\n";

// get lines 2-6
$lines = array_slice($data, 1, 5);
echo implode("\n", $lines);
?>
```

Write a custom function that uses the `fgets()` and `fseek()` calls to pick one or more lines out of a file:

```php
<?php
// function to get an arbitrary range of lines
// from a file
function getLines($file, $startLineNum, $endLineNum) {
    // check for valid range endpoints
    if ($endLineNum < $startLineNum) {
        die("Ending line number must be greater than or ⏎
equal to starting line number!");
    }

    // initialize line counter
    $lineCounter = 0;

    // open the file for reading
    $fp = fopen($file, "rb") or die("Cannot open file");

    // read contents line by line
    while (!feof($fp) && $lineCounter <= $endLineNum)  {
        // once the starting line number is attained
        // save contents to an array
        // until the ending line number is attained
        $lineCounter++;
        $line = fgets($fp);
        if ($lineCounter >= $startLineNum && $lineCounter <= ⏎
$endLineNum) {
            $lineData[] = $line;
        }
    }

    // close the file
    fclose($fp) or die ("Cannot close file");
```

```
        // return line range to caller
        return $lineData;
}

// return lines 2-6 of file as array
$lines = getLines("fortunes.txt", 2, 6);
print_r($lines);
?>
```

Comments

Extracting one or more lines from a file is one of the more common problems developers face, and it's no surprise that there are so many creative solutions to it. The first listing outlines the simplest approach, storing the lines of a file in an array with PHP's file() function and then using array indexing to extract specific lines by number.

The second listing offers a more complicated approach, wherein a custom getLines() function accepts three arguments: a file path, a starting line number, and an ending line number (for a single line, the latter two will be equal). It then iterates through the named file, incrementing a counter as each line is processed. Lines that fall within the supplied range will be saved to an array, which is returned to the caller once the entire file is processed.

You can also get the first and last lines of a file with a combination of fseek() and fgets() function calls, as illustrated here:

```
<?php
// open file
$fp = fopen('fortunes.txt', "rb") or die("Cannot open file");

// get first line
fseek($fp, 0, SEEK_SET);
echo fgets($fp);

// get last line
fseek($fp, 0, SEEK_SET);
while (!feof($fp)) {
    $line = fgets($fp);
}
echo $line;

// close file
fclose($fp) or die ("Cannot close file");
?>
```

Here, the `fseek()` function moves the internal file pointer to a specific location in the file, and the `fgets()` function retrieves all the data beginning from the pointer location until the next newline character. To obtain the first line, set the file pointer to position 0 and call `fgets()` once; to obtain the last line, keep calling `fgets()` until the end of the file is reached and the last return value will represent the last line.

You should also take a look at the listing in "6.5: Reading Byte Ranges from a File" for a variant that extracts file contents by bytes instead of lines.

6.5 Reading Byte Ranges from a File

Problem

You want to read a particular byte or byte range from a file.

Solution

Write a custom function encapsulating a combination of `fseek()`, `ftell()`, and `fgetc()` calls:

```php
<?php
// function to get an arbitrary number of bytes
// from a file
function getBytes($file, $startByte, $endByte) {
    // check for valid range endpoints
    if ($endByte < $startByte) {
        die("Ending byte number must be greater than or ↵
equal to starting byte number!");
    }

    // open the file for reading
    $fp = fopen($file, "rb") or die("Cannot open file");

    // seek to starting byte
    // retrieve data by character
    // until ending byte
    fseek ($fp, $startByte, SEEK_SET);
    while (!(ftell($fp) > $endByte)) {
        $data .= fgetc($fp);
    }
```

```php
    // close the file
    fclose($fp) or die ("Cannot close file");

    // return data to caller
    return $data;
}

// return first 10 bytes of file
echo getBytes("fortunes.txt", 0, 9);
?>
```

Comments

The user-defined getBytes() function is similar to the getLines() function illustrated in the first listing in "6.4: Reading Line Ranges from a File," with the primary difference lying in its use of fgetc() instead of fgets().The function accepts three arguments: a file path, a starting byte number, and an ending byte number. It then sets the internal file pointer to the starting byte value and loops over the file character by character, appending the result at each stage to a variable, until the ending byte value is reached. The variable containing the saved bytes is then returned to the caller as a string.

6.6 Counting Lines, Words, and Characters in a File

Problem

You want to count the number of lines, words, and characters in a file.

Solution

Use PHP's file_get_contents(), strlen(), and str_word_count() functions to count words and characters in a file:

```php
<?php
// set file name and path
$file = "dummy.txt";
```

```
// read file contents into string
$str = file_get_contents($file) or die ("Cannot read from file");

// read file contents into array
$arr = file ($file) or die ("Cannot read from file");

// count lines
echo "Counted ". sizeof($arr) . " line(s).\n";

// count characters, with spaces
$numCharsSpaces = strlen($str);
echo "Counted $numCharsSpaces character(s) with spaces.\n";

// count characters, without spaces
$newStr = ereg_replace('[[:space:]]+', '', $str);
$numChars = strlen($newStr);
echo "Counted $numChars character(s) without spaces.\n";

// count words
$numWords = str_word_count($str);
echo "Counted $numWords words.\n";
?>
```

Comments

It's fairly easy to count the number of lines in a file—simply read the file into an array with `file()`, which stores each line as an individual array element, and then count the total number of elements in the array.

Counting words and characters is a little more involved, and requires you to first read the file into a string with a function such as `file_get_contents()`. The number of words and characters (including spaces) can then be obtained by running the `str_word_count()` and `strlen()` functions on the string.

To obtain the number of characters excluding spaces, simple remove all spaces from the string with `ereg_replace()` and then obtain the size of the string with `strlen()`. You can read more about how this works in the listing in "1.4: Removing Whitespace from Strings," and users whose PHP builds don't support the relatively-newer `str_word_count()` function will find an alternative way of counting words in the listing in "1.13: Counting Words in a String."

6.7 Writing Files

Problem

You want to write a string to a file.

Solution

Use the `file_put_contents()` function:

```php
<?php
// define string to write
$data = "All the world's a stage\r\nAnd all the men and ↵
women merely players";

// write string to file
file_put_contents('shakespeare.txt', $data) or die("Cannot write to ↵
file"); echo "File successfully written.";
?>
```

Comments

The `file_put_contents()` function provides an easy way to write data to a file. The file will be created if it does not already exist, and overwritten if it does. The return value of the function is the number of bytes written.

> **TIP**
>
> To have `file_put_contents()` *append to an existing file rather than overwrite it completely, add the optional* `FILE_APPEND` *flag to the function call as its third argument.*

If you're using an older PHP build that lacks the `file_put_contents()` function, you can use the `fwrite()` function to write to a file instead. Here's how:

```php
<?php
// define string to write
$data = "All the world's a stage\r\nAnd all the men and ↵
women merely players";

// open file
$fp = fopen('shakespeare.txt', "wb+") or die ("Cannot open file");
```

```
// lock file
// write string to file
if (flock($fp, LOCK_EX)) {
    fwrite($fp, $data) or die("Cannot write to file");
    flock($fp, LOCK_UN);
    echo "File successfully written.";
} else {
    die ("Cannot lock file");
}

// close file
fclose($fp) or die ("Cannot close file");
?>
```

Here, the `fwrite()` function is used to write a string to an open file pointer, after the file has been opened for writing with `fopen()` and the w+ parameter. Notice the call to `flock()` before any data is written to the file—this locks the file, stops other processes from writing to the file, and thereby reduces the possibility of data corruption. Once the data has been successfully written, the file is unlocked. Locking is discussed in greater detail in the listing in "6.8: Locking and Unlocking Files."

TIP

To have `fwrite()` *append to an existing file, rather than overwrite it completely, change the file mode to* `ab+` *in the* `fopen()` *call.*

NOTE

The `flock()` *function is not supported on certain file systems, such as the File Allocation Table (FAT) system and the Network File System (NFS). For an alternative file-locking solution for these file systems, look at the listing in "6.8: Locking and Unlocking Files," and read more about* `flock()` *caveats at* `http://www.php.net/flock`.

6.8 Locking and Unlocking Files

Problem

You want to lock a file before writing to it.

Solution

Use the `flock()` function:

```php
<?php
// open file
$fp = fopen('dummy.txt', "wb+") or die ("Cannot open file");

// lock file
// write string to file
if (flock($fp, LOCK_EX)) {
    fwrite($fp, "This is a test.") or die("Cannot write to file");
    flock($fp, LOCK_UN);
} else {
    die ("Cannot lock file");
}

// close file
fclose($fp) or die ("Cannot close file");
echo "File successfully written.";
?>
```

Comments

PHP implements both shared and exclusive file locks through its `flock()` function, which accepts a file pointer and a flag indicating the lock type (`LOCK_EX` for exclusive lock, `LOCK_SH` for shared lock, and `LOCK_UN` for unlock). Once a file is locked with `flock()`, other processes attempting to write to the file have to wait until the lock is released; this reduces the possibility of multiple processes trying to write to the same file simultaneously and corrupting it.

NOTE

PHP's file locking is advisory, which means that it only works if all processes attempting to access the file respect PHP's locks. This may not always be true in the real world—just because a file is locked with PHP `flock()` doesn't mean that it can't be modified with an external text editor like `vi`—so it's important to always try and ensure that the processes accessing a file use the same type of locking and respect each other's locks.

So long as your file is only written to by a PHP process, `flock()` will usually suffice; if, however, your file is accessed by multiple processes, or scripts in different languages, it might be worth your time to create a customized locking system that can be understood and used by all accessing programs. The listing in this section contains some ideas to get you started.

On certain file systems, the `flock()` function remains unsupported and will always return false. Users of older Windows versions are particularly prone to this problem, as `flock()` does not work with the FAT file system. If file locking is still desired on such systems, it becomes necessary to simulate it by means of a user-defined lock/unlock API. The following listing illustrates this:

```php
<?php
// function to set lock for file
function lock($file) {
    return touch("$file.lock");
}

// function to remove lock for file
function unlock($file) {
    return unlink ("$file.lock");
}

// function to check if lock exists
function isLocked($file) {
    clearstatcache();
    return file_exists("$file.lock") ? true : false;
}

// set file name
$file = "dummy.txt";

while ($attemptCount <= 60) {
    // if file is not in use
    if (!isLocked($file)) {
        // lock file
        lock($file);

        // perform actions
        $fp = fopen($file, "ab") or die("Cannot open file");
        fwrite($fp, "This is a test.") or die("Cannot write to file");
        fclose($fp) or die("Cannot close file");

        // unlock file
        unlock($file);
        echo "File successfully written.";
```

```
            // break out of loop
            break;
      } else {
      // if file is in use
            // increment attempt counter
            $attemptCount++;

            // sleep for one second
            sleep(1);

            // try again
      }
}
?>
```

This simple locking API contains three functions: one to lock a file, one to unlock it, and one to check the status of the lock. A lock is signaled by the presence of a lock file, which serves as a semaphore; this file is removed when the lock is released.

The PHP script first checks to see if a lock exists on the file, by looking for the lock file. If no lock exists, the script obtains a lock and proceeds to make changes to the file, unlocking it when it's done. If a lock exists, the script waits one second and then checks again to see if the previous lock has been released. This check is performed 60 times, once every second; at the end of it, if the lock has still not been released, the script gives up and exits.

NOTE

If `flock()` *is not supported on your file system, or if you're looking for a locking mechanism that can be used by both PHP and non-PHP scripts, the previous listing provides a basic framework to get started. Because the lock is implemented as a file on the system and all programming languages come with functions to test files, it is fairly easy to port the API to other languages and create a locking system that is understood by all processes.*

6.9 Removing Lines from a File

Problem

You want to remove a line from a file, given its line number.

Solution

Use PHP's `file()` function to read the file into an array, remove the line, and then write the file back with the `file_put_contents()` function:

```php
<?php
// set the file name
$file = "fortunes.txt";

// read file into array
$data = file($file) or die("Cannot read file");

// remove third line
unset ($data[2]);

// re-index array
$data = array_values($data);

// write data back to file
file_put_contents($file, implode($data)) or die("Cannot write to file");
echo "File successfully written.";
?>
```

Comments

The simplest way to erase a line from a file is to read the file into an array, remove the offending element, and then write the array back to the file, overwriting its original contents. An important step in this process is the re-indexing of the array once an element has been removed from it—omit this step and your output file will display a blank line at the point of surgery.

If your PHP build doesn't support the `file_put_contents()` function, you can accomplish the same result with a combination of `fgets()` and `fwrite()`. Here's how:

```php
<?php
// set the file name
$file = "fortunes.txt";

// set line number to remove
$lineNum = 3;
```

```
// open the file for reading
$fp = fopen($file, "rb") or die("Cannot open file");

// read contents line by line
// skip over the line to be removed
while (!feof($fp)) {
    $lineCounter++;
    $line = fgets($fp);
    if ($lineCounter != $lineNum) {
        $data .= $line;
    }
}

// close the file
fclose($fp) or die ("Cannot close file");

// open the file again for writing
$fp = fopen($file, "rb+") or die("Cannot open file");

// lock file
// write data to it
if (flock($fp, LOCK_EX)) {
    fwrite($fp, $data) or die("Cannot write to file");
    flock($fp, LOCK_UN);
} else {
    die ("Cannot lock file for writing");
}

// close the file
fclose($fp) or die ("Cannot close file");
echo "File successfully written.";
?>
```

The fgets() function reads the file line by line, appending whatever it finds to a string. A line counter keeps track of the lines being processed, and takes care of skipping over the line to be removed so that it never makes it into the data string. Once the file has been completely processed and its contents have been stored in the string (with the exception of the line to be removed), the file is closed and reopened for writing. A lock secures access to the file, and the fwrite() function then writes the string back to the file, erasing the original contents in the process.

6.10 Processing Directories

Problem

You want to iteratively process all the files in a directory.

Solution

Use PHP's `scandir()` function:

```php
<?php
// define directory path
$dir = './test';

// get directory contents as an array
$fileList = scandir($dir) or die ("Not a directory");

// print file names and sizes
foreach ($fileList as $file) {
    if (is_file("$dir/$file") && $file != '.' && $file != '..') {
        echo "$file: " . filesize("$dir/$file") . "\n";
    }
}
?>
```

Comments

PHP's `scandir()` function offers a simple solution to this problem—it returns the contents of a directory as an array, which can then be processed using any loop construct or array function.

An alternative approach is to use the Iterators available as part of the Standard PHP Library (SPL). *Iterators* are ready-made, extensible constructs designed specifically to loop over item collections, such as arrays and directories. To process a directory, use a DirectoryIterator, as illustrated here:

```php
<?php
// define directory path
$dir = './test';

// create a DirectoryIterator object
$iterator = new DirectoryIterator($dir);
```

```
// rewind to beginning of directory
$iterator->rewind();

// iterate over the directory using object methods
// print each file name
while($iterator->valid()) {
if ($iterator->isFile() && !$iterator->isDot())  {
        print $iterator->getFilename() . ": " .↵
$iterator->getSize() .  "\n";
    }
    $iterator->next();
}
?>
```

Here, a DirectoryIterator object is initialized with a directory name, and the object's `rewind()` method is used to reset the internal pointer to the first entry in the directory. You can then use a `while()` loop, which runs so long as a valid() entry exists, to iterate over the directory. Individual file names are retrieved with the `getFilename()` method, while you can use the `isDot()` method to filter out the entries for the current (`.`) and parent (`..`) directories. The `next()` method moves the internal pointer forward to the next entry.

You can read more about the DirectoryIterator at `http://www.php.net/~helly/php/ext/spl/`.

6.11 Recursively Processing Directories

Problem

You want to process all the files in a directory and its subdirectories.

Solution

Write a recursive function to process the directory and its children:

```
<?php
// function to recursively process
// a directory and all its subdirectories
function dirTraverse($dir) {
    // check if argument is a valid directory
    if (!is_dir($dir)) { die("Argument '$dir' is not a directory!"); }
```

```
    // declare variable to hold file list
    global $fileList;

    // open directory handle
    $dh = opendir($dir) or die ("Cannot open directory '$dir'!");

    // iterate over files in directory
    while (($file = readdir($dh)) !== false)  {
        // filter out "." and ".."
        if ($file != "." && $file != "..") {
            if (is_dir("$dir/$file")) {
                // if this is a subdirectory
                // recursively process it
                dirTraverse("$dir/$file");
            } else    {
                // if this is a file
                // do something with it
                // for example, reverse file name/path and add to array
                $fileList[] = strrev("$dir/$file");
            }
        }
    }

    // return the final list to the caller
    return $fileList;
}

// recursively process a directory
$result = dirTraverse('./test');
print_r($result);
?>
```

Comments

As illustrated in the listing in "6.10: Processing Directories," it's fairly easy to process the contents of a single directory with the `scandir()` function. Dealing with a series of nested directories is somewhat more complex. The previous listing illustrates the standard technique, a recursive function that calls itself to travel ever deeper into the directory tree.

The inner workings of the `dirTraverse()` function are fairly simple. Every time the function encounters a directory entry, it checks to see if that value is a file or a directory. If it's a directory, the function calls itself and repeats the process until it reaches the end of the directory tree. If it's a file, the file is processed—the previous listing simply reverses the file name and adds it to an array, but you can obviously replace this with your own custom routine—and then the entire performance is repeated for the next entry.

Another option is to use the Iterators available as part of the Standard PHP Library (SPL). Iterators are ready-made, extensible constructs designed specifically to loop over item collections such as arrays and directories. A predefined Recursive DirectoryIterator already exists and it's not difficult to use this for recursive directory processing. Here's how:

```php
<?php
// initialize an object
// pass it the directory to be processed
$iterator  = new RecursiveIteratorIterator( new ↵
 RecursiveDirectoryIterator('./test') );

// iterate over the directory
foreach ($iterator as $key=>$value) {
   print strrev($key) . "\n";
}
?>
```

The process of traversing a series of nested directories is significantly simpler with the SPL at hand. First, initialize a RecursiveDirectoryIterator object and pass it the path to the top-level directory to be processed. Next, initialize a RecursiveIterat orIterator object (this is an Iterator designed solely for the purpose of iterating over other recursive Iterators) and pass it the newly minted RecursiveDirectoryIterator. You can now process the results with a `foreach()` loop.

You can read more about the RecursiveDirectoryIterator and the RecursiveIterator Iterator at `http://www.php.net/~helly/php/ext/spl/`.

For more examples of recursively processing a directory tree, see the listings in "6.11: Recursively Processing Directories," "6.15: Copying Directories," n "6.17: Deleting Directories," and "6.20: Searching for Files in a Directory." You can also read about recursively processing arrays in the listing in "4.3: Processing Nested Arrays."

6.12 Printing Directory Trees

Problem

You want to print a hierarchical listing of a directory and its contents.

Solution

Write a recursive function to traverse the directory and print its contents:

```php
<pre>
<?php
// function to recursively process
// a directory and all its subdirectories
// and print a hierarchical list
function printTree($dir, $depth=0) {
    // check if argument is a valid directory
    if (!is_dir($dir)) { die("Argument is not a directory!"); }

    // open directory handle
    $dh = opendir($dir) or die ("Cannot open directory");

    // iterate over files in directory
    while (($file = readdir($dh)) !== false)  {
        // filter out "." and ".."
        if ($file != "." && $file != "..") {
            if (is_dir("$dir/$file")) {
                // if this is a subdirectory (branch)
                // print it and go deeper
                echo str_repeat("  ", $depth) . " [$file]\n";
                printTree("$dir/$file", ($depth+1));
            } else     {
                // if this is a file (leaf)
                // print it
                echo str_repeat("  ", $depth) . " $file\n";
            }
        }
    }
}

// recursively process and print directory tree
printTree('./test/');
?>
</pre>
```

Comments

This listing is actually a variant of the technique outlined in the listing in "6.11: Recursively Processing Directories." Here, a recursive function travels through the named directory and its children, printing the name of every element found. A depth counter is incremented every time the function enters a subdirectory; the str_ repeat() function uses this depth counter to pad the listing with spaces and thus simulate a hierarchical tree.

For more examples of recursively processing a directory tree, see the listings in "6.15: Copying Directories" and "6.17: Deleting Directories."

6.13 Copying Files

Problem

You want to copy a file from one location to another.

Solution

Use PHP's copy() function:

```php
<?php
// set file name
$source = "dummy.txt";
$destination = "dummy.txt.backup";

// copy file if it exists, else exit
if (file_exists($source)) {
    copy ($source, $destination) or die ("Cannot copy file '$source'");
    echo "File successfully copied.";
} else {
    die ("Cannot find file '$source'");
}
?>
```

Comments

In PHP, creating a copy of a file is as simple as calling the copy() function and passing it the source and destination file names and paths. The function returns true if the file is successfully copied.

If what you really want is to create a copy of a directory, visit the listing in "6.15: Copying Directories."

NOTE

If the destination file already exists, it will be overwritten with no warning by `copy()`*. If this is not what you want, implement an additional check for the target file with* `file_exists()` *and exit with a warning if the file already exists.*

6.14 Copying Remote Files

Problem

You want to create a local copy of a file located on a remote server.

Solution

Use PHP's `file_get_contents()` and `file_put_contents()` functions to read a remote file and write the retrieved data to a local file:

```php
<?php
// increase script execution time limit
ini_set('max_execution_time', 600);

// set URL of file to be downloaded
$remoteFile = "http://www.some.domain/remote.file.tgz";

// set name of local copy
$localFile = "local.file.tgz";

// read remote file
$data = file_get_contents($remoteFile) or ↵
die("Cannot read from remote file");

// write data to local file
file_put_contents($localFile, $data) or ↵
die("Cannot write to local file");

// display success message
echo "File [$remoteFile] successfully copied to [$localFile]";
?>
```

Comments

Most of PHP's file functions support reading from remote files. In this listing, this capability is exploited to its fullest to create a local copy of a remote file. The `file_get_contents()` function reads the contents of a remote file into a string, and the `file_put_contents()` function then writes this data to a local file, thereby creating an exact copy. Both functions are binary-safe, so this technique can be safely used to copy both binary and non-binary files.

6.15 Copying Directories

Problem

You want to copy a directory and all its contents, including subdirectories.

Solution

Write a recursive function to travel through a directory, copying files as it goes:

```php
<?php
// function to recursively copy
// a directory and its subdirectories
function copyRecursive($source, $destination) {
    // check if source exists
    if (!file_exists($source)) { die("'$source' is not valid"); }

    if (!is_dir($destination)) {
        mkdir ($destination);
    }

    // open directory handle
    $dh = opendir($source) or die ("Cannot open directory '$source'");

    // iterate over files in directory
    while (($file = readdir($dh)) !== false) {
        // filter out "." and ".."
        if ($file != "." && $file != "..") {
            if (is_dir("$source/$file")) {
                // if this is a subdirectory
                // recursively copy it
                copyRecursive("$source/$file", "$destination/$file");
            } else {
```

```
                    // if this is a file
                    // copy it
                    copy ("$source/$file", "$destination/$file")↵
or die ("Cannot copy file '$file'");
            }
        }
    }

    // close directory
    closedir($dh);
}

// copy directory recursively
copyRecursive("www/template", "www/site12");
echo "Directories successfully copied.";
?>
```

Comments

This listing is actually a combination of techniques discussed in the listings in "6.11: Recursively Processing Directories" and "6.13: Copying Files." Here, the custom `copyRecursive()` function iterates over the source directory and, depending on whether it finds a file or directory, copies it to the target directory or invokes itself recursively. The recursion ends when no further subdirectories are left to be traversed. Note that if the target directory does not exist at any stage, it is created with the `mkdir()` function.

6.16 Deleting Files

Problem

You want to delete a file.

Solution

Use PHP's `unlink()` function:

```
<?php
// set file name
$file = "shakespeare.asc";
```

```
// check if file exists
// if it does, delete it
if (file_exists($file)) {
    unlink ($file) or die("Cannot delete file '$file'");
    echo "File successfully deleted.";
} else {
    die ("Cannot find file '$file'");
}
?>
```

Comments

To delete a file with PHP, simply call the `unlink()` function with the file name and path. The function returns true if the file was successfully deleted.

> **NOTE**
>
> *Typically, PHP will not be able to delete files owned by other users; the PHP process can only delete files owned by the user it's running as. This is a common cause of errors, so keep an eye out for it!*

6.17 Deleting Directories

Problem

You want to delete a directory and its contents, including subdirectories.

Solution

Write a recursive function to travel through a directory and its children, deleting files as it goes:

```php
<?php
// function to recursively delete
// a directory and its subdirectories
function deleteRecursive($dir) {
    // check if argument is a valid directory
    if (!is_dir($dir)) { die("'$dir' is not a valid directory"); }

    // open directory handle
    $dh = opendir($dir) or die ("Cannot open directory '$dir'");
```

```
            // iterate over files in directory
            while (($file = readdir($dh)) !== false)  {
                // filter out "." and ".."
                if ($file != "." && $file != "..") {
                    if (is_dir("$dir/$file")) {
                        // if this is a subdirectory
                        // recursively delete it
                        deleteRecursive("$dir/$file");
                    } else {
                        // if this is a file
                        // delete it
                        unlink ("$dir/$file") or die ("Cannot delete file ↵
'$file'");
                    }
                }
            }
        // close directory
        closedir($dh);

        // remove top-level directory
        rmdir($dir);
}

// delete directory recursively
deleteRecursive("junk/robert/");
echo "Directories successfully deleted.";
?>
```

Comments

In PHP, the function to remove a directory a `rmdir()`. Unfortunately, this function only works if the directory in question is empty. Therefore, to delete a directory, it is first necessary to iterate over it and delete all the files within it. If the directory contains subdirectories, those need to be deleted too; you do this by entering them and erasing their contents.

The most efficient way to accomplish this task is with a recursive function such as the one in the previous listing, which is a combination of the techniques outlined in the listing in "6.11: Recursively Processing Directories" and the listing in "6.16: Deleting Files." Here, the `deleteRecursive()` function accepts a directory path and name and goes to work deleting the files in it. If it encounters a directory, it invokes itself recursively to enter that directory and clean it up. Once all the contents of a directory are erased, you use the `rmdir()` function to remove it completely.

6.18 Renaming Files and Directories

Problem

You want to move or rename a file or directory.

Solution

Use PHP's `rename()` function:

```php
<?php
// set old and new file/directory names
$oldFile = "home/john";
$newFile = "home/jane";

// check if file/directory exists
// if it does, move/rename it
if (file_exists($oldFile)) {
    rename ($oldFile, $newFile)↵
or die("Cannot move/rename file '$oldFile'");
    echo "Files/directories successfully renamed.";
} else {
    die ("Cannot find file '$oldFile'");
}
?>
```

Comments

A corollary to PHP's `copy()` function, you can use the `rename()` function to both rename and move files. Like `copy()`, `rename()` accepts two arguments, a source file and a destination file, and attempts to rename the former to the latter. It returns true on success.

6.19 Sorting Files

Problem

You want to sort a file listing.

Solution

Save the file list to an array, and then use the `array_multisort()` function to sort it by one or more attributes:

```php
<?php
// define directory
$dir = "./test/a";

// check if it is a directory
if (!is_dir($dir)) { die("Argument '$dir' is not a directory!"); }

// open directory handle
$dh = opendir($dir) or die ("Cannot open directory '$dir'!");

// iterate over files in directory
while (($file = readdir($dh)) !== false)  {
    // filter out "." and ".."
    if ($file != "." && $file != "..") {
        // add an entry to the file list for this file
        $fileList[] = array("name" => $file, "size" => ⏎
filesize("$dir/$file"), "date" => filemtime("$dir/$file"));
    }
}

// close directory
closedir($dh);

// separate all the elements with the same key
// into individual arrays
foreach ($fileList as $key=>$value) {
   $name[$key]   =   $value['name'];
   $size[$key]   =   $value['size'];
   $date[$key]   =   $value['date'];
}

// now sort by one or more keys
// sort by name
array_multisort($name, $fileList);
print_r($fileList);
```

```
// sort by date and then size
array_multisort($date, $size, $fileList);
print_r($fileList);
?>
```

Comments

Here, PHP's directory functions are used to obtain a list of the files in a directory, and place them in a two-dimensional array. This array is then processed with PHP's `array_multisort()` function, which is especially good at sorting symmetrical multidimensional arrays.

The `array_multisort()` function accepts a series of input arrays and uses them as sort criteria. Sorting begins with the first array; values in that array that evaluate as equal are sorted by the next array, and so on. This makes it possible to sort the file list first by size and then date, or by name and then size, or any other permutation thereof. Once the file list has been sorted, it can be processed further or displayed in tabular form.

6.20 Searching for Files in a Directory

Problem

You want to find all the files matching a particular name pattern, starting from a top-level search directory.

Solution

Write a recursive function to search the directory and its children for matching file names:

```php
<?php
// function to recursively search
// directories for matching filenames
function searchRecursive($dir, $pattern) {
    // check if argument is a valid directory
    if (!is_dir($dir)) { die("Argument '$dir' is not a directory!"); }

    // declare array to hold matches
    global $matchList;
```

```
    // open directory handle
    $dh = opendir($dir) or die ("Cannot open directory '$dir'!");

    // iterate over files in directory
    while (($file = readdir($dh)) !== false) {
        // filter out "." and ".."
        if ($file != "." && $file != "..") {
            if (is_dir("$dir/$file")) {
            // if this is a subdirectory
                // recursively process it
                searchRecursive("$dir/$file", $pattern);
            } else {
            // if this is a file
                // check for a match
                // add to $matchList if found
                if (preg_match("/$pattern/", $file))    {
                    $matchList[] = "$dir/$file";
                }
            }
        }
    }

    // return the final list to the caller
    return $matchList;
}

// search for file names containing "ini"
$fileList = searchRecursive("c:/windows", "ini");
print_r($fileList);
?>
```

Comments

This listing is actually a variant of the technique outlined in the listing in "6.11: Recursively Processing Directories." Here, a recursive function travels through the named directory and its children, using the `preg_match()` function to check each file name against the name pattern. Matching file names and their paths are stored in an array, which is returned to the caller once all subdirectories have been processed.

An alternative approach here involves using the PEAR File_Find class, available from `http://pear.php.net/package/File_Find`. This class exposes a `search()` method, which accepts a search pattern and a directory path and performs a recursive search in the named directory for files matching the search pattern. The return value of the method is an array containing a list of paths to the matching files.

Here's an illustration of this class in action:

```php
<?php
// include File_Find class
include "File/Find.php";

// search recursively for file names containing "tgz"
// returns array of paths to matching files
$fileList = File_Find::search("tgz", "/tmp");
print_r($fileList);
?>
```

For more examples of recursively processing a directory tree, see the listings in "6.11: Recursively Processing Directories," "6.15: Copying Directories," and "6.17: Deleting Directories."

6.21 Searching for Files in PHP's Default Search Path

Problem

You want to check if a particular file exists in PHP's default search path, and obtain the full path to it.

Solution

Scan PHP's include_path for the named file and, if found, obtain the full path to it with PHP's realpath() function:

```php
<?php
// function to check for a file
// in the PHP include path
function searchIncludePath($file) {
    // get a list of all the directories
    // in the include path
    $searchList = explode(";", ini_get('include_path'));
```

```php
    // iterate over the list
    // check for the file
    // return the path if found
    foreach ($searchList as $dir)     {
        if (file_exists("$dir/$file")) { return realpath("$dir/$file"); }
    }
    return false;
}


// look for the file "DB.php"
$result = searchIncludePath('DB.php');
echo $result ? "File was found in $result" : "File was not found";
?>
```

Comments

A special PHP variable defined through the *php.ini* configuration file, the `include_path` variable typically contains a list of directories that PHP will automatically look in for files `include`-d or `require`-d by your script. It is similar to the Windows `$PATH` variable, or the Perl `@INC` variable.

In this listing, the directory list stored in this variable is read into the PHP script with the `ini_get()` function, and a `foreach()` loop is then used to iterate over the list and check if the file exists. If the file is found, the `realpath()` function is used to obtain the full file system path to the file.

6.22 Searching and Replacing Patterns Within Files

Problem

You want to perform a search/replace operation within one or more files.

Solution

Use PEAR's File_SearchReplace class:

```php
<?php
// include File_SearchReplace class
include "File/SearchReplace.php";
```

```
// initialize object
$fsr = new File_SearchReplace('PHP',↵
'PHP: Hypertext Pre-Processor', array('chapter_01.txt', ↵
'chapter_02.txt'));

// perform the search
// write the changes to the file(s)
$fsr->doReplace();

// get the number of matches
echo $fsr->getNumOccurences() . " match(es) found.";
?>
```

Comments

To perform search-and-replace operations with one or more files, you'll need the PEAR File_SearchReplace class, available from `http://pear.php.net/package/File_SearchReplace`. Using this class, it's easy to replace patterns inside one or more files.

The object constructor requires three arguments: the search term, the replacement text, and an array of files to search in. The search/replace operation is performed with the `doReplace()` method, which scans each of the named files for the search term and replaces matches with the replacement text. The total number of matches can always be obtained with the `getNumOccurences()` method.

> ### TIP
> *You can use regular expressions for the search term, and specify an array of directories (instead of files) as an optional fourth argument to the object constructor. It's also possible to control whether the search function should comply with Perl or PHP regular expression matching norms. More information on how to accomplish these tasks can be obtained from the class documentation and source code.*

6.23 Altering File Extensions

Problem

You want to change all or some of the file extensions in a directory.

Solution

Use PHP's `glob()` and `rename()` functions:

```php
<?php
// define directory path
$dir = './test';

// define old and new extensions
$newExt = "asc";
$oldExt = "txt";

// search for files matching pattern
foreach (glob("$dir/*.$oldExt") as $file) {
    $count++;
    // extract the file name (without the extension)
    $name = substr($file, 0, strrpos($file, "."));
    // rename the file using the name and new extension
    rename ($file, "$name.$newExt") ↵
or die ("Cannot rename file '$file'!");
}
echo "$count file(s) renamed.";
?>
```

Comments

PHP's `glob()` function builds a list of files matching a particular pattern, and returns an array with this information. It's then a simple matter to iterate over this array, extract the filename component with `substr()`, and rename the file with the new extension.

6.24 Finding Differences Between Files

Problem

You want to perform a UNIX `diff` on two files.

Solution

Use PEAR's Text_Diff class:

```
<pre>
<?php
// include Text_Diff class
include "Text/Diff.php";
include "Text/Diff/Renderer.php";
include "Text/Diff/Renderer/unified.php";

// define files to compare
$file1 = "rhyme1.txt";
$file2 =  "rhyme2.txt";

// compare files
$diff = &new Text_Diff(file($file1), file($file2));

// initialize renderer and display diff
$renderer = &new Text_Diff_Renderer_unified();
echo $renderer->render($diff);
?>
</pre>
```

Comments

The UNIX `diff` program is a wonderful way of quickly identifying differences between two strings. PEAR's Text_Diff class, available from `http://pear.php.net/package/Text_Diff`, brings this capability to PHP, making it possible to easily compare two strings and returning the difference in standard `diff` format.

The input arguments to the Text_Diff object constructor must be two arrays of string values. Typically, these arrays contain the lines of the files to be compared, and are obtained with the `file()` function. The Text_Diff_Renderer class takes care of displaying the comparison in UNIX `diff` format, via the `render()` method of the object.

As an illustration, here's some sample output from this listing:

```
@@ -1,2 +1,3 @@
 They all ran after the farmer's wife,
-Who cut off their tales with a carving knife.
+Who cut off their tails with a carving knife,
+Did you ever see such a thing in your life?
```

6.25 "Tailing" Files

Problem

You want to "tail" a file, or watch it update in real time, on a Web page.

Solution

Display the output of the UNIX tail program on an auto-refreshing Web page:

```
<html>
<head>
<meta http-equiv="refresh" content="5;url=<?=$_SERVER['PHP_SELF']?>">
</head>

<body>
<pre>
<?php
// set name of log file
$file = "/tmp/rootproc.log";

// set number of lines to tail
$limit = 10;

// run the UNIX "tail" command and display the output
system("/usr/bin/tail -$limit $file");
?>
</pre>
</body>
</html>
```

Comments

UNIX administrators commonly use the tail program to watch log files update in real time. A common requirement in Web applications, especially those that interact with system processes, is to have this real-time update capability available within the application itself.

The simplest—though not necessarily most elegant—way to do this is to use PHP's `system()` function to fork an external tail process and display its output on a Web page. A `<meta http-equiv="refresh" ... />` tag at the top of the page causes it to refresh itself every few seconds, thereby producing an almost real-time update.

NOTE

Forking an external process from PHP is necessarily a resource-intensive process. To avoid excessive usage of system resources, tune the page refresh interval in this listing to correctly balance the requirements of real-time monitoring and system resource usage.

6.26 Listing Available Drives or Mounted File Systems

Problem

You want a list of available drives (Windows) or mounted file systems (UNIX).

Solution

Use the is_dir() function to check which drive letters are valid (Windows):

```php
<?php
// loop from "a" to "z"
// check which are active drives
// place active drives in an array
foreach(range('a','z') as $drive) {
    if (is_dir("$drive:")) {
        $driveList[] = $drive;
    }
}

// print array of active drive letters
print_r($driveList);
?>
```

Read the /etc/mtab file for a list of active mount points (UNIX):

```php
<?php
// read mount information from mtab file
$lines = file("/etc/mtab") or die ("Cannot read file");

// iterate over lines in file
// get device and mount point
// add to array
foreach ($lines as $line) {
```

```
    $arr = explode(" ", $line);
    $mountList[$arr[0]] = $arr[1];
}

// print array of active mounts
print_r($mountList);
?>
```

Comments

For Web applications that interact with the file system—for example, an interactive file browser or disk quota manager—a common requirement involves obtaining a list of valid system drives (Windows) or mount points (UNIX). The previous listings illustrate simple solutions to the problem.

Windows drive letters always consist of a single alphabetic character. So, to find valid drives, use the `is_dir()` function to test the range of alphabetic characters, from A to Z, and retain those for which the function returns true.

A list of active UNIX mounts is usually stored in the system file `/etc/mtab` (although your UNIX system may use another file, or even the `/proc` virtual file system). So, to find valid drives, simply read this file and parse the information within it.

6.27 Calculating Disk Usage

Problem

You want to calculate the total disk space used by a disk partition or directory.

Solution

Use PHP's `disk_free_space()` and `disk_total_space()` functions to calculate the total disk usage for a partition:

```
<?php
// define partition
// for example, "C:" for Windows
// or "/" for UNIX
$dir = "c:";

// get free space in MB
$free = round(disk_free_space($dir)/1048576);
```

```php
// get total available space in MB
$total = round(disk_total_space($dir)/1048576);

// calculate used space in MB
$used = $total - $free;
echo "$used MB used";
?>
```

Write a recursive function to calculate the total disk space consumed by a particular directory:

```php
<?php
// function to recursively process
// a directory and all its subdirectories
function calcDirUsage($dir) {
    // check if argument is a valid directory
    if (!is_dir($dir)) { die("Argument '$dir' is not a directory!"); }

    // declare variable to hold running total
    global $byteCount;

    // open directory handle
    $dh = opendir($dir) or die ("Cannot open directory '$dir'!");

    // iterate over files in directory
    while (($file = readdir($dh)) !== false) {
        // filter out "." and ".."
        if ($file != "." && $file != "..") {
            if (is_dir("$dir/$file")) {
                // if this is a subdirectory
                // recursively process it
                calcDirUsage("$dir/$file");
            } else {
                // if this is a file
                // add its size to the running total
                $byteCount += filesize("$dir/$file");
            }
        }
    }

    // return the final list to the caller
    return $byteCount;
}
```

```
// calculate disk usage for directory in MB
$bytes = calcDirUsage("c:/windows");
$used = round($bytes/1048576);
echo "$used MB used";
?>
```

Comments

PHP's `disk_total_space()` and `disk_free_space()` functions return the maximum and available disk space for a particular drive or partition respectively, in bytes. Subtracting the latter from the former returns the number of bytes currently in use on the partition.

Obtaining the disk space used by a specific directory and its subdirectories is somewhat more complex. The task here involves adding the sizes of all the files in that directory and its subdirectories to arrive at a total count of bytes used. The simplest way to accomplish this is with a recursive function such as the one outlined in the previous listing, where file sizes are calculated and added to a running total. Directories are deal with recursively, in a manner reminiscent of the technique outlined in the listing in "6.11: Recursively Processing Directories." The final sum will be the total bytes consumed by the directory and all its contents (including subdirectories).

TIP

To convert byte values to megabyte or gigabyte values for display, divide by 1048576 or 1073741824 respectively.

6.28 Creating Temporary Files

Problem

You want to create a temporary file with a unique name, perhaps as a flag or semaphore for other processes.

Solution

Use PHP's `tempnam()` function:

```
<?php
// create temporary file with prefix "tmp"
$filename = tempnam("/tmp", "tmp");
echo "Temporary file [$filename] successfully created";
?>
```

Comments

PHP's `tempnam()` function accepts two arguments, a directory name and a file prefix, and attempts to create a file using the prefix and a randomly generated identifier in the specified directory. If the file is successfully created, the function returns the complete path and name to it—this can then be used by other file functions to write data to it.

This listing offers an easy way to quickly create a file for temporary use, perhaps as a signal to other processes. Note, however, that the file created by `tempnam()` must be manually deleted with `unlink()` once it's no longer required.

TIP

PHP's `tmpfile()` *function creates a unique, temporary file that exists only for the duration of the script. Read more about this function at* `http://www.php.net/tmpfile`.

6.29 Finding the System Temporary Directory

Problem

You want to retrieve the path to the system's temporary directory.

Solution

Use PHP's `tempnam()` function to create a temporary file, and then obtain the path to it:

```php
<?php
// create a temporary file and get its name
// result: "Temporary directory is /tmp"
$tmpfile = tempnam("/this/directory/does/not/exist", "tmp");
unlink ($tmpfile);
echo "Temporary directory is " . dirname($tmpfile);
?>
```

Comments

The `tempnam()` function provides an easy way to create a temporary file on the system. Such a file is typically used as a semaphore or flag for other processes—for example, it can be used for file locking processes or status indicators. The return value of the `tempnam()` function is the full path to the newly minted file. Given this file is always created in the system's temporary directory, running the `dirname()` function on the complete file path produces the required information.

NOTE

In this listing, the first parameter to `tempnam()` *is a nonexistent directory path. Why? Well,* `tempnam()` *normally requires you to specify the directory in which the temporary file is to be created. Passing a nonexistent directory path forces the function to default to the system's temporary directory, thereby making it possible to identify the location.*

An alternative approach consists of using the PEAR File_Util class, available at `http://pear.php.net/package/File`. This class exposes a `tmpDir()` method, which returns the path to the system temporary directory. Take a look:

```php
<?php
// include File_Util class
include "File/Util.php";

// get name of system temporary directory
// result: "Temporary directory is /tmp"
$tmpdir = File_Util::tmpDir();
echo "Temporary directory is $tmpdir";
?>
```

6.30 Converting Between Relative and Absolute File Paths

Problem

You want to convert a relative path to an absolute path.

Solution

Use PHP's `realpath()` function:

```php
<?php
// result: "/usr/local/apache/htdocs" (example)
echo realpath(".");
```

```
// result: "/usr/local/apache"   (example)
echo realpath("..");

// result: "/usr/local/"
echo realpath("/usr/local/mysql/data/../..");
?>
```

Comments

To convert a relative path to an absolute file path, use PHP's `realpath()` function. This function performs "path math," translating all the relative locations in a path string to return a complete absolute file path.

> ### NOTE
>
> On a tangential note, take a look at PEAR's File_Util class, available from `http://pear .php.net/package/File`, which comes with a method to calculate the difference between two file paths. The following simple example illustrates:
>
> ```
> <?php
> // include File_Util class
> include "File/Util.php";
>
> // define two locations on the filesystem
> $begin = "/usr/local/apache";
> $end = "/var/spool/mail";
>
> // figure out how to get from one to the other
> // result: "../../../var/spool/mail"
> echo File_Util::relativePath($end, $begin, "/");
> ?>
> ```

6.31 Parsing File Paths

Problem

You want to extract the path, file name, or extension path from a file path.

Solution

Use PHP's `pathinfo()` function to automatically split the file path into its constituent parts:

```php
<?php
// define path and filename
$path = "/etc/sendmail.cf";

// decompose path into constituents
$data = pathinfo($path);
print_r($data);
?>
```

Comments

The `pathinfo()` function is one of PHP's more useful path manipulation functions. Pass it a file path, and `pathinfo()` will split it into its individual components. The resulting associative array contains separate keys for directory name, file name, and file extension. You can then easily access and use these keys for further processing— for example, the variable `$data['dirname']` will return the value `/etc`.

> **TIP**
>
> When parsing file paths, also consider using the `basename()`, `dirname()`, and `realpath()` functions. You can read about these functions in the PHP manual at `http://www.php.net/filesystem`.

CHAPTER 7

Working with HTML and Web Pages

IN THIS CHAPTER:

O ne of PHP's biggest selling points, and a big part of its current popularity, is the ease with which it can be used for Web development. By making it simple to include variables and functions calls in regular HTML pages, PHP reduces the pain of constructing interactive, data-driven sites and Web applications. The fact that it's extremely user-friendly and is supported with an extensive online manual and user community is just icing on the cake.

This chapter is meant for developers who use PHP on a regular basis to interact with Web applications and HTML pages. The recipe lineup includes marking up ASCII files for display in a Web browser; turning text URLs into HTML hyperlinks; generating DHTML menu trees from data in a flat file or database; tracking and visually displaying the progress of server tasks; caching page output; and paginating large volumes of content into smaller segments.

7.1 Displaying Text Files

Problem

You want to display the contents of a text file on a Web page.

Solution

Use PHP's `readfile()` function to read and display the file:

```php
<?php
// override default header
header("Content-Type: text/plain");

// display file contents
readfile("data.txt");
?>
```

Comments

The `readfile()` function reads a file and writes its content to the output buffer—in this case, the HTTP client. This function provides a handy one-line shortcut to display the contents of an external file in your Web application.

Note that PHP's default configuration causes it to send the client a header indicating that the following page is an HTML document. In this case, because the file being displayed is a text file, it's a good idea to override this default header with one telling the client that what follows is plain text. This also forces the client to preserve line breaks and carriage returns when rendering the file's contents.

7.2 Highlighting PHP Syntax

Problem

You want to display one or more lines of PHP source code with syntax highlighting.

Solution

Use PHP's `highlight_file()` or `highlight_string()` functions:

```php
<?php
// set PHP source file
$sourceFile = "count-matches.php";
// highlight and display source
highlight_file($sourceFile);

// set PHP code string
$sourceStr = "<?php echo round(60*2)/7; ?>";
// highlight and display source
highlight_string($sourceStr);
?>
```

Comments

If you'd like users to be able to inspect the source code of your PHP scripts, PHP's `highlight_file()` and `highlight_string()` functions provide an easy way to generate color-coded versions of PHP source code. The default colors used by these functions can be configured in the php.ini file.

You might also want to try Aidan Lister's PHP_Highlight class from `http://www.aidanlister.com/repos/`, which not only highlights syntax but also adds line numbers and links function calls to their descriptions in the online manual. Here's an illustration of this alternative:

```php
<?php
// include PHP_Highlight class
include "PHP_Highlight.php";
```

```php
// initialize PHP_Highlight object
$highlight = new PHP_Highlight;

// set PHP source file
$source = "count-matches.php";

// load source file
$highlight->loadFile($source);

// print source as ordered list
$highlight->toList(false);
?>
```

7.3 Wrapping Text

Problem

You want text on a Web page to wrap at a particular column width.

Solution

Run the text through PHP's `wordwrap()` function:

```php
<?php
// define string
$text = "Fans of the group will have little trouble recognizing the
group's distinctive synthesized sounds and hypnotic dance beats, since
these two elements are present in almost every song on the album;
however, the lack of diversity and range is troubling, and I'm hoping
we see some new influences in the next album. More intelligent lyrics
might also help.";

// wrap string when displaying
echo nl2br(wordwrap($text,10));
?>
```

Comments

PHP's `wordwrap()` function limits text display to a particular column size, thereby allowing precise control over how text is rendered on a Web page. By default, `wordwrap()` wraps strings at column 75 using the standard newline sequence, but both these parameters are configurable; the previous listing illustrates this by wrapping the string at column 10. The `nl2br()` function then translates the wrapped text for display on a Web page by converting the newline sequence into the HTML line break element `<br />`.

7.4 Activating Embedded URLs

Problem

You want to turn text URLs into active HTML hyperlinks.

Solution

Scan the text for URL patterns and replace them with HTML anchors using the `eregi_replace()` function:

```php
<?php
// function to turn URLs in text
// into HTML hyperlinks
function activateUrls($text) {
    return eregi_replace("([[:alnum:]]+://[^[:space:]]*[[:alnum:]↵
#?/&= +%_:]]*)", "<a href=\"\\1\">\\1</a>", $text);
}


// activate URLs in text block
// result: text with hyperlinks
print activateUrls("There are innumerable ways in which metacharacters ↵
can be combined to create powerful pattern-matching rules. For an ↵
in-depth introduction, take a look at ↵
http://www.melonfire.com/community/columns/trog/article.php?id=2 ↵
and the PHP manual pages at ↵
http://www.php.net/manual/en/ref.regex.php. ↵
You can also find sample regular expressions at http://www.regexlib ↵
.com/");
?>
```

Comments

Although the custom `activateUrls()` function in this listing appears daunting, it's actually fairly simple—all it does is scan the supplied string for patterns matching the typical format of an URL and surrounds those patterns with the HTML code for a hyperlink. Notice how the code incorporates the matching text segment (the URL itself) into the replacement string (the anchor element) with a backreference.

TIP

To turn a text file containing embedded URLs into an HTML document, combine this listing with the technique outlined in the listing in "7.21: Extracting URLs."

7.5 Protecting Public E-mail Addresses

Problem

You want to protect a publicly-displayed e-mail address from being captured by an e-mail address harvester.

Solution

Mangle the address so that it is readable by a human but not recognizable as a standard e-mail address to a computer program:

```php
<?php
// function to protect
// publicly-displayed e-mail addresses
// replace @ with "at"
//          . with "dot"
//          - with "dash"
//          _ with "underscore"
function protectEmail($email) {
// define array of search and replacement terms
    $search = array(".", "-", "_", "@");
    $replace = array(" dot ", " dash ", " underscore ", " at ");

    // perform search and replace operation
    return str_replace($search, $replace, $email);
}

// result: "john dot doe at blue dash viper dot domain dot net"
print protectEmail("john.doe@blue-viper.domain.net");
?>
```

Comments

With the advent of e-mail harvesters, protecting publicly displayed e-mail addresses on a Web page has become a necessity. The technique discussed in this listing is used on many popular Web sites, including the interactive version of the PHP manual.

This listing replaces the special symbols in an e-mail address with English words, making the e-mail address unrecognizable as such to an address harvester. So @ becomes at, _ becomes underscore, and - becomes dash.

An alternative solution involves encrypting the e-mail address and using client-side JavaScript to decrypt and display it. This solution is implemented fairly elegantly in the PEAR HTML_Crypt class, available from http://pear.php .net/package/HTML_Crypt. Here's an example:

```php
<?php
// include HTML_Crypt class
include "HTML/Crypt.php";

// initialize object with e-mail address
$c = new HTML_Crypt('john@some.domain.com', 8);

// add mailto: link
$c->addMailTo();

// send encrypted output to client
$c->output();
?>
```

Here, the HTML_Crypt() object encrypts an e-mail address, and turns into a clickable hyperlink with the addMailTo() method. The output() method then sends the encrypted string to the client, together with all the necessary JavaScript code to turn it into a readable hyperlink in an HTTP client. Address harvesters that examine the source of the page will only see an encrypted string and assorted JavaScript code; the original e-mail address will not be visible to them (try it for yourself and see!).

TIP

You can also encrypt your HTML source code with the HTML_Crypt class, to prevent users from examining it. Here's an illustration:

```html
<html>
<head></head>
<body>
<div>The secret handshake is
<?php
// include HTML_Crypt class
include "HTML/Crypt.php";
```

```
                    // initialize object with HTML/Javascript code
                    $c = new HTML_Crypt('up-down-diagonal-smack-down-up', 8);

                    // send encrypted output to client
                    $c->output();
                    ?>
                    </div>
                    </body>
                    </html>
```

7.6 Generating Tables

Problem

You want to generate an HTML table using PHP method calls.

Solution

Use PEAR's HTML_Table class:

```php
<?php
// include HTML_Table class
include "HTML/Table.php";

// initialize object
$table = new HTML_Table(array("border" => 1, "cellpadding" => 5));

// set default value for empty cells
$table->setAutoFill("Unavailable");

// define data for table
$data = array(
    array("Name", "Skype", "Yahoo", "AIM", "MSN"),
    array("Luke", "luke09", null, null, "luke.skywalker"),
    array("Ben", null, "obiwan21", null, "obiwan.kenobi"),
    array("Darth", null, null, "darkdude", null)
);
```

```
// process data
// add cells as required
$rowCount = 0;
foreach ($data as $person) {
    $colCount = 0;
    foreach ($person as $p)      {
        $table->setCellContents($rowCount,↵
$colCount, $data[$rowCount][$colCount]);
        $colCount++;
    }
    $rowCount++;
}

// arbitrarily add some more cells
$table->setCellContents(4, 0, "Leia");
$table->setCellContents(4, 4, "leia46");

// render and display table
echo $table->toHTML();
?>
```

Comments

PEAR's HTML_Table class, available from `http://pear.php.net/package/` `HTML_Table`, makes it easy to generate the HTML source code for a multirow, multicolumn table using PHP method calls. Once an object of the class has been initialized, you can use the `setCellContents()` method to create table cells and attach content to them. You can add individual rows and columns with the `addRow()` and `addCol()` method, respectively, while the `toHTML()` method translates the in-memory table structure to valid HTML markup.

NOTE

This example also requires the HTML_Common class from `http://pear.php.net/` `package/HTML_Common`.

Figure 7-1 illustrates the output of this listing.

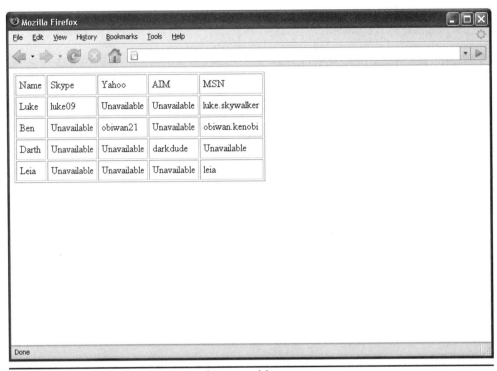

Figure 7-1 *A dynamically generated HTML table*

7.7 Generating Random Quotes

Problem

You want to display a random quotation or tag line in your page.

Solution

Use PHP's `exec()` function to run the UNIX `fortune` program and save the output to a variable:

```php
<?php
// run the UNIX "fortune" command
// result: "Make yourself at home! Clean my kitchen." (example)
exec("/usr/bin/fortune", $results);
echo join("\n", $results);
?>
```

Create a file containing quotations or tag lines and use PHP's `array_rand()` function to pick one at random:

```php
<?php
// read file containing data
$lines = file("fortunes.txt") or die("Cannot read file");

// extract a random line from the file
// result: "Make yourself at home! Clean my kitchen." (example)
echo $lines[array_rand($lines)];
?>
```

Comments

In order to add an element of dynamism to a Web page, many page authors like to include a randomly selected quotation or tag line. The easiest way to do this, especially on a UNIX-based Web server, is to capture the output of the UNIX `fortune` program and display it in the page. The first listing of the previous two does just this, using PHP's `exec()` function to run the `fortune` program and save its output to a variable.

Users who don't have access to the UNIX `fortune` program, but would still like to simulate this feature, can create a file containing quotations or taglines, one on each line, and then use the `file()` function to read the file into an array. The `array_rand()` function can then be used to pick a line at random.

7.8 Generating Hierarchical Lists

Problem

You want to display a series of nested arrays as an indented HTML list.

Solution

Write a recursive function to traverse the array and print its contents as a series of nested, unordered HTML list elements.

```php
<?php
// define hierarchical data set
$data = array (
    "bread",
    "eggs",
```

```php
        "cheese" => array("parmesan", "mozzarella"),
        "meat" => array("white" => array("fish", "chicken"),↵
"red" => array("beef", "lamb")),
        "milk"
);

// function to recursively traverse
// a series of nested arrays
function arrayTraverse($arr) {
    // check if input is array
    if (!is_array($arr)) { die ("Argument is not array!"); }

    // start HTML list
    echo "<ul>";

    // iterate over array
    foreach($arr as $key=>$value) {
        if (is_array($value)) {
            // if a nested array
            // print key
            // recursively traverse and
            // start a new, inner list
            print "<li>$key</li>";
            arrayTraverse($value);
        } else {
        // if not an array
            // print value as list item
            print "<li>$value</li>";
          }
    }

    // close HTML list
    echo "</ul>";
}

// process the hierarchical list
// print values
// use list indentation to indicate hierarchy
arrayTraverse($data);
?>
```

Comments

As discussed in the listing in "4.3: Processing Nested Arrays," the usual technique to process a series of nested arrays is to use a recursive function. In this listing, every time the `arrayTraverse()` function moves down a level in the array hierarchy, it generates an opening list element. Scalar elements at that level are then printed as list items, while array elements are processed by recursively calling `arrayTraverse()`. Once all the elements at a particular depth in the hierarchy are processed, a closing list element is used to visually mark the end of the level. Indentation is automatically handled by the HTTP client when it encounters the nested list elements.

Figure 7-2 demonstrates what the output looks like.

Figure 7-2   *A recursively-built, unordered, hierarchical list*

7.9 Using Header and Footer Templates

Problem

You want to use a common header and footer on all your Web pages.

Solution

Create separate files for the page header and footer, and use PHP's `include` construct to include them at the top and bottom of your Web pages:

File: header.php
```
<!-- header.php BEGIN -->
<html>
<head></head>
<body>
<center>This is the page header. Server time is
<?php echo date("H:i", time()); ?>.</center>
<!-- header.php END -->
```

File: footer.php
```
<!-- footer.php BEGIN -->
<p></p> <p></p>
<center>Content on this page is &copy; myCompany. Be good.
We have lawyers.</center>
</body>
</html>
<!-- footer.php END -->
```

File: main.php
```
<?php include "header.php"; ?>

<b><font size="+1">
<p>This is the page content.<p>
<p>It can contain <a href="http://www.w3.org/MarkUp/">HTML</a>,
client-side code like <script language="Javascript">document.
writeln("JavaScript");</script> and
server-side code like <?php echo "PHP"; ?>.</p>
</font></b>

<?php include "footer.php"; ?>
```

Comments

PHP's include construct makes it easy to pull external files into your PHP script. These files may contain markup or program code; they are executed "in place" when they are read into the script.

This listing demonstrates one application of the include construct: dynamically importing header and footer templates into an HTML page. As it illustrates, the page header and footer are stored in separate files, called header.php and footer .php, respectively. The include() construct takes care of reading and displaying these templates at the top and bottom of every page of the site. Naturally, any change to the header or footer template will be immediately reflected in all pages that include them.

As this listing illustrates, files include-d in this manner can contain static markup as well as program code. Code placed in <?php...?> tags will be executed by the parser in place as it is encountered.

7.10 Charting Task Status with a Progress Bar

Problem

You want to visually display elapsed and remaining time for a task to complete.

Solution

Use PEAR's HTML_Progress2 class:

```php
<?php
// increase script execution time limit
ini_set('max_execution_time', 600);

// include HTML_Progress class
include "HTML/Progress2.php";

// create object
$progress = new HTML_Progress2();

// define function to
// check if a number is a prime number
```

```php
function testPrime($num) {
    // divide each number
    // by all numbers lower than it (excluding 1)

    // if even one such operation returns no remainder
    // the number is not a prime
    for ($x=($num-1); $x>1; $x--) {
        if (($num%$x) == 0) { return false; }
    }
    return true;
}
?>
<html>
<head>
<?php
echo $progress->getStyle(false);
echo $progress->getScript(false);
?>
</head>
<body>

<div id="progress" style="position: absolute; left: 35%">
<?php
// initialize progress bar display
$progress->display();
?>
</div>

<div id="output" style="position: absolute; top: 100px">
<?php
// initialize counter
$count = 0;

// numbers to check for prime-ness
$limit = 10000;

// loop
while ($count <= $limit) {
    // test if counter value is a prime number
    // print if so
    if (testPrime($count)) { echo "$count "; }
```

```
    // on every 50th number
    // get percentage of task completed
    // refresh the progress bar
    if ($count % 50 == 0) {
        $percentDone = intval($count/$limit*100);
        $progress->moveStep($percentDone);
    }

    // increment counter
    $count++;
}

?>
</div>
</body>
</html>
```

Comments

In a typical HTTP transaction, a client requests a script and the server; and after processing the request, it returns the output of the script to the client. Most of the time, the time lag between request and response is trivial; however, in certain situations—for example, when uploading a large file or querying a large database— the time required to process the request is significant. And because the stateless nature of HTTP precludes event notification or task progress reports, the user is usually left watching a blank page as the server works its way through the script.

It is precisely to alleviate this situation that the PEAR HTML_Progress2 class was developed. Available at `http://pear.php.net/package/HTML_Progress2`, this class enables developers to provide users with visual notification of task progress through a DHTML progress bar. With this class, a developer can check the progress of a task and update the progress bar on a periodic basis, providing the user with a clear estimate of elapsed and remaining time.

The previous example illustrates this, by calculating all the prime numbers between 0 and 10,000, and using a progress bar to visually display task progress. First, an object of the `HTML_Progress2()` class is initialized, and then the `getStyle()` and `getScript()` methods are used to generate the layout and JavaScript code is needed to display the progress bar. Next, a `while()` loop is set to run 10,000 times, testing every number between and 0 and 10,000 to see if it is prime. On every 50th number, the percentage of task completion is calculated, and the object's `moveStep()` method is used to refresh the progress bar with the latest status.

Figure 7-3 demonstrates what the output looks like.

Here's another example, this one using a progress bar to track a remote file download:

```php
<?php
// increase script execution time limit
ini_set('max_execution_time', 600);

// include HTML_Progress class
include "HTML/Progress2.php";

// include HTTP_Request class
include "HTTP/Request.php";

// set URL of file to be downloaded
$remoteFile = "http://www.some.domain/files/remote.file.zip";
```

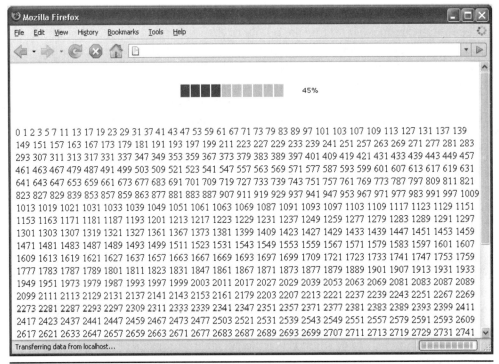

Figure 7-3   *A dynamic indicator to chart task progress*

```php
// set name of local copy
$localFile = "downloads/local.file.zip";

// create objects
$progress = new HTML_Progress2();
$request = &new HTTP_Request();

// perform an HTTP request
// get size of file to be downloaded
$request->setUrl($remoteFile);
$request->setMethod("HEAD");
$request->sendRequest(false);
$actualSize = $request->getResponseHeader("Content-Length");
?>
<html>
<head>
<?php
echo $progress->getStyle(false);
echo $progress->getScript(false);
?>
</head>
<body>

<div id="progress" style="position: absolute; left: 0px">
<?php
// initialize progress bar display
$progress->display();
?>
</div>

<div id="output" style="position: absolute; top: 100px">
<?php
// open the URL
$rfp = fopen($remoteFile, "rb") or die("Cannot open remote file");;

// open local file
$lfp = fopen($localFile, "wb") or die("Cannot open local file");;

// read the remote file in chunks
// calculate percentage left at each stage
// update progress bar in 10% increments
while ($chunk = fread($rfp, 1024)) {
    fwrite($lfp, $chunk) or die("Cannot write to local file");
```

```
    $recdSize += strlen($chunk);
    $percent = intval(($recdSize*100)/$actualSize);
    if (($percent % 10 == 0)) {
        $progress->moveStep($percent);
        // flag to improve performance
        // prevent unnecessary calling of display()
    }
}
}

// close URL pointer
fclose($rfp) or die("Cannot close remote file");

// close file
fclose($lfp) or die("Cannot close local file");

// display success message
echo "File [$remoteFile] successfully copied to [$localFile]";
?>
</div>
</body>
</html>
```

Here, in order to display the progress of the download, it is necessary to first know the actual size of the file being downloaded. This information is obtained by sending a HEAD request to the remote URL and checking the Content-Length header to retrieve the file size in bytes.

Next, a progress bar object is initialized and PHP's fopen() and fread() functions are used to read the remote file and copy it to a local file. As the read/write operation takes place, a counter keeps track of the total number of bytes downloaded. At regular intervals, the current file size is compared to the actual file size to calculate what percentage of the transaction is complete. This percentage value is then used to update the progress bar via the moveStep() method.

NOTE

These examples also require the HTTP_Request class and the Event_Dispatcher class from http://pear.php.net/package/HTTP_Request *and* http://pear.php.net/package/Event_Dispatcher.

7.11 Dynamically Generating a Tree Menu

Problem

You want to display a hierarchical tree menu that uses client-side scripting to expand and collapse tree nodes on demand.

Solution

Use PEAR's HTML_TreeMenu class:

```php
<?php
// include HTML_TreeMenu class
include "HTML/TreeMenu.php";

// initialize menu object
$root = new HTML_TreeMenu();

// set up first level
$a2h = new HTML_TreeNode(array("text" => "A-H", "link" => null));
$i2p = new HTML_TreeNode(array("text" => "I-P", "link" => null));
$q2z = new HTML_TreeNode(array("text" => "Q-Z", "link" => null));

// set up second level
$apparel = new HTML_TreeNode(array("text" => "Apparel",↵
"link" => "catalog/apparel.html"));
$accessories = new HTML_TreeNode(array("text" => "Accessories",↵
"link" => "catalog/accessories.html"));
$hdecor = new HTML_TreeNode(array("text" => "Home Decor",↵
"link" => "catalog/hdecor.html"));
$jewelery = new HTML_TreeNode(array("text" => "Jewelry",↵
"link" => "catalog/jewelry.html"));
$pharma = new HTML_TreeNode(array("text" => "Pharmacy",↵
"link" => "catalog/pharmacy.html"));
$shoes = new HTML_TreeNode(array("text" => "Shoes",↵
"link" => "catalog/shoes.html"));
$toys = new HTML_TreeNode(array("text" => "Toys",↵
"link" => "catalog/toys.html"));
```

```php
// set up third level
$men = new HTML_TreeNode(array("text" => "Men", "link" =>↵
"catalog/shoes-men.html"));
$women = new HTML_TreeNode(array("text" => "Women",↵
"link" => "catalog/shoes-women.html"));

// start linking nodes
// attach first level to root
$root->addItem($a2h);
$root->addItem($i2p);
$root->addItem($q2z);

// attach second-level items
// A-H
$a2h->addItem($apparel);
$a2h->addItem($accessories);
$a2h->addItem($hdecor);
// I-P
$i2p->addItem($jewelery);
$i2p->addItem($pharma);
// Q-Z
$q2z->addItem($shoes);
$q2z->addItem($toys);

// attach third-level items
$apparel->addItem($men);
$apparel->addItem($women);
$shoes->addItem($men);
$shoes->addItem($women);
?>
<html>
<head>
<!-- link in the JavaScript code for expanding/collapsing the tree -->
<script src="TreeMenu.js" language="JavaScript"↵
type="text/javascript"></script>
</head>
<body>
<?php
// initialize menu interface
// set options: path for tree images
//              frame to load click targets
$menu = new HTML_TreeMenu_DHTML($root,↵
array("linkTarget" => "rhframe", "images" => "images/"));
```

```
// print menu tree
$menu->printMenu();
?>
</body>
</html>
```

Comments

PEAR's HTML_TreeMenu class, available from `http://pear.php.net/` `package/HTML_TreeMenu`, offers a PHP interface to build an expandable/ collapsible menu tree. The class uses two primary objects—`HTML_TreeMenu()`, representing the menu tree, and `HTML_TreeNode()`, representing a node on the tree—and offers various methods to link nodes to each other and thereby create parent-child relationships between different levels of the menu.

Every `HTML_TreeNode()` object is initialized with a label and a target URL, and exposes an `addItem()` method that is used to link it to other `HTML_TreeNode()`s. Once `HTML_TreeNode()` objects have been created for every item of the menu, and all the items have been correctly linked, an `HTML_TreeMenu_DHTML()` object is initialized and the menu tree is generated, complete with all the JavaScript needed to display and hide tree nodes.

Figure 7-4 demonstrates what the output of the listing looks like.

NOTE

This package requires you to separately install the menu's JavaScript source file and tree node images in the directory containing your PHP script(s). These items are included in the downloadable version of the PEAR package.

TIP

The tree menu generated by HTML_TreeMenu is extremely customizable. The things you can change include the node and branch images, the initial state of each node (whether expanded/ collapsed), the frame in which link targets appear, and whether the menu should retain its last state across sessions.

Of course, in the real world, it's more than likely that your menu will come from a database, rather than be hard-coded into your script. Therefore, it's also worthwhile to see how the HTML_TreeMenu class can be used to dynamically generate a menu tree from records stored in a MySQL database.

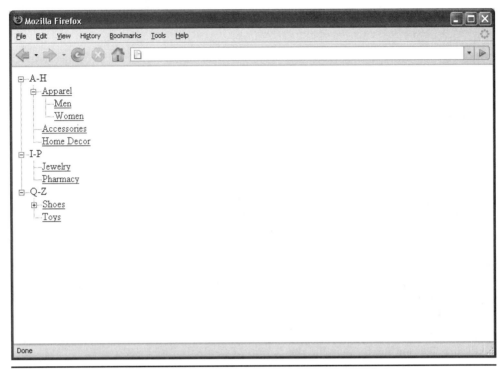

Figure 7-4 *A collapsible HTML tree menu*

Assume that the menu information is stored in a MySQL table, like this:

```
+----+------------------------------+--------------+--------+
| id | link                         | label        | parent |
+----+------------------------------+--------------+--------+
|  2 |                              | A-H          |      1 |
|  3 | catalog/apparel.html         | Apparel      |      2 |
|  4 | catalog/accessories.html     | Accessories  |      2 |
|  5 | catalog/hdecor.html          | Home Decor   |      2 |
|  6 | catalog/apparel-men.html     | Men          |      3 |
|  7 | catalog/apparel-women.html   | Women        |      3 |
|  8 |                              | I-P          |      1 |
|  9 | catalog/jewelry.html         | Jewelry      |      8 |
| 10 | catalog/pharmacy.html        | Pharmacy     |      8 |
| 11 |                              | Q-Z          |      1 |
| 12 | catalog/shoes.html           | Shoes        |     11 |
| 13 | catalog/shoes-men.html       | Men          |     12 |
| 14 | catalog/shoes-women.html     | Women        |     12 |
| 15 | catalog/toys.html            | Toys         |     11 |
+----+------------------------------+--------------+--------+
```

In this schema, parent-child relationships are determined by the interaction of the `id` and `parent` columns. Every record is identified by a unique `id`; when this `id` appears in the `parent` column of a record, it sets up a parent-child relationship between the corresponding records. All records with parent 1 are assumed to be at the root level.

The following code reads the menu information and converts it into a collapsible tree menu with the HTML_TreeMenu class:

```php
<?php
// include HTML_TreeMenu class
include "HTML/TreeMenu.php";

// initialize menu object
$root = new HTML_TreeMenu();

// create the first node (node id 1)
$node1 = new HTML_TreeNode(array("text" => "Sitemap", "link" => ""));
$root->addItem($node1);

// open connection
$connection = mysql_connect("localhost", "user", "pass")↵
or die ("Unable to connect!");

// select database
mysql_select_db("db1") or die ("Unable to select database!");

// create query
$query = "SELECT id, link, label, parent FROM menu ORDER BY parent";

// execute query
$result = mysql_query($query)↵
or die ("Error in query: $query. " . mysql_error());

// dynamically create nodes for each parent/child combination
// attach each child to its parent
if (mysql_num_rows($result) > 0) {
    while ($row = mysql_fetch_assoc($result)) {
        $parentObjName = "node" . $row['parent'];
        $childObjName = "node" . $row['id'];
        $$childObjName = new HTML_TreeNode(↵
array("text" => $row["label"], "link" => $row["link"]));
        $$parentObjName->addItem($$childObjName);
    }
}
```

```
// free result set memory
mysql_free_result($result);

// close connection
mysql_close($connection);
?>
<html>
<head>
<!-- link in the JavaScript code for expanding/collapsing the tree -->
<script src="TreeMenu.js" language="JavaScript"↵
 type="text/javascript"></script>
</head>
<body>
<?php
// initialize menu interface
// set options: path for tree images
//          frame to load click targets
$menu = new HTML_TreeMenu_DHTML($root,↵
array("linkTarget" => "rhframe", "images" => "images/"));

// print menu tree
$menu->printMenu();
?>
</body>
</html>
```

Here, a MySQL query retrieves all the nodes from the database, and a `while()` loop is used to create `HTML_TreeNode()` objects for each one. The child nodes are then linked to the parent nodes by means of the `parent` and `id` fields, and the menu tree is rendered via the `printMenu()` method. Note that the query orders the result set by parent ID, to avoid the situation of child nodes being created before their parents.

7.12 Dynamically Generating a Cascading Menu

Problem

You want to display a cascading menu that uses client-side scripting to hide and show menu levels.

Solution

Use the phpLayersMenu class:

```
<html>
<head>
<link rel="stylesheet" href="layersmenu-gtk2.css" ⏎
type="text/css"></link>
<script language="JavaScript" type="text/javascript"⏎
src="libjs/layersmenu-browser_detection.js"></script>
<script language="JavaScript" type="text/javascript"⏎
src="libjs/layersmenu-library.js"></script>
<script language="JavaScript" type="text/javascript" ⏎
src="libjs/layersmenu.js"></script>
</head>
<body>

<?php
// include PHPLayers class
include "lib/PHPLIB.php";
include "lib/layersmenu-common.inc.php";
include "lib/layersmenu.inc.php";

// initialize menu object
$menu = new LayersMenu();

// define file paths
$menu->setDirroot(".");
$menu->setImgwww("menuimages/");
$menu->setIconwww("menuicons/");

// set menu templates
$menu->setHorizontalMenuTpl ⏎
("templates/layersmenu-horizontal_menu.ihtml");
$menu->setSubMenuTpl("templates/layersmenu-sub_menu.ihtml");

// define menu as string
// this menu has 2 main menu items
$menuStr =<<< END
.|Meals|||
..|Breakfast|breakfast.html||
...|Cornflakes|breakfast.html#corn||
...|Toast|breakfast.html#toast||
..|Lunch|lunch.html||
...|Pasta Amatriciana|lunch.html#specials||
```

```
..|Dinner|dinner.html||
...|Roast Pork|dinner.html#option1||
...|Fried Trout with Scallions|dinner.html#option2||
.|Movies|||
..|Romance|http://some.domain.com/show.php?genre=Romance||
...|Sleepless In Seattle|http://some.domain.com/review.php?id=84||
..|Comedy|http://some.domain.com/show.php?genre=Comedy||
...|Meet The Parents|http://some.domain.com/review.php?id=9||
...|Four Weddings And A Funeral|http://some.domain.com/ ↵
review.php?id=17||
..|Action|http://some.domain.com/show.php?genre=Action||
...|Rambo: First Blood|http://some.domain.com/review.php?id=54||
END;

// parse menu string
$menu->setMenuStructureString($menuStr);
$menu->parseStructureForMenu("myMenu");

// generate menu
$menu->newHorizontalMenu("myMenu");

// render and display menu
$menu->printHeader();
$menu->printMenu("myMenu");
$menu->printFooter();
?>
</body>
</html>
```

Comments

The phpLayersMenu class, available from `http://phplayersmenu.sourceforge
.net/`, is a free, open-source PHP interface to a variety of menu types, including
cascading menus. Developed by Marco Pratesi, phpLayersMenu can read a menu
structure from a text file or database, and generate horizontal or vertical cascading
menus using client-side scripting.

The phpLayersMenu class comes with many different menu templates and, once
a `LayersMenu()` object is initialized, one of the first things you will do is decide
which template to use for the primary and secondary menus. This information is
defined through the `setHorizontalMenuTpl()` and `setSubMenuTpl()` methods,
respectively.

The menu structure itself may be retrieved from a string, a flat file, or a database.
In string or file format, a node on the menu tree is represented by a line containing

a series of pipe-separated values, with parents and children arranged in descending order. The previous listing illustrates this format:

```
.|Meals|||
..|Breakfast|breakfast.html||
...|Cornflakes|breakfast.html#corn||
..|Lunch|lunch.html||
...|Pasta Amatriciana|lunch.html#specials||
```

The `setMenuStructureString()` method attaches this menu structure to the `LayersMenu()` object, and the `parseStructureForMenu()` method then parses it and creates an in-memory representation of the menu. The `newHorizontalMenu()` method generates the menu, and the `printHeader()`, `printFooter()`, and `printMenu()` methods take care of translating the menu into HTML.

Figure 7-5 illustrates what the output of the previous listing looks like.

If you found the menu structure string in the previous listing somewhat awkward, don't worry, because phpLayersMenu makes it extremely easy to retrieve your

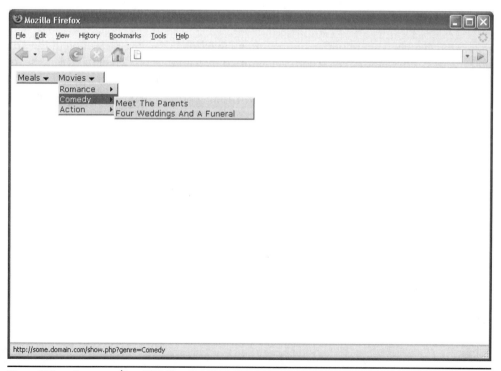

Figure 7-5 *A cascading HTML menu*

menu nodes and relationships from a database. To illustrate, consider the following MySQL table, which contains a complete set of menu items:

```
+----+---------------------------+-------------+--------+
| id | link                      | label       | parent |
+----+---------------------------+-------------+--------+
|  2 |                           | A-H         |   1 |
|  3 | catalog/apparel.html      | Apparel     |   2 |
|  4 | catalog/accessories.html  | Accessories |   2 |
|  5 | catalog/hdecor.html       | Home Decor  |   2 |
|  6 | catalog/apparel-men.html  | Men         |   3 |
|  7 | catalog/apparel-women.html| Women       |   3 |
|  8 |                           | I-P         |   1 |
|  9 | catalog/jewelry.html      | Jewelry     |   8 |
| 10 | catalog/pharmacy.html     | Pharmacy    |   8 |
| 11 |                           | Q-Z         |   1 |
| 12 | catalog/shoes.html        | Shoes       |  11 |
| 13 | catalog/shoes-men.html    | Men         |  12 |
| 14 | catalog/shoes-women.html  | Women       |  12 |
| 15 | catalog/toys.html         | Toys        |  11 |
+----+---------------------------+-------------+--------+
```

In this schema, parent-child relationships are determined by the interaction of the id and parent columns. Every record is identified by a unique id; when this id appears in the parent column of a record, it sets up a parent-child relationship between the corresponding records. All records with parent 1 are assumed to be at the root level.

The following code reads the menu information and converts it into a cascading menu with the phpLayersMenu class:

```
<html>
<head>
<link rel="stylesheet" href="layersmenu-gtk2.css" type="text/css"> ↵
</link>
<script language="JavaScript" type="text/javascript" ↵
src="libjs/layersmenu-browser_detection.js"></script>
<script language="JavaScript" type="text/javascript" ↵
src="libjs/layersmenu-library.js"></script>
<script language="JavaScript" type="text/javascript"↵
src="libjs/layersmenu.js"></script>
</head>
<body>
<?php
```

```php
// include PHPLayers class
include "lib/PHPLIB.php";
include "lib/layersmenu-common.inc.php";
include "lib/layersmenu.inc.php";

// include PEAR and DB classes for database connectivity
include "PEAR.php";
include "DB.php";

// initialize menu object
$menu = new LayersMenu();

// define file paths
$menu->setDirroot(".");
$menu->setImgwww("menuimages/");
$menu->setIconwww("menuicons/");

// set menu templates
$menu->setHorizontalMenuTpl ↵
("templates/layersmenu-horizontal_menu.ihtml");
$menu->setSubMenuTpl("templates/layersmenu-sub_menu.ihtml");

// define database connection parameters as DSN
$menu->setDBConnParms('mysql://user:pass@localhost/db1');

// set name of menu table
$menu->setTableName('menu');

// map table fields
$menu->setTableFields(array(
    "id" => "id",
    "parent_id"     => "parent",
    "text" => "label",
    "href" => "link",
    "title" => "label",
    "icon" => "",
    "target" => "",
    "orderfield" => "",
    "expanded" => ""));
```

```
// retrieve menu information
$menu->scanTableForMenu("myMenu");

// generate menu
$menu->newHorizontalMenu("myMenu");

// render and display menu
$menu->printHeader();
$menu->printMenu("myMenu");
$menu->printFooter();
?>
</body>
</html>
```

Here, the PEAR DB class is used to open a connection to the menu database, and the `setTableFields()` method is used to map specific table fields into the phpLayersMenu format. The `scanTableForMenu()` method then builds an in-memory structure representing the menu, and the `printMenu()` function renders it to the Web page.

NOTE

This example also requires the DB class from `http://pear.php.net/package/DB`.

7.13 Calculating Script Execution Times

Problem

You want to calculate and display how long it took PHP to render a particular page.

Solution

Use PHP's `microtime()` function to time how long the script takes:

```php
<?php
// start timer
$start = (float) array_sum(explode(' ', microtime()));

// execute some time-consuming code
// function to check if a number is prime
function testPrime($num) {
    for ($x=($num-1); $x>1; $x--) {
        if (($num%$x) == 0) {
```

```
            return false;
        }
    }
    return true;
}

// test first 1000 numbers for prime-ness
while ($count <= 1000) {
    // test if counter value is a prime number
    // print if so
    if (testPrime($count)) {
        echo "$count ";
    }
    $count++;
}

// end timer
$end = (float) array_sum(explode(' ', microtime()));

// calculate and print elapsed time
// result: "Total processing time was 0.627 seconds" (example)
echo "Total processing time was " . sprintf("%.4f",↵
($end-$start)) . " seconds";
?>
```

Comments

PHP's `microtime()` function returns the current UNIX timestamp in microseconds. This extra precision makes it useful for timing script execution and other tasks involving performance benchmarks. In the previous listing, two timestamps are generated, one at the start of the script and the other at the end. The difference between the two is the time taken for script execution.

7.14 Generating Multiple Web Pages from a Single Template

Problem

You want to add an element of reusability to your Web pages by creating standard templates and changing their content as required.

Solution

First, create a template for your page, using variable placeholders for the dynamic content:

File: chapter.tmpl
```
<!-- template for book chapter -->
<html>
<head></head>
<body>

<!-- chapter number and title -->
<div id="header" style="font-weight: bolder; font-style: italic;↵
padding-bottom: 15px">
Chapter {$chapterNum}: {$chapterTitle}
</div>

<!-- chapter text -->
<div id="content">{$chapterContents}</div>

<!-- page number -->
<div id="pagecount" style="text-align: right; font-size: smaller">
Page {$currentPage} of {$totalPages}
</div>

</body>
</html>
```

Then, use the Smarty template engine to replace the placeholders with actual data and render the page:

```php
<?php
// include Smarty class
include "Smarty.class.php";

// create object
$tmpl = new Smarty();

// set directory locations
$tmpl->template_dir = "./";
$tmpl->compile_dir = "./";

// set values for template variables
$tmpl->assign("chapterNum", 8);
$tmpl->assign("chapterTitle", "Welcome to Woohoo-Land!");
```

```
$tmpl->assign("chapterContents", "The mice jumped over the cat,⏎
giggling madly as the moon exploded into green and purple confetti. ⏎
\"Ah\", sighed the orange rabbit, \"It's so nice to be home in spring!⏎
It's enough to put a spring into anyone's step.\"");

$tmpl->assign("currentPage", 1);
$tmpl->assign("totalPages", 17);

// parse and display the template
$tmpl->display("chapter.tmpl");
?>
```

Comments

It's generally considered a Good Thing for an application's user interface to be independent of the business logic that drives it. This separation of the presentation layer from the functional layer affords both developers and designers a fair degree of independence when it comes to altering how the application looks and works, and also produces cleaner, more readable code (because PHP function calls are no longer interspersed within HTML markup).

The easiest way to accomplish this separation is by using page templates to separate presentation and layout information from program code, and a template engine to combine the two as needed. In this context, a *template* is simply a text file, containing both static elements (HTML code, ASCII text, et al) and special variable placeholders. When the template engine parses such a template, it automatically replaces the variable placeholders with actual values (referred to as *variable interpolation*). These values may be defined by the developer at run time, and may be either local to a particular template, or global across all the templates within an application.

This listing uses the popular Smarty template engine, available from http:// smarty.php.net/. Here, a template is defined for a Web page, with variable placeholders for dynamic elements such as the title and page number. Then, a PHP script initializes the template engine and uses its assign() method to assign values to the placeholders. Once all variable placeholders have been assigned values, the display() method is used to render the final page. Figure 7-6 illustrates the result:

To generate a new page from the same template, simply set new values for the template variables with assign() and call display() to render the page again.

Of course, you can do a lot more with Smarty (or, in fact, any template engine) than just this basic assign-and-display operation. Displaying parts of a page conditionally, creating reusable HTML blocks, nesting one template within another, and repeatedly rendering a single subtemplate to create a list, are some of the tasks a template engine makes possible. Learn more about this in the tutorial available at http://www.melonfire.com/community/columns/trog/article .php?id=130.

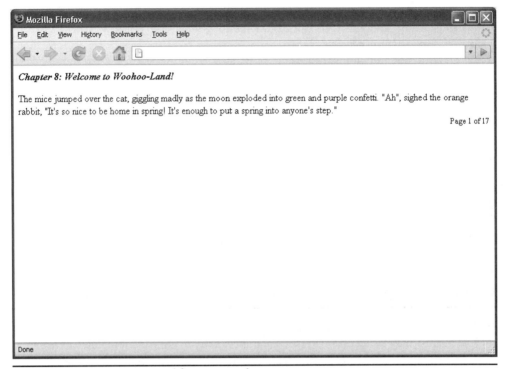

Figure 7-6   *A page generated from a template engine*

NOTE

The values assigned in this particular listing are hard-coded into the PHP script for illustrative purposes; in the real world, it's far more likely that these values will be produced from a database or other content source.

7.15 Caching Script Output

Problem

You want to improve response times by caching the output of frequently used scripts or scripts that perform time-consuming tasks whose output doesn't change very frequently.

Solution

Use PEAR's Cache class to implement a page cache:

```php
<?php
// include Cache class
include "Cache.php";

// initialize Cache object
$cache = new Cache('file', array('cache_dir' => 'cache/') );

// generate an ID for this page
$id = $cache->generateID("thisPage");

if ($page = $cache->get($id)) {
    // if the page is already cached
    // get it and print it
    print "\n[CACHED DATA]\n";
    print $page;
} else {
    // if the page is not cached
    // generate and store it in the cache
    $output = "The sum of the numbers 1 to 99000 is: " .↵
 array_sum(range(1,99000));
    echo $output;
    $cache->save($id, $output, 60);
}
?>
```

Comments

Complex business logic increases the time taken for a script to execute, and affects the user's perception of how slow or fast a server is. So, to improve response time, it's a good idea to cache the output of frequently accessed scripts. A simple caching mechanism can be implemented via PEAR's Cache class, available from http://pear.php.net/package/Cache.

The business logic to use a Cache object instance is fairly simple: check if the required data already exists in the cache, retrieve and use it if it does, generate it and save a copy to the cache if it doesn't. Most of this logic is accomplished via the get() and save() methods of the Cache() object. The get() method checks to see if the data exists in the cache and returns it if so, while the save() method saves data to the cache. Input arguments to the save() method are the data to be cached and a unique identifier that is later used to retrieve the cached data.

The previous listing illustrates this logic, calculating the sum of the first 99,000 numbers and displaying it as a Web page. Because performing this calculation is a time-intensive process and the output isn't likely to change at all, it makes sense to perform it once and then cache the page so that subsequent requests are dealt with quickly.

In this listing, a `Cache()` object is initialized and a unique ID is generated for the page. When a request arrives for the page, PHP checks to see if a cached version of the page exists via the `get()` method. If a cached version does not exist, the calculation is performed and the page is generated and `save()`-d to the output buffer. The contents of the output buffer are then cached and simultaneously sent to the client. Subsequent requests are served directly from the cache.

NOTE

For this script to work, you must manually create a directory for the cache, and tell the class about it in the class constructor.

The data in the cache remains valid for the duration specified in the Cache object's `save()` method—in this case, for 60 seconds. The page will be regenerated and re-cached for requests outside this time window.

In most cases, your page will not contain a single string, but will be generated in a composite manner from SQL query output, calculations, HTML markup, headers and footers, and images and forms. In these situations, you can combine a cache with an output buffer, which provides an easy way to save the final page to the cache. Here's an example:

```php
<?php
// include Cache class
include "Cache.php";

// initialize Cache object
$cache = new Cache('file', array('cache_dir' => 'cache/') );

// generate an ID for this page
$id = $cache->generateID("myPage");

// see if the page is cached
// if so, get it and print it
// if it is not cached
// generate the page
// and store it in the output buffer
if ($data = $cache->get($id)) {
    print "\n[CACHED DATA]\n";
    print $data;
} else {
```

```php
    // initialize the output buffer
    ob_start();

    // do whatever is needed
    // to generate the page:
    // - perform SQL queries
    // - parse, read, write files
    // - print HTML header, body, footer
    ?>

    <font size="+1">

    <?php include "header.php"; ?>

    <p>This is the page content.<p>
    <p>It can contain <a href="http://www.w3.org/MarkUp/">HTML</a>,↵
client-side code like <u><script↵
language="Javascript">document.writeln("JavaScript");</script></u>↵
and server-side code like <u><?php echo "PHP"; ?></u>.</p>

    <p>It can include calculations: <br /><u>
    <?php
    echo "The product of the numbers 1 to 99 is ";
    $product = 1;
    foreach (range(1,99) as $num) {
        $product = $num * $product;
    }
    echo $product;
    ?></u></p>

    <p>It can include the output of SQL queries: <br /><u>
    <?php
    echo "The MySQL server has been up for ";
    $connection = mysql_connect("localhost", "root", "")↵
or die ("Unable to connect!");
    $result = mysql_query("SHOW STATUS LIKE 'Uptime'")↵
or die ("Error in query: $query. " . mysql_error());
    $row = mysql_fetch_assoc($result);
    echo $row['Value'] . " seconds.";
    mysql_close($connection);
    ?></u>

    <p>The current server time is <u>↵
<?php echo date("H:i:m", time()); ?></u></p>
```

```php
    <?php include "footer.php"; ?>

    </font>

    <?php
    // complete page is now stored in the output buffer
    // save buffer contents to the cache
    // set cached data to expire after 1 minute
    $cache->save($id, ob_get_contents(), 60);

      // dump buffer contents to the client
    ob_end_flush();
}
?>
```

In the previous listing, the final page is generated from external header and footer templates, the result of a calculation, the result of an SQL query, the output of various PHP function calls, and some client-side JavaScript. In fact, this is representative of how most Web pages are generated, and the approach to use is to wrap the page in calls to PHP's output buffer functions. Once the page has been generated, the ob_get_contents() function is used to retrieve the final content of the buffer and save it to the cache; the ob_end_flush() function then dumps the same output to the client. Any subsequent request for the page will then receive the cached version (at least until the cache reaches its expiry value).

7.16 Paginating Content

Problem

You want to make a collection of records more readable, by splitting it into "pages."

Solution

Use PEAR's Pager class to break a data set into smaller pages and generate navigation links between them:

```php
<html>
<head></head>
<body>
<?php
// include Pager class
include "Pager/Pager.php";
```

```php
// define directory path
$dir = '/home/user/downloads';

// check if it is a directory
if (is_dir($dir)) {
    // open directory handle
    $dh = opendir($dir) or die ("Cannot open directory '$dir'!");

    // iterate over files in directory
    while (($file = readdir($dh)) !== false) {
        // optional, filter out "." and ".."
        if ($file != "." && $file != "..") {
            // store the file list and file size in an array
            $fileList[] = array($file, filesize($dir . "/" . $file));
        }
    }

    // close directory
    closedir($dh);
} else {
    die("Argument '$dir' is not a directory!");
}

// set up the paging engine
// define items per page
$options = array(
    "itemData" => $fileList,  // data set
    "perPage" => 10,          // items per page
    "delta" => 8,             // number of page numbers to display
    "mode"  => "Jumping"      // paging mode
);

// initialize object
$pager = &Pager::factory($options);

// get items for this page as array
$items = $pager->getPageData();

// get page numbers and links for this page
$links = $pager->getLinks();

// get total number of pages
$totalPages = $pager->numPages();
```

```php
// get current page number
$currentPage = $pager->getCurrentPageID();
?>

<p align="center" />

<?php
// header
// print next, previous links
// print page number links
echo $links['all'];
?>

<p align="left" />

<?php
// print items on this page
// file name and size
foreach ($items as $item) {
    echo $item[0] . " (" . $item[1] . " bytes)<p />";
}
?>

<p align="right" />

<?php
// footer
// print current page number and total pages
echo "Page $currentPage of $totalPages";
?>
</body>
</html>
```

Comments

It's usually not very user friendly to display a large volume of data on a single HTML page, as doing so forces the user to scroll up and down endlessly to view the results. This is where *pagination*   the act of breaking up large data sets into smaller subsets and displaying them one page at a time—can help. By breaking the large mass of data into smaller, more easily navigable pages, you increase the usability of your application, and you also avoid overwhelming the user with mountains of data at once.

PEAR's Pager class, available from `http://pear.php.net/package/Pager`, takes all the pain out of paginating large data sets. Given an array of values, the Pager class breaks the array into discrete "pages" of smaller elements and generates navigation links to move back and forth between the pages.

The previous listing demonstrates the Pager class in action. The data set here is a list of all the files in a directory; this list is broken into pages of ten items each, with the Pager class providing the navigation between pages.

The data set is passed to the Pager object via the `$options` array. This array also sets various paging parameters, such as the number of items per page and the number of pages accessible through the navigation links. The `getPageDate()` method retrieves, as an array, the list of items for the current page, while the `getLinks()` method generates an array of "next page" and "previous page" navigation links, together with a clickable list of page numbers for easy access to any part of the collection.

Figure 7-7 demonstrates what the output looks like.

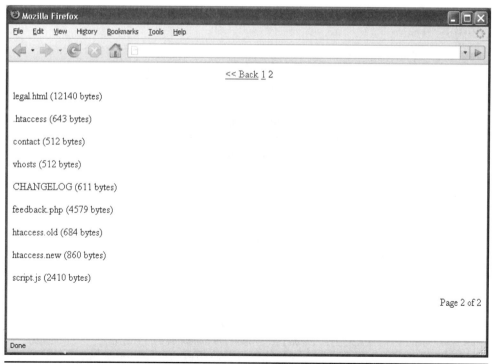

Figure 7-7 *A directory listing, broken up into pages*

7.17 Detecting Browser Type and Version

Problem

You want to identify the user's browser type and version number.

Solution

Use PHP's get_browser() function:

```php
<?php
// get browser information
$browser = get_browser(null, true);
// result: "Your browser is Firefox 2.0" (example)
print "Your browser is " . $browser['browser'] . " " . ↵
$browser['version'];
?>
```

Comments

The get_browser() function evaluates the $_SERVER['HTTP_USER_AGENT']
string and returns information about the client currently accessing the script. This
information includes the client identification string and version number, together
with detailed information on the client's capabilities. All this information is returned
as an associative array, which might look something like Figure 7-8.

You can use the information supplied by get_browser() to selectively display
code optimized for particular browser types and version numbers. Here's an
example:

```php
<?php
if (($browser['browser'] == "Opera" ) && ($browser['version'] >= 6)) {
    // code for Opera 6.x
}
?>
```

NOTE

In order to use the get_browser() *function, you must have configured PHP to point to a
valid* browscap.ini *file on your system. You can obtain a* browscap.ini *file from*
http://www.garykeith.com/browsers/downloads.asp, *or you can visit
the PHP manual page at* http://www.php.net/get-browser *for more information.*

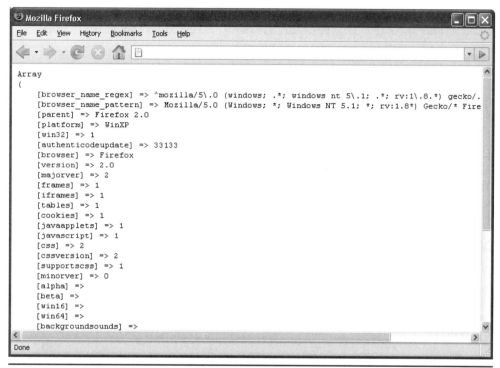

Figure 7-8   *Output of the get_browser() function*

An alternative here is to use the phpSniff class, available from `http://phpsniff.sourceforge.net/`. This class, like the `get_browser()` function, evaluates the user agent string and returns information on the client's capabilities and type. Here's an example of how it can be used:

```php
<?php
// include phpSniff library
include "phpSniff.class.php";

// initialize object
$sniffer = new phpSniff($_SERVER['HTTP_USER_AGENT']);

// get browser name, version and platform
$browser = $sniffer->get_property('browser');
$version = $sniffer->get_property('version');
$platform = $sniffer->get_property('platform');
$os = $sniffer->get_property('os');
```

```
// result: "Your browser is mz 1.8.1 running on win xp" (example)
print "Your browser is $browser $version running on $platform $os";
?>
```

7.18 Triggering Browser Downloads

Problem

You want to send the user's browser a file and manually trigger its download mechanism.

Solution

Send the browser appropriate `Content-Type` and `Content-Disposition` headers, to force it to begin downloading the file:

```php
<?php
// set the filename
$filename = "/tmp/photos.zip";

// send headers to client to initiate file download
header ("Content-Type: application/octet-stream");
header ("Content-Length: " . filesize($filename));
header ("Content-Disposition: attachment; filename=" .
basename($filename));

// send file to client
readfile($filename);
?>
```

Comments

If your PHP application needs to save a file to the client's disk, it must first trigger the client's file download mechanism. The easiest way to do this is to send the client a series of headers, telling it that what follows is a binary file and should be saved to disk instead of being rendered. Once the headers have been sent, the `readfile()` function can be used to stream the file to the client.

NOTE

Microsoft Internet Explorer suffers from a bug that causes some versions to not respond to these headers with an appropriate input dialog. For a list of possible hacks around this flaw, visit `http://www.php.net/header.`

NOTE

The call to PHP's `header()` *function must precede any script output, unless output buffering is enabled.*

7.19 Redirecting Browsers

Problem

You want to redirect the user's browser from one URL to another.

Solution

Send the browser an appropriate `Location` header to send it to a new URL:

```php
<?php
// send the browser a header
// with the new location
header("Location: http://www.google.com");
exit;
?>
```

Comments

To transparently redirect an HTTP client from one URL to another, all that's needed is to send it a `Location` HTTP header with the new URL. This can be easily accomplished via PHP's `header()` function, as illustrated in this listing. This listing is commonly used to redirect a client to an error page if, for example, user credentials or form data values are found to be invalid.

NOTE

The call to PHP's `header()` *function must precede any script output, unless output buffering is enabled.*

7.20 Reading Remote Files

Problem

You want to retrieve the contents of a remote file.

Solution

Use PHP's `file_get_contents()` function to read data from the corresponding file URL:

```php
<?php
// read and display file contents
header ("Content-Type: text/plain");
$data = file_get_contents("http://some.domain.com/index.html")↵
or die("Cannot open URL");
echo $data;
?>
```

Comments

Reading the source code of a Web page over HTTP is easy, given that PHP's file functions can all be used to read remote files. In this listing, the `file_get_contents()` function is used to read a remote URL and store the retrieved data in a PHP variable, which may be processed or displayed.

An alternative technique of retrieving the source code for a remote file consists of using the PEAR HTTP_Request class to generate and send a GET request for the URL. The content of the URL is contained in the body of the server's response to such a request. Here's what the code looks like:

```php
<?php
// send content header
header ("Content-Type: text/plain");

// include HTTP_Request class
include "HTTP/Request.php";

// create object
$request = &new HTTP_Request();
```

```
// perform an HTTP request
// get body
$request->setUrl("http://some.domain.com/index.html");
$request->setMethod("GET");
$request->sendRequest();
echo $request->getResponseBody();
?>
```

> **NOTE**
>
> The `text/plain` header in these examples is used to force the client to render the data is receives "as is." Without this header, the client would attempt to render any HTML code in the response body instead of displaying it.

7.21 Extracting URLs

Problem

You want to extract a list of all the URLs on a Web page.

Solution

Scan the HTML source of the page for URL patterns using the `preg_match_all()` function:

```
<?php
// read URL contents into a string
$dataStr = file_get_contents("http://www.some.domain.com/page.html")↵
or die ("Cannot open URL");

// look for URLs
// defined as strings beginning with http(s) or ftp
preg_match_all("/(http|https|ftp):\/\/[^<>[:space:]]+[[: ↵
alnum:]#?\/&=+%_]/", $dataStr, $matches);

// place matches in a separate array
$urlList = $matches[0];
print_r($urlList);
?>
```

Comments

Chapter 1 has numerous examples of the `preg_match_all()` function being used
to extract a list of matching substrings from a larger string. In this case, the substring
to be matched is a pattern representing the typical Web URL, and the text to be
scanned is the source code of a Web page. Matches, if any, are placed in a separate
array for further processing.

An alternative technique, based on suggestions posted in the online PHP manual,
involves scanning the page source for `href` and `src` attributes and retrieving their
values. Here's how:

```php
<?php
// read URL contents into a string
$dataStr = file_get_contents("http://www.some.domain.com/page.html")↵
or die ("Cannot open URL");

// look for URLs
// defined as strings referenced in <a> or <img> elements
preg_match_all("/(href|src)=(\"|')*([^<>[:space.]]+[[:alnum:]#?\/&=+%_])↵
(\"|')*/i", $dataStr, $matches);

// place matches in a separate array
$urlList = $matches[3];
print_r($urlList);
?>
```

This technique has the advantage of returning both relative and absolute URLs
from image and anchor elements in the page, and may be suitable for some
applications—for example, a Web spider. Notice the use of parentheses within
the regular expression to isolate and index particular segments of the matched
substrings.

7.22 Generating HTML Markup from ASCII Files

Problem

You want to mark up an ASCII file as a Web page.

Solution

Use PHP's nl2br() and htmlentities() functions to turn ASCII text into its HTML equivalent:

```php
<?php
// read ASCII data
$ascii = file("shoppinglist.txt") or die("Cannot read from file");

// attach custom page header
$html =<<< HEADER
<html>
<head></head>
<body>
Rendered page follows: <hr />
HEADER;

// add page contents
// convert ASCII data to HTML
$html .= nl2br(htmlentities(implode("", $ascii)));

// add custom page footer
$html .=<<< FOOTER
<hr />Rendered page ends.
</body>
</html>
FOOTER;

// display page
echo $html;
?>
```

Comments

Given an ASCII file, this listing reads it into an array and then runs two functions on it to make it suitable for display in a Web browser: the htmlentities() function replaces special characters like ", &, <, and > with the corresponding HTML entity values, while the nl2br() function helps to retain the original formatting of the text by converting newline characters to HTML <br /> elements. The HTML-ized content is surrounded with the standard HTML header and footer markup.

> **TIP**
>
> If the ASCII file contains hyperlinks, you can convert them to HTML anchor elements with the technique outlined in the listing in "7.4: Activating Embedded URLs."

7.23 Generating Clean ASCII Text from HTML Markup

Problem

You want to strip the HTML tags from a Web page to generate a "clean" ASCII version.

Solution

Use PHP's strip_tags() and html_entity_decode() functions to turn HTML markup into plain ASCII text:

```
<pre>
<?php
// read URL contents into a string
$html = file_get_contents("page.html") or die ("Cannot open URL");

// strip out HTML tags
// replace HTML entities with their ASCII counterparts
$ascii = html_entity_decode(strip_tags($html));

// compress multiple lines to a single like
$ascii = preg_replace("/([\r\n])[\s]+/", "\\1", trim($ascii));

// display ASCII
echo $ascii;
?>
</pre>
```

Comments

In this listing, PHP's file_get_contents() function is used to read the HTML source of a Web page into a string and the strip_tags() function is then used to remove all HTML and PHP code from the string. The html_entity_decode() function, new in PHP 5.x, is then used to convert HTML entities into their ASCII equivalents, and the `preg_replace()` and `trim()` functions are used to remove extra whitespace from the string. The end result is a "clean" ASCII version of the original Web page.

7.24 Generating an HTML Tag Cloud

Problem

You want to build a *tag cloud* to visually display the frequency of tag occurrence on your Web pages.

Solution

Calculate the frequency of each tag's appearance and use this to determine how large a space it occupies in the cloud relative to other tags:

```
<html>
<head>
<style type="text/css">
    span { padding: 5px; }
    .smallest { font-size: 10pt; }
    .small { font-size: 15pt; }
    .medium { font-size: 20pt; }
    .large { font-size: 25pt; }
    .largest { font-size: 30pt; }
</style>
</head>
<body>

<?php
// initialize array for tag information
$tags = array();

// query database for tags
$connection = mysql_connect("localhost", "user", "pass")↵
or die ("Unable to connect!");
mysql_select_db("db1") or die ("Unable to select database!");
$query = "SELECT tag, tagCount FROM tags  ORDER BY tag";
$result = mysql_query($query) ↵
or die ("Error in query: $query. " . mysql_error());
```

```php
    // process query results, convert to associative array
    if (mysql_num_rows($result) > 0) {
        while ($row = mysql_fetch_assoc($result)) {
            $tags[$row['tag']] = $row['tagCount'];
        }
    }

    // close connection
    mysql_close($connection);

    // get max/min tag frequency and range
    // calculate "bins" for font sizes
    $max = max($tags);
    $min = min($tags);
    $diff = $max-$min;
    $stepVal = round($diff/5);

    // iterate through tag list
    // decide which font size to use
    // based on tag frequency
    foreach ($tags as $tag => $count) {
        switch ($count) {
        case ($count <= ($min + $stepVal)):
            echo "<span class='smallest'>↵
<a href='http://www.wikipedia.com/wiki/$tag'>$tag</a> ↵
</span>";
            break;

        case ($count <= ($min + $stepVal*2)):
            echo "<span class='small'>↵
<a href='http://www.wikipedia.com/wiki/$tag'>$tag</a> ↵
</span>";
            break;

        case ($count <= ($min + $stepVal*3)):
            echo "<span class='medium'>↵
<a href='http://www.wikipedia.com/wiki/$tag'>$tag</a> ↵
</span>";
            break;

        case ($count <= ($min + $stepVal*4)):
            echo "<span class='large'>↵
<a href='http://www.wikipedia.com/wiki/$tag'>$tag</a> ↵
```

```
</span>";
        break;

    case ($count <= ($min + $stepVal*5)):
        echo "<span class='largest'>↵
<a href='http://www.wikipedia.com/wiki/$tag'>$tag</a> ↵
</span>";
        break;
    }
}
?>

</body>
</html>
```

Comments

A *tag cloud* is a visual representation of how often particular tags occur in a Web page or application. More frequently occurring tags are typically rendered in a larger font, and are usually hyperlinked to appropriate Web pages. Tag clouds thus provide an easy way to gauge the popularity of particular tags, and are most frequently seen on community-oriented sites such as Flickr and Digg.

To generate a tag cloud, it is necessary to first have a list of unique tags, as well as a count of how frequently each appears. For simplicity, this listing assumes that this data is available in the following MySQL database table:

```
+-----------+----------+---------------------+
| tag       | tagCount | tagCountLastUpdate  |
+-----------+----------+---------------------+
| Wharton   |      112 | 2006-10-27 23:04:53 |
| Stanford  |      232 | 2006-10-27 23:05:07 |
| Harvard   |      225 | 2006-10-27 23:05:25 |
| Oxford    |       73 | 2006-10-27 23:05:36 |
| Cambridge |       87 | 2006-10-27 23:05:44 |
| NYU       |      187 | 2006-10-27 23:06:09 |
| Yale      |       54 | 2006-10-27 23:06:28 |
| Berkeley  |      190 | 2006-10-27 23:06:39 |
| MIT       |      211 | 2006-10-27 23:07:00 |
+-----------+----------+---------------------+
```

The preceding listing begins by obtaining a list of tags and their corresponding frequency, via a SELECT query to the database table shown previously. The results of the query are turned into a PHP associative array named $tags with elements of the form (tag => frequency). PHP's max() and min() functions are then used to obtain the highest and lowest frequency values, and calculate the range between them.

For easy visual differentiation, five sizes of font will be used to render the tag cloud. The frequency range calculated in the previous step is therefore divided by five to obtain "bins" into which each tag will be placed. A foreach() loop is then used to iterate over the $tags array; the loop checks each tag's frequency, compares it to the size "bins" to decide which one is most appropriate, and then generates appropriate HTML and CSS code to render the tag. Each tag is also hyperlinked to the Wikipedia Web site.

When viewed in a browser, each tag is rendered in a size corresponding to its frequency, using the CSS rules described for the corresponding bin. Figure 7-9 provides an example of what the output might look like:

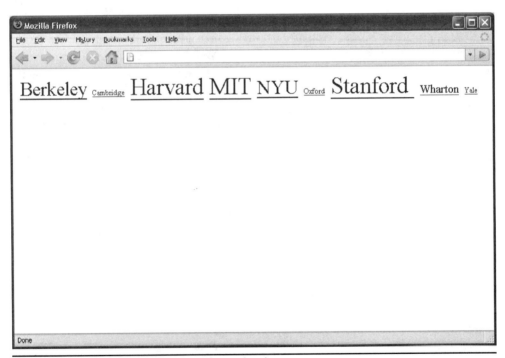

Figure 7-9   *A dynamically generated tag cloud*

An alternative approach is to use PEAR's HTML_TagCloud class, which provides prebuilt methods for rendering tags based on their frequency. Here's an example of this in action:

```php
<?php
// include TagCloud class
include "HTML/TagCloud.php";

// initialize object
$cloud = new HTML_TagCloud(50,30);

// query database for tags
$connection = mysql_connect("localhost", "user", "pass")↵
or die ("Unable to connect!");
mysql_select_db("db1") or die ("Unable to select database!");
$query = "SELECT tag, tagCount FROM tags";
$result = mysql_query($query)↵
or die ("Error in query: $query. " . mysql_error());

// add element for each tag with frequency
if (mysql_num_rows($result) > 0) {
    while ($row = mysql_fetch_assoc($result)) {
        $cloud->addElement($row['tag'],↵
"http://www.wikipedia.com/wiki/" . $row['tag'], $row['tagCount']);
    }
}

// close connection
mysql_close($connection);

// output tag cloud
print $cloud->buildAll();
?>
```

Here, a list of tags and their corresponding frequencies is obtained via a SELECT query to the database, as before. The class' addElement() method is then used to attach each tag, with its frequency, to the tag cloud. The buildAll() method then performs the necessary calculations and renders the cloud using different font sizes. Notice that the range of allowed font sizes is specified in the class constructor.

TIP

Read more about tag clouds at http://en.wikipedia.org/wiki/Tag_cloud.

Working with Forms, Sessions, and Cookies

IN THIS CHAPTER:

One of the most critical things you can do to ensure the stability of your Web application is to verify the input it receives through online forms. This might seem trivial, but a failure to build in basic input validation routines can snowball into serious problems, such as data corruption or inconsistent calculations.

With this in mind, a good part of this chapter focuses on forms and input validation: processing form input; validating e-mail addresses, URLs, and credit card numbers; uploading files through forms; preserving data across multipage forms; and dynamically generating form elements.

That's not all, though—unlike many other languages, PHP comes with native session and cookie management support, making it possible to track individual client sessions on a Web site and create highly customized Web pages. This chapter explores these features, discussing how to store and retrieve session variables; set and delete cookies; customize how session data is stored; authenticate users and protect pages from unauthorized access; build a session-based shopping cart; and create persistent objects.

NOTE

You'll find the SQL code needed to create the database tables in this chapter in the code archive for this book, at `http://www.php-programming-solutions.com`.

8.1 Generating Forms

Problem

You want to generate an HTML form using PHP method calls.

Solution

Use PEAR's HTML_QuickForm class:

```
<html>
<head></head>
<body>
<?php
// include HTML_QuickForm class
include "HTML/QuickForm.php";
```

```php
// initialize form object
$form = new HTML_QuickForm("pizzaOrder");

// add text input box
$form->addElement("text", "name", "Name:", array("size" => 30));

// add check box
$form->addElement("checkbox", "new_account", "Create an account for me");

// add selection list
$select = $form->addElement("select", "size", "Pizza size:",↵
array("8-inch", "12-inch", "16-inch"));

// add radio button group
$radio[] =& HTML_QuickForm::createElement("radio", null, null,↵
"Deep Dish", "D");
$radio[] =& HTML_QuickForm::createElement("radio", null, null,↵
"Thin and Crisp", "C");
$form->addGroup($radio, "base", "Pizza base:");

// add textarea
$form->addElement("textarea", "comments", "Special requests:");

// add submit button
$form->addElement("submit", null, "Place Order");

// render and display the form
$form->display();
?>
</body>
</html>
```

Comments

PEAR's HTML_QuickForm class, available from `http://pear.php.net/package/HTML_QuickForm`, is a sophisticated PHP class designed for on-the-fly form generation. Once an object of the class has been initialized, you can use the `addElement()` method to create and attach different types of input elements to the form. Typically, between three and four arguments are passed to `addElement()`: the element type, the element name, the element label (or value), and an optional array of additional attributes or information. Once the elements have been created, the `display()` method renders the form in HTML.

Figure 8-1 illustrates the output of this listing.

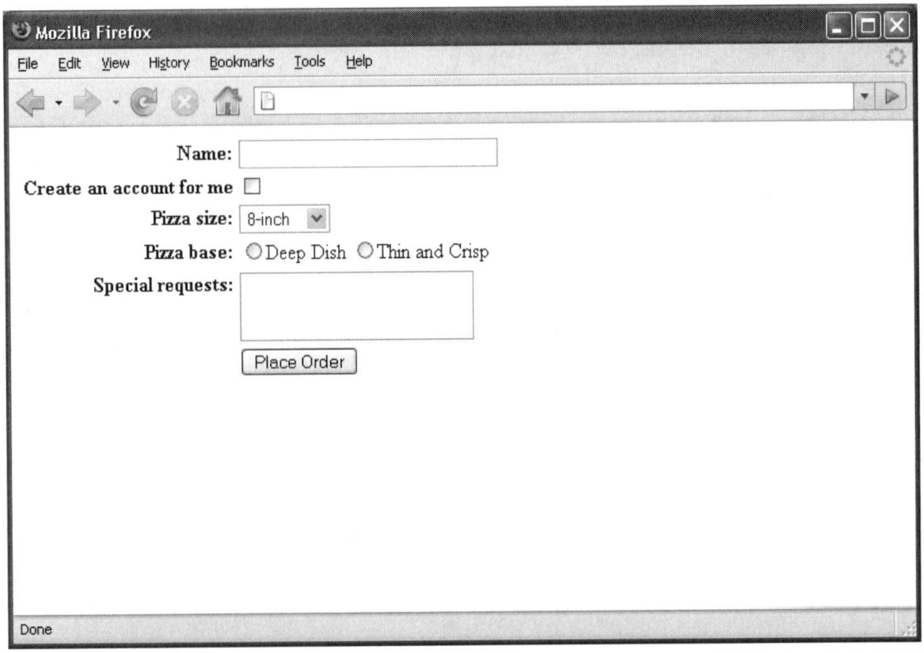

Figure 8-1   A Web form

See more examples of HTML_QuickForm in the listings in "8-5: Creating Dependent Drop-Down Lists," "8-6: Validating Form Input," "8-16: Uploading Files Through Forms," and "8-17: Preserving User Input Across Form Pages."

> ### TIP
>
> In addition to the standard form input types, the HTML_QuickForm class also provides some custom built-ins for linking and grouping form elements. Read more about this at `http://pear.php.net/package/HTML_QuickForm`, or look at an example in the listing in "8-5 Creating Dependent Drop-Down Lists."

8.2 Processing Form Input

Problem

You want to use the data submitted in a form.

Solution

Access the data through the $_POST or $_GET arrays:

```php
<?php
// iterate through POST-ed form data
// display each field and its value
foreach ($_POST as $key => $value) {
    echo "$key = $value";
    echo "<br />";
}

// display the value of a specific field
echo $_POST['email'];
?>
```

Comments

Whenever a form is submitted to a PHP script, all variable-value pairs within that form automatically become available for use within the script through one of two associative arrays: $_POST or $_GET. It's easy to iterate through these arrays and retrieve the submitted values, or even access specific values by key.

> ### NOTE
> *Remember that data submitted through a form may not necessarily be valid, and it must be checked before it can be saved or used in a calculation. The listing in "8.6: Validating Form Input" discusses how you may do this.*

> ### TIP
> *To quickly view data submitted in a form, use the* `print_r()` *function with the* $_POST *and* $_GET *arrays, like this:*
> ```php
> <?php
> print_r($_POST);
> ?>
> ```

8.3 Combining a Form and Its Result Page

Problem

You want to use a single PHP script for both a form and its result page.

Solution

Use the presence or absence of the form `<submit>` element to decide whether to display the form or its result page:

```
<html>
<head></head>
<body>
<?php
if (!$_POST['submit']) {
// if $_POST['submit'] does not exist
// display initial page
?>
    <form action="<?=$_SERVER['PHP_SELF']?>" method="post">
    Enter your age: <input name="age" size="2" maxlength="2">
    <input type="submit" name="submit" value="Go">
    </form>
<?php
} else {
// if $_POST['submit'] exists
// process form data
    $age = $_POST['age'];
    echo ($age >= 21) ? "You're an adult" : "You're a child";
}
?>
</body>
</html>
```

Comments

Normally, when creating and processing forms in PHP, you would place the HTML form in one file, and handle form processing through a separate PHP script. However, with the power of conditional statements at your disposal, you can combine both pages into one.

To do this, simply assign a name to the form's `<submit>` control, and then check whether the special `$_POST` container variable contains that name each time the script runs. If it does, it means that the form has already been submitted, and you can process the data; if it does not, it means that the user has not submitted the form and you therefore need to generate the initial unfilled form. Thus, by testing for the presence or absence of this variable, a clever PHP programmer can use a single PHP script to generate both the initial form and the output after it has been submitted.

Notice also the use of the $_SERVER['PHP_SELF'] variable in the form's action element; this variable always holds the path and name of the currently executing script and ensures that the form submits user input back to itself (a so-called *postback*).

NOTE

You can also do this with HTML_QuickForm. Look at the listing in "8.6: Validating Form Input" for an example.

8.4 Creating Drop-Down Lists

Problem

You want to create a drop-down list of options from an array.

Solution

Use a foreach() loop to process the array and convert it to a series of <option> elements:

```php
<?php
// define array of items for <select>
$colors = array("red", "green", "blue", "orange", "black", "silver");
?>

<html>
<head></head>
<body>
<form>
Color: <select name="color">
<?php
foreach ($colors as $k=>$v) {
    echo "<option value=\"$k\">$v</option>\n";
}
?>
</select>
</form>
</body>
</html>
```

Comments

To dynamically generate a drop-down option list in a form, store the options in an array and use PHP's `foreach()` loop to iterate through the array and print HTML `<option>` elements corresponding to its contents.

If you prefer to do this using pure PHP instead of a mixture of HTML code and PHP functions calls, use PEAR's HTML_QuickForm class, available from `http://pear.php.net/package/HTML_QuickForm`. This class enables you to add a drop-down list with the `addElement()` method, and specify the list items as an input argument to the method. Take a look:

```
<html>
<head></head>
<body>
<?php
// include HTML_QuickForm class
include "HTML/QuickForm.php";

// initialize form object
$form = new HTML_QuickForm("colors");

// define array of items for <select>
$colors = array("red", "green", "blue", "orange", "black", "silver");

// add <select> element
$form->addElement("select", "color", "Color:", $colors);

// render and display
$form->display();
?>
</body>
</html>
```

To create drop-down lists that dynamically change their contents on selection, see the listing in "8.5: Creating Dependent Drop-Down Lists."

8.5 Creating Dependent Drop-Down Lists

Problem

You want to create a series of dependent drop-down lists, such that a choice in one alters the available choices in another.

Solution

Use PEAR's HTML_QuickForm class:

```
<html>
<head></head>
<body>

<?php
// include HTML_QuickForm class
include "HTML/QuickForm.php";

// initialize form object
$form = new HTML_QuickForm("storeFinder");

// define array of items for parent <select>
$firstLevel = array();
$firstLevel[1] = "A-H";
$firstLevel[2] = "I-P";
$firstLevel[3] = "Q-Z";

// define array of items for child <select>
$secondLevel = array();
$secondLevel[1][1] = "Apparel";
$secondLevel[1][2] = "Cosmetics";
$secondLevel[2][1] = "Jewelery";
$secondLevel[2][2] = "Linen";
$secondLevel[2][3] = "Pets";
$secondLevel[3][1] = "Shoes";

// add hierarchical <select> element
$select =& $form->addElement("hierselect", "store", "Store:");

// attach parent and child data
$select->setMainOptions($firstLevel);
$select->setSecOptions($secondLevel);

// render and display
$form->display();
?>

</body>
</html>
```

Comments

PEAR's HTML_QuickForm class, available from `http://pear.php.net/package/HTML_QuickForm`, comes with a special built-in element, `hierselect`, which is designed specifically to create dependent drop-down lists in forms.

Here, the item choices for both primary and secondary drop-down lists are stored in arrays, with the index numbers of the primary array serving as keys to the corresponding items in the multidimensional secondary array. The `setMainOptions()` and `setSecOptions()` methods are used to link the arrays to the `<select>` object. The `display()` method renders the form, together with the client-side code necessary to change the contents of the secondary drop-down list once a selection is made from the primary one.

8.6 Validating Form Input

Problem

You want to validate the data submitted in a form.

Solution

Check the submitted data using either built-in or custom data validation routines, and only proceed to use it if it's valid:

```
<html>
<head></head>
<body>
<?php
if (!$_POST['submit']) {
    // not submitted
    // display form
?>
    <form action="<?php echo $_SERVER['PHP_SELF']; ?>" method="post">
    Username: <br /> <input type="text" name="username"> <br />
    Password (6 or more characters): <br />
    <input type="password" name="password"> <br />
    E-mail: <br /> <input type="text" name="email">    <br />
    Age: <br /><input type="text" name="age" size="2"> <br />
    <input type="submit" name="submit">
    </form>
```

```php
<?php
} else {
    // submitted
    // initialize array to hold validation errors
    $errorList = array();

    // check if required input is present
    if (!isset($_POST['username']) || ↵
trim($_POST['username']) == "")      {
        $errorList[] = "ERROR: Missing value 'username'";
    }

    // check if input is of correct type
    if (!is_numeric($_POST['age'])) {
        $errorList[] = "ERROR: Incorrect data type for value 'age'";
    }

    // check if input is of correct length
    if (strlen($_POST['password']) < 6) {
        $errorList[] = "ERROR: Incorrect length for value 'password'";
    }

    // check if input conforms to a pattern
    if (!eregi("^([a-z0-9_-]|\.)+@(([a-z0-9_-])+\.)+[a-z]↵
{2,6}$", $_POST['email'])) {
        $errorList[] = "ERROR: Incorrect format for value 'email'";
    }

    // check to see if any validation errors occurred

    if (sizeof($errorList) > 0) {
        // if errors occurred
        // display error list
        // and terminate script processing
        echo "Please review and correct the following errors: <br />";
        foreach ($errorList as $e) {
            echo "$e <br />";
        }
    } else {
        // if no errors occurred
        // process input
        // for example, save to a database or file
```

```
            // display success message
            echo "Thank you for your submission";
        }
    }
?>
</body>
</html>
```

Comments

When dealing with form input, many novice programmers immediately save the submitted data to a database, or use it in a calculation. This is a serious mistake, as there is no guarantee that the data submitted through a form is valid. Therefore, to avoid errors or database corruption, form input must always be tested for validity before it is used.

The previous listing illustrates the basic procedure to validate form input:

▶   Test each input value for validity using either a built-in or custom function and add any validation errors to an error stack (here, a simple PHP array).

▶   Once all the input values have been tested, check the error stack.

▶   If the error stack is empty, it implies that some of the data is invalid. Display a list of the errors, and terminate processing.

▶   If the error stack is not empty, it implies that all of the input is valid, and you can safely use it for further processing.

PHP offers a number of built-in functions to test form input. The previous listing illustrates some of the common ones, and it's always possible to roll your own as well (see the listings in "8.7: Validating Numbers" to "8.15: Validating URLs" for some ideas).

NOTE

It's common practice to use client-side scripting languages such as JavaScript or VBScript for client-side input validation. However, this type of client-side validation is not foolproof—if a user turns off JavaScript in the client, all your client-side code will become nonfunctional. That's why it's a good idea to couple client-side validation (which is faster) with server-side validation (which is more secure).

An alternative approach, and one that will appeal to fans of Object-Oriented Programming (OOP), is to use the PEAR HTML_QuickForm class, available from http://pear.php.net/package/HTML_QuickForm. HTML_QuickForm comes with numerous built-in input validation rules that significantly ease the task of validating form input. To illustrate this, compare the previous listing with the code that follows, which is equivalent:

```
<html>
<head></head>
<body>
<?php
// include HTML_QuickForm class
include "HTML/QuickForm.php";

// initialize form object
$form = new HTML_QuickForm("userReg");

// add text input boxes
$form->addElement("text", "name", "Name:", array("size" => 30));
$form->addElement("password", "password", "Password:", ⏎
array("size" => 30));
$form->addElement("text", "age", "Age:", array("size" => 2));
$form->addElement("text", "email", "E-mail address:");

// add submit button
$form->addElement("submit", null, "Submit");

// run filters on input values
$form->applyFilter(array("name", "password", "age", "email"), "trim");

// define input validation rules
$form->addRule("name", "ERROR: Missing value", "required");
$form->addRule("password", "ERROR: Missing value", "required");
$form->addRule("password", "ERROR: Incorrect length", "minlength", 6);
$form->addRule("age", "ERROR: Missing value", "required");
$form->addRule("age", "ERROR: Incorrect data type", "numeric");
$form->addRule("email", "ERROR: Missing value", "required");
$form->addRule("email", "ERROR: Incorrect format", "email");

// validate input
if ($form->validate()) {
    // if valid, freeze the form
    $form->freeze();

    // retrieve submitted data as array
    $data = $form->exportValues();
```

```
        // process input
        // for example, save to a database or file

        // display success message and exit
        echo "Thank you for your submission";
        exit;
    }

// render and display the form
$form->display();
?>

</body>
</html>
```

Here, the addRule() method is used to attach built-in validation rules ("required", "minlength", "email") to each form element, together with the error message to be displayed if the input fails validation. Once the validate() method is called, HTML_QuickForm tests each input value using the defined rules and, in the event of validation errors, redisplays the form with the flawed values highlighted. Only when all the form values are valid and the validate() method returns true, will the script proceed to use the submitted data.

TIP

For a complete list of HTML_QuickForm's built-in input tests, check the online manual at `http://pear.php.net/package/HTML_QuickForm`.

8.7 Validating Numbers

Problem

You want to test if a value is a number.

Solution

Use a regular expression to check if the supplied value contains only numbers, a negative sign (optional), and a decimal point (optional):

```php
<?php
// function to validate an integer
function validateInteger($str) {
    // test if input is an integer, optionally signed
    return preg_match("/^-?([0-9])+$/", $str);
}

// function to validate a float
function validateFloat($str) {
    // test if input is a floating-point number, optionally signed
    return preg_match("/^-?([0-9])+([\.|,]([0-9])*)?$/", $str);
}

// result: "Is an integer"
echo validateInteger("123456") ? "Is an integer" : "Is not an integer";

// result: "Is not an integer"
echo validateInteger("123456.506") ? "Is an integer" : ↵
"Is not an integer";

// result: "Is not an integer"
echo validateInteger("12a3456.506") ? "Is an integer" : ↵
"Is not an integer";

// result: "Is a float"
echo validateFloat("123456") ? "Is a float" : "Is not a float";

// result: "Is a float"
echo validateFloat("123456.506") ? "Is a float" : "Is not a float";
?>
```

Comments

While PHP does offer the built-in is_numeric(), is_float(), and is_int()
functions to check numeric input, you might often prefer to implement custom
number-checking routines for more stringent validation. This listing illustrates two
such validation routines, validateInteger() and validateFloat(), useful
for testing the format of integer and decimal input, respectively. In both cases, the
regular expression pattern matches numbers in the range 0-9, with an optional sign
prefix; in the latter case, the pattern also supports a decimal point and following
values.

An alternative is to use PHP's `ctype_digit()` function, which returns true only if every character of the supplied input argument is a number. As the next listing demonstrates, it thus returns false for every value except positive integers:

```php
<?php
// result: "Is a number"
echo ctype_digit("123456") ? "Is a number" : "Is not a number";

// result: "Is not a number"
echo ctype_digit("123456.506") ? "Is a number" : "Is not a number";

// result: "Is not a number"
echo ctype_digit("12a3456.506") ? "Is a number" : "Is not a number";
?>
```

8.8 Validating Alphabetic Strings

Problem

You want to test if a value is an alphabetic string.

Solution

Use a regular expression to check if the supplied value contains only alphabetic characters:

```php
<?php
function validateAlpha($str) {
    // test if input contains only alphabetic characters
    return preg_match("/^[a-z]+$/i", $str);
}

// result: "Is alphabetic"
echo validateAlpha("abc") ? "Is alphabetic" : "Is not alphabetic";

// result: "Is not alphabetic"
echo validateAlpha("abc1") ? "Is alphabetic" : "Is not alphabetic";
?>
```

Comments

PHP lets you test strings with the `is_string()` function, but this function doesn't distinguish between alphabetic, alphanumeric, and numeric strings. If you'd like more stringent validation, consider the `validateAlpha()` function in this listing, which only passes strings containing alphabetic characters (strings with numbers or symbols will be rejected). Notice the function's use of the `i` modifier, which performs case-insensitive matching.

An alternative is to use PHP's `ctype_alpha()` function, which returns true only if every character of the supplied input argument is an alphabetic character. Here's an example:

```php
<?php
// result: "Is alphabetic"
echo ctype_alpha("abc") ? "Is alphabetic" : "Is not alphabetic";

// result: "Is not alphabetic"
echo ctype_alpha("abc1") ? "Is alphabetic" : "Is not alphabetic";
?>
```

8.9 Validating Alphanumeric Strings

Problem

You want to test if a value is an alphanumeric string.

Solution

Use a regular expression to check if the supplied value contains only alphabetic characters and numbers:

```php
<?php
function validateAlphaNum($str) {
    // test if input contains alphabetic and numeric characters
    return preg_match("/^[a-z0-9]*$/i", $str);
}

// result: "Is an alphabetic string"
echo validateAlphaNum("abc") ? "Is an alphabetic string" :
"Is not an alphabetic string";

// result: "Is an alphabetic string"
echo validateAlphaNum("abc1") ? "Is an alphabetic string" :
"Is not an alphabetic string";
```

```
// result: "Is not an alphabetic string"
echo validateAlphaNum("abc?") ? "Is an alphabetic string" :↵
"Is not an alphabetic string";
?>
```

Comments

PHP lets you test strings with the is_string() function, but this function doesn't distinguish between alphabetic, alphanumeric, and numeric strings. If you need more precise validation, consider the validateAlphaNum() function in this listing, which tests strings for alphabetic or numeric characters and rejects those containing symbols or special characters outside the alphabetic or numeric range. Notice also the function's use of the i modifier, for case-insensitive matching.

You could also perform this check with PHP's ctype_alnum() function, which returns true only if every character of the supplied input argument belongs to either the alphabetic or numeric set. Here's an example:

```
<?php
// result: "Is an alphabetic string"
echo ctype_alnum("abc") ? "Is an alphabetic string" :↵
"Is not an alphabetic string";

// result: "Is an alphabetic string"
echo ctype_alnum("abc1") ? "Is an alphabetic string" :↵
"Is not an alphabetic string";

// result: "Is not an alphabetic string"
echo ctype_alnum("abc?") ? "Is an alphabetic string" : ↵
"Is not an alphabetic string";
?>
```

8.10 Validating Credit Card Numbers

Problem

You want to validate the format of a credit card number or expiration date.

Solution

Use a regular expression to test the format of the supplied number and date:

```php
<?php
// function to validate a credit card number
function validateCCNum($str) {
    // test if input is of the form dddddddddddddddd
    return preg_match("/^\d{16}$/" ,$str);
}


// function to validate a credit card expiry date
function validateCCExpDate($str) {
    // test if input is of the form mm/yyyy
    return preg_match("/(0[1-9]|1[0-2])\/20[0-9]{2}$/", $str);
}

// result: "Is a valid 16-digit number"
echo validateCCNum("4476269198125132") ? "Is a valid 16-digit number" :↵
"Is not a 16-digit number";

// result: "Is a valid date string"
echo validateCCExpDate("12/2013") ? "Is a valid date string" :↵
"Is an invalid date string";
?>
```

Comments

Credit card numbers are typically sixteen digits long, and their expiration dates are usually in the format mm/yyyy. In this listing, the `validateCCNum()` and `validateCCExpDate()` both contain relatively trivial regular expressions to test input values and see if they conform to these patterns. Note that the regular expression used in the `validateCCExpDate()` function is somewhat stringent to ensure that only month values in the range 01–12 are accepted.

For more stringent validation, you might want to consider using PEAR's Payment_Process or Validate classes, available from `http://pear.php` `.net/package/Payment_Process` and `http://pear.php.net/package/` `Validate_Finance_CreditCard`, respectively. Both classes include intelligence to check the validity of a credit card number, using either the Luhn algorithm or specific knowledge of the valid number range for each card brand. Here's an example:

```php
<?php
// include Payment_Process class
include "Payment/Process.php";
```

```
// initialize object
$card = &Payment_Process_Type::factory("CreditCard");

// set card data
$card->type = PAYMENT_PROCESS_CC_MASTERCARD;
$card->cardNumber = "5548111111111111";
$card->expDate = "12/2005";

// result: "Is a properly-formatted card number"
echo Payment_Process_Type::isValid($card) ? "Is a properly-formatted⏎
card number" : "Is an improperly-formatted card number";
?>
<?php
// include Validate class
include "Validate/Finance/CreditCard.php";

// test credit card number using Luhn algorithm
// result: "Is an improperly-formatted card number"
echo Validate_Finance_CreditCard::type("5548111111121111", ⏎
"AmericanExpress") ? "Is a properly-formatted card number" : ⏎
"Is an improperly-formatted card number";

// result: "Is a properly-formatted card number"
echo Validate_Finance_CreditCard::type("5548111111121111",⏎
"MasterCard") ? "Is a properly-formatted card number" :⏎
"Is an improperly-formatted card number";
?>
```

TIP

Read more about the Luhn algorithm at http://www.webopedia.com/TERM/L/ Luhn_formula.html.

8.11 Validating Telephone Numbers

Problem

You want to validate the format of an international telephone number.

Solution

Use a regular expression to test the format of the supplied value:

```php
<?php
// function to validate an international phone number
function validateIntlPhone($str) {
    // test if input is of the form +cc aa nnnn nnnn
    return preg_match("/^(\+|00)[1-9]{1,3}(\.|\s|-)?([0-9]{1,5}↵
(\.|\s|-)?){1,3}$/", $str);
}

// result: "Is a properly-formatted phone number"
echo validateIntlPhone("+1 301 111 1111") ? "Is a properly-formatted↵
phone number" : "Is an improperly-formatted phone number";

// result: "Is a properly-formatted phone number"
echo validateIntlPhone("0091-11-2123-7574") ? "Is a properly-formatted↵
phone number" : "Is an improperly-formatted phone number";

// result: "Is a properly-formatted phone number"
echo validateIntlPhone("+612 9555-5555") ? "Is a properly-formatted↵
phone number" : "Is an improperly-formatted phone number";

// result: "Is an improperly-formatted phone number"
echo validateIntlPhone("12346") ? "Is a properly-formatted phone↵
number" : "Is an improperly-formatted phone number";
?>
```

Comments

There are numerous ways of writing an international telephone number, and the previous regular expression tries to match all of them. The expression used here expects a number with country and area code, and enables you to prefix the country code with a + symbol or a pair of zeroes; separate the country, area, and local codes with spaces, periods, or hyphens; and write the local number as a single set of numbers or split it into spaced blocks.

If you find this regular expression a little too generous, you can alter it to be more restrictive, or to only support local numbers. As an illustration, consider the following variants, which validate local U.S. and Indian telephone numbers only:

```php
<?php
// function to validate a US phone number
function validateUSPhone($str) {
    // test if input is of the form aaa-nnn-nnnn
    return preg_match("/^[2-9]\d{2}-\d{3}-\d{4}$/", $str);
}
```

```php
// function to validate an Indian phone number
function validateIndiaPhone($str) {
    // test if input is of the form (0aa) nnnn nnnn
    return preg_match("/^\(0\d{2}\)\s?\d{8}$/", $str);
}


// result: "Is a properly-formatted phone number"
echo validateUSPhone("301-111-1111") ? "Is a properly-formatted↵
phone number" : "Is an improperly-formatted phone number";


// result: "Is a properly-formatted phone number"
echo validateIndiaPhone("(022) 22881111") ? "Is a properly-formatted↵
phone number" : "Is an improperly-formatted phone number";
?>
```

8.12 Validating Social Security Numbers

Problem

You want to validate the format of a U.S. Social Security number.

Solution

Use a regular expression to test the format of the supplied number:

```php
<?php
// function to validate U.S. Social Security number
function validateSSN($str) {
    // test if input is of the form ddd-dd-dddd
    return preg_match("/^\d{3}\-\d{2}\-\d{4}$/", $str);
}


// result: "Is a properly-formatted SSN"
echo validateSSN("123-45-6789") ? "Is a properly-formatted SSN" :↵
"Is an improperly-formatted SSN";


// result: "Is an improperly-formatted SSN"
echo validateSSN("123456789") ? "Is a properly-formatted SSN" :↵
"Is an improperly-formatted SSN";
?>
```

Comments

Social Security numbers in the USA are usually nine digits long, with hyphens after the third and fifth digits. This listing simply encapsulates this pattern into a regular expression, and uses the `preg_match()` function to test input against this pattern.

8.13 Validating Postal Codes

Problem

You want to validate the format of a postal ("zip") code.

Solution

Use a regular expression to test the format of the supplied value:

```php
<?php
// function to validate a zip code
function validateZip($str) {
    // test if input is of the form ddddd
    return preg_match("/^\d{6}$/" ,$str);
}

// result: "Is a properly-formatted zip code"
echo validateZip("123456") ? "Is a properly-formatted zip code" :↵
"Is an improperly-formatted zip code";

// result: "Is an improperly-formatted zip code"
echo validateZip("56456") ? "Is a properly-formatted zip code" :↵
"Is an improperly-formatted zip code";
?>
```

Comments

Postal codes differ from country to country, so there's no one-size-fits-all solution to the problem. Usually, you will need to customize the regular expression to local conventions before you can use the `validateZip()` function. This listing assumes a postal code of six digits; however, it's quite likely that you might have a nine-digit code separated with a hyphen (as in the USA) or a six-character code containing both letters and numbers (as in the UK). Here are some variants illustrating these local conventions:

```php
<?php
// function to validate a US zip code
function validateUSZip($str) {
    // test if input is of the form dddd-ddddd
    return preg_match("/^\d{5}(-\d{4})?$/" ,$str);
}

// function to validate a UK zip code
function validateUKZip($str) {
    // test if input is of the form ssdd dss
    return eregi("^[a-z]{1,2}[0-9]{1,2}([a-z])?[[:space:]]?[0-9][a-z]↵
{2}$" ,$str);
}

// result: "Is a properly-formatted US zip code"
echo validateUSZip("10113-1243") ? "Is a properly-formatted US↵
zip code" : "Is an improperly-formatted US zip code";

// result: "Is a properly-formatted UK postcode"
echo validateUKZip("NW3 5ED") ? ↵
"Is a properly-formatted UK postcode" :↵
"Is an improperly-formatted UK postcode";
?>
```

8.14 Validating E-mail Addresses

Problem

You want to validate the format of an e-mail address.

Solution

Use a regular expression to test the format of the supplied value:

```php
<?php
// function to validate
// an e-mail address
function validateEmailAddress($str) {
```

```
    // test if input matches e-mail pattern
    return eregi("^([a-z0-9_-])+([\.a-z0-9_-])*@([a-z0-9-])+↵
(\.[a-z0-9-]+)*\.([a-z]{2,6})$", $str);
}

// result: "Is a properly-formatted e-mail address"
echo validateEmailAddress("joe@some.domain.com") ?↵
"Is a properly-formatted e-mail address" : "Is an improperly-formatted ↵
e-mail address";

// result: "Is an improperly-formatted e-mail address"
echo validateEmailAddress("joe@dom.") ?↵
"Is a properly-formatted e-mail address" : "Is an improperly-formatted ↵
e-mail address";
?>
```

Comments

E-mail address validation is one of the most common types of input validation, and there's no shortage of regular expressions available online to match e-mail address patterns. The previous listing uses one of the more stringent patterns, restricting the range of characters in both username and domain parts and requiring the length of the top-level domain to be between two and six characters.

An alternative to rolling your own regular expression is to use the one provided by the PEAR Validate class, available from `http://pear.php.net/package/Validate`. The following listing illustrates this:

```
<?php
// include Validate class
include "Validate.php";

// test e-mail address
// result: "Is a properly-formatted e-mail address"
echo Validate::email("john@doe.info") ? "Is a properly-formatted e-mail↵
address" : "Is an improperly-formatted e-mail address";

// result: "Is an improperly-formatted e-mail address"
echo Validate::email("#$@nothing") ? "Is a properly-formatted e-mail↵
address" : "Is an improperly-formatted e-mail address";
?>
```

Looking for a more sophisticated regex? Try this one:

```php
<?php
function validateEmailAddress($str) {
    // test if input matches e-mail pattern
    return preg_match('/[^\x00-\x20()<>@,;:\\".
[\]\x7f-\xff]+(?:\.[^\x00-\x20()<>@,;:\\".[\]
\x7f-\xff]+)*\@[^\x00-\x20()<>@,;:\\".[\]
\x7f-\xff]+(?:\.[^\x00-\x20()<>@,;:\\".[\]
\x7f-\xff]+)+/i', $str);
}
?>
```

8.15 Validating URLs

Problem

You want to validate the format of a URL.

Solution

Use a regular expression to test the format of the supplied value:

```php
<?php
// function to validate a URL
function validateUrl($str) {
    // test if input matches URL pattern
    return preg_match("/^(http|https|ftp):\/\/([a-z0-9]([a-z0-9_-]*↵
[a-z0-9])?\.)+[a-z]{2,6}\/?([a-z0-9\?\._-~&#=+%]*)?/", $str);
}

// result: "Is valid"
echo validateUrl("http://www.example.com/html/index.php") ? ↵
"Is valid" : "Is invalid";

// result: "Is valid"
echo validateUrl("http://www.some.site.info") ? ↵
"Is valid" : "Is invalid";

// result: "Is invalid"
echo validateUrl("http://some") ? "Is valid" : "Is invalid";
?>
```

Comments

URLs come in all shapes and colors and, as with e-mail addresses, you can be generous or strict in the regular expression you choose to validate them. The expression used here restricts the protocol to HTTP, HTTPS, or FTP, requires the top-level domain to be between two and six characters long, and supports trailing path/file names or anchors.

8.16 Uploading Files Through Forms

Problem

You want to upload a file through a form.

Solution

Use PHP's built-in file upload capabilities, which support POST-ing a file in a form and accessing it via the $_FILES array:

```
<html>
<head></head>
<body>
<?php
// display file upload form
if (!$_POST['submit']) {
?>
    <form enctype="multipart/form-data"↵
action="<?=$_SERVER['PHP_SELF']?>" method="post">
    <input type="hidden" name="MAX_FILE_SIZE" value="8000000">
    Select file:
    <input type="file" name="data">
    <input type="submit" name="submit" value="Upload File">
    </form>
<?php
} else {
    // check uploaded file size
    if ($_FILES['data']['size'] == 0) {
        die("ERROR: Zero byte file upload");
    }

    // check if file type is allowed (optional)
    $allowedFileTypes = array("image/gif", "image/jpeg", ↵
"image/pjpeg");
```

```
    if (!in_array($_FILES['data']['type'], $allowedFileTypes))      {
        die("ERROR: File type not permitted");
    }

    // check if this is a valid upload
    if (!is_uploaded_file($_FILES['data']['tmp_name']))      {
        die("ERROR: Not a valid file upload");
    }

    // set the name of the target directory
    $uploadDir = "./uploads/";

    // copy the uploaded file to the directory
    move_uploaded_file($_FILES['data']['tmp_name'], $uploadDir . ↵
$_FILES['data']['name']) or die("Cannot copy uploaded file");

    // display success message
    echo "File successfully uploaded to " . $uploadDir .↵
 $_FILES['data']['name'];
}
?>
</body>
</html>
```

Comments

PHP significantly simplifies the task of uploading files through a Web form, by exposing a special $_FILES array which contains information on files sent through the POST method.

There are two components to this listing, the file upload form and the business logic that processes the submitted form.

1. The form must be submitted using POST, and must contain the enctype="multipart/form-data" attribute, to ensure that the file is correctly uploaded. The hidden form variable MAX_FILE_SIZE specifies the maximum allowed upload size, in bytes; files larger than this will be rejected.

2. Once a file has been uploaded, it is stored in a temporary directory and information on its size, type, and original and temporary names is saved to the $_FILES array. The temporary file name is then provided to the move_uploaded_file() function, which is used to copy the file from the temporary directory to a new location.

It's generally considered a good idea to verify the integrity of the upload before accepting it. Typical checks include ensuring the file is not a zero-byte file with the `'size'` key of the `$_FILES` array, and verifying that the file was indeed uploaded through a POST operation (and not "injected" into the script artificially by a malicious user) with the `is_uploaded_file()` function. You may also choose to test the file type if your application only allows particular types of files to be uploaded.

> **TIP**
>
> *Don't use the file extension to determine the file type, as it's easy to rename an executable file with a "safe" extension. Instead, use the `'type'` key of the `$_FILES` array to check the Multipurpose Internet Mail Extensions (MIME) type of the file, and only allow those types you deem to be safe.*

Understanding PHP's File Upload Variables

There are six important PHP configuration variables influencing POST file uploads:

- ▶ **`"file_uploads"`**   This variable, a Boolean, indicates whether or not file uploads should be permitted. Set this to true if your application supports file uploads.

- ▶ **`"max_execution_time"`**   This variable determines the number of seconds a PHP script can run before it is forcibly terminated by the engine. If your application expects large file uploads, or if a slow network link is used for the file transfer, increase this value to avoid your script automatically terminating in the middle of a long upload.

- ▶ **`"max_input_time"`**   This variable controls the maximum amount of time a script has to receive input data, including POST-ed files. As with the `max_execution_time` variable, increase this value if you anticipate large files or slow transfers.

- ▶ **`"upload_max_filesize"`**   This variable determines the maximum size of an uploaded file, and it gets higher priority than the hidden `MAX_FILE_SIZE` form field.

- ▶ **`"post_max_size"`**   This variable determines the maximum size of data PHP can accept in a single POST request, including file uploads. This should be at least equal to the value defined in `"upload_max_filesize"`; in most cases, it is larger.

- ▶ **`"upload_tmp_dir"`**   This variable determines the temporary directory used for uploaded files. It defaults to the system's temporary directory.

In case you're confused by the interaction between these variables, think of it this way: `"upload_max_filesize"` applies to each of the files being uploaded to the server and `"post_max_size"` defines how many of them (or how much of them) can come through in a single POST request. This is why you'd typically want `"post_max_size"` to be larger than `"upload_max_filesize"`.

Users who prefer a more object-oriented approach to file uploads may be interested in the HTML_QuickForm class, available from `http://pear.php .net/package/HTML_QuickForm`. As you will see after comparing the next listing with the previous one, HTML_QuickForm's built-in element and rule types can significantly reduce the code needed to manage and validate a file upload:

```
<html>
<head></head>
<body>
<?php
// include HTML_Quickform class
include "HTML/QuickForm.php";

// initialize form object
$form = new HTML_QuickForm("uploadFile");

// add file upload element
$file =& $form->addElement("file", "filedata", "Select image file:");

// add submit button
$form->addElement("submit", null, "Upload Image");

// add file input validation rules
$form->addRule("filedata", "Please select a file for⏎
upload", "uploadedfile");
$form->addRule("filedata", "Please upload only images",⏎
"mimetype", array("image/gif", "image/jpeg", "image/pjpeg"));

// validate file input
if ($form->validate()) {
    // if valid upload
    // move file to upload area
    // print success message
    $uploadDir = "./uploads/";
    if ($file->isUploadedFile())  {
        $info = $file->getValue();
        $file->moveUploadedFile($uploadDir);
```

```
        echo "File successfully uploaded to $uploadDir" . ↵
$info['name'];
    } else    {
        echo "Not a valid file upload";
    }
    exit;
}


// render and display form
$form->display();
?>
</body>
</html>
```

When working with uploaded files, the form-processing segment of the script is only executed after the file has been completely uploaded, and it's not uncommon for users to see a blank page while the upload is in progress. So, for large file uploads, it's generally a good idea to display some form of task notification to the user, to indicate that the upload is in progress. This is usually a pop-up window with a message, but you could also display a progress bar using the PEAR HTML_ Progress2 package first discussed in the listing in "7.10: Charting Task Status with a Progress Bar." Here's how:

```
<html>
<head></head>
<body>
<?php
// display file upload form
if (!$_POST['submit']) {
    // generate unique ID for this transfer
    $id = md5(uniqid(rand(), true));
?>
    <form enctype="multipart/form-data"↵
action="<?=$_SERVER['PHP_SELF']?>" method="post"↵
onSubmit="javascript:window.open('example03-progress.php?id=<?=$id;?>',↵
'pb', 'height=100,width=200,location=no,menubar=no,↵
resizable=no,scrollbars=no,status=no,toolbar=no');">↵
    <input type="hidden" name="MAX_FILE_SIZE" value="8000000">
    <input type="hidden" name="id" value="<?=$id;?>">
    Select file:
    <input type="file" name="data">
    <input type="submit" name="submit" value="Upload File">
    </form>
```

```php
<?php
} else {
    // ensure ID is present
    $id = $_POST['id'];
    if (trim($id) == "") {
        die ("ERROR: No file ID present");
    }

    // upload done
    // write a semaphore file
    // to tell the progress bar window to close
    $fp = fopen("upld$id", "wb")
or die("ERROR: Cannot open semaphore file");
    fclose($fp) or die("ERROR: Cannot close semaphore file");

    // check uploaded file size
    if ($_FILES['data']['size'] == 0) {
        die("ERROR: Zero byte file upload");
    }

    // check if this is a valid upload
    if (!is_uploaded_file($_FILES['data']['tmp_name']))     {
        die("ERROR: Not a valid file upload");
    }

    // set the name of the target directory
    $uploadDir = "./uploads/";

    // copy the uploaded file to the directory
    move_uploaded_file($_FILES['data']['tmp_name'], $uploadDir .
 $_FILES['data']['name']) or die("Cannot copy uploaded file");

    // display success message
    echo "File successfully uploaded to " . $uploadDir .
$_FILES['data']['name'];
}
?>
</body>
</html>
```

In this variant, every file upload is associated with a unique ID, generated through a combination of md5() and uniqid() calls. When the form is submitted, client-side code is used to open a new window containing the progress bar and passing it the identifier. Once the form has been successfully uploaded, a semaphore file is created using the unique ID, to signal the progress bar window to close.

Here's the code used by the script running in the progress bar window:

```php
<?php
// increase script execution time limit
ini_set('max_execution_time', 600);

// include HTML_Progress class
include "HTML/Progress2.php";

// create objects
$progress = new HTML_Progress2();

// ensure ID is present
$id = $_GET['id'];
if (trim($id) == "") {
    die ("ERROR: No file ID present");
}

// custom handler for progress bar ticks
function customHandler($progressValue, &$obj) {
    // retrieve file transfer ID
    global $id;

    // check for semaphore file
    // if it exists, file upload is complete
    // close this popup
    // if not,
    // sleep 2 seconds and try again
    if (file_exists("upld$id")) {
        unlink("upld$id");
        echo "<script language='javascript'>self.close()</script>";
    } else {
        sleep(2);
    }
}
?>
<html>
<head>
<title>Upload In Progress</title>
```

```php
<?php
echo $progress->getStyle(false);
echo $progress->getScript(false);
?>
</head>
<body>

<div id="progress">
<?php
// set bar speed and increment value
$progress->setAnimSpeed(100);
$progress->setIncrement(10);

// place bar in indeterminate mode
$progress->setIndeterminate(true);

// set user-defined function
// this will check when upload is complete
// and switch bar back to indeterminate mode
$progress->setProgressHandler('customHandler');

// initialize progress bar display
$progress->display();
$progress->run();
?>
</div>

</body>
</html>
```

This script receives the unique file upload ID, and initializes a progress bar object using the HTML_Progress2 package. It then defines a custom handler for the progress bar, which checks for the presence of the semaphore file every few seconds. Once the semaphore file appears, it indicates that the file has been uploaded, and is thus a signal to the progress window to close. When the window closes, it also deletes the semaphore file. The file upload ID is used to connect the two scripts, and serves as an identification tag in an environment where multiple uploads may be taking place simultaneously.

TIP

Read more about HTML_Progress2 in the listing in "7.10: Charting Task Status with a Progress Bar," and on the Web at `http://pear.php.net/package/HTML_Progress2`.

8.17 Preserving User Input Across Form Pages

Problem

You want to preserve user input across multiple form pages.

Solution

Attach input from a prior form submission to subsequent pages as hidden data:

```
<html>
<head></head>
<body>
<?php
// function to rewrite submitted values
// as hidden form fields
function importPrevPageData() {
    $hiddenDataStr = "<!-- input carried forward begins -->\n";
    foreach ($_POST as $key => $value) {
        $hiddenDataStr .= "<input type=\"hidden\" name=\"" .↵
htmlentities($key) . "\" value=\"" .↵
htmlentities(stripslashes($value)) . "\">\n";
    }
    $hiddenDataStr .= "<!-- input carried forward ends -->\n";
    echo $hiddenDataStr;
}

// look for the page number
// if not available, assume page 1
$pageID = isset($_POST['pageID']) ? $_POST['pageID'] : 1;

// display pages by number
switch ($pageID) {
    case 1:
?>
        <!-- page 1 -->
        <form method="post" action="<?php echo $_SERVER['PHP_SELF']; ?>">
        Name:
        <br />
        <input type="text" name="name" size="30">
        <br />
        E-mail address:
```

```
        <br />
        <input type="text" name="email">
        <br />
        Telephone:
        <br />
        <input type="text" name="tel" size="10">
        <br />
        <input type="hidden" name="pageID" ↵
value=<?php echo ($pageID+1); ?>>
        <input type="submit" name="submit" value="Go to Page 2">
        </form>
<?php
        break;

    case 2:
        // perform validation of page 1 data
        // if errors, display error list
        // if no errors, display page 2
?>
        <!-- page 2 -->
        <form method="post" action="<?php echo $_SERVER['PHP_SELF']; ?>">
        Card type:
        <br />
        <select name="cctype">
            <option value="V">Visa</option>
            <option value="M">MasterCard</option>
            <option value="A">AmEx</option>
        </select>
        <br />
        Name on credit card:
        <br />
        <input type="ccname" name="ccname" size="30">
        <br />
        Credit card expiration date (MM/YYYY):
        <br />
        <input type="text" name="ccexp" size="7">
        <br />
        Email invoice:
        <br />
        <input type="radio" name="email_invoice" value="Y">Yes
        <input type="radio" name="email_invoice" value="N">No
        <br />
```

```php
            <input type="hidden" name="pageID" ⌐
value=<?php echo ($pageID+1); ?>>
<?php
        // remove unnecessary form elements
        unset($_POST['submit']);
        unset($_POST['pageID']);

        // import previous form submission
            importPrevPageData();
?>
            <input type="submit" name="submit" value="Place Order">
            </form>
<?php
        break;

    case 3:
        // perform validation of page 2 data
        // if errors, display error list
        // if no errors, display page 3

        // remove unnecessary form elements
        unset($_POST['submit']);
        unset($_POST['pageID']);

        // get all the submitted data as an array
        $data = $_POST;

        // process the data
        // for example, save to a database or file
        print_r($data);

        // print success message
        echo "Thank you for your order";
        break;
}
?>
</body>
</html>
```

Comments

A basic problem when dealing with forms spanning two or more pages involves
transferring the data entered by the user from one page to the next. To illustrate the

problem, consider a three-page form that asks for the user's name (page 1) and e-mail address (page 2) before saving both to the database (page 3). To avoid errors, data submitted on the first page must be retained until the third page has completed processing.

The first solution to this problem involves rewriting the data submitted at each stage as a series of hidden form elements, and adding them to the next form page. This carries forward form data from page to page, until it can all be processed on the final page. You can see how this might work based on the previous listing, which calls the importPrevPageData() function each page of the form. On each invocation, importPrevPageData() reads the $_POST array and rewrites its contents as a series of <input type="hidden" /> elements, which are then attached to the existing form and carried forward to the next page. On the final page, the $_POST array will contain the data submitted over all the previous form pages. This data can then be validated and processed in the usual manner.

The second solution to the problem involves using a session to store the data submitted at each stage, and processing it all at once on the final page. This is somewhat less tedious than the previous alternative, mostly because of PHP's excellent built-in session handling capabilities, but it can fail if the client browser lacks (or has disabled) cookie support. Here's the previous listing, rewritten to illustrate this approach:

```php
<?php
// function to save submitted values
// as session variables
function importPrevPageData() {
    foreach ($_POST as $key => $value) {
        $_SESSION['form'][$key] = htmlentities(stripslashes($value));
    }
}
// look for the page number
// if not available, assume page 1
$pageID = isset($_POST['pageID']) ? $_POST['pageID'] : 1;

// import previous session
session_start();
?>
<html>
<head></head>
<body>
<?php
// display pages by number
switch ($pageID) {
```

```
    case 1:
?>
        <!-- page 1 -->
        <form method="post" ↵
action="<?php echo $_SERVER['PHP_SELF']; ?>">
        Name:
        <br />
        <input type="text" name="name" size="30">
        <br />
        E-mail address:
        <br />
        <input type="text" name="email">
        <br />
        Telephone:
        <br />
        <input type="text" name="tel" size="10">
        <br />
        <input type="hidden" name="pageID" ↵
value=<?php echo ($pageID+1); ?>>
        <input type="submit" name="submit" value="Go to Page 2">
        </form>
<?php
        break;

    case 2:
        // perform validation of page 1 data
        // if errors, display error list
        // if no errors, display page 2
?>
        <!-- page 2 -->
        <form method="post" ↵
action="<?php echo $_SERVER['PHP_SELF']; ?>">
        Card type:
        <br />
        <select name="cctype">
            <option value="V">Visa</option>
            <option value="M">MasterCard</option>
            <option value="A">AmEx</option>
        </select>
        <br />
        Name on credit card:
        <br />
        <input type="ccname" name="ccname" size="30">
        <br />
```

```
                Credit card expiration date (MM/YYYY):
                <br />
                <input type="text" name="ccexp" size="7">
                <br />
                Email invoice:
                <br />
                <input type="radio" name="email_invoice" value="Y">Yes
                <input type="radio" name="email_invoice" value="N">No
                <br />
                <input type="hidden" name="pageID" ⏎
value=<?php echo ($pageID+1); ?>>
<?php
        // remove unnecessary form elements
        unset($_POST['submit']);
        unset($_POST['pageID']);

        // add previous submission to session
        importPrevPageData();
?>
        <input type="submit" name="submit" value="Place Order">
        </form>
<?php
        break;

    case 3:
        // perform validation of page 2 data
        // if errors, display error list
        // if no errors, display page 3

        // remove unnecessary form elements
        unset($_POST['submit']);
        unset($_POST['pageID']);

        // add previous submission to session
        importPrevPageData();

        // get all the submitted data from the session
        $data = $_SESSION['form'];

        // process the data
        // for example, save to a database or file
        print_r($data);
```

```
            // print success message
            echo "Thank you for your order";
            break;
}
?>
</body>
</html>
```

Here, the `importPrevPageData()` function merely iterates through the `$_POST` array on each invocation, creating a copy of the POST-ed data in the `$_SESSION['form']` array. On the final page, the `$_SESSION['form']` array will contain the data submitted over all the previous form pages. This data can then be validated and processed in the usual manner.

If you don't like the thought of manually managing the task of preserving data across a multipage form, there is a third alternative: use PEAR's HTML_QuickForm_Controller class, available from `http://pear.php.net/package/HTML_QuickForm_Controller`, to handle it for you automatically. The HTML_QuickForm_Controller class is an add-on to the HTML_QuickForm package, designed specifically to deal with multipage forms. Here's how you might use it:

```
<?php
// include HTML_QuickForm class
include "HTML/QuickForm.php";

// include HTML_Quickform_Controller class
include "HTML/QuickForm/Controller.php";
include "HTML/QuickForm/Action.php";

// initialize session
// form input is stored here
// during page transitions
session_start();

// custom class for form pages
class checkoutPage extends HTML_QuickForm_Page {
    // override default method
    function buildForm() {
        $this->_formBuilt = true;

        // get page name
        // build appropriate form elements
        switch($this->getAttribute("id")) {
            // first page
            case 'persInfo':
```

```
                    //--- form elements here ---//

                    // add header
                    $this->addElement("header", null, ↵
"Personal Information");

                    // add input boxes
                    $this->addElement("text", "name", "Name:",↵
array("size" => 30));
                    $this->addElement("text", "email", "E-mail address:");
                    $this->addElement("text", "tel", "Telephone:",↵
array("size" => 10));

                    // add submit button
                    $this->addElement("submit", null, "Go to Page 2");

                    //--- form validation rules here ---//

                    // for example
                    $this->applyFilter(array("name", "email", "tel"), ↵
"trim");
                    $this->addRule("name", "Please enter your name", ↵
"required");
                    $this->addRule("email", "Please enter a valid↵
e-mail address", "email");

                    break;

                // second page
                case 'pymtInfo':

                    //--- form elements here ---//

                    // add header
                    $this->addElement("header", null, ↵
"Payment Information");

                    // add card selection list
                    $select = $this->addElement("select", "cctype",↵
"Card type:", array("V" -> "Visa", "M" => "MasterCard", ↵
"A" => "AmEx"));

                    // add input box for card name
                    $this->addElement("text", "ccname", ↵
"Name on credit card:", array("size" => 25));
```

```php
                // add input box for card expiry date
                $this->addElement("text", "ccexp", "Credit card↵
expiration date (MM/YYYY):", array("size" => 7));

                // add radio button group
                $radio[] =& HTML_QuickForm::createElement("radio", ↵
null, null, "Yes", "Y");
                $radio[] =& HTML_QuickForm::createElement("radio", ↵
null, null, "No", "N");
                $this->addGroup($radio, "email_invoice", ↵
"Email invoice:");

                // add submit button
                    $this->addElement("submit", null, "Place Order");

                //--- form validation rules here ---//

                // for example
                $this->applyFilter(array("ccname", "ccexp"), "trim");
                $this->addRule("ccname", "Please enter the↵
card holder's name", "required");

                break;

            // add cases for additional pages as needed
        }

        // once page is validated and submitted
        // go to next page
        $this->setDefaultAction("next");
    }
}

// custom class for form action
class checkoutAction extends HTML_QuickForm_Action {
    function perform(&$page, $actionName) {
        // get all the submitted data as an array
        $data = $page->controller->exportValues();

        // process the data
        // for example, save to a database or file
        print_r($data);
```

```
        // print success message
        echo "Thank you for your order";
    }
}

// initialize form controller
$formMulti =& new HTML_QuickForm_Controller("orderCheckout");

// add pages to form
// each page appears only after previous
// page has been submitted with valid data
$formMulti->addPage(new checkoutPage("persInfo"));
$formMulti->addPage(new checkoutPage("pymtInfo"));

// add more pages here as needed

// add action for final page
$formMulti->addAction("process", new checkoutAction());

// generate form
$formMulti->run();
?>
```

This might look immensely complicated, but it really isn't. The HTML_
QuickForm_Controller package provides two basic classes, HTML_QuickForm_
Page and HTML_QuickForm_Action, representing a single page of a multipage
form and the action to be taken on the final page respectively. Both these must be
subclassed before they can be used to build a multipage form.

In this listing, a custom checkoutPage class first extends the base HTML_
QuickForm_Page class. Form pages are then represented as object instances of
checkoutPage class, and incorporate standard HTML_QuickForm elements and
validation tests. Because this form contains two input pages, two such form page
objects are generated, named persInfo and pymtInfo, respectively. These objects
are attached to the top-level HTML_QuickForm_Controller object by means of the
addPage() method.

Next, a custom checkoutAction class, representing the action to be taken on the
final page, extends the base HTML_QuickForm_Action class. This subclass defines
a perform() method, which contains the code to be executed once all the pages
of the form have been submitted with valid data. The action object is attached to

the top-level HTML_QuickForm_Controller object by means of the `addAction()` method.

Once both the form's pages and actions are defined, the `run()` method of the HTML_QuickForm_Controller object is used to generate the form. Submissions are internally handled by the HTML_QuickForm_Controller engine, with form generation and data validation performed by the HTML_QuickForm class.

NOTE

As this listing illustrates, the HTML_QuickForm_Controller class is fairly complex, and requires more detailed explanation than is possible here. If you plan to use it to generate a multipage form, refer to the class documentation at `http://pear.php.net/package/` `HTML_QuickForm_Controller` *to obtain a better understanding of how it works. You can also refer to the listings in "8.1: Generating Forms," "8.6: Validating Form Input," "8.16: Uploading Files Through Forms" for more examples of the base HTML_QuickForm package in action.*

8.18 Protecting Form Submissions with a CAPTCHA

Problem

You want to verify that a human, rather than an automated script or "bot," submitted a form.

Solution

First, use PEAR's Text_CAPTCHA package to dynamically generate a CAPTCHA (Completely Automated Public Turing test to tell Computers and Humans Apart) image:

File: captcha-generator.php

```php
<?php
// include class
include "Text/CAPTCHA.php";

// set font options
$options = array(
```

```
      "font_size" => 24,
      "font_path" => "C:/windows/fonts/",
      "font_file" => "ARIAL.TTF"
);

// configure CAPTCHA options
$captcha = Text_CAPTCHA::factory('Image');
$captcha->init(250, 150, null, $options)↵
or die ("ERROR: Cannot generate CAPTCHA");

// get CAPTCHA string
$str = $captcha->getPhrase();

// start session
// store MD5 signature of CAPTCHA string in session variable
session_start();
$_SESSION['captcha'] = md5($str);

// send CAPTCHA image as output to client
header("Content-Type: image/jpeg");
print $captcha->getCAPTCHAAsJPEG();
exit();
?>
```

Then attach the CAPTCHA to a form and verify that the CAPTCHA is correctly solved before processing the form submission:

File: form.php

```php
<?php session_start(); ?>
<html>
 <head></head>
 <body>
<?php
// if form has not been submitted
// generate form
if (!$_POST['submit'])
{
?>
    <form action-"<?php echo $_SERVER['PHP_SELF']; ?>" method="POST">
    <p>
    Name: <br />
     <input type="text" name="name" size="20" />
    </p>
```

```
   <p>
   Message: <br />
    <textarea name="message"></textarea>
   </p>
   <p>
   Enter the text in the image below to verify that this is↵
a genuine message. <input type="text" name="captcha" size="15" /> <br />
   <img src="captcha-generator.php" />
   </p>
   <p>
    <input type="submit" name="submit" value="Send Message">
   </p>
   </form>
<?php
// if form has been submitted
// check if MD5 signature of input CAPTCHA string
// matches that generated by the original CAPTCHA
} else {
    if (md5($_POST['captcha']) == $_SESSION['captcha']) {
        // destroy CAPTCHA session variable
        // print success message and POST-ed data
        unset($_SESSION['captcha']);
        unset($_POST['captcha']);
        echo "Your submission was successful.";
        var_dump($_POST);
    } else {
        echo "Your submission was not accepted. <a ↵
href='{$_SERVER['PHP_SELF']}'>Try again</a>.";
    }
}
?>
 </body>
</html>
```

Comments

PEAR's Text_CAPTCHA package, freely available from `http://pear.php`
`.net/package/Text_Captcha`, takes all the hassle out of actually generating
a CAPTCHA image. As the first listing (`captcha-generator.php`) illustrates,
generating a CAPTCHA begins by initializing an instance of the Text_CAPTCHA
class, and setting options such as the height and width of the image and the font file
to use for the CAPTCHA string. The `getPhrase()` method returns the solution
of the CAPTCHA as a string, while the `getCAPTCHAAsJPEG()` method prints the
CAPTCHA as a JPEG image (other image formats are also supported).

Using this CAPTCHA in combination with a form is somewhat more involved.

1. The simple CAPTCHA generation script described previously (`captcha-generator.php`) must be modified to store the CAPTCHA solution in a session variable. This enables it to be used by other scripts operating in the context of the same user session. For greater security, it's also possible to store an MD5 signature of the solution (rather than the solution itself), as the first listing does.

2. It's necessary to modify the form (`form.php`) with some additional elements. First, the CAPTCHA image itself must be displayed; this is accomplished by referencing `captcha-generator.php` in an `<img />` tag. A text input field should also be added, to enable a user to input the CAPTCHA solution.

3. The form processing script must create an MD5 signature of the user's input, and check this signature against that originally stored in the session by the `captcha-generator.php` script. If the signatures match, it may be assumed that a human solved the CAPTCHA, and form processing can continue. If the signatures do not match, it could be for one of two possible reasons: (a) a human attempted to submit the form but was unable to solve the CAPTCHA; (b) the form was submitted by an automated script. In either case, the appropriate response is to reject the form submission and offer the user the chance to resubmit with a different CAPTCHA and solution.

NOTE

A CAPTCHA, or Completely Automated Public Turing test to tell Computers and Humans Apart, is a common challenge-response test used to identify if the entity at the other end of a connection is a human being or a computer. On the Web, the typical form of a CAPTCHA is a distorted sequence of random alphanumeric characters, operating on the principle that a computer will be unable to see past the distortion, but a human, with greater powers of perception, will be able to correctly identify the sequence. Such CAPTCHAs are typically attached to input forms on the Web (for example, user registration forms), and must be solved correctly before the input will be processed by the host application. CAPTCHAs need not always be visual; audio CAPTCHAs are also possible, and are most appropriate for visuallyhandicapped users.

Read more about CAPTCHAs at `http://en.wikipedia.org/wiki/Captcha`.

8.19 Storing and Retrieving Session Data

Problem

You want to make one or more variables persistent across a client session.

Solution

Use PHP's `session_start()` function to start a new session (or import a previous one), and register variables in the session by adding them to the `$_SESSION` associative array:

```php
<?php
// start new session
// or import previous session
session_start();

// add session variables
$_SESSION['type'] = "Porsche Boxster";
$_SESSION['colors'] = array("black", "silver", "red");
print_r($_SESSION);
?>
```

Retrieve previously saved session variables by accessing the keys of the `$_SESSION` associative array:

```php
<?php
// start session
session_start();

// check if session variables exist
if (isset($_SESSION['type']) && isset($_SESSION['colors'])) {
    // do something with them
    echo "You would like a " . $_SESSION['type'] . " in " .↲
implode(" and ", $_SESSION['colors']);
}
?>
```

Comments

To start a session in PHP, use the `session_start()` function. Once a session has been initialized, register session variables by adding them to the special `$_SESSION` associative array as key-value pairs. In subsequent scripts, calling the `session_start()` function re-creates the session environment by importing the contents of the `$_SESSION` associative array into the current symbol table. You can then retrieve the values of previously registered session variables from the `$_SESSION` array, by key.

To delete session data, see the listing in "8.20: Deleting Session Data."

NOTE

The call to `session_start()` *must take place before any output is generated by the script. This is because of restrictions in the HTTP protocol that require cookie, session, and HTTP headers to be sent before any script output. To bypass these restrictions, see the listing in "8.30: Bypassing Protocol Restrictions on Session and Cookie Headers."*

8.20 Deleting Session Data

Problem

You want to delete a single session variable, or destroy all the variables associated with a session.

Solution

Use PHP's `unset()` function to selectively remove session variables:

```php
<?php
// start session
session_start();

// remove a session variable
if (isset($_SESSION['type'])) {
    unset($_SESSION['type']);
}
print_r($_SESSION);
?>
```

Use PHP's `session_destroy()` function to destroy all the variables registered in a session:

```php
<?php
// start session
session_start();

// reset session array
$_SESSION = array();

// destroy session
session_destroy();
print_r($_SESSION);
?>
```

Comments

To remove a previously registered session variable, simply unset() the corresponding key in the `$_SESSION` array. To delete all the data associated with a session, reset the `$_SESSION` array and use the `session_destroy()` function to erase session data. Note that before you can call `session_destroy()`, you need to first re-create the session environment with `session_start()`.

To find out more about setting and retrieving session variables, see the listing in "8.19: Storing and Retrieving Session Data."

8.21 Serializing Session Data

Problem

You want to serialize session data into a string, or restore a session using a previously serialized string.

Solution

Use PHP's `session_encode()` function to serialize session variables, and PHP's `session_decode()` function to deserialize the encoded data and re-create the session:

```php
<?php
// start session
session_start();
```

```
// register session variables
$_SESSION['parrot'] = "Polly";
$_SESSION['dog'] = array("Sparky", "Mr. Sparks");

// encode session data into string
$encodedStr = session_encode();

// destroy session
$_SESSION = array();
session_destroy();

// recreate session
// decode session data from string
session_start();
session_decode($encodedStr);
print_r($_SESSION);
?>
```

Comments

The session_encode() function encodes the variables and values of the current session into a string. The session_decode() function reads this encoded string and re-creates the session from it. These functions are useful to create a persistent snapshot of a session in a file or database.

NOTE

The session_start() *function must be used to start a session before* session_encode() *or* session_decode() *can be used.*

8.22 Sharing Session Data

Problem

You want to share the information stored in a PHP session with a script written in another language—for example, one written in Perl (Practical Extraction and Report Language) or JSP (Java Server Pages).

Solution

Encode the contents of the PHP session and send it as an HTTP POST request to the receiving script:

```php
<?php
// include HTTP_Request class
include "HTTP/Request.php";

// start session
session_start();

// create object
$request = &new HTTP_Request();

// define receiver URL and method
$request->setUrl("/cgi-bin/respond.cgi");
$request->setMethod("POST");

// dump session variables
foreach ($_SESSION as $key=>$value) {
    $request->addPostData($key, $value);
}

// send data via POST
$request->sendRequest();

// get response body
$body = $request->getResponseBody();
echo $body;
?>
```

Comments

In a perfect world, everything would be written in PHP. In the real world, however, it's quite likely that you'll be working in an environment that has multiple scripting languages coexisting with each other. In this situation, you might need to send data stored in a PHP session to scripts written in other languages for calculation or further processing (and then perhaps import the response back into PHP).

One way to do this is to serialize the $_SESSION array and save it to a file, which the external process can then read and use. In a multiuser, multiprocess environment, though, this option increases the potential for data corruption, and requires careful planning to be successful. It also has a significant drawback in that both source and target processes must be running on the same physical system, or must have access to a shared data storage area.

An alternative option is the one outlined in this listing. Assuming an HTTP-compliant environment with CGI (Common Gateway Interface) support, it's fairly easy to encode the PHP session into a POST request packet and submit it, as though it were a form, to the target script through CGI. The previous listing uses the PEAR HTTP_Request class, available from `http://pear.php.net/package/HTTP_Request` to create a POST packet; it then iterates through the `$_SESSION` array and adds each variable-value pair found to the packet using the `addPostData()` object method. The request is then submitted over HTTP to the target script. If a response is forthcoming, this response can be read with the `getResponseBody()` method, and handled in the most appropriate manner.

The target CGI script treats the input data as though it were a POST-ed form, which means that standard language constructs can be used to process it. In Perl, for example, you can use the CGI.pm package to retrieve and reconstitute the POST-ed data into native Perl structures.

TIP

This listing demonstrates how to transfer the contents of a PHP session to a script written in another language. However, you can use this technique to share the contents of any PHP variable, scalar, or array with scripts written in other languages, so long as those scripts support CGI and know how to extract data from an HTTP POST request.

You can see a few more examples of the HTTP_Request class in action in the listings in "7.10: Charting Task Status with a Progress Bar" and "7.20: Reading Remote Files."

8.23 Storing Objects in a Session

Problem

You want to make an object persistent across a session.

Solution

Start a session and add the object to the `$_SESSION` array:

```php
<?php
// include HTML_Page class
include "HTML/Page2.php";
```

```php
// create object
$page = &new HTML_Page2();

// set an object property
$page->setTitle("Black Tree Cliff");

// start session
session_start();

// save object in session
$_SESSION['html_page_obj'] = $page;
?>
```

To access the object at any time during the session, load the class definition, import the session data, and retrieve the object from the $_SESSION array:

```php
<?php
// include HTTP_Request class
include "HTML/Page2.php";

// start session
session_start();

// retrieve object from session
$obj = $_SESSION['html_page_obj'];

// returns "Black Tree Cliff"
$title = $obj->getTitle();
echo $title;
?>
```

Comments

Storing an object in a session is identical to storing a scalar or array variable—simply add it to the $_SESSION array. When retrieving it, though, it's critical that the corresponding class definition be loaded first, before any attempt is made to retrieve the object from the $_SESSION array. Failure to follow this sequence will result in PHP errors about "incomplete objects."

This listing illustrates the process, initializing an instance of the HTML_Page2 class and setting the value of an object property with the setTitle() method. The object is then stored in the $_SESSION array. Following this, in another script, the class definition is loaded, the session data is reimported and the object is retrieved from the $_SESSION array. The object's getTitle() method is then used to verify that the object has been reimported correctly, with no loss of data.

8.24 Storing Sessions in a Database

Problem

You want to store session information in a database instead of a session cookie.

Solution

First, create a (MySQL) database table to hold session information:

```
+------------+--------------+------+-----+-------------------+-------+
| Field      | Type         | Null | Key | Default           | Extra |
+------------+--------------+------+-----+-------------------+-------+
| sid        | varchar(255) |      | PRI |                   |       |
| sdata      | text         | YES  |     | NULL              |       |
| stimestamp | timestamp    | YES  |     | CURRENT_TIMESTAMP |       |
+------------+--------------+------+-----+-------------------+-------+
```

Then, use PHP's `session_set_save_handler()` function to register custom handlers to store session data in this table:

```php
<?php
// define database connection parameters
$host = "localhost";
$user = "user";
$pass = "pass";
$db = "db1";
$table = "sessions";

// function to open session record
// function receives session path and name
function _sess_open($sessionPath, $sessionName) {
    // uncomment this for debugging
    // echo "Opening...\n";

    // retrieve database parameters
    global $host, $user, $pass, $db, $table, $connection;

    // open connection to database
    $connection = mysql_connect($host, $user, $pass)↵
or die ("Unable to connect!");
```

```
    // select database
    mysql_select_db($db, $connection) or die ↵
("Unable to select database!");

    // return
    return true;
}

// function to close session record
function _sess_close() {
    // uncomment this for debugging
    // echo "Closing...\n";

    // retrieve database connection handle
    global $connection;

    // close connection and return
    return mysql_close($connection);
}

// function to read session record
// function receives session ID
function _sess_read($sessionID) {
    // retrieve database connection handle and table name
    global $table, $connection;

    // initialize variable
    $data = "";

    // create query to get session data
    $query = "SELECT sdata FROM $table WHERE sid = '$sessionID'";

    // execute query
    $result = mysql_query($query, $connection)↵
or die ("Error in query: $query. " . mysql_error());

    // if data exists
    // retrieve it
    if (mysql_num_rows($result) > 0) {
        $row = mysql_fetch_object($result);
        $data = $row->sdata;
    }
```

```
        // uncomment this for debugging
        // echo "Reading [$data]...\n";

        // return session data string
        return $data;
}

// function to write session
// function receives session ID and data to write
function _sess_write($sessionID, $sessionData) {
        // uncomment this for debugging
        // echo "Writing [$sessionData]...\n";

        // retrieve database connection handle and table name
        global $table, $connection;

        // create query to see if session record exists
        $query1 = "SELECT * FROM $table WHERE sid = '$sessionID'";

        // execute query
        $result1 = mysql_query($query1, $connection)↵
or die ("Error in query: $query1 . " . mysql_error());

        // if session record exists
        // update it
        // if session record does not exist
        // create new record
        if (mysql_num_rows($result1) > 0) {
             $query2 = "UPDATE $table SET sdata = '" . ↵
mysql_escape_string($sessionData) . "', stimestamp =↵
FROM_UNIXTIME('" . mktime() . "') WHERE sid = '$sessionID'";
        } else {
             $query2 = "INSERT INTO $table (sid, sdata,↵
stimestamp) VALUES('$sessionID', '" . ↵
mysql_escape_string($sessionData) . "', FROM_UNIXTIME('" .↵
mktime() . "'))";
        }

        // execute query
        $result2 = mysql_query($query2, $connection)↵
or die ("Error in query: $query2. " . mysql_error());

        // return
```

```php
        return true;
    }


    // function to erase session record
    // function receives session ID
    function _sess_destroy($sessionID) {
        // uncomment this for debugging
        // echo "Deleting...\n";

        // retrieve database connection handle and table name
        global $table, $connection;

        // create query to remove session record
        $query = "DELETE FROM $table WHERE sid = '$sessionID'";

        // execute query
        $result = mysql_query($query, $connection)
or die ("Error in query: $query. " . mysql_error());

        // return
        return true;
    }


    // function to remove expired session records
    function _sess_gc($sessionLife) {
        // uncomment this for debugging
        // echo "Cleaning up...\n";

        // retrieve database connection handle and table name
        global $table, $connection;

        // check timestamps of session records
        // remove all those more than (session.gc_maxlifetime) seconds old
        $query = "DELETE FROM $table
WHERE UNIX_TIMESTAMP(stimestamp) +
$sessionLife < UNIX_TIMESTAMP(NOW())";

        // execute query
        $result = mysql_query($query, $connection)
or die ("Error in query: $query. " . mysql_error());

        // return
        return true;
    }
```

```
// register custom session handling functions
session_set_save_handler("_sess_open", "_sess_close",↵
"_sess_read", "_sess_write", "_sess_destroy", "_sess_gc");

// start session
session_start();

// register session variables
$_SESSION['uname'] = "jimbo";
$_SESSION['uid'] = "745626";

// destroy session
session_destroy();
?>
```

Comments

By default, PHP stores session data in a cookie and reimports this data into a script when the session_start() function is called. However, in certain situations, you may prefer to use a database table to store this information.

As this listing illustrates, the table used for session data must contain fields for the session ID, session values, and a timestamp. Once it has been initialized, override PHP's built-in session handlers by using the session_set_save_handler() function to define replacement functions for opening, closing, reading, writing, destroying, and cleaning up sessions. In the previous listing, these replacement functions are named _sess_open(), _sess_close(), _sess_read(), _sess_write(), _sess_destroy(), and _sess_gc(), respectively, and they're passed to session_set_save_handler() as string arguments.

Internally, each of these functions interacts with the database server, reading and writing data to and from the session database, as follows:

▶ The _sess_open() function opens a connection to the database.

▶ The _sess_read() function uses the session ID to obtain a list of currently registered session variables and values.

▶ The _sess_write() function creates a new session record, or, if one already exists, updates it with the latest session variables and values.

▶ The _sess_close() function closes the database connection.

▶ The _sess_destroy() function removes the session record from the database.

▶ The _sess_gc() function uses the session timestamp to identify and remove expired session records.

Once these functions have been registered with `session_set_save_handler()`, all session data will be saved to the database. You can verify this by calling `session_start()` and adding some data to the session while simultaneously watching the MySQL table.

TIP

To see your custom session handler in action, uncomment the debugging statements in each handler function.

8.25 Creating a Session-Based Shopping Cart

Problem

You want to allow users to select items from a catalog and save them to a persistent "shopping cart" for later access.

Solution

First, create a (SQLite) database table to hold a catalog of items:

productSKU	productName	productUnitCost
100	Leopard-skin throw rug	89.99
200	Sunblock	4.99
300	Can o' worms	9.99
400	Boomerang	15.99
500	Ivory cigar holder	450.00

Then, create a persistent variable to hold the items selected by the user, and write code to add and delete items from it:

```php
<?php
// start session
session_start();

// initialize session shopping cart
if (!isset($_SESSION['cart'])) {
    $_SESSION['cart'] = array();
}

// get product list //
```

```php
// open database
$handle = sqlite_open("products.db")↵
or die ("ERROR: Unable to open database!");

// generate and execute query
$query = "SELECT productSKU, productName, ↵
productUnitCost FROM products";
$result = sqlite_query($handle, $query)↵
or die ("ERROR: Cannot execute $query. " .
sqlite_error_string(sqlite_last_error($handle)));

// save product list as array
if (sqlite_num_rows($result) > 0) {
    while($row = sqlite_fetch_object($result)) {
        $sku = $row->productSKU;
        $productInfo[$sku] = array();
        $productInfo[$sku]['name'] = $row->productName;
        $productInfo[$sku]['price'] = $row->productUnitCost;
    }
} else {
    die ("ERROR: Cannot retrieve product information");
}

// close connection
sqlite_close($handle);


// define cart actions //

switch($_POST['action']) {
    // when items are added
    case 'add':
        // iterate over POST-ed data
        // get SKU and quantity
        foreach ($_POST['addQty'] as $sku => $quantity) {
            // add item SKU and quantity to cart
            if (isset($quantity) && $quantity > 0) {
                $_SESSION['cart'][$sku] += $quantity;
            }
        }
        break;

    // when cart is updated
```

```php
        case 'update':
            // iterate over POST-ed data
            // get SKU and quantity
            foreach ($_POST['updateQty'] as $sku => $quantity) {
                // if quantity = 0
                // remove item from cart
                if ($quantity == 0 && trim($quantity) != "") {
                    unset($_SESSION['cart'][$sku]);
                }

                // if quantity > 0
                // set new quantity
                if ($quantity > 0) {
                    $_SESSION['cart'][$sku] = $quantity;
                }
            }
            break;

    // when cart is reset
    case 'reset':
        // destroy the cart
        $_SESSION['cart'] = array();
        break;
}
?>
<html>
<head></head>
<body>

<table border="0" width="100%" cellpadding="10">
<tr>
<td valign="top">
    <!-- complete product list -->
    <u>Available Products</u>
    <form action="<?=$_SERVER['PHP_SELF']?>" method="post">
    <ol>
<?php
    // print the product list
    foreach ($productInfo as $sku => $item) {
        echo "<li><b>" . $item['name'] . "</b><br />\n";
        echo "Unit price: " . $item['price'] . "<br />\n";
        echo "Quantity: <input type=text size=4 ↵
name=addQty[$sku] />\n";
```

```
            echo "</li><p />\n";
        }
?>
    </ol>
    <input type="hidden" name="action" value="add">
    <input type="submit" value="Add To Cart">
    </form>
    </td>
<td valign="top">
    <!-- current shopping cart-->
    <u>Selected Products</u>
<?php
if (sizeof($_SESSION['cart']) > 0) {
?>
    <form action="<?=$_SERVER['PHP_SELF']?>" method="post">
    <ol>
<?php
    // print the currently selected items
    foreach ($_SESSION['cart'] as $sku => $quantity) {
        echo "<li><b>" . $productInfo[$sku]['name'] . "</b><br />\n";
        echo $quantity . " units @ " . $productInfo[$sku]['price'] .↵
" each<br />\n";
        $subtotal = $quantity * $productInfo[$sku]['price'];
        $total += $subtotal;
        echo "Subtotal: " . number_format($subtotal, 2) . "<br />\n";
        echo "New quantity: <input type=text size=4 ↵
name=updateQty[$sku] />\n";
        echo "</li><p />\n";
    }
?>
    </ol>
    <b>TOTAL: <?php echo number_format($total, 2); ?></b>
    <p />
    <input type="hidden" name="action" value="update">
    <input type="submit" value="Update Cart">
    </form>

    <form action="<?=$_SERVER['PHP_SELF']?>" method="post">
    <input type="hidden" name="action" value="reset">
    <input type="submit" value="Reset Cart">
    </form>
```

```php
<?php
} else {
?>
    <p />
    No products selected.
<?php
}
?>

</body>
</html>
```

Comments

In this listing, a SQLite database is used to store a list of items and their prices. PHP's SQLite API is used to query the database and retrieve the item list for display. A Web page is then generated, containing three forms: one lists the available items in the catalog, one lists the selected items in the shopping cart, and one displays a cart reset button. Both catalog and cart forms contain input fields, enabling the user to either add specific quantities of an item from the catalog to the cart, or update existing quantities in the cart. The "cart" itself is nothing but an associative array containing codes and quantities for the selected products; it is stored as `$_SESSION['cart']`.

Figure 8-2 illustrates what this looks like.

Depending on which of the three forms is submitted, a hidden action field activates the appropriate branch of the `switch()` conditional statement to update the `$_SESSION['cart']` array. As items are added to (or removed from) the cart, the `$_SESSION['cart']` array is updated with the corresponding product codes and quantities, and the various totals and subtotals are recalculated. Setting an item quantity to zero deletes the corresponding product code from the `$_SESSION['cart']` array, while resetting the cart deletes all the product codes and quantities from `$_SESSION['cart']`.

TIP

It's easy to extend this listing for more complex requirements—simply add a new action button to the form, and a new branch to the `switch()` conditional statement to handle the action.

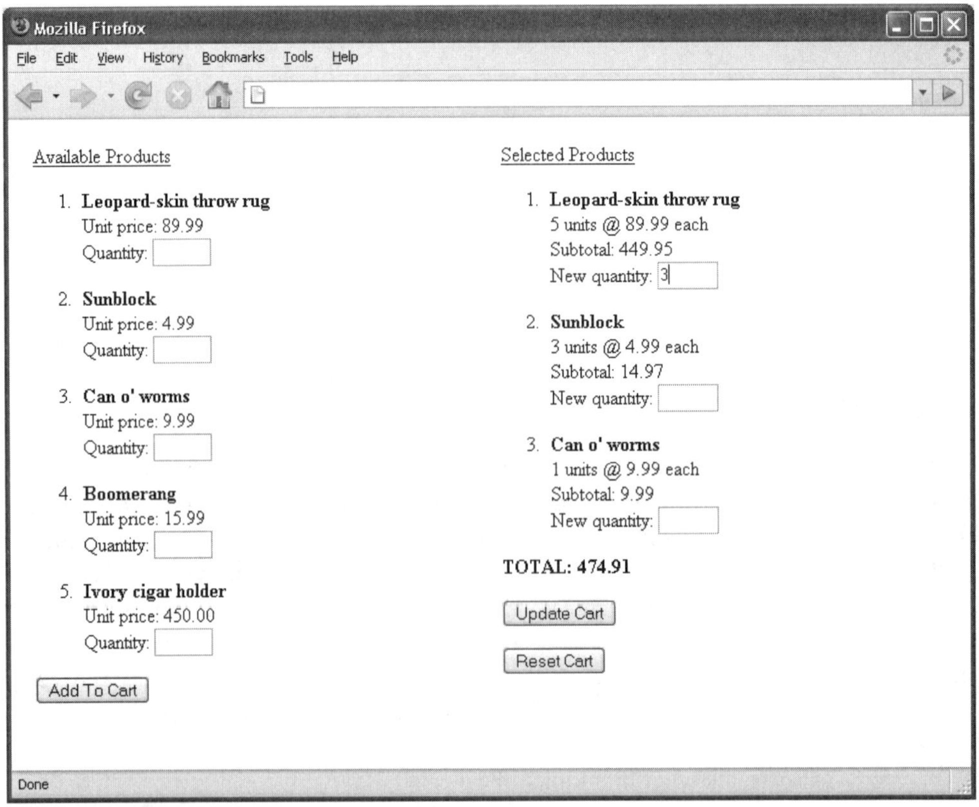

Figure 8-2 *A shopping cart form*

8.26 Creating a Session-Based User Authentication System

Problem

You want users to authenticate themselves with a valid password before granting access to a protected resource.

Solution

First, create a (MySQL) database table for authentication parameters:

```
+----+----------+------------------+
| id | username | password         |
+----+----------+------------------+
|  1 | john     | 2ca0ede551581d29 |
|  2 | joe      | 7b57f28428847751 |
|  3 | tom      | 675bd1463e544441 |
|  4 | bill     | 656d52cb5d0c13cb |
+----+----------+------------------+
```

Then, request the user's credentials through a login form and grant access if the credentials match the information stored in the database:

```php
<?php
// form not submitted
if (!$_POST['submit']) {
?>
<html>
<head></head>
<body>
    <table border="0" cellspacing="5" cellpadding="5">
    <form action="<?php echo $_SERVER['PHP_SELF']; ?>" method="POST">
    <tr>
        <td>Username</td>
        <td><input type="text" size="10" name="username"></td>
    </tr>
    <tr>
        <td>Password</td>
        <td><input type="password" size="10" name="password"></td>
    </tr>
    <tr>
        <td colspan="2" align="center"><input type="submit"⏎
name="submit" value="Log In"></td>
    </tr>
    </form>
    </table>
</body>
</html>
```

```php
<?php
} else {
// form submitted
    // check for username
    if (!isset($_POST['username']) || trim($_POST['username']) == "") {
        die ("You must enter a username!");
    }

    // check for password
    if (!isset($_POST['password']) || trim($_POST['password']) == "") {
        die ("You must enter a password!");
    }

    // assign to variables and escape
    $inputUser = mysql_real_escape_string($_POST['username']);
    $inputPass = mysql_real_escape_string($_POST['password']);

    // connect and execute SQL query
    $connection = mysql_connect("localhost", "user", "pass")
or die ("Unable to connect!");
    mysql_select_db("db1");

        $query = "SELECT id from users WHERE username = '$inputUser'
AND password = PASSWORD('$inputPass')";
    $result = mysql_query($query, $connection)
or die ("Error in query: $query. " . mysql_error());

    if (mysql_num_rows($result) == 1) {
    // if row exists
        // user/pass combination is correct
        // start a session
        session_start();

        // register a session variable
        $_SESSION['authorizedUser'] = 1;

        // redirect browser to protected resource
        header("Location: success.php");
    } else {
    // if row does not exist
        // user/pass combination is wrong
        // redirect browser to error page
        header("Location: fail.php");
    }
}
?>
```

Comments

Many Web applications require a user to authenticate himself or herself, by providing a valid password, before granting access to protected information. This is usually implemented as a login form, with input fields for the user's account name and password. On submission, the credentials supplied are verified against the user database and, if they're found to be correct, are used to grant access.

Figure 8-3 illustrates what this looks like.

This listing outlines the PHP business logic behind such an authentication system. The top half of the script is concerned with the display of the login form and its two input fields. The bottom half verifies that both fields have been filled in, opens a connection to the MySQL database, and executes a SELECT query to retrieve the

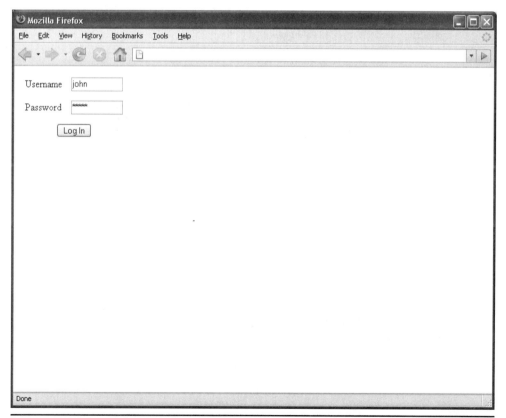

Figure 8-3   *A log-in form*

user record corresponding to the supplied name and password. The response to the SELECT query is all-important: If the user name and password are correct, it will contain a single result row and if not, it will not contain any data.

Depending on the MySQL response, the client is redirected appropriately: Invalid credentials lead to an error page, while valid ones grant access to the protected area. If the login is valid, a session variable is also registered indicating this fact; this session variable may be used to verify the user's status on subsequent page requests (to see how, flip to the listing in "8.27: Protecting Data with Sessions").

8.27 Protecting Data with Sessions

Problem

You want to display a page only to specified users—for example, to successfully logged-in users.

Solution

Use a session variable as a flag to determine whether or not the page should be displayed:

```php
<?php
// start session
session_start();

// check session for flag
if ($_SESSION['authorizedUser'] != 1) {
    // if flag is absent
    // the user does not have view privileges
    // print error message
    echo "You are not authorized to view this page.";

    // terminate processing
    // kick the client out
    exit();
} else {
    echo "Welcome!";
}
?>
```

Comments

Web sites and applications that distinguish between user types often use a session variable to determine whether or not a user is authorized to view a particular page. In its simplest form, this technique consists of first setting a session variable with the user's privilege level following authentication, and then checking the value of this session variable on all subsequent accesses to determine whether or not the page should be displayed. The previous listing demonstrates how such a check may be performed at the beginning of every page.

8.28 Storing and Retrieving Cookies

Problem

You want to make one or more variables persistent across multiple client requests.

Solution

Use PHP's `setcookie()` function to store the variable(s) in a client-side cookie:

```php
<?php
// set cookie
setcookie("freqFlyerMiles", "26789", mktime()+86400, "/");
?>
```

Retrieve previously saved session variables by accessing the keys of the `$_COOKIE` associative array:

```php
<?php
// check if cookie variables exists
if (isset($_COOKIE['seatClass']) && isset($_COOKIE['freqFlyerMiles'])) {
    // do something with them
    if ($_COOKIE['seatClass'] == "B" && ↵
$_COOKIE['freqFlyerMiles'] > 20000)
    {
            $upgradeFlag = 1;
    }
}
?>
```

Comments

In PHP, cookies are set with the setcookie() function, which accepts six arguments: the cookie name, its value, its expiration date (in UNIX timestamp format), the path and domain for which it is valid, and a Boolean flag indicating its security status. Only the first argument is required; all the rest are optional. On subsequent requests, the cookie is automatically imported into the $_COOKIE associative array, and it can be retrieved by name.

To delete cookies, see the listing in "8.29: Deleting Cookies."

NOTE

The call to setcookie() *must take place before any output is generated by the script. This is because of restrictions in the HTTP protocol that require cookie, session, and HTTP headers to be sent before any script output. To bypass these restrictions, see the listing in "8.30: Bypassing Protocol Restrictions on Session and Cookie Headers."*

8.29 Deleting Cookies

Problem

You want to delete a cookie.

Solution

Use the setcookie() function to set the cookie's expiration date to a value in the past:

```php
<?php
// delete cookie
if (isset($_COOKIE['freqFlyerMiles'])) {
    setcookie("freqFlyerMiles", NULL, mktime()-10000, "/");
}
?>
```

Comments

PHP doesn't offer any specific function to delete a cookie. The easiest way to accomplish this is to simply rewrite the cookie with an expiration date in the past, and have the client remove it automatically. The previous listing illustrates this, using the `mktime()` function to generate a timestamp in the past.

To find out more about setting and retrieving cookies, see the listing in "8.28: Storing and Retrieving Cookies."

8.30 Bypassing Protocol Restrictions on Session and Cookie Headers

Problem

You want to send a cookie, session header, or HTTP header even though your script has already begun generating output.

Solution

Use PHP's output buffering functions:

```php
<?php
// start output buffering
ob_start();

// send some output
echo "Attempting to set a cookie...";

// set cookie
@setcookie("freqFlyerMiles", "26789", mktime()+86400, "/")↵
or die("Unable to set cookie.");

// send some more output
echo "Cookie set.";

// dump the buffer to the client
ob_end_flush();
?>
```

Comments

Normally, a PHP script can only send HTTP headers (including session and cookie headers) to a client if the script has not yet generated any output. If the script has generated even a single character of output, calls to the `session_start()`, setcookie(), header() and related functions will fail. This is a restriction imposed by the HTTP protocol itself; it is not a PHP constraint.

This restriction may be avoided through use of PHP's output buffering functions, as illustrated in the previous listing. Here, output generated by the script is not written directly to the standard output device (the client), but to a special memory buffer instead. The client receives the output only when the contents of the buffer are specifically released with the ob_end_flush() function. Given the contents of the buffer are invisible until ob_end_flush() is invoked, HTTP headers can be sent at any point in the script up until the call to ob_end_flush().

8.31 Building GET Query Strings

Problem

You want to convert a PHP array to a GET query string.

Solution

Use PHP's http_build_query() function:

```php
<?php
// define array of key-value pairs
$data = array(
    "princess" => "leia",
    "bad guys" => array("darth vader", "the emperor"),
    "heroes" => array("luke", "han", "chewbacca"),
    "teacher" => "yoda");

// convert array to query string
// result: "princess=leia&bad+guys%5B0%5D=darth+vader&
// bad+guys%5B1%5D =the+emperor&heroes%5B0%5D=luke
// &heroes%5B1%5D=han&heroes%5B2%5D=chewbacca
// &teacher=yoda"
$queryString = http_build_query($data);
echo $queryString;
?>
```

Comments

PHP's `http_build_query()` function accepts an associative or numerically indexed array of data and converts it to a GET query string, complete with URL encoding and separators. Nested arrays are supported as well.

8.32 Extracting Variables from a URL Path

Problem

You want to create a PHP associative array from the variable-value pairs encoded in a URL path.

Solution

Parse the `$_SERVER['PATH_INFO']` variable and create an array of key-value pairs from it:

```php
<?php
// extract variables encoded in an URL path
if (isset($_SERVER['PATH_INFO'])) {
    // define variable to hold key-value pairs
    $urlParams = array();

    // split string on slashes
    $elements = explode("/", $_SERVER['PATH_INFO']);

    // remove first (empty) element
    array_shift($elements);

    // link keys to values
    for ($x=0; $x<sizeof($elements); $x += 2) {
        $key = $elements[$x];
        $value = $elements[($x+1)];
        $urlParams[$key] = $value;
    }
}
print_r($urlParams);
?>
```

Comments

To make their pages more attractive to search engines, many dynamic Web sites prefer to encode script variables as part of the URL path itself, rather than in the more traditional GET query string (which is unwieldy and hard for search engines to decipher). Thus, for example, the URL `http://www.some.domain.com/display.php?id=45&page=2` would instead be written as `http://www.some.domain.com/display.php/id/45/page/2`.

Variables encoded in a GET query string can be easily accessed through PHP's `$_GET` array. However, accessing variables encoded in a URL path requires a little more work. First, the string of encoded variables must be separated from the rest of the URL path, and second, it must be parsed and converted into key-value pairs.

These tasks are accomplished by using PHP's special `$_SERVER['PATH_INFO']` variable, which stores a string containing the information following the script file name in a URL path. This string is `explode()`-d into an array of individual values, and a `for()` loop is used to create an associative array from these values.

CHAPTER 9

Working with Databases

One of the most compelling things PHP has going for it is its support for a variety of Relational Database Management Systems (RDBMSs), including MySQL, PostgreSQL, Oracle, and SQL Server. By virtue of this support, PHP developers can create sophisticated data-driven Web applications at a fraction of the time and cost required by competing alternatives. And this, naturally, is a Good Thing.

This chapter is devoted to solutions involving PHP and databases. In addition to discussing the basics of connecting, querying, and fetching data from some of today's most well-known database systems, it also provides solutions to other common tasks—retrieving a subset of an SQL result set; writing portable database code; performing transactions; protecting special characters in query strings; and storing binary data in a table.

Before getting started, however, you should be aware of the following:

▶ Most of the listings in this chapter make use of three linked tables, illustrated in Figure 9-1. The SQL code needed to generate these tables (in MySQL and SQLite) can be obtained from the downloadable code archive, at `http://www.php-programming-solutions.com`.

▶ Before attempting to use any of the listings in this chapter, you must ensure that your PHP build includes support for the appropriate database extension. On Windows systems, this support can be enabled by activating the appropriate DLL; on *NIX systems, it usually involves activating the appropriate extension and recompiling PHP. Look in the PHP manual, at `http://www.php.net/manual/en/`, for specific instructions on how to activate each extension.

With those caveats out of the way, let's get started!

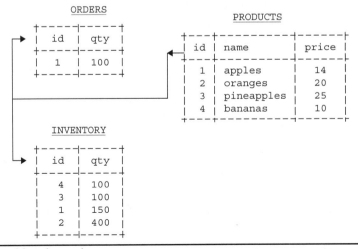

Figure 9-1 *Table relationships*

9.1 Working with MySQL

Problem

You want to execute SQL commands on a MySQL server.

Solution

Use PHP's MySQLi extension:

```php
<?php
// open connection
$connection = mysqli_connect('localhost', 'user', 'pass', 'db1')↵
or die ("ERROR: Cannot connect");

// create and execute INSERT query
$sql = "INSERT INTO products (id, name) VALUES ('5', 'pears')";
mysqli_query($connection, $sql) or die ("ERROR: " .↵
mysqli_error($connection) . " (query was $sql)");

// create and execute SELECT query
$sql = "SELECT id, name FROM products";
$result = mysqli_query($connection, $sql)↵
or die ("ERROR: " . mysqli_error($connection) . " (query was $sql)");

// check for returned rows
// print if available
if (mysqli_num_rows($result) > 0) {
    while($row = mysqli_fetch_row($result)) {
        echo $row[0] . " = " . $row[1] . "\n";
    }
} else {
    echo "No records found!";
}

// close connection
mysqli_close($connection);
?>
```

Comments

PHP's MySQLi (Improved MySQL) extension makes it possible to easily connect to, and execute queries on, a MySQL database server. Connections are initialized with a call to mysqli_connect(), which must be supplied with valid server access credentials—the server host name, a user name and password, and a database name. SQL commands are executed via the mysqli_query() function, which returns an SQL result object for SELECT, SHOW, DESCRIBE, and EXPLAIN queries, and a Boolean value indicating success or failure for other query types (including INSERT, UPDATE, and DELETE queries).

A number of methods exist to process the result set returned by mysqli_query(). This listing demonstrates the mysqli_fetch_row() function, which returns each row of the result set as a numerically indexed array that can easily be processed with a while() or for() loop. Alternatives to the mysqli_fetch_row() function include the mysqli_fetch_object() function, which returns each row as an object that exposes field values as object properties; the mysqli_fetch_assoc() function, which returns each row as an associative array; and the mysqli_fetch_array() function, which returns each row as both an associative array and a numerically indexed array.

Useful utility functions in this context include the mysqli_num_rows() function, used to count the number of rows returned by a query, and the mysqli_affected_rows() function (demonstrated in the listing in "9.10: Counting Altered Records"), used to count the number of records affected by an INSERT, UPDATE, or DELETE query. Connections can be terminated explicitly via a call to mysqli_close(), although PHP will automatically close open connections once the script ends. Errors, if any, can be retrieved via a call to mysqli_error(), which returns the last error message generated by the server.

You can also use the MySQLi extension in an object-oriented way, wherein each task—connecting, querying, fetching—is actually a method of the mysqli() object. Take a look at this alternative version of the previous listing, which illustrates this:

```php
<?php
// open connection
$mysqli = new mysqli('localhost', 'user', 'pass', 'db1');
if (mysqli_connect_errno()) {
    die("ERROR: Cannot connect. " . mysqli_connect_error());
}

// create and execute INSERT query
$sql = "INSERT INTO products (id, name) VALUES ('5', 'pears')";
if (!$mysqli->query($sql)) {
    die("ERROR: " . $mysqli->error . " (query was $sql)");
}
```

```
// create and execute SELECT query
// check for returned rows
// print if available
$sql = "SELECT id, name FROM products";
if ($result = $mysqli->query($sql)) {
    if ($result->num_rows > 0) {
        while($row = $result->fetch_row()) {
            echo $row[0] . " = " . $row[1] . "\n";
        }
    } else {
        echo "No records found!";
    }
    $result->close();
} else {
    die("ERROR: " . $mysqli->error . " (query was $sql)");
}

// close connection
$mysqli->close();
?>
```

Here, the new keyword is used to instantiate an object of the class mysqli() and pass the object constructor connection parameters. The resulting object, stored in $mysqli, then exposes methods and properties to perform the tasks of querying, fetching and processing rows, and handling errors. A close comparison of the procedural and object-oriented approaches will reveal the similarities in function (method) names and arguments.

You can retain compatibility with PHP versions earlier than PHP 5.0 by using the "standard" MySQL extension. Although this older extension does not support the new features of MySQL 4.1 and later, it is nevertheless more than adequate for the basic tasks of connecting, querying, and fetching. The next listing illustrates how it can be used:

```
<?php
// open connection
$connection = mysql_connect('localhost', 'user', 'pass')↵
or die ("ERROR: Cannot connect");

// select database
mysql_select_db('db1') or die ("ERROR: Cannot select database");

// create and execute INSERT query
$sql = "INSERT INTO products (id, name) VALUES ('5', 'pears')";
mysql_query($sql) or die ("ERROR: " . mysql_error() . ↵
" (query was $sql)");
```

```php
// create and execute SELECT query
$sql = "SELECT id, name FROM products";
$result = mysql_query($sql) or die ("ERROR: " . mysql_error() .⏎
" (query was $sql)");

// check for returned rows
// print if available
if (mysql_num_rows($result) > 0) {
    while($row = mysql_fetch_row($result)) {
        echo $row[0] . " = " . $row[1] . "\n";
    }
} else {
    echo "No records found!";
}

// close connection
mysql_close($connection);
?>
```

NOTE

As the listings in this section illustrate, code written for the new ext/mysqli *extension looks very similar to that written for the older* ext/mysql *extension. However, there are a whole bunch of differences under the hood:* ext/mysqli *is faster, more secure, and more powerful than regular* ext/mysql, *and it also includes support for prepared statements, bound result sets, multiple simultaneous queries, transactions, and other new features available only in MySQL 4.1 and later. In most cases, given a choice,* ext/mysqli *will serve you better than* ext/mysql.

9.2 Working with PostgreSQL

Problem

You want to execute SQL commands on a PostgreSQL server.

Solution

Use PHP's PostgreSQL extension:

```php
<?php
// open connection
$connection = pg_connect("host=localhost dbname=db1⏎
user=user password=pass") or die ("ERROR: Cannot connect");
```

```
// create and execute INSERT query
$sql = "INSERT INTO products (id, name) VALUES ('5', 'pears')";
pg_query($connection, $sql) or die ("ERROR: " .↵
pg_last_error($connection) . " (query was $sql)");

// create and execute SELECT query
$sql = "SELECT id, name FROM products";
$result = pg_query($connection, $sql)↵
or die ("ERROR: " . pg_last_error($connection) . ↵
" (query was $sql)");

// check for returned rows
// print if available
if (pg_num_rows($result) > 0) {
    while($row = pg_fetch_row($result)) {
        echo $row[0] . " = " . $row[1] . "\n";
    }
} else {
    echo "No records found!";
}

// close connection
pg_close($connection);
?>
```

Comments

PHP supports PostgreSQL databases through its PostgreSQL extension. Connections to a PostgreSQL database server are initialized by calling the pg_connect() function with appropriate credentials. Once a connection has been established, SQL commands can be executed with the pg_query() function, which returns either an SQL result object or a Boolean value indicating success or failure. The server connection can be terminated with a call to pg_close(), with error messages (if any) retrieved through pg_last_error().

The pg_fetch_row() function is one of many functions available to process query results. This function returns each row of the result set as a numerically indexed array, suitable for processing in a loop. Alternatives to this approach include the pg_fetch_assoc() function, which returns each record as an associative array; the pg_fetch_object() function, which returns each row as an object; the pg_fetch_result() function, which returns the value of an individual field given row and columns coordinates; and the pg_fetch_all() function, which returns all the rows in the result set at once as a multidimensional array.

9.3 Working with SQLite

Problem

You want to execute SQL commands on a SQLite database.

Solution

Use PHP's SQLite extension:

```php
<?php
// open database file
$handle = sqlite_open('products.db') or ⏎
die ("ERROR: Cannot open database");

// create and execute INSERT query
$sql = "INSERT INTO products (id, name) VALUES ('5', 'pears')";
sqlite_query($handle, $sql)⏎
or die ("ERROR: " . sqlite_error_string(sqlite_last_error($handle)) .⏎
" (query was $sql)");

// create and execute SELECT query
$sql = "SELECT id, name FROM products";
$result = sqlite_query($handle, $sql)⏎
or die ("ERROR: " . sqlite_error_string(sqlite_last_error($handle)) .⏎
" (query was $sql)");

// check for returned rows
// print if available
if (sqlite_num_rows($result) > 0) {
    while($row = sqlite_fetch_array($result)) {
        echo $row[0] . " = " . $row[1] . "\n";
    }
}

// close database file
sqlite_close($handle);
?>
```

Comments

PHP 5 supports reading and writing SQLite databases via its SQLite extension. This listing illustrates the process, by adding a record to a SQLite table with an INSERT query and then reading records from a SQLite table with a SELECT query.

The process starts with a call to the sqlite_open() function, which attempts to open the database file named as argument. If the call is successful, a database handle is returned; if not, an empty database file is created with the supplied name. SQL commands can be executed with the sqlite_query() function, which accepts the database handle and query string as arguments and returns either a Boolean value (for non-SELECT-type queries) or a result object (for SELECT-type queries). The result object can then be processed with the sqlite_fetch_array() object, which retrieves each row as both a numerically indexed array and an associative array. The database connection is then closed with the sqlite_close() function.

Alternatives to the sqlite_fetch_array() function include the sqlite_fetch_object() function, which returns each row as an object; the sqlite_fetch_single() function, which returns the value of the first column of each row; and the sqlite_fetch_all() function, which returns all the rows in the result set at once as a multi-dimensional array. Useful ancillary function include sqlite_num_rows(), which returns the number of records in the result set; sqlite_changes(), which returns the number of rows changed by a query; sqlite_last_error(); which returns the last error code generated; and sqlite_error_string(), which converts an error code into a human-readable error message.

You can also use the SQLite extension in an object-oriented way, wherein each of the previous functions becomes a method of the SQLiteDatabase() object. Take a look at this next listing, which is equivalent to the preceding one:

```php
<?php
// create database object
$db = new SQLiteDatabase('products.db')
or die ("ERROR: Cannot open database");↵

// create and execute INSERT query
$sql = "INSERT INTO products (id, name) VALUES ('5', 'pears')";
$db->query($sql) or die ("ERROR: " .↵
sqlite_error_string(sqlite_last_error($handle)) . ↵
" (query was $sql)");
```

```
// create and execute SELECT query
$sql = "SELECT id, name FROM products";
$result = $db->query($sql) or die ("ERROR: " .↵
sqlite_error_string(sqlite_last_error($handle)) .
" (query was $sql)");

// check for returned rows
// print if available
if ($result->numRows() > 0) {
    while($row = $result->fetch()) {
        echo $row[0] . " = " . $row[1] . "\n";
    }
}

// close database file
unset($db);
?>
```

Here, the new keyword is used to instantiate an object of the class
SQLiteDatabase() and pass the object constructor the database file name and
path. The resulting object, stored in $db, then exposes methods and properties to
perform the tasks of querying, fetching and processing rows, and handling errors.
A close comparison of the procedural and object-oriented approaches will reveal the
similarities in function (method) names and arguments.

9.4 Working with Sybase

Problem

You want to execute SQL commands on a Sybase server.

Solution

Use PHP's Sybase extension:

```
<?php
// open connection
$connection = sybase_connect('localhost', 'user', 'pass')↵
or die ("ERROR: Cannot connect");

// select database
sybase_select_db('db1') or die ("ERROR: Cannot select database");
```

```
// create and execute INSERT query
$sql = "INSERT INTO products (id, name) VALUES ('5', 'pears')";
sybase_query($sql, $connection) or die ("ERROR: " .↵
sybase_get_last_message() . " (query was $sql)");

// create and execute SELECT query
$sql = "SELECT id, name FROM products";
$result = sybase_query($sql, $connection) or die ("ERROR: " .↵
sybase_get_last_message() . " (query was $sql)");

// check for returned rows
// print if available
if (sybase_num_rows($result) > 0) {
    while($row = sybase_fetch_row($result)) {
        echo $row[0] . " = " . $row[1] . "\n";
    }
} else {
    echo "No records found!";
}

// close connection
sybase_close($connection);
?>
```

Comments

PHP supports Sybase databases through its Sybase extension. Connections to a Sybase database server are initialized by calling the `sybase_connect()` function with appropriate credentials. Once a connection has been established, a database is selected with `sybase_select_db()`, and SQL queries are performed with the `sybase_query()` function. The return value of `sybase_query()` is either a SQL result object (for SELECT-type queries) or a Boolean value indicating success or failure (for non-SELECT-type queries). Once all SQL operations have been concluded, the server connection can be terminated with a call to `sybase_close()`, with error messages (if any) retrieved through `sybase_last_error_message()`.

The result set returned by a query can be processed with a number of functions, of which `sybase_fetch_row()` is one example. The `sybase_fetch_row()` function returns each row of the result set as a numerically indexed array, suitable for processing in a loop. Alternatives to this approach include the `sybase_fetch_assoc()` function, which returns each row as an associative array; the `sybase_fetch_object()` function, which returns each row as an object with properties corresponding to field values; the `sybase_fetch_array()` function, which returns each row as both an associative and numerically indexed array; and the `sybase_result()` function, which returns the value of a particular field, given its row and column offset.

9.5 Working with Oracle

Problem

You want to execute SQL commands on an Oracle server.

Solution

Use PHP's Oracle extension:

```php
<?php
// open connection
$connection = oci_connect('user', 'pass', 'db1');

// create and execute INSERT query
$sql = "INSERT INTO products (id, name) VALUES ('5', 'pears')";
$stmt = oci_parse($connection, $sql)⏎
or die ("ERROR: " . oci_error($connection));
oci_execute($stmt) or die ("ERROR: " . oci_error($stmt));

// create and execute SELECT query
$sql = "SELECT id, name FROM products";
$stmt = oci_parse($connection, $sql)⏎
or die ("ERROR: " . oci_error($connection));
oci_execute($stmt) or die ("ERROR: " . oci_error($stmt));

// print returned records
while($row = oci_fetch_row($stmt)) {
    echo $row[0] . " = " . $row[1] . "\n";
}

// close connection
oci_close($connection);
?>
```

Comments

PHP supports Oracle7, Oracle8, and Oracle9 databases through its Oracle extension, which uses the Oracle Call Interface (OCI) to communicate with the server. Here, a server connection is initialized with the `oci_connect()` function. Once the connection is established, SQL commands are prepared for use with the `oci_parse()` function, which returns a statement identifier; this identifier is then passed to the `oci_execute()` function to actually be executed on the server. The server connection can be terminated with a call to `oci_close()`.

For queries that return a result set, the `oci_fetch_row()` function can be used in combination with a loop to iterate over the result set and retrieve each record as an enumerated array. Alternatives to this function include `oci_fetch_assoc()`, which retrieves each record as an associative array; `oci_fetch_object()`, which represents each record as an object with properties corresponding to field values; `oci_result()`, which retrieves the value of an individual field of a record; and `oci_fetch_all()`, which returns all the records in the result set as a single multidimensional array. Errors in connection or statement execution can be retrieved with a call to `oci_error()`.

9.6 Working with Microsoft SQL Server

Problem

You want to execute SQL commands on a Microsoft SQL server.

Solution

Use PHP's MS-SQL extension:

```php
<?php
// open connection
$connection = mssql_connect('localhost', 'user', 'pass')↵
or die ("ERROR: Cannot connect");

// select database
mssql_select_db('db1') or die ("ERROR: Cannot select database");
```

```
// create and execute INSERT query
$sql = "INSERT INTO products (id, name) VALUES ('5', 'pears')";
mssql_query($connection, $sql) or die ("ERROR: " .↵
mssql_get_last_message() . " (query was $sql)");

// create and execute SELECT query
$sql = "SELECT id, name FROM products";
$result = mssql_query($connection, $sql)↵
or die ("ERROR: " . mssql_get_last_message() . ↵
" (query was $sql)");

// check for returned rows
// print if available
if (mssql_num_rows($result) > 0) {
    while($row = mssql_fetch_row($result)) {
        echo $row[0] . " = " . $row[1] . "\n";
    }
} else {
    echo "No records found!";
}

// close connection
mssql_close($connection);
?>
```

Comments

PHP supports Microsoft SQL Server databases through its MS-SQL extension.
Connections to a MS-SQL database server are initialized by calling the `mssql_connect()` function with appropriate credentials. Once a connection has been
established, a database is selected with the `mssql_select_db()` function, and SQL
commands are executed with the `mssql_query()` function. The server connection
can be terminated with a call to `mssql_close()`.

The `mssql_fetch_row()` function returns each row of the result set as a
numerically indexed array, suitable for processing in a loop. Alternatives to this
approach include the `mssql_fetch_assoc()` function, which returns each record
as an associative array; the `mssql_fetch_object()` function, which returns each
row as an object; and the `mssql_result()` function, which returns the value of an
individual field given row and column offsets.

Useful ancillary function include `mssql_num_rows()`, which returns the number
of records in the result set; `mssql_rows_affected()`, which returns the number

of rows changed by a query; and `mssql_get_last_message()`, which returns the last message generated by the server.

9.7 Working with ODBC

Problem

You want to execute SQL commands using Open Database Connectivity (ODBC).

Solution

Use PHP's ODBC extension:

```php
<?php
// open connection
$connection = odbc_connect('DBI', 'user', 'pass')↵
or die ("ERROR: Cannot connect");

// create and execute INSERT query
$sql = "INSERT INTO products (id, name) VALUES ('5', 'pears')";
odbc_exec($connection, $sql) or die ("ERROR: " .↵
odbc_errormsg($connection) . " (query was $sql)");

// create and execute SELECT query
$sql = "SELECT id, name FROM products";
$result = odbc_exec($connection, $sql) or die ("ERROR: " .↵
odbc_errormsg($connection) . " (query was $sql)");

// check for returned rows
// print if available
if (odbc_num_rows($result) > 0) {
    while($row = odbc_fetch_row($result)) {
        echo $row[0] . " = " . $row[1] . "\n";
    }
} else {
    echo "No records found!";
}

// close connection
odbc_close($connection);
?>
```

Comments

PHP supports interacting with ODBC-compliant databases through its ODBC extension. To open a connection to such a database, invoke the `odbc_connect()` function with an appropriate Data Source Name (DSN), user name, and password. Once a connection has been established, SQL queries may be executed with the `odbc_exec()` function. For queries that return data, the `odbc_fetch_row()` function can be used to iterate over the result set, and the database connection can be closed with the `odbc_close()` function.

Alternatives to `odbc_fetch_row()` include the `odbc_fetch_array()` function, which returns each record as an associative array; the `odbc_fetch_object()` function, which returns each row as an object; and the `odbc_result()` function, which returns the value of an individual field in the current row, given the field offset. Other functions include `odbc_num_rows()`, which returns the number of records in the result set, and `odbc_errormsg()`, which returns the last error message generated.

9.8 Writing Database-Independent Code

Problem

You want to write code that is portable across different RDBMS implementations.

Solution

Use a database abstraction layer, such as `ext/pdo`:

```php
<?php
// attempt a connection
try {
    $pdo = new PDO('mysql:dbname=db1;host=localhost', 'user', 'pass');
} catch (PDOException $e) {
    die("ERROR: Cannot connect: " . $e->getMessage());
}

// create and execute INSERT query
$sql = "INSERT INTO products (id, name) VALUES ('5', 'pears')";
$pdo->exec($sql) or die("ERROR: " . implode(":", $pdo->errorInfo()));
```

```
// create and execute SELECT query
$sql = "SELECT id, name FROM products";
$rslt = $pdo->query($sql) or die("ERROR: " . implode(":",↵
$pdo->errorInfo()));
while ($row = $rslt->fetch()) {
    echo $row[0] . " = " . $row[1] . "\n";
}

// close connection
unset($pdo);
?>
```

Comments

If you've worked with different databases, you've probably seen that each database operates in a slightly different manner from the others. The data types aren't always uniform, and many of them come with proprietary extensions (transactions, stored procedures, and so on) that aren't supported elsewhere. Additionally, the API to interact with these databases is not uniform; as this chapter amply illustrates, PHP itself comes with a different API for each supported database type.

For all these reasons, switching from one database to another is typically a complex process, and one that usually involves porting data from one system to another (with the assorted datatyping complications), rewriting your code to use the new database API, and testing it to make sure it all works. And that's where a database abstraction layer can help.

Typically, a database abstraction layer functions as a wrapper around your database interaction code, exposing a set of generic methods to interact with a database server. These generic methods are internally mapped to the native API for each corresponding database, with the abstraction layer taking care of ensuring that the correct method is called for your selected database type. Additionally, most abstraction layers also incorporate a generic superset of datatypes, which get internally converted into datatypes native to the selected RDBMS. With an abstraction layer in place, therefore, you can transparently use a single generic call and have the abstraction layer convert it into the native API call. This makes it simple to switch between databases with minimal impact on code.

A number of different abstraction layers are available for PHP; this listing uses the PHP Data Objects (PDO) extension, an attempt to bring a Perl-style DBI interface to PHP. PDO offers database programmers a consistent API that is portable across different RDBMS by serving as a wrapper around drivers that actually "talk" to the database server and perform actions on it. When a function call is made through the PDO extension, PDO transmits the properly formatted information over to the relevant driver. Once the driver is through, PDO picks up the response and returns it to the caller. The driver to be used is stated as the first parameter in the DSN passed to the class constructor; to use a different driver, simply alter this parameter, leaving the rest of the code unchanged.

An alternative is to use the ADOdb Database Abstraction Library for PHP, freely available from `http://adodb.sourceforge.net/`. Here, a database connection is represented as an instance of the ADOConnection class. The `Connect()` and `Close()` methods initialize and terminate connections to the server, respectively, while the `Execute()` method executes SQL commands. Query results are represented as instances of the ADORecordset class, and expose methods to retrieve result rows.

Instances of the ADOConnection class are initialized by passing the database type to the class constructor. This can be seen in the next listing, which uses the type `"mysql"` to initialize the ADOdb MySQL driver. In addition to MySQL, the ADOdb abstraction layer supports a variety of database types, including Oracle, Sybase, Firebird, dBASE, PostgreSQL, SQLite, and ODBC. In the event of an RDBMS change, the argument passed to the class constructor must be altered to reflect the new type; the remaining code can remain untouched, because the abstraction layer will then internally use a different driver to communicate with the new RDBMS.

Here's an example of ADOdb in action:

```php
<?php
// include the DB abstraction layer
include "adodb/adodb.inc.php";

// open database connection
$dbh =& NewADOConnection("mysql");
$dbh->Connect('localhost', 'user', 'pass', 'db1')
or die("ERROR: Cannot connect");

// create and execute INSERT query
$sql = "INSERT INTO products (id, name) VALUES ('5', 'pears')";
$result = $dbh->Execute($sql) or die("ERROR: " . $dbh->ErrorMsg() .
" (query was $sql)");

// create and execute SELECT query
$sql = "SELECT id, name FROM products";
$result = $dbh->Execute($sql) or die("ERROR: " . $dbh->ErrorMsg() .
" (query was $sql)");

// check for returned rows
// print if available
if ($result->RecordCount() > 0) {
    while (!$result->EOF) {
            echo $result->fields[0] . " = " . $result->fields[1] . "\n";
```

```
        $result->MoveNext();
    }
} else {
    echo "No records found!";
}

// close connection
$dbh->Close();
?>
```

> **NOTE**
>
> *Using an abstraction layer is more inefficient than using native PHP functions, because of the extra lines of code involved in translating the generic function call into a native PHP function, in keeping track of abstraction layer variables and in converting between generic and native datatypes. Also, it's worth keeping in mind that switching from one RDBMS to another is no small task; careful planning is needed to ensure that your code, queries, and data types work optimally on the target system and such switches should not be undertaken lightly.*

As of this writing, PDO drivers are available for Sybase, Microsoft SQL Server, Firebird, MySQL, Oracle, ODBC, PostgreSQL, and SQLite.

9.9 Retrieving the Last-Inserted Record ID

Problem

You want to retrieve the ID of the last inserted record in a table.

Solution

Use PDO's `lastInsertId()` method:

```
<?php
// attempt a connection
try {
    $pdo = new PDO('mysql:dbname=db1;host=localhost', 'user', 'pass');
} catch (PDOException $e) {
    die("ERROR: Cannot connect: " . $e->getMessage());
}
```

```php
// create and execute INSERT query
$sql = "INSERT INTO products (id, name) VALUES (NULL, 'pears')";
$pdo->exec($sql) or die("ERROR: " . implode(":", $pdo->errorInfo()));

// get ID of inserted record
echo "Record successfully inserted with ID " . $pdo->lastInsertId();

// close connection
unset($pdo);
?>
```

Comments

The technique to obtain the last inserted ID varies from database to database—for example, Sybase and MS-SQL users must run the command SELECT @@identity, while SAP-DB users must run the command SELECT table.CURRVAL FROM DUAL. The PDO abstraction layer lets you make some sense of these different implementations, by wrapping them all in a generic Insert_ID() method, as illustrated in the previous listing.

If you're performing an INSERT or UPDATE query on a MySQL table containing an AUTO_INCREMENT primary key, you can obtain the last auto-increment ID generated with the mysqli_insert_id() function. This is equivalent to executing a SELECT LAST_INSERT_ID() command on the MySQL server. The following listing demonstrates this:

```php
<?php
// open connection
$connection = mysqli_connect('localhost', 'user', 'pass', 'db1')↵
or die ("ERROR: Cannot connect");

// create and execute INSERT query
$sql = "INSERT INTO products (id, name) VALUES (NULL, 'pears')";
mysqli_query($connection, $sql) or die("ERROR: " .↵
mysqli_error($connection) . " (query was $sql)");

// get ID of inserted record
echo "Record successfully inserted with ID " .↵
mysqli_insert_id($connection);

// close connection
mysqli_close($connection);
?>
```

9.10 Counting Altered Records

Problem

You want to count the number of records changed by the last INSERT, UPDATE, or DELETE query.

Solution

Use the return value of PDO's exec() method:

```php
<?php
// attempt a connection
try {
    $pdo = new PDO('mysql:dbname=db1;host=localhost', 'user', 'pass');
} catch (PDOException $e) {
    die("ERROR: Cannot connect: " . $e->getMessage());
}

// create and execute UPDATE query
$sql = "UPDATE products SET price = price * 1.1 WHERE price < 20";
$numRows = $pdo->exec($sql) or die("ERROR: " . implode(":",
$pdo->errorInfo()));

// get number of rows changed
echo $numRows . " record(s) updated";

// close connection
unset($pdo);
?>
```

Comments

The name of the PHP function to obtain the number of rows affected by a query varies from database to database—for example, SQLite users can use the PHP function sqlite_changes(), while Informix users must use the function ifx_affected_rows(). PHP's PDO extension offers a more generic technique: the number of rows affected by a query may be retrieved from the return value of the corresponding call to exec(), as illustrated in the previous listing.

If you're working only with MySQL, the `mysqli_affected_rows()` function serves an equivalent function, as illustrated in the next listing:

```php
<?php
// open connection
$connection = mysqli_connect('localhost', 'user', 'pass', 'db1')↵
or die ("ERROR: Cannot connect");

// create and execute UPDATE query
$sql = "UPDATE products SET price = price * 1.1 WHERE price < 20";
mysqli_query($connection, $sql) or die ("ERROR: " .↵
mysqli_error($connection) . " (query was $sql)");

// get number of rows changed
echo mysqli_affected_rows($connection) . " record(s) updated";

// close connection
mysqli_close($connection);
?>
```

9.11 Protecting Special Characters

Problem

You want to protect special characters, such as quotes or slashes, in a query string.

Solution

Use PDO's `quote()` method to protect these special characters with a backslash:

```php
<?php
// define input data
$realname = "Frank D'Souza";

// attempt a connection
try {
    $pdo = new PDO('mysql:dbname=db1;host=localhost', 'user', 'pass');
} catch (PDOException $e) {
    die("ERROR: Cannot connect: " . $e->getMessage());
}
```

```
// escape special characters in input
$realname = $pdo->quote($realname);

// create and execute INSERT query
$sql = "INSERT INTO users (realname) VALUES ('$realname')";
$pdo->exec($sql) or die("ERROR: " . implode(":", $pdo->errorInfo()));
echo "Record successfully inserted with query: $sql";

// close connection
unset($pdo);
?>
```

Comments

It is usually necessary to escape special characters, such as quotes or slashes, in strings intended for use in an SQL query. For example, to maintain the integrity of the string "Frank D'Souza" when saving it to a table, it is necessary to protect the single quote by preceding it with a backslash (\) character. PDO's quote() method will automatically do this for you, by finding and protecting all single quotes ('), double quotes(") and backslashes (\) in a string.

An alternative is to use the addslashes() function, which does the same thing:

```
<?php
// define input data
$realname = "Frank D'Souza";

// open connection
$connection = mysqli_connect('localhost', 'user', 'pass', 'db1')↵
or die ("ERROR: Cannot connect");

// escape special characters in input
$realname = addslashes($connection, $realname);

// create and execute INSERT query
$sql = "INSERT INTO users (realname) VALUES ('$realname')";
mysqli_query($connection, $sql) or die ("ERROR: " .↵
mysqli_error($connection) . " (query was $sql)");
echo "Record successfully inserted with query: $sql";

// close connection
mysqli_close($connection);
?>
```

> **NOTE**
>
> *PHP comes with a configuration directive,* `magic_quotes_gpc`, *which automatically escapes all special characters submitted through a form or retrieved through a cookie with backslashes, just as* `addslashes()` *does. If this directive is enabled (the default situation), you should not run* `addslashes()` *on form or cookie data prior to using it in an SQL query. Using* `addslashes()` *in this situation could corrupt your data (by placing a double set of backslashes before every special character). Read the information provided at* `http://www.php.net/ manual/en/ref.info.php#ini.magic-quotes-gpc` *for more.*

9.12 Limiting Query Results

Problem

You want to retrieve a subset of the records returned by a SELECT query.

Solution

Use a LIMIT clause in the SQL query (MySQL):

```php
<?php
// open connection
$connection = mysqli_connect('localhost', 'user', 'pass', 'db1')↵
or die ("ERROR: Cannot connect");

// create and execute SELECT query
// limit result set to 2 records starting with #3
$sql = "SELECT id, name FROM products LIMIT 2, 2";
$result = mysqli_query($connection, $sql) or die ("ERROR: " .↵
mysqli_error($connection) . " (query was $sql)");

// check for returned rows
// print if available
if (mysqli_num_rows($result) > 0) {
    while($row = mysqli_fetch_array($result, MYSQLI_BOTH)) {
        echo $row['id'] . " = " . $row['name'] . "\n";
    }
} else {
    echo "No records found!";
}
```

```
// close connection
mysqli_close($connection);
?>
```

Comments

With MySQL, it's easy to retrieve a subset of the total records in a result set by adding a `LIMIT` clause to the query string. This clause takes two parameters, which specify the record offset to start with and the number of records to display from that offset. So the query `SELECT * FROM tbl LIMIT 2,2` would return records #3 and #4 only.

However, all databases do not support the `LIMIT` clause—some ignore it altogether, while others use modified variants (for example, the equivalent statement in PostgreSQL would be `SELECT * FROM tbl LIMIT 2 OFFSET 2`, while in Sybase, it would be `SET ROWCOUNT 2`). Generically, then, you can solve the problem by using the ADOdb abstraction layer, freely available from `http://adodb.sourceforge.net/`. This layer comes with a `SelectLimit()` method, which can be used to restrict the number of rows retrieved and which internally performs the translation needed for each RDBMS. Here's an example of it in action:

```
<?php
// include the DB abstraction layer
include "adodb/adodb.inc.php";

// open database connection
$dbh =& NewADOConnection("postgres");
$dbh->Connect('localhost', 'user', 'pass', 'db1')↵
or die("ERROR: Cannot connect");

// create and execute SELECT query
// limit result set to 2 records starting with #3
$sql = "SELECT id, name FROM products";
$dbh->SetFetchMode(ADODB_FETCH_ASSOC);
$result = $dbh->SelectLimit($sql, 2, 2)↵
or die("ERROR: " . $dbh->ErrorMsg() . " (query was $sql)");

// check for returned rows
// print if available
if ($result->RecordCount() > 0) {
    while (!$result->EOF) {
            echo $result->fields['id'] . " = " .↵
```

```
$result->fields['name'] . "\n";
            $result->MoveNext();
    }
} else {
    echo "No records found!";
}


// close connection
$dbh->Close();
?>
```

> **TIP**
>
> If you're curious about the SQL command(s) to limit record ranges in your RDBMS, you'll find it instructive to look at the source code for the `SelectLimit()` function in the ADOdb driver for your RDBMS.

9.13 Using Prepared Statements

Problem

You want to execute an SQL command multiple times, with different values each time.

Solution

Use a prepared statement with the PDO extension:

```
<?php
// define data array
$data = array(
    "10" => "tomatoes",
    "11" => "potatoes",
    "12" => "carrots",
    "13" => "onions",
    "14" => "beans"
);

// attempt a connection
try {
    $pdo = new PDO('mysql:dbname=db1;host=localhost', 'user', 'pass');
```

```
} catch (PDOException $e) {
    die("ERROR: Cannot connect: " . $e->getMessage());
}

// create prepared statement
$sql = "INSERT INTO products (id, name) VALUES (?, ?)";
$stmt = $pdo->prepare($sql) or die("ERROR: " . implode(":",↵
$pdo->errorInfo()));

// bind parameters to statement
$stmt->bindParam(1, $id);
$stmt->bindParam(2, $name);

// process data array
// execute prepared statement with different values
// on each iteration
foreach ($data as $id => $name) {
    $stmt->execute() or die("ERROR: " . ↵
implode(":", $stmt->errorInfo()));
}

// display message
echo "Record(s) successfully added.";

// close connection
unset($pdo);
?>
```

Comments

In the event that you need to execute a particular query multiple times with different values—for example, a series of INSERT statements—it's a good idea to use a *prepared statement* to save time and overhead. A prepared statement is like a regular SQL statement, except that it contains placeholders for variable data; these placeholders are replaced with actual values each time the statement is executed.

With PDO, a prepared statement is created by passing PDO's prepare() method a SQL statement containing query placeholders, as in the previous listing. These placeholders can then be bound to variables with the statement object's bindParam() method (which must be called for each placeholder), and the statement can then executed with the object's execute() method. In the previous listing, the data for the query comes from a predefined array, and a loop is used to repeatedly execute the prepared statement, assigning the placeholders new values from the array on each iteration.

If you're using MySQL, a prepared statement is created with the `mysqli_prepare()` function, which returns a statement handle. Parameters are bound to the variable placeholders in the statement with the `mysqli_stmt_bind_param()` function, which accepts as arguments the statement handle, a string indicating the data types of the various variable placeholders (*s* for string, *i* for integer, *d* for double-precision number), and variables representing each of the placeholders. The `mysqli_stmt_execute()` function then executes the prepared query, iterating over the list of values and assigning them to the variable placeholders in a loop. This process is clearly illustrated in the next listing:

```php
<?php
// define data array
$data = array(
    "10" => "tomatoes",
    "11" => "potatoes",
    "12" => "carrots",
    "13" => "onions",
    "14" => "beans"
);

// open connection
$connection = mysqli_connect('localhost', 'user', 'pass', 'db1')↵
or die ("ERROR: Cannot connect");

// create prepared statement
$sql = "INSERT INTO products (id, name) VALUES (?, ?)";
$stmt = mysqli_prepare($connection, $sql) or die("ERROR: " .↵
mysqli_error($connection));

// bind parameters to statement
mysqli_stmt_bind_param($stmt, 'is', $id, $name);

// process data array
// execute prepared statement with different values
// on each iteration
foreach ($data as $id => $name) {
    mysqli_stmt_execute($stmt) or ↵
die("ERROR: " . mysqli_stmt_error($stmt));
}

// close statement
mysqli_stmt_close($stmt);
```

```
// close connection
mysqli_close($connection);

// display message
echo "Record(s) successfully added.";
?>
```

Using a prepared statement can provide performance benefits when you have a single query to be executed a large number of times with different values, as only the variable data is transmitted to the server each time, not the complete query. However, this benefit is only available if the database system supports prepared queries (MySQL, InterBase, and Oracle do, just to name a few); in all other cases, only simulated functionality is available and `prepare()` becomes equivalent to a simple `exec()`, with no inherent performance gain.

9.14 Performing Transactions

Problem

You want to execute a series of linked SQL commands as an atomic unit (a transaction), but roll them back in the event of an error.

Solution

Use PDO's `commit()` and `rollBack()` methods:

```php
<?php
// attempt a connection
try {
    $pdo = new PDO('mysql:dbname=db1;host=localhost', 'user', 'pass');
    $pdo->setAttribute(PDO::ATTR_ERRMODE, PDO::ERRMODE_EXCEPTION);
} catch (PDOException $e) {
    die("ERROR: Cannot connect: " . $e->getMessage());
}

try {
    // begin a new transaction
    $pdo->beginTransaction();
```

```
    // create and execute two DML queries
    // in case of errors, roll back transaction
    $sql = "INSERT INTO orders (id, qty) VALUES ('4', '20')";
    $pdo->exec($sql);
    $sql = "UPDATE inventory SET qty = qty-20 WHERE id = 4";
    $pdo->exec($sql);

    // commit the changes
    $pdo->commit();
    echo "Transaction completed successfully";
} catch (PDOException $e) {
    // in case of error
    // roll back the transaction
    $pdo->rollBack();
    die("ERROR: " . $e->getMessage());
}

// close connection
unset($pdo);
?>
```

Comments

In the SQL world, the term *transaction* refers to a series of SQL statements that are treated as a single unit by the RDBMS. Typically, a transaction is used to group together SQL statements that are interdependent; a failure in even one of them is considered a failure of the group as a whole. Thus, a transaction is said to be successful only if all the individual statements within it are executed successfully.

The previous listing illustrates this by executing two SQL statements as a transaction. First, the beginTransaction() method is used to mark the start of a transaction and turn off database auto-commit—this tells the database that it should not commit the changes made by each statement until explicitly told to do so. Next, the SQL statements are executed. If no error occurs, the commit() method is invoked and the changes are committed to the database permanently. If PDO generates an exception when executing either of the statements, control passes to the catch block, which calls the rollBack() method to reset the table to the state it was in prior to beginning the transaction.

If you're using MySQL 4.x or later, you can benefit from the native transactional functions built into ext/mysqli. Here, the mysqli_autocommit() function first turns off database auto-commit; the mysqli_commit() function saves changes to the system; and the `mysqli_rollback()` function rolls changes back in the event of an error. The following listing illustrates this in greater detail:

```php
<?php
// open connection
$connection = mysqli_connect('localhost', 'user', 'pass', 'db1')↵
or die ("ERROR: Cannot connect");

// turn off transaction auto-commit
mysqli_autocommit($connection, FALSE);

// begin a new transaction
// create and execute two DML queries
// in case of errors, roll back transaction
$sql = "INSERT INTO orders (id, qty) VALUES ('4', '20')";
if (mysqli_query($connection, $sql) !== TRUE) {
    echo "ERROR: " . mysqli_error($connection) . " (query was $sql)";
    mysqli_rollback($connection);
    exit();
}

$sql = "UPDATE inventory SET qty = qty-20 WHERE id = 4";
if (mysqli_query($connection, $sql) !== TRUE) {
    echo "ERROR: " . mysqli_error($connection) . " (query was $sql)";
    mysqli_rollback($connection);
    exit();
}

// no errors
// commit the transaction
mysqli_commit($connection);
echo "Transaction completed successfully";

// close connection
mysqli_close($connection);
?>
```

NOTE

As of MySQL 4.x, native ACID-compliant (Atomicity, Consistency, Isolation, and Durability) transactions are only possible with InnoDB and BerkeleyDB tables. For other table types, transactional environments need to be implemented at the application level, through the use of table locks or other mechanisms.

9.15 Executing Multiple SQL Commands at Once

Problem

You want to execute two or more SQL commands at once.

Solution

Use a subquery:

```php
<?php
// attempt a connection
try {
    $pdo = new PDO('mysql:dbname=db1;host=localhost', 'user', 'pass');
} catch (PDOException $e) {
    die("ERROR: Cannot connect: " . $e->getMessage());
}

// create nested query
$sql = "SELECT name, price FROM products where id IN (SELECT id↵
FROM inventory WHERE qty <= 200)";
$rslt = $pdo->query($sql) or die("ERROR: " . implode(":",↵
$pdo->errorInfo())));
while ($row = $rslt->fetch()) {
    echo $row[0] . " = " . $row[1] . "\n";
}

// close connection
unset($pdo);
?>
```

Comments

Subqueries, as the name suggests, are queries nested inside other queries. They make it possible to use the results of one query directly in the conditional tests or FROM clauses of other queries. The most common type of subquery is a SELECT within a SELECT (also called a *subselect*), such that the results of the inner SELECT serve as values for the WHERE clause of the outer SELECT. This is the type illustrated in the previous listing, and it's handled in exactly the same manner as any other SQL query—executed with PDO's query() method and processed with its fetch() or similar method.

Many database systems also support *multistatement queries*, wherein multiple SQL statements are concatenated into a single query string with semicolons and executed together as a single block. This is illustrated in the listing that follows, which uses the `mysqli_multi_query()` function to execute one such statement block in a MySQL database. Individual record sets resulting from the multistatement query are retrieved with the `mysqli_store_result()` function, and processed in the usual way.

```php
<?php
// open connection
$connection = mysqli_connect('localhost', 'user', 'pass', 'db1')⏎
or die ("ERROR: Cannot connect");

// create array of queries
$queries[] = "SELECT name, price FROM products";
$queries[] = "SELECT name, qty FROM products,orders WHERE⏎
products.id = orders.id";

// join individual queries into composite query
$multiQuery = implode(";", $queries);

// execute composite query
// process the results
$multiResult = mysqli_multi_query($connection, $multiQuery)⏎
or die("ERROR: An error occurred in one of the queries");
$count = 0;
do {
    // get next result set
    if ($result = mysqli_store_result($connection)) {
        // print the corresponding query string
        echo "\n" . $queries[$count] . ":\n";
        // print the records
        while ($row = mysqli_fetch_row($result)) {
          echo $row[0] . " = " . $row[1] . "\n";
        }
        // free the result set
        mysqli_free_result($result);
    }
    // increment counter
    // repeat for next result set
    $count++;
} while (mysqli_next_result($connection));
```

```
// close connection
mysqli_close($connection);
?>
```

9.16 Storing and Retrieving Binary Data

Problem

You want to save a binary file to a table, or retrieve binary data from a table and save it to a file.

Solution

To save a binary file to a database, create a table containing a field of type BLOB and write a PHP script to read the file's contents and INSERT it into the BLOB field:

```
<?php
// set file name
$file = "img1008.jpg";

// read file contents into variable
// make sure script has read permissions!
if (file_exists($file)) {
    $fileData = addslashes(file_get_contents($file));
} else {
    die ("ERROR: Cannot find file");
}

// attempt a connection
try {
    $pdo = new PDO('mysql:dbname=db1;host=localhost', 'user', 'pass');
    $pdo->setAttribute(PDO::ATTR_ERRMODE, PDO::ERRMODE_EXCEPTION);
} catch (PDOException $e) {
    die("ERROR: Cannot connect: " . $e->getMessage());
}

try {
    // create and execute INSERT query
    $sql = "INSERT INTO bindata (data, name) VALUES ('$fileData',↵
'" . basename($file) . "')";
    $pdo->exec($sql);
```

```
    // display success message
    echo "File successfully added to database with ID " .↵
$pdo->lastInsertId();
} catch (PDOException $e) {
    // in case of error
    // display error message
    die("ERROR: " . $e->getMessage());
}

// close connection
unset($pdo);
?>
```

To retrieve binary data from a table, use a SELECT query to obtain the contents of the BLOB field and write the data to a file:

```
<?php
// attempt a connection
try {
    $pdo = new PDO('mysql:dbname=db1;host=localhost', 'user', 'pass');
    $pdo->setAttribute(PDO::ATTR_ERRMODE, PDO::ERRMODE_EXCEPTION);
} catch (PDOException $e) {
    die("ERROR: Cannot connect: " . $e->getMessage());
}

// create and execute SELECT query
// use record ID returned by previous script
// to retrieve the binary data
try {
    $sql = "SELECT data, name FROM bindata WHERE id = 1";
    $rslt = $pdo->query($sql);
    $row = $rslt->fetch();
    file_put_contents($row[1] . '.new', $row[0]);
    echo "File saved to [" . $row[1] . ".new]";
} catch (PDOException $e) {
    // in case of error
    // display error message
    die("ERROR: " . $e->getMessage());
}

// close connection
unset($pdo);
?>
```

Comments

Most databases support the **Binary Large Ob**ject data type, intended specifically for use with binary data. Adding (retrieving) binary data to (from) such a database is then simply a matter of manipulating the contents of the BLOB field with SQL.

The previous listings illustrate the two parts of the process. The first script reads the contents of the file into a string with the binary-safe file_get_contents() function and saves it to the database with an INSERT query (after first protecting special characters in the binary data string with addslashes()). The second uses a SELECT query to retrieve the binary data and save it to disk with the file_put_contents() function. The file name is stored in the database with the binary data to make recomposing the file into its original form easier.

A common application of this listing is a Web-based file upload tool, which enables users to upload binary files to a database through their Web clients. This is easily accomplished by using PHP's file upload support in combination with a MySQL table containing a BLOB field, as illustrated here:

```php
<?php
// display file upload form
if (!$_POST['submit']) {
?>
    <form enctype="multipart/form-data" ⏎
action="<?=$_SERVER['PHP_SELF']?>" method="post">
    <input type="hidden" name="MAX_FILE_SIZE" value="8000000">
    Select file:
    <input type="file" name="data">
    <input type="submit" name="submit" value="Upload File">
    </form>
<?php
// if form has been submitted
// process the upload
} else {
    // check uploaded file size
    if ($_FILES['data']['size'] == 0) {
        die("ERROR: Zero byte file upload");
    }

    // check if this is a valid upload
    if (!is_uploaded_file($_FILES['data']['tmp_name'])) {
        die("ERROR: Not a valid file upload");
    }
```

```
    // read file contents into variable
    $fileData = addslashes(file_get_contents($_FILES['data']↵
['tmp_name']));

    // get file type and name
    $fileType = $_FILES['data']['type'];
    $fileName = $_FILES['data']['name'];

    // open connection to MySQL server
    $connection = mysqli_connect('localhost', 'user', 'pass', 'db1')↵
or die ("ERROR: Cannot connect");

    // create and execute INSERT query
    $sql = "INSERT INTO bindata (data, name, type) VALUES↵
('$fileData', '$fileName', '$fileType')";
    mysqli_query($connection, $sql) or die ("ERROR: " . ↵
mysqli_error($connection) . " (query was $sql)");

    // display success message
    echo "File successfully added to database with ID " .↵
mysqli_insert_id($connection);

    // close connection
    mysqli_close($connection);
}
?>
```

Here, an HTML form enables the user to select a local file and upload it to the server. After some basic checks to ensure that the upload is valid, an INSERT query saves the contents of the file to the table. In addition to saving file contents, this script also takes note of the original file name and file type, storing those details in the database as well.

TIP

Read more about form-based file uploads with PHP in the listing in "8.16: Uploading Files Through Forms."

Of course, this is only half of the puzzle—the other half involves retrieving the file from the database. Here's the code to accomplish this:

```php
<?php
// open connection to MySQL server
$connection = mysqli_connect('localhost', 'user', 'pass', 'db1')↵
or die ("ERROR: Cannot connect");

// if file ID provided
// retrieve file and prompt user
// to save to disk
if ($_GET['id'] && is_numeric($_GET['id'])) {
    $sql = "SELECT data, name, type FROM bindata WHERE id = ↵
" . $_GET['id'];
    $result = mysqli_query($connection, $sql) or die ("ERROR: " . ↵
mysqli_error($connection) . " (query was $sql)");
    if (mysqli_num_rows($result) == 1) {
        $row = mysqli_fetch_row($result);
        header("Content-Type: " . $row[2]);
        header("Content-Disposition: attachment; filename=" . $row[1]);
        echo $row[0];
    } else {
        echo "No records found!";
    }
// if no file ID provided
// display file list
} else {
    $sql = "SELECT id, name FROM bindata";
    $result = mysqli_query($connection, $sql)↵
or die ("ERROR: " . mysqli_error($connection) . " (query was $sql)");
    if (mysqli_num_rows($result) > 0) {
        while($row = mysqli_fetch_row($result)) {
            echo "<a href=" . $_SERVER['PHP_SELF'] . "?id=" . $row[0]  .↵
">" . $row[1] . "</a><br />";
        }
    } else {
        echo "No records found!";
    }
}

// close connection
mysqli_close($connection);
?>
```

This script actually performs one of two actions depending on whether or not it is called with a file ID. If called without any parameters, it connects to the database server and retrieves a list of all files currently stored in it. Each file name in the list is hyperlinked, via its unique file ID, back to the same script. Note the use of the special $_SERVER['PHP_SELF'] variable for this purpose.

Clicking any such hyperlink causes the script to be called again, this time with a file ID; the script uses this file ID to retrieve the contents of the corresponding BLOB field. The script also sends the user's browser HTTP headers indicating that what follows is binary data; this triggers a user dialog asking for a location to save the data. Once saved to disk, the file can be displayed with an appropriate viewer.

9.17 Caching Query Results

Problem

You want to improve response times by caching the output of frequently used SELECT queries.

Solution

Use the ADOdb abstraction layer to implement a query cache:

```
<html>
<head></head>
<body>

<?php
// include the DB abstraction layer
include "adodb/adodb.inc.php";

// set the cache location
$ADODB_CACHE_DIR = "cache/";

// open database connection
$dbh =& NewADOConnection("mysql");
$dbh->Connect('localhost', 'user', 'pass', 'db1') ↵
or die("ERROR: Cannot connect");
```

```php
// create and execute SELECT query
// use previously-cached result if available
$sql = "SELECT products.id, products.name, inventory.qty ↵
FROM products,inventory WHERE products.id = inventory.id";
$result = $dbh->CacheExecute(180, $sql) or die("ERROR: " .↵
$dbh->ErrorMsg() . " (query was $sql)");

// check for returned rows
// print as table, if available
if ($result->RecordCount() > 0) {
    echo "<table border=1 cellspacing=0 cellpadding=5>";
    while (!$result->EOF) {
        echo "<tr>\n";
        echo "<td>" . $result->fields[0] . "</td>\n";
        echo "<td>" . $result->fields[1] . "</td>\n";
        echo "<td>" . $result->fields[2] . "</td>\n";
        echo "</tr>\n";
        $result->MoveNext();
    }
    echo "</table>";
} else {
    echo "No records found!";
}

// close connection
$dbh->Close();
?>

</body>
</html>
```

Comments

Complex queries take longer to execute and can significantly affect the response time of your script, especially when coupled with a slow or overloaded database server. For this reason, it's a good idea to cache the output of frequently accessed scripts. A simple caching mechanism can be implemented via the ADOdb database abstraction layer, available from http://adodb.sourceforge.net/ and is discussed in the listing in "9.8: Writing Database-Independent Code."

The business logic to use a query cache is fairly simple: check if the required data already exists in the cache, retrieve and use it if it does, generate it and save a copy to the cache if it doesn't. With ADOdb, most of this is handled internally by the class; all you really need to do is replace the usual call to Execute() with a call to CacheExecute().

This listing illustrates the process, caching the results of the SELECT query for 3 minutes (180 seconds) following the initial request. Other requests for the same query within this time period will be served from the cache, without any connection being made to the database server.

The first argument to CacheExecute() is the number of seconds to cache the query results; the second is, obviously, the query string itself. The remainder of the script remains unchanged—a cached resultset is processed in exactly the same manner as a non-cached one.

TIP

You can use the CacheFlush() *method to flush all queries from the cache.*

NOTE

If you're using MySQL 4.x, you should know that the RDBMS includes a built-in query cache, which can substantially improve performance by caching the results of common queries and returning this cached data to the caller without having to re-execute the query each time. Read more about this feature at http://dev.mysql.com/doc/mysql/en/query-cache.html.

CHAPTER

10

Working with XML

IN THIS CHAPTER:

A s XML has become more and more ubiquitous on (and off) the Web, so too has PHP's support for it improved. A few years ago, parsing an XML file with PHP meant struggling with custom element handlers, unintuitive tree navigation functions, and an XML implementation that often differed from release to release. All of this has changed: PHP now has a standard XML implementation based on the GNOME XML library, and has significantly improved its XML parsing capabilities with its SimpleXML extension.

This chapter covers common listings for parsing and using XML documents with PHP, including processing node and attribute values; creating custom node collections; validating XML against Document Type Definitions (DTDs) or Schemas; transforming XML with XSLT style sheets; creating and parsing RSS feeds; and interfacing with external Web services.

NOTE

The listings in this chapter use PHP's SimpleXML, DOM (Document Object Model), XSLT (XSL Transformations), and SOAP (Simple Object Access Protocol) extensions. The SimpleXML and DOM extensions are usually enabled by default, while the SOAP and XSLT extensions must be activated manually. On Windows systems, this support can be enabled by activating the appropriate DLL (Dynamic Link Library) file; on *NIX systems, it usually involves activating the appropriate extension and recompiling PHP. Look in the PHP manual, at `http://www.php.net/ manual/en/` *for specific instructions on how to activate each extension.*

The example XML files used in this chapter can be obtained from the downloadable code archive, at `http://www.php-programming-solutions.com.`

10.1 Retrieving Node and Attribute Values

Problem

You want to retrieve the value of a specific node or attribute from an XML document instance.

Solution

Use SimpleXML to locate the node or attribute and retrieve its value:

```
<?php
// define XML data string
$xmlData = <<< END
```

```
<?xml version="1.0"?>
<data>
    <color red="128" green="0" blue="128">purple</color>
</data>
END;

// read XML data string
$xml = simplexml_load_string($xmlData)⏎
or die("ERROR: Cannot create SimpleXML object");

// read attribute values
$hexColor = sprintf("#%02x%02x%02x", $xml->color['red'],⏎
$xml->color['green'], $xml->color['blue']);

// read node data
// result: "The color purple is #800080 in hexadecimal"
echo "The color " . $xml->color . " is " . $hexColor . " in hexadecimal";
?>
```

Comments

In this listing, a call to `simplexml_load_string()` converts the XML data into a SimpleXML object. Once such an object has been initialized, elements are represented as object properties and attribute collections as associative arrays. Node values can thus be accessed using standard `object->property` notation, beginning with the root element and moving down the hierarchical path of the document tree, while attribute values can be accessed as keys of the attribute array associated with each object property.

If there is more than one element with the same name at a particular level of the XML hierarchy, it is represented, with its partners, in a numerically indexed array. Such a collection can be processed with a `foreach()` loop, as in the following listing:

```
<?php
// create XML data string
$xmlData =<<< END
<?xml version="1.0"?>
<collection>
    <color>red</color>
    <color>blue</color>
    <color>green</color>
    <color>yellow</color>
</collection>
END;
```

```
// read XML data
$xml = simplexml_load_string($xmlData) ↵
or die("ERROR: Cannot create SimpleXML object");

// process node collection
// result: "red blue green yellow"
foreach ($xml->color as $color) {
    echo "$color ";
}
?>
```

Or, if you don't know the element name, use the children() method to iterate over all the children of a particular node:

```
<?php
// create XML data string
$xmlData =<<< END
<?xml version="1.0"?>
<collection>
    <color>red</color>
    <color>blue</color>
    <color>green</color>
    <color>yellow</color>
</collection>
END;

// read XML data
$xml = simplexml_load_string($xmlData) ↵
or die("ERROR: Cannot create SimpleXML object");

// process node collection
// result: "color: red color: blue color: green color: yellow "
foreach ($xml->children() as $name => $data) {
    echo "$name: $data ";
}
?>
```

Note that you can also iterate over the attribute collection for a specific element with the attributes() method, as illustrated here:

```
<?php
// define XML data string
$xmlData = <<< END
```

```
<?xml version="1.0"?>
<data>
    <element shape="rectangle" height="10" width="5" length="7" />
</data>
END;

// read XML data string
$xml = simplexml_load_string($xmlData)↵
or die("ERROR: Cannot create SimpleXML object");

// print attributes
// result: "shape: rectangle; height: 10; width: 5; length: 7; "
foreach ($xml->element->attributes() as $name => $data) {
    echo "$name: $data; ";
}
?>
```

10.2 Modifying Node and Attribute Values

Problem

You want to alter the value of a node or an attribute in an XML document.

Solution

Use SimpleXML to read the XML file, assign new values to elements or attributes, and save the changes back to the file:

```
<?php
// read XML tree
$xml = simplexml_load_file("data.xml")↵
or die("ERROR: Cannot create SimpleXML object");

// alter value of node <weight>
$xml->weight = 3000;

// alter value of attribute <weight units=>
$xml->weight['units'] = "gm";
```

```
// write modified tree back to file as XML string
file_put_contents("data.xml", $xml->asXML()) ↵
or die("ERROR: Could not write to file");
echo "XML file successfully updated";
?>
```

Comments

In this listing, the original XML file is first read in, and elements and attributes are altered by assigning new values to the corresponding object properties and arrays. The asXML() method, typically used to output the XML tree as a string, is combined with the file_put_contents() function to overwrite the original XML document with the new data.

> **TIP**
>
> *You can also modify node or attribute values with the DOM extension's* replaceChild() *method. See the listing in "10.5: Adding or Removing XML Nodes" for an example.*

10.3 Processing XML

Problem

You want to recursively process an XML document.

Solution

Write a recursive function to traverse the XML document tree:

```
<?php
// create XML data string
$xmlData =<<< END
<?xml version="1.0"?>
<movie>
    <title>The Matrix</title>
    <credits>
        <actor>
            <name>Keanu Reeves</name>
            <character>Neo</character>
        </actor>
```

```
        <actor>
            <name>Laurence Fishburne</name>
            <character>Morpheus</character>
        </actor>
        <actor>
            <name>Carrie-Anne Moss</name>
            <character>Trinity</character>
        </actor>
        <director>
            <name>Andy Wachowski</name>
        </director>
        <director>
            <name>Larry Wachowski</name>
        </director>
    </credits>
    <year>1999</year>
    <duration units="min">120</duration>
</movie>
END;

// read XML data
$xml = simplexml_load_string($xmlData)↵
or die("ERROR: Cannot create SimpleXML object");

// function to recursively iterate over XML tree
// printing node names and values
function xmlTraverse($node) {
    foreach ($node->children() as $name => $data) {
        if (trim($data) != "") {
            echo "$name: [$data, " . strlen($data) . "]\n";
        }
        xmlTraverse($data);
    }
}

// traverse XML tree
// result: "title: [The Matrix, 10] name: [Keanu Reeves, 12] ..."
xmlTraverse($xml);
?>
```

Comments

Because an XML document is a hierarchical tree of nested elements, the most efficient way to process it is with a recursive function that calls itself to traverse the entire tree. This is the technique illustrated in the previous listing.

The recursive `xmlTraverse()` function begins with the root element and looks for children with SimpleXML's `children()` function. If children exist, the function loops over the child list, repeatedly calling itself to process each node until it reaches the end of the list. The process continues until no further nodes remain to be processed. At each stage, the current node name and value are printed.

Alternatively, consider using an Iterator from the Standard PHP Library (SPL). Iterators are ready-made, extensible constructs designed specifically to loop over item collections—directories, files, class methods, and XML trees. A predefined SimpleXMLIterator already exists and it's not difficult to extend this for recursive array processing. Here's how:

```php
<?php
// create XML data string
$xmlData =<<< END
<?xml version="1.0"?>
<movie>
    <title>The Matrix</title>
    <credits>
        <actor>
            <name>Keanu Reeves</name>
            <character>Neo</character>
        </actor>
        <actor>
            <name>Laurence Fishburne</name>
            <character>Morpheus</character>
        </actor>
        <actor>
            <name>Carrie-Anne Moss</name>
            <character>Trinity</character>
        </actor>
        <director>
            <name>Andy Wachowski</name>
        </director>
        <director>
            <name>Larry Wachowski</name>
        </director>
    </credits>
```

```
    <year>1999</year>
    <duration units="min">120</duration>
</movie>
END;

// read XML data
$xml = simplexml_load_string($xmlData, "SimpleXMLIterator")↵
or die("ERROR: Cannot create SimpleXML object");

// recursively iterate over XML tree
foreach(new RecursiveIteratorIterator($xml, true) as $name => $data)
{
    if (trim($data) != "") {
        echo "$name: [$data, " . strlen($data) . "]\n";
    }
}
?>
```

The process of traversing a series of nested directories is significantly simpler with the SPL at hand. First, initialize a SimpleXMLIterator() object and pass it the XML tree to be processed. Next, initialize a RecursiveIteratorIterator() object (this is an Iterator designed solely for the purpose of iterating over other recursive Iterators) and pass it the newly-minted `SimpleXMLIterator()`. You can now process the results with a `foreach()` loop.

You can read more about the SimpleXMLIterator and the RecursiveIteratorIterator at `http://www.php.net/~helly/php/ext/spl/`.

10.4 Creating XML

Problem

You want to generate an XML document using PHP method calls.

Solution

Use PHP's DOM extension to create a DOM tree and append nodes to it:

```
<?php
// initialize DOM object
$xml = new DOMDocument("1.0");
```

```php
// add root node <listing>
$root = $xml->createElement("list");
$xml->appendChild($root);

// add element <description> to root
$desc = $xml->createElement("description");
$root->appendChild($desc);

// add <description> content
$desc->appendChild($xml->createTextNode("Sam's Shopping List"));

// add comment
$root->appendChild($xml->createComment("item list follows"));

// add <item> child element
// add quantities as attributes
$items = $xml->createElement("items");
$root->appendChild($items);

$item = $xml->createElement("item");
$items->appendChild($item);
$item->appendChild($xml->createTextNode("eggs"));
$item->setAttribute("units", 3);
unset($item);

$item = $xml->createElement("item");
$items->appendChild($item);
$item->appendChild($xml->createTextNode("salt"));
$item->setAttribute("units", "100 gm");

// add CDATA block
$items->appendChild($xml->createCDATASection("You can't make
an omelette without breaking eggs"));

// add PI
$root->appendChild($xml->createProcessingInstruction(
"xml-dummy-pi", "shop('now')"));

// display final tree as HTML...
$xml->formatOutput = true;
echo "<xmp>" . $xml->saveXML() . "</xmp>";

// ...or write it to a file as XML
$xml->save("list.xml") or die("ERROR: Could not write to file");
?>
```

Comments

PHP's SimpleXML extension does not support node creation, so this task is better handled with PHP's DOM extension, which comes with a wide array of methods designed to help you design an XML document instance dynamically. To get started, create an instance of the DOMDocument class, and then use its `createElement()` method to create element objects. These element objects may then be attached to a parent node by calling the parent node object's `appendChild()` method. The process is illustrated in the previous listing.

Of course, an XML document is much more than just elements—which is why the DOM extension also offers `createTextNode()`, `createCDATASection()`, `createProcessingInstruction()`, and `createComment()` methods to attach text, CDATA blocks, PIs (Processing Instructions), and comments to the DOM tree respectively. Attributes for an element are set by calling the corresponding element object's `setAttribute()` method with appropriate parameters.

Once the tree has been generated, it may be retrieved as a string with the primary DOMDocument object's `saveXML()` method, or written to a file with the object's `save()` method.

10.5 Adding or Removing XML Nodes

Problem

You want to add (remove) nodes to (from) an XML document instance.

Solution

Use the `appendChild()`, `replaceChild()`, and `removeChild()` methods from PHP's DOM extension:

```
<?php
// define XML data string
$xmlData = <<< END
<?xml version="1.0"?>
<favorites>
    <pet>Humphrey Hippo</pet>
    <flavor>chocolate</flavor>
    <movie>Star Wars</movie>
</favorites>
END;
```

```php
// read XML data
$xml = new DOMDocument();
$xml->formatOutput = true;        // format output
$xml->preserveWhiteSpace = false; // discount whitespace
$xml->loadXML($xmlData) or die("ERROR: ↵
Cannot create DOMDocument object");

// print the original XML tree
echo "<xmp>OLD:\n" . $xml->saveXML() . "</xmp>";

// get document element
$root = $xml->documentElement;

// add a node before <movie>
$movie = $root->childNodes->item(2);
$book = $xml->createElement("book");
$root->insertBefore($book, $movie);
$book->appendChild($xml->createTextNode("The Lord Of The Rings"));

// add a node after <movie>
$toy = $xml->createElement("toy");
$toy->appendChild($xml->createTextNode("Stuffed bear"));
$root->appendChild($toy);

// replace <flavor> with <icecream>
$flavour = $root->childNodes->item(1);
$icecream = $xml->createElement("icecream");
$icecream->appendChild($xml->createTextNode("strawberry"));
$root->replaceChild($icecream, $flavour);

// delete <movie>
$movie = $root->childNodes->item(3);
$root->removeChild($movie);

// print the modified XML tree
echo "<xmp>NEW:\n" . $xml->saveXML() . "</xmp>";
?>
```

Comments

PHP's SimpleXML extension doesn't support node addition or removal, so this task is best addressed with PHP's DOM extension. Adding a node to an existing DOM tree is fairly simple—create a new object with the appropriate create*Item*() method, and append it to the tree by using the parent node object's appendChild() method to link the two. Removing a node is also fairly easy—use the primary DOMDocument object's `removeChild()` method and pass it the node to be removed.

> **NOTE**
>
> *If what you're really after is modifying a node value, take a look at the listing in "10.2: Modifying Node and Attribute Values," which shows you how to do it with SimpleXML.*
>
> *For those XML elements that cannot be modified via SimpleXML (for example, Comments and PIs), the listing in "10.5: Adding or Removing XML Nodes" also illustrates the process of modifying a node with PHP's DOM extension: create a new node object with the appropriate* `createItem()` *method and then use the* `replaceChild()` *method to overwrite an existing node with the newly minted one.*

10.6 Collapsing Empty XML Elements

Problem

You want to collapse empty tags in an XML document.

Solution

Use PEAR's XML_Util class:

```php
<?php
$xmlData =<<< END
<?xml version="1.0" encoding="UTF-8"?>
<!DOCTYPE html PUBLIC "-//W3C//DTD XHTML 1.0 Transitional//EN"
"http://www.w3.org/TR/xhtml1/DTD/xhtml1-transitional.dtd">
<html xmlns="http://www.w3.org/1999/xhtml">
 <head></head>
 <body>
  <div>Content here.</div>
  <p></p>
  <div>Content here.</div>
 </body>
</html>
END;

// include class
include "XML/Util.php";
```

```
// collapse empty tags and print
echo XML_Util::collapseEmptyTags($xmlData);
?>
```

Comments

For elements that have no content, such as <name></name>, the XML specification suggests the use of empty-element tags, such as <name />. Available from http://pear.php.net/package/XML_Util, PEAR's XML_Util class provides an automated way to accomplish this change via its collapseEmptyTags() method. One of the most common uses for this method is illustrated in the previous listing: replace HTML's <p></p> sequence with the "better" <p /> sequence.

10.7 Counting XML Element Frequency

Problem

You want to count the frequency of occurrence of a particular element or attribute in an XML document.

Solution

Use PEAR's XML_Statistics class:

```
<?php
$xmlData =<<< END
<?xml version='1.0'?>
<library>
    <movie>
        <title>The Matrix</title>
        <cast>
            <person>Keanu Reeves</person>
            <person>Laurence Fishburne</person>
            <person>Carrie-Anne Moss</person>
        </cast>
    </movie>
    <movie>
        <title rating="3">Mission: Impossible III</title>
        <cast>
            <person>Tom Cruise</person>
```

```
            <person>Ving Rhames</person>
            <person>Laurence Fishburne</person>
        </cast>
    </movie>
    <movie>
        <title rating="5">Minority Report</title>
        <cast>
            <person>Tom Cruise</person>
            <person>Max von Sydow</person>
        </cast>
    </movie>
</library>
END;

// include class
include "XML/Statistics.php";

// analyze XML string
$obj = new XML_Statistics();
$obj->analyzeString($xmlData);

// count total number of elements
// result: "Total number of elements: 18"
echo "Total number of elements: " . $obj->countTag() . "\n";

// count total number of <person> elements
// result: "Total number of  elements: 8"
echo "Total number of <person> elements: " .↵
$obj->countTag('person') . "\n";

// count total number of attributes
// result: "Total number of attributes: 2"
echo "Total number of attributes: " . $obj->countAttribute() . "\n";

// count total number of text elements
// result: "Total number of text elements: 11"
echo "Total number of text elements: " . $obj->countDataChunks() . "\n";
?>
```

Comments

PEAR's XML_Statistics class, available from http://pear.php.net/
package/XML_Statistics, enables you to retrieve information on the number
of elements, attributes, CDATA blocks, PIs, and entities within an XML file

or string. Once an object of the class is initialized, the `analyzeString()` or `analyzeFile()` method statistically analyzes the XML data and builds an internal frequency table for the data within it. The `countTag()`, `countAttribute()`, and `countDataChunks()` methods can then be used to obtain totals for the number of elements, attributes, and character data blocks respectively; these totals may be further filtered by supplying a specific element or attribute name to the corresponding method.

> **NOTE**
>
> *This example also requires the XML_Parser class from* `http://pear.php.net/package/XML_Parser`.

10.8 Filtering XML Nodes by Namespace

Problem

You want to find only those nodes belonging to a particular namespace.

Solution

Use SimpleXML's `children()` method with the namespace URI (Universal Resource Identifier):

```php
<?php
// define XML data string
// containing namespaces
$xmlData = <<< END
<?xml version="1.0"?>
<data xmlns:home="http://www.some.domain/xmlns/home" ↵
xmlns:work="http://www.some.domain/xmlns/work">
    <home:file>music.txt</home:file>
    <work:file>accounts.dat</work:file>
    <work:file>inbox.mbx</work:file>
    <home:file>expenses.xls</home:file>
    <home:file>addressbook.doc</home:file>
</data>
END;

// read XML data
$xml = simplexml_load_string($xmlData);
```

```
// process nodes in "work" namespace
// result: "accounts.dat inbox.mbx "
foreach ($xml->children("http://www.some.domain/xmlns/work") as $file)
{
    echo "$file ";
}
?>
```

Comments

It's easy to isolate only those child nodes belonging to a particular namespace if
you're using SimpleXML: just pass the namespace URI to the `children()` method
as an additional argument. In this example, this technique has been used to isolate all
the nodes in the `"work"` namespace under the document element. The resulting node
collection can then be processed in the usual manner, with a `foreach()` or other
loop.

10.9 Filtering XML Nodes with XPath

Problem

You want to find only those nodes matching a particular XPath location path.

Solution

Use SimpleXML's `xpath()` method:

```
<?php
$xmlData =<<< END
<?xml version="1.0"?>
<data>
    <item>
        <id>20</id>
        <name>mangoes</name>
        <price>11</price>
    </item>
    <item>
        <id>22</id>
        <name>strawberries</name>
        <price>5</price>
    </item>
```

```
    <item>
        <id>23</id>
        <name>grapes</name>
        <price>25</price>
    </item>
</data>
END;

// read XML data
$xml = simplexml_load_string($xmlData)↵
or die("ERROR: Cannot create SimpleXML object");

// create a custom collection of <name> nodes
// using an XPath query
// result: "mangoes strawberries grapes "
foreach ($xml->xpath('//name') as $name) {
    echo "$name ";
}
```

Comments

XPath provides a standard addressing mechanism for an XML document, making it easy to access and manipulate every element, attribute, and text node on the XML document tree.

SimpleXML supports building custom node collections via its xpath() method. This method accepts an XPath location path (either absolute or relative) and selects all the nodes matching that path. In this example, the //name shortcut selects <name> elements anywhere below the document element and returns them as a node collection that can be processed in a loop.

TIP

For a friendly introduction to XPath, visit http://www.melonfire.com/ community/columns/trog/article.php?id=83.

10.10 Validating XML

Problem

You want to validate an XML document instance against a DTD or XML Schema.

Solution

Use PHP's DOM extension to perform validation using the `validate()` method for a DTD:

```php
<?php
// read XML data
$xml = new DOMDocument();
$xml->load("data-1.xml") or die("ERROR: Cannot create DOMDocument ↵
object");

// validate XML against DTD
// result: "Valid data"
echo $xml->validate() ? "Valid data" : "Invalid data";
?>
```

Use PHP's DOM extension to perform validation using the `schemaValidate()` method for an XML Schema:

```php
<?php
// read XML data
$xml = new DOMDocument();
$xml->load("data-2.xml") or die("ERROR: Cannot create DOMDocument ↵
object");

// validate XML against XML Schema
// result: "Valid data"
echo $xml->schemaValidate("data.xsd") ? "Valid data" : "Invalid data";
?>
```

Comments

Data validation is an important part of parsing an XML document instance. As of this writing, SimpleXML merely ensures that XML documents are well-formed; it offers no way of testing them against DTDs or the new XML Schemas. Therefore, to test an XML document for validity, it is necessary to use PHP's DOM extension, which offers `validate()` and `schemaValidate()` methods for this purpose.

The `validate()` method automatically looks up the name of the DTD file in the XML document instance, while the `schemaValidate()` method requires you to specify the name and path to the schema file as an argument. Both methods return false if the document instance does not match the rules laid down in the DTD/Schema, and the `validate()` method also returns false if no DTD declaration exists within the document instance.

10.11 Transforming XML

Problem

You want to transform an XML document instance using an XSLT style sheet.

Solution

Use PHP's DOM and XSLT extensions together:

```php
<?php
// read XML data
$xml = new DOMDocument;
$xml->load('review.xml');

// read XSL stylesheet data
$xsl = new DOMDocument;
$xsl->load('review.xsl');

// initialize XSLT engine
$xslp = new XSLTProcessor;

// attach XSL stylesheet object
$xslp->importStyleSheet($xsl);

// perform transformation
echo $xslp->transformToXML($xml);
?>
```

Comments

XSL, the Extensible Style Language, is a powerful language that makes it possible to apply presentation rules to XML documents, and convert—or transform—them from one format to another. For example, you could use different XSL transformations to create an HTML Web page, a WML deck, and an ASCII text file... all from the same source XML.

An XSL Transformation essentially consists of converting an XML *source tree* into a new—and usually completely different—*result tree*. This is accomplished by means of an XSLT stylesheet, which contains one or more *template rules*. A template rule performs two functions: It first identifies a pattern to match in the source tree, and then describes the structure of the desired result tree. It is this process of *transforming* the source tree into the result tree that gives XSLT its name.

The previous listing demonstrates how this works in PHP. Here, two instances of the DOMDocument class are created, one for the XML data and the other for the XSLT style sheet. Next, the XSLT engine is initialized by creating an object of the XSLTProcessor class, and the object's `importStyleSheet()` method is used to import the XSLT style sheet. Once the style sheet has been successfully parsed, the `transformToXML()` method is used to apply the style rules to the XML document, "transform" it, and return the result.

10.12 Exporting Data to XML

Problem

You want to export an SQL result set as an XML file.

Solution

Turn the result set into an XML document with PHP's DOM functions:

```php
<?php
// open connection
$mysqli = new mysqli("localhost", "user", "pass", "db1");
if (mysqli_connect_errno()) {
    die("ERROR: Cannot connect. " . mysqli_connect_error());
}

// create and execute SELECT query
$sql = "SELECT id, name, price FROM products";
if ($result = $mysqli->query($sql)) {
    // if results exist
    // initialize DOM object
    $xml = new DOMDocument("1.0");

    // add root node
    $root = $xml->createElement("resultset");
    $xml->appendChild($root);

    // iterate over result set
    // print <record>s and <field>s
    if ($result->num_rows > 0) {
        while($row = $result->fetch_row()) {
            $record = $xml->createElement("record");
```

```
                $root->appendChild($record);
                $fieldCount = 0;
                while ($fieldCount < $mysqli->field_count) {
                        $field = $xml->createElement("field");
                        $record->appendChild($field);
                        $field->appendChild(↵
$xml->createTextNode($row[$fieldCount]));
                        $fieldCount++;
                }
            }
        }
        $result->close();
} else {
        die("ERROR: " . $mysqli->error . " (query was $sql)");
}

// close connection
$mysqli->close();

// display XML result set as HTML...
$xml->formatOutput = true;
echo "<xmp>" . $xml->saveXML() . "</xmp>";

// ...or write it to a file as XML
$xml->save("results.xml") or die("ERROR: Could not write to file");
?>
```

Comments

There are a number of reasons why you might want to export a SQL result set to an XML file: to make the data more usable and portable, to reduce your application's dependence on a database server, or to improve performance (because it's usually faster to read from a disk file than from a network connection).

The previous listing shows you how, by executing a SELECT query and then converting the resulting data set into a series of <record> and <field> elements. PHP's DOM extension, which comes with built-in support for dynamically adding nodes to an XML document tree, takes care of the heavy lifting with its createElement(), createTextNode(), and appendChild() methods (these methods are discussed in greater detail in the listings in "10.4: Creating XML" and "10.5: Adding or Removing XML Nodes"). Once the document has been completely generated, it may be written to a file via the save() method, or returned as a string suitable for display with the saveXML() method.

You can also do the reverse: read data from an XML file and write it to a database. The next listing demonstrates this, using SimpleXML to parse an XML file and generate a series of SQL INSERT statements from it:

```php
<?php
$xmlData =<<< END
<?xml version="1.0"?>
<data>
    <item>
        <id>20</id>
        <name>mangoes</name>
        <price>11</price>
    </item>
    <item>
        <id>22</id>
        <name>strawberries</name>
        <price>5</price>
    </item>
    <item>
        <id>23</id>
        <name>grapes</name>
        <price>25</price>
    </item>
</data>
END;

// read XML data string
$xml = simplexml_load_string($xmlData)
or die("ERROR: Cannot create SimpleXML object");

// open MySQL connection
$connection = mysqli_connect("localhost", "user", "pass", "db1")
or die ("ERROR: Cannot connect");

// process node data
// create and execute INSERT queries
foreach ($xml->item as $item) {
    $id = $item->id;
    $name = mysqli_real_escape_string($connection, $item->name);
    $price = $item->price;
    $sql = "INSERT INTO products (id, name, price)
```

```
VALUES ('$id', '$name', '$price')";
    mysqli_query($connection, $sql) or die ("ERROR: " .↵
mysqli_error($connection) . " (query was $sql)");
}

// close connection
mysqli_close($connection);
?>
```

In this listing, SimpleXML is used to iterate over each <item> in the XML document and generate an SQL INSERT statement from the values contained within it. PHP's ext/mysqli functions are then used to execute each INSERT statement on the database server, thus writing the data to the database.

> **TIP**
>
> Metabase is a PHP-based database abstraction layer that uses XML to express table relationships, structures and records. Read more about it at `http://www.phpclasses.org/ metabase`.

10.13 Working with RDF Site Summaries

Problem

You want to create or parse an RDF Site Summary (RSS) feed.

Solution

Create an RSS feed by importing data from an external data source (such as a database) into an RSS template:

```
<?php
// send XML header
header("Content-Type: text/xml");
echo "<?xml version=\"1.0\" encoding=\"iso-8859-1\"?>";
?>
<rss version="2.0">
    <channel>
        <title>Trog</title>
        <link>http://www.melonfire.com/community/columns/trog/</link>
        <description>Tutorials on PHP and other languages</description>
```

```php
<?php
// open connection
$connection = mysqli_connect("localhost", "user", "pass", "db1")↵
or die ("ERROR: Cannot connect");

// create and execute SELECT query
$sql = "SELECT url, title, synopsis FROM content LIMIT 10";
$result = mysqli_query($connection, $sql)↵
or die ("ERROR: " . mysqli_error($connection) . ↵
" (query was $sql)");

// check for returned rows
// print as <item>s if available
if (mysqli_num_rows($result) > 0) {
    while($row = mysqli_fetch_assoc($result)) {
?>
                <item>
                  <title><?php echo htmlentities($row['title']); ?>↵
</title>
                  <link><?php echo $row['url']; ?></link>
                  <description>
                    <?php echo htmlentities($row['synopsis']); ?>
                  </description>
                </item>
<?php
    }
}

// close connection
mysqli_close($connection);
?>
    </channel>
</rss>
```

Parse an RSS feed by using SimpleXML to read the RSS stream and parse and display the contents of each <item> element:

```html
<html>
<head></head>
<body>

<?php
// a bare-bones RSS reader
```

```
// read RSS data
$xml = simplexml_load_file("http://some.domain.com/data.rss")↵
or die("ERROR: Cannot create SimpleXML object");

// print channel information
echo "CHANNEL: " . $xml->channel->title . "<br />";
echo "DESCRIPTION: " . $xml->channel->description . "<br />";
echo "<br />";

// iterate over item list
// print first 200 characters of each item
// after stripping out embedded HTML elements
$count = 1;
foreach ($xml->channel->item as $item) {
    echo "($count) " . strtoupper($item->title) . "<br />";
    echo "URL: <a href='" . $item->link . "'>" . $item->link . "</a><br
/><br />";
    echo substr(strip_tags($item->description), 0, 200) . "...<br />↵
<br />";
    $count++;
}
?>
</pre>
</body>
</html>
```

Comments

RSS is an XML-based format originally devised by Netscape to distribute information about the content on its My.Netscape.Com portal. RSS makes it possible to distribute a frequently updated list of the latest information about a particular Web site, thus opening the door to content syndication over the Web.

An RSS document follows all the rules of XML markup, and typically contains a list of resources (URLs), marked up with descriptive metadata. A <channel> block contains general information and encloses multiple <item> elements, each of which describes a single resource in greater detail by providing a title, a URL, and a description of that resource.

If you're a content publisher looking to create an RSS document for your Web site, and you have a database or other external data source to populate the feed, all you need to do is build an RSS template and "plug in" data at appropriate spots. This process is illustrated in the first listing, which reads resource information from a MySQL database and plugs it into a template to dynamically create an RSS feed.

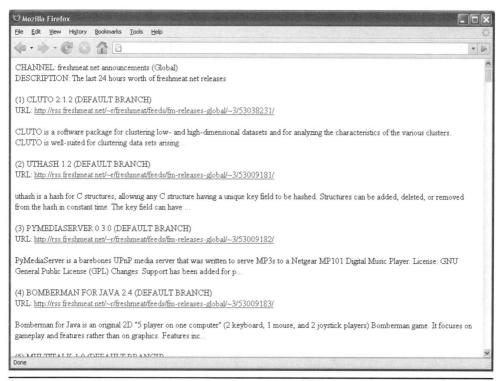

Figure 10-1 *A bare-bones RSS reader*

If, on the other hand, your task is to parse an RSS feed generated by someone else, the second listing demonstrates the process: use SimpleXML to read the remote RSS data and retrieve channel and resource information using standard `object->property` notation. SimpleXML's ability to loop over node collections further simplifies the task of processing `<item>` elements and iteratively building an HTML (or other format) document from them. If item information contains embedded HTML elements, you may optionally choose to remove these with the `strip_tags()` method. Figure 10-1 illustrates what the output might look like.

10.14 Using the Google Web APIs

Problem

You want to perform a Google.com search.

Solution

Use PHP's SOAP functions with the Google Web APIs to execute a search on Google.com and process the results:

```php
<html>
<head></head>
<body>

<?php
if (!isset($_POST['submit'])) {
?>

    <form method="post" action="<?php echo $_SERVER['PHP_SELF'];?>">
        Search Google for: <input type="text" name="q">
        <input type="submit" name="submit" value="Search">
    </form>

<?php
} else {
    // initialize SOAP client
    $client = new SoapClient("http://api.google.com/GoogleSearch.wsdl");

    // set up input parameters to be
    // passed to the remote procedure
    $key = 'xxxxxx';       // insert your Google key here
    $q   = $_POST['q'];    // search term
    $start = 0;            // start from result n
    $maxResults = 10;      // show a total of n results
    $filter = false;       // remove similar results
    $restrict = '';        // restrict by topic
    $safeSearch = false;   // remove adult links
    $lr = '';              // restrict by language
    $ie = '';              // input encoding
    $oe = '';              // output encoding

    // try the code
    try {
        // invoke the method on the server
            $result = $client->doGoogleSearch($key, $q, $start,↵
$maxResults, $filter, $restrict, $safeSearch, $lr, $ie, $oe);
    // catch exceptions
        } catch (SoapFault $fault) {
        die("ERROR: " . $fault->faultstring);
    }
```

```
    // else print results
    echo "<h2>Search Results</h2>";
    echo $result->estimatedTotalResultsCount . " hits found in " .↵
$result->searchTime . " ms";
    echo "<ul>";
    if (is_array($result->resultElements)) {
        foreach ($result->resultElements as $r) {
            echo "<li><a href=\"" . $r->URL . "\">" . $r->title . "</a>";
            echo "<br>";
            echo $r->snippet . "(" . $r->cachedSize . ")";
            echo "<p></p>";
        }
    }
    echo "</ul>";
}
?>

</body>
</html>
```

Comments

The Google Web APIs enable developers to query the complete Google database using a series of SOAP-based remote procedure calls. PHP 5 supports the SOAP, making it possible to transparently execute SOAP-based remote procedure calls over HTTP. These two facts make it easy to interface a PHP application with the Google.com Web site.

This script actually contains two parts, separated by a conditional test. The first part displays an HTML form into which the user can input one or more query terms. Once the form is submitted, the second part initializes a SOAP client and passes it the URL to Google.com's Web Services Description Language (WSDL) file; once this file is read, it becomes possible to access Google Web API methods as though they were local methods of the SOAPClient object.

Given the task here is to perform a search for the user's query term(s), the doGoogleSearch() method is invoked next, and parameters such as the license key, the query term, the number of matches to display, the language to search in, and the character encoding of the result set are passed to it. The request is transmitted to the SOAP server, and the result is converted into a native PHP object holding a series of result elements, together with some statistics on the search itself. With this information at hand, it becomes a simple matter to create an HTML page containing a properly formatted list of matches. Errors, if any, are returned as SOAPFault objects, and can easily be detected and processed by wrapping the method call in a try-catch() block.

Figure 10-2 illustrates the result of a search for "tim berners-lee".

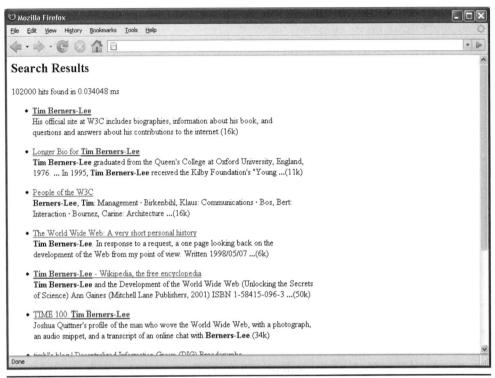

Figure 10-2   *The results of a search conducted using the Google Web APIs*

An alternative is to use the PEAR SOAP class, freely available from `http://pear.php.net/package/SOAP`. This class provides a good replacement for PHP's native SOAP protocol support; this is illustrated by the next listing, which uses it to create a script equivalent to the previous one:

```
<html>
<head></head>
<body>

<?php
if (!isset($_POST['submit'])) {
?>

    <form method="post" action="<?php echo $_SERVER['PHP_SELF'];?>">
        Search Google for: <input type="text" name="q">
        <input type="submit" name="submit" value="Search">
    </form>
```

```php
<?php
} else {
    // include SOAP class
    include "SOAP/Client.php";

    // initialize SOAP client
    $soapclient = new ⏎
SOAP_Client("http://api.google.com/GoogleSearch.wsdl");

    // set up an array containing input parameters to be
    // passed to the remote procedure
    $params = array( 'key' => 'xxxxx',        // insert your Google key
                                              //   here
                     'q'    => $_POST['q'],   // search term
                     'start' => 0,            // start from result n
                     'maxResults' => 10,      // show a total of n
                                              //   results
                     'filter' => false,       // remove similar results
                     'restrict' => '',        // restrict by topic
                     'safeSearch' => false,   // remove adult links
                     'lr' => '',              // restrict by language
                     'ie' => '',              // input encoding
                     'oe' => '');             // output encoding

    // invoke the method on the server
    $result = $soapclient->call("doGoogleSearch", $params,⏎
array('namespace' => 'urn:GoogleSearch'));

    // check for an error
    if (get_class($result) == "soap_fault") {
        die("ERROR: " . $result->message);
    }
    // else print results
    echo "<h2>Search Results</h2>";
    echo $result->estimatedTotalResultsCount . " hits found in " .⏎
$result->searchTime . " ms";
    echo "<ul>";
    if (is_array($result->resultElements)) {
        foreach ($result->resultElements as $r) {
            echo "<li><a href=\"" . $r->URL . "\">" . $r->title . ⏎
"</a>";
```

```
            echo "<br>";
            echo $r->snippet . "(" . $r->cachedSize . ")";
            echo "<p></p>";
        }
    }
    echo "</ul>";
}
?>
</body>
</html>
```

Here, an instance of the SOAP_Client class is created, and then the class' call() method is used to invoke the remote doGoogleSearch() method with an array of parameters. The result is processed in the same manner as it is in the first listing in this section. Errors, if any, are generated as soap_fault() objects, and can be detected with a call to get_class().

> **NOTE**
>
> A Google license key must accompany each request made through the Google Web APIs, or else the API call(s) will fail. Therefore, you need to obtain a license key and place it in the scripts described in this listing before they will work as advertised.

10.15 Using the Amazon E-Commerce Service

Problem

You want to interface with the Amazon.com product catalog.

Solution

Use PHP's SOAP functions with the Amazon E-Commerce Service (ECS) to perform product searches on Amazon.com:

```
<html>
<head></head>
<body>

<?php
if (!isset($_POST['submit'])) {
?>
```

```php
    <form method="post" action="<?php echo $_SERVER['PHP_SELF'];?>">
        Search Amazon.com for ISBN: <input type="text" name="isbn">
        <input type="submit" name="submit" value="Search">
    </form>

<?php
} else {
    // initialize SOAP client
    $client = new ↵
SoapClient("http://webservices.amazon.com/AWSECommerceService/↵
AWSECommerceService.wsdl");

    // set operation parameters
    $params->{"ItemId"} = $_POST['isbn'];      // ISBN number

    // generate request object
    $request->{"Request"} = $params;
    $request->{"SubscriptionId"} = "xxxxx";  // insert your ↵
ECS key here

    // try the code
    try {
        // invoke AWS method on server
        $result=$client->ItemLookup($request);
    // catch exceptions
    } catch (SoapFault $fault) {
        die("ERROR: " . $fault->faultstring);
    }

    // print results
    echo "<h2>Search Results</h2>";
    echo "ASIN: " . $result->Items->Item->ASIN . "<br />";
    echo "Title: " . $result->Items->Item->ItemAttributes->Title . ↵
"<br />";
    echo "Author: " . $result->Items->Item->ItemAttributes->Author .↵
"<br />";
    echo "<a href=\"" . $result->Items->Item->DetailPageURL . "\">↵
Read more</a>...";
}
?>
</body>
</html>
```

Comments

The Amazon ECS enables developers to query the complete Amazon.com product catalog using a series of SOAP-based remote procedure calls. PHP 5 supports SOAP, making it possible to transparently execute SOAP-based remote procedure calls over HTTP. This makes it easy to interface a PHP application with the Amazon.com online store.

This script is made up of two sections: the first displays an HTML form that the user can input an ISBN number into (an ISBN number is a unique number used to reference a book), and the second initializes a SOAP client and passes it the URL to Amazon.com's WSDL file. Once this file is read, it becomes possible to access Amazon ECS methods as though they were local methods of the SOAPClient object.

As an example, assume the task is to look up a book by its International Standard Book Number (ISBN). A review of the ECS documentation suggests that the ItemLookup() method is most appropriate for this task, as it accepts an ISBN number and returns meta-information for the corresponding book. Thus, the previous listing creates a request object and initializes it with the ECS subscription ID and the ISBN to search. This request object is then transmitted to the SOAP server, and the result is converted into a native PHP object holding a series of result elements. It is now a simple matter to process the SOAP response and extract the book's title, author, and Amazon.com page URL from it. Errors, if any, are returned as SOAPFault objects, and they can be detected and processed by wrapping the method call in a try-catch() block.

> **TIP**
>
> To see this script in action, try it with the number 1592640079—the ISBN number for Oliver Twist by Charles Dickens.

Users of PHP versions without SOAP support may instead prefer to use the PEAR SOAP class, freely available from http://pear.php.net/package/SOAP. This class provides a good replacement for PHP's native SOAP protocol support; this is illustrated by the next listing, which uses it to create a script equivalent to the previous one:

```
<html>
<head></head>
<body>

<?php
if (!isset($_POST['submit'])) {
?>
```

```
    <form method="post" action="<?php echo $_SERVER['PHP_SELF'];?>">
        Search Amazon.com for ISBN: <input type="text" name="isbn">
        <input type="submit" name="submit" value="Search">
    </form>

<?php
} else {
    // include SOAP class
    include "SOAP/Client.php";

    // initialize SOAP client (non-WSDL)
    $soapclient = new SOAP_Client("http://webservices.amazon.com/onca/↵
soap? Service=AWSECommerceService");

    // set up an array of input parameters
    // passed to the remote procedure
    $params = array( 'Service' => 'AWSECommerceService',  // service
                     'SubscriptionId' => 'xxxx',    // insert your ↵
ECS key here
                     'ItemId' => $_POST['isbn'] );     // ISBN number

    // invoke the method on the server
    $result = $soapclient->call("ItemLookup", $params);

    // check for an error
    if (get_class($result) == "soap_fault") {
        die("ERROR: " . $result->message);
    }
    // else print results
    echo "<h2>Search Results</h2>";
    echo "ASIN: " . $result['Items']->Item->ASIN . "<br />";
    echo "Title: " . $result['Items']->Item->ItemAttributes->Title .↵
"<br />";
    echo "Author: " . $result['Items']->Item->ItemAttributes->Author .↵
"<br />";
    echo "<a href=\"" . $result['Items']->Item->DetailPageURL . "\">↵
Read more</a>...";
}
?>
</body>
</html>
```

Here, an instance of the SOAP_Client class is created, and then the class' `call()` method is used to invoke the remote `ItemLookup()` method with an array of parameters. The result is processed in the same manner as in the first listing in this section. Errors, if any, are generated as `soap_fault()` objects, and can be detected with a call to `get_class()`.

NOTE

An ECS subscription key must accompany each request made through the ECS service, or else the request will fail. Therefore, you need to obtain a subscription key and place it in the scripts described in this listing before they will work as advertised. You can obtain such a key free of charge from `http://www.amazon.com/webservices`.

TIP

In addition to performing item lookups, ECS also lets you search Amazon.com for keywords, titles, wish lists, zShops, and Amazon Marketplace sellers; create and remotely manipulate Amazon.com shopping carts; browse categories; sort results by different criteria; and refine the level of search detail. Additionally, you may also use the techniques and script template used in this listing to access newer Amazon.com services, such as the Simple Queue Service (SQS), Elastic Compute Cloud (EC2) and Mechanical Turk. Look in the online documentation at `http://www.amazon.com/webservices` *for more details.*

10.16 Creating Trackbacks

Problem

You want to manually set a trackback to a blog post, or a Web page that accepts trackbacks.

Solution

Use PEAR's Services_Trackback class:

```php
<?php
$trackbackData = array(
    'id'        => 1,
    'title'     => 'What I Think Of What They Said (testing, PL IGNORE)',
    'excerpt'   => 'Here, I refer to the post at originating.blog,↵
```

```
which I thought made some powerful statements.',
    'url'        => 'http://my.blog/url/to/my/post',
    'blog_name' => 'My Blog',
    'trackback_url' => 'http://originating.blog/url/to/↵
trackback?postID=19',);

// include class
include "Services/Trackback.php";

// initialize new instance
$trackback = new Services_Trackback();

// set object properties
foreach ($trackbackData as $k => $v) {
        $trackback->set($k, $v);
}

// send trackback
$ret = $trackback->send();
if (PEAR::isError($ret)) {
    echo "Trackback failed: " . $ret->getMessage();
} else {
    echo "Trackback successful";
}
?>
```

Comments

Trackbacks provide an easy way for content authors to notify each other when they refer to each other's published material on their blogs or Web pages. A trackback is an XML-formatted message, used to create a link between the original content source and its referrer. Once a trackback has been posted, it usually becomes visible on the original content source, thereby facilitating discussion among readers. Most modern blogging applications support the trackback protocol; this listing provides a solution for those that don't.

PEAR's Services_Trackback class, available from `http://pear.php.net/ package/Services_Trackback`, provides routines to create and format a trackback message in XML, and send it to a target URL. As the previous listing illustrates, this message has various components: a title and excerpt for the trackback message, the URL and name of the referring blog or page, and the URL to which the trackback must be posted at the original source of the content. These components are stored in a PHP associative array and passed to an instance of the Services_ Trackback class via the set() method, which takes care of formatting them into XML. The instance's send() method is then used to actually post the trackback to the destination URL.

TIP

Read more about trackbacks at http://en.wikipedia.org/wiki/ Trackback, *and about the trackback protocol at* http://www.sixapart.com/ pronet/docs/trackback_spec.

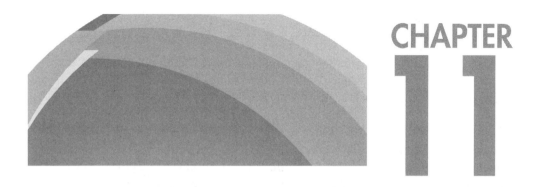

CHAPTER
11

Working with Different File Formats and Network Protocols

P HP comes with innumerable extensions, all designed to let developers interface the language with as many servers, protocols and formats as possible. This all-embracing approach is one of the reasons for PHP's primacy as a Web scripting language—it's hard to think of a single format or protocol that you *can't* hook a PHP script up to!

This chapter is the proof of the pudding: It includes recipes for connecting to File Transfer Protocol (FTP) servers; reading mail in Post Office Protocol 3 (POP3) mailboxes; querying Domain Name System (DNS) and WHOIS servers; extracting thumbnails from digital Joint Photographic Experts Group (JPEG) files; dynamically generating Portable Document Format (PDF) files; creating Multipurpose Internet Mail Extensions (MIME) -compliant e-mail messages; and many more. Enter, and prepare to be amazed!

11.1 Pinging Remote Hosts

Problem

You want to check if a particular network host is "alive."

Solution

Use the system's `ping` command:

```php
<?php
// ping remote host
exec("/bin/ping -c 5 host.name", $output);
echo "<pre>" . join("\r\n", $output) . "</pre>";
?>
```

Comments

The `ping` command, which sends the target host a data packet and checks for a response, is the quickest way to find out if a network host is functional. The previous listing directly calls the system-specific ping command with `exec()` to check a host's status.

> **NOTE**
>
> Remember to alter the path to the `ping` binary so that it is correct for your system.

For OS-independent code, you might prefer to use PEAR's Net_Ping class, freely available from `http://pear.php.net/package/Net_Ping`. This class chooses the appropriate `ping` command for the operating system and executes it with the target host as parameter. A result object is created from the response; this object can be used to access individual elements of the response, such as the response time or latency, or to view the raw output of the command with the `getRawData()` method. Here's an example of it in action:

```php
<?php
// include class
include "Net/Ping.php";

// create object
$ping = Net_Ping::factory();

// ping remote host
// print results
$response = $ping->ping("host.name");
echo "<pre>" . join("\r\n", $response->getRawData()) . "</pre>";
?>
```

11.2 Tracing Network Routes

Problem

You want to trace the route between the current host and a remote host.

Solution

Use the system's `traceroute` command:

```php
<?php
// ping remote host
exec("/usr/bin/traceroute host.name", $output);
echo "<pre>" . join("\r\n", $output) . "</pre>";
?>
```

Comments

The `traceroute` (sometimes called `tracert` on Windows systems) command displays the path a data packet must take in order to arrive at a named remote host.

This command is a good way to measure the Internet distance between two hosts, as well as the time taken to cross that distance. The previous listing directly calls the system's `traceroute` command with `exec()` to obtain this distance. Remember to alter the path to the `traceroute` binary so that it is correct for your system.

For OS-independent code, you might prefer to use PEAR's Net_Traceroute class, freely available from `http://pear.php.net/package/Net_Traceroute`. This class searches the disk for the `traceroute` program for the operating system and executes it with the target host as parameter. A result object is created from the response; this object can be used to access individual elements of the response, or to view the raw output of the command with the `getRawData()` method. Here's an example of it in action:

```php
<?php
// include class
include "Net/Traceroute.php";

// create object
$trace = Net_Traceroute::factory();

// trace route to remote host
// print results
$response = $trace->traceroute("host.name");
echo "<pre>" . join("\r\n", $response->getRawData()) . "</pre>";
?>
```

11.3 Performing WHOIS Queries

Problem

You want to retrieve ownership information for a domain.

Solution

Use PEAR's Net_Whois class:

```php
<?php
// include class
include "Net/Whois.php";

// create object
$whois = new Net_Whois();
```

```php
// perform WHOIS query
// print results
$response = $whois->query("host.name");
echo "<pre>" . $response . "</pre>";
?>
```

Comments

A WHOIS query returns ownership and administrative information for a particular domain. To perform such a query with PHP, use the PEAR Net_Whois class, freely available from `http://pear.php.net/package/Net_Whois`. This class first obtains the registrar of record for the named domain, and then queries that registrar to obtain detailed information on the billing, administrative, and technical contact for that domain.

11.4 Performing DNS Queries

Problem

You want to query the DNS for a domain record.

Solution

Use PEAR's Net_DNS class:

```php
<?php
// include class
include "Net/DNS.php";

// create object
$dns = new Net_DNS_Resolver();

// get IP for host
// print results
$host = "host.name";
$response = $dns->search($host, "MX");
print_r($response);
?>
```

Comments

PEAR's Net_DNS class, freely available from `http://pear.php.net/package/Net_DNS`, is your one-stop Solution for any DNS query operation. The class provides a `search()` method, which accepts a host name or IP address, together with optional type and class identifiers. It then queries the DNS and returns matching DNS records as a series of objects containing the required information. The previous listing illustrates the process of querying the DNS to find the mail exchanger (MX) for a domain.

TIP

By default, Net_DNS uses the default nameserver for queries. You can alter this by specifying one or more nameservers (as an array) in the object constructor.

NOTE

PHP has some built-in functions for DNS queries: `dns_get_record()`, `dns_get_mx()`, `dns_check_record()`, `getmxrr()`, *and* `checkdnsrr()`. *However, these functions are not implemented on the Windows platform and so it's worthwhile to check the PHP manual for compatibility before using them in your code.*

11.5 Mapping Names to IP Addresses

Problem

You want to find the IP address corresponding to a host name, or vice versa.

Solution

Use PHP's `gethostbyname()` and `gethostbyaddr()` functions:

```php
<?php
// get IP for host
$host = "host.name";
echo "$host = " . gethostbyname($host) . "\n";

// get host name for IP
$ip = "127.0.0.1";
echo "$ip = " . gethostbyaddr($ip) . "\n";
?>
```

Comments

PHP's `gethostbyname()` function accepts a domain name and returns the IP address corresponding to that name; the `gethostbyaddr()` function accepts an IP address and returns the corresponding domain name.

An alternative is to use PEAR's Net_DNS class, freely available from `http://pear.php.net/package/Net_DNS`. You can use the class' `search()` method to perform name-to-IP-address translation by querying for an A record, as illustrated here:

```php
<?php
// include class
include "Net/DNS.php";

// create object
$dns = new Net_DNS_Resolver();

// get IP for host
// print results
$host = "host.name";
$response = $dns->search($host, "A");
echo "$host = " . $response->answer[0]->address . "\n";

// get host name for IP
$ip = "127.0.0.1";
$response = $dns->search($host, "A");
echo "$ip = " . $response->answer[0]->name . "\n";
?>
```

11.6 Performing IP-Based Geographic Lookups

Problem

You want to identify a user's current geographic location.

Solution

Use PEAR's Net_GeoIP class in combination with the MaxMind country database to map the user's IP address to a country name:

```php
<?php
// include class
include "Net/GeoIP.php";
```

```
// create object
// set path to country database
$geoip = Net_GeoIP::getInstance("GeoIP.dat");

// print results
echo "IP address: " . getenv('REMOTE_ADDR') . "\n";
echo "Country: " . $geoip->lookupCountryName(getenv('REMOTE_ADDR')) . ↵
"\n";

// print MaxMind compulsory license notice
echo "This product includes GeoIP data created by MaxMind, available ↵
from http://maxmind.com/";
?>
```

Comments

To find out which country and city a user is physically located in, it is necessary to obtain the user's IP address and map it to a country. IP address blocks are assigned to countries by the Internet Assigned Numbers Authority (IANA). So, by identifying the block from which an IP address has been assigned, it's usually possible to identify the user's location.

A number of organizations offer IP-to-country mapping databases for this purpose. MaxMind (`http://www.maxmind.com/`) and NetGeo (`http://www.caida .org/tools/utilities/netgeo/`) are two popular options. The previous listing uses the free MaxMind country database, with PEAR's Net_GeoIP class (`http:// pear.php.net/package/Net_GeoIP`) providing an interface to this database via its `lookupCountryName()` and `lookupCountryCode()` methods.

NOTE

In order to use the Net_GeoIP class, you must first download the MaxMind country database from `http://www.maxmind.com/`.

A common application of IP-based geo-location is to serve targeted advertising to Web site visitors. In this case, the client's IP address is used to identify its current location, and an advertisement relevant to that location is displayed. Here's an example of how this might be done:

```
<html>
<head></head>
<body>
<center>
<?php
// include class
include "Net/GeoIP.php";
```

```
// create object
// set path to country database
$geoip = Net_GeoIP::getInstance("GeoIP.dat");

// get country code
$code = $geoip->lookupCountryCode(getenv('REMOTE_ADDR'));

// retrieve and display image advertisement
// corresponding to country code
echo "<img src=\"images/ads/" . $code . ".gif\" alt=\"banner ad\">\n";

// print MaxMind compulsory license notice
echo "This product includes GeoIP data created by MaxMind,
available from http://maxmind.com/";↵
?>
</center>
</body>
</html>
```

An alternative to the MaxMind GeoIP database is PEAR's Net_Geo class, freely available from `http://pear.php.net/package/Net_Geo`. This class also maps IP addresses to geographic locations and, unlike the MaxMind product, its database provides both city and country information free of charge. The flip side of this: The Net_Geo database is not actively maintained and so is more likely to produce inaccurate results.

Here's an example demonstrating its usage:

```
<?php
// include class
include "Net/Geo.php";

// get location data for requesting
// client IP address
$geo = new Net_Geo();
$data = $geo->getRecord(getenv('REMOTE_ADDR'));

// print results
echo "IP address: " . $data['TARGET'] . "\n";
echo "Owner: " . $data['NAME'] . "\n";
echo "City: " . $data['CITY'] . "\n";
echo "State: " . $data['STATE'] . "\n";
echo "Country: " . $data['COUNTRY'] . " [" . $data['LAT'] .↵
" lat./" . $data['LONG'] . " long.]\n";
?>
```

11.7 Transferring Files over FTP

Problem

You want to upload or download a file over FTP.

Solution

Use PHP's FTP extension:

```php
<?php
// set access parameters
$host = "ftp.some.domain.dom";
$user = "joe";
$pass = "secret";
$dir = "/pub";

// open connection to FTP server
$conn = ftp_connect($host) or die ("ERROR: Cannot connect");

// log in
ftp_login($conn, $user, $pass) or die ("ERROR: Cannot log in");

// get file listing
$list = ftp_nlist($conn, ".") or die("ERROR: Cannot list files");
foreach ($list as $file) {
    echo "$file\n";
}

// download a file
$remote = "code.zip";
$local = "code_020605.zip";
ftp_get($conn, $local, $remote, FTP_BINARY)↵
or die ("ERROR: Cannot download file: $remote");
echo "File [$remote] successfully downloaded as [$local]\n";

// upload a file
$local = "photo556.jpg";
$remote = "photo556.jpg";
ftp_put($conn, $remote, $local, FTP_BINARY)↵
or die ("ERROR: Cannot upload file: $local");
echo "File [$local] successfully uploaded as [$remote]\n";
```

```
// delete a file
$remote = "addresses.tmp";
ftp_delete($conn, $remote) or die ("ERROR: Cannot delete file: $remote");
echo "File [$remote] successfully deleted\n";

// disconnect
ftp_close($conn);
?>
```

Comments

PHP comes with built-in support for the FTP file transfer protocol, making it easy to interface with FTP servers for file transfers. The previous listing illustrates the process. First, a connection to the FTP server is initialized with a call to `ftp_connect()`; this function returns a connection handle that is used in all subsequent calls. The `ftp_login()` function is then used to log in to the server, while the `ftp_close()` function is used to terminate the connection and end the session.

Between the calls to `ftp_connect()` and `ftp_disconnect()`, it is possible to perform all the actions commonly associated with an FTP session. The previous listing illustrates four of the most common: listing files using `ftp_nlist()`; uploading files with `ftp_put()`; downloading files with `ftp_get()`; and deleting files with `ftp_delete()`. Note that `ftp_put()` and `ftp_get()` must be supplied with the remote and local file name, together with the transfer type (binary or ASCII).

11.8 Accessing POP3 Mailboxes

Problem

You want to read and retrieve messages from a POP3-compliant mailbox.

Solution

Use PEAR's Net_POP3 class to connect to and interact with the POP3-compliant mail server:

```
<?php
// include class
include "Net/POP3.php";
```

```php
// set mailbox access parameters
$host = "mail.server.com";
$user = "john";
$pass = "secret";
$port = "110";

// create object
$pop3 =& new Net_POP3();

// connect to host
if(PEAR::isError($ret = $pop3->connect($host, $port))){
    die("ERROR: " . $ret->getMessage());
}

// log in
if(PEAR::isError($ret = $pop3->login($user, $pass, 'USER'))){
    die("ERROR: " . $ret->getMessage());
}

// get number of messages and mailbox size
echo $pop3->numMsg() . " messages in mailbox, " .↵
$pop3->getSize() . " bytes\n\n";

// get message listing
// print message headers and first 300 characters of body
for ($x=1; $x<=$pop3->numMsg(); $x++) {
    $msgData = $pop3->getParsedHeaders($x);
    $msgBody = $pop3->getBody($x);
    echo "To: " . $msgData['To'] . "\n";
    echo "From: " . $msgData['From'] . "\n";
    echo "Subject: " . $msgData['Subject'] . "\n";
    echo "Date: " . $msgData['Date'] . "\n";
    echo "\n" . substr($msgBody, 0, 300) . "...\n";
    echo " -- END OF MESSAGE --";
    echo "\n\n";
}

// delete message #1
$pop3->deleteMsg(1);

// disconnect
$pop3->disconnect();
?>
```

Comments

PEAR's Net_POP3 class, freely available from `http://pear.php.net/package/Net_POP3`, is designed specifically to interact with, and read messages from, POP3 servers. In this illustrative listing, the ball starts rolling with a call to the `connect()` method; this method is passed the POP3 server name and port as arguments. Next, an attempt is made to access the contents of the user's mailbox, using the supplied credentials as input to the `login()` method. If successful, a number of utility methods become available to interact with the mailbox. The session can be terminated at any point with a call to the `disconnect()` method.

The utility functions available include: the `numMsg()` method, which returns the number of messages in the mailbox; the `getSize()` method, which returns the mailbox size in bytes; the `getParsedHeaders()` method, which returns an array of message headers; the `getBody()` method, which returns the message body; the `getMsg()` method, which retrieves the entire message (both header and body); and the `deleteMsg()` method, which deletes an individual message.

11.9 Generating and Sending E-mail

Problem

You want to generate and send an e-mail message.

Solution

Use PHP's `mail()` function:

```php
<?php
// set message headers and body
$to = "Joe Doe <joe.doe@some.domain.com>";
$from = "Paul Froe <paul@dummy>";
$subject = "Happy Birthday!";
$body =<<< END
Hey Joe,
Just wanted to wish you a happy 30th! Have a good one!
Paul
END;
```

```php
// send mail
if (mail($to, $subject, $body, "From: $from")) {
    echo "Message successfully delivered to mail agent";
} else {
    echo "Message could not be delivered to mail agent";
}
?>
```

Comments

PHP's `mail()` function is the simplest way to send e-mail messages from PHP. The function accepts four arguments: the recipient e-mail address, the message subject, the message body, and a series of optional headers separated by the \r\n sequence (among the optional headers, the `From:` header is mandatory). The `mail()` function then hands the message to the local mail agent or the specified SMTP server (see the Note about the Windows implementation of `mail()` in this section for more information on this topic) for delivery. The previous listing illustrates this process.

The return value of `mail()` merely indicates whether or not the message was delivered to the local mail agent/specified SMTP server. It offers no indication of whether or not the message has reached the intended recipient.

You can send the same message to multiple recipients by using a comma-separated recipient list, as illustrated here:

```php
<?php
// set message headers and body
$to = "sarab.b@host.domain, joe.doe@other.domain";
$from = "Paul Froe <paul@dummy>";
$subject = "Happy Birthday!";
$body =<<< END
Hello all,
Just wanted to wish you a happy 30th! Have a good one!
Paul
END;

// send mail
if (mail($to, $subject, $body, "From: $from")) {
    echo "Message successfully delivered to mail agent";
} else {
    echo "Message could not be delivered to mail agent";
}
?>
```

NOTE

In case you thought you could use `mail()` *to send bulk e-mail by iterating over an address list in a loop, think again: because* `mail()` *opens a separate socket connection each time it is invoked, it is inefficient and not at all suited for bulk mail transmission.*

NOTE

Windows and *NIX implementations of PHP differ in the way their `mail()` *function works. In *NIX implementations,* `mail()` *delivers the message to the local mail agent while in Windows implementations,* `mail()` *sends the message via the SMTP server specified in the php.ini file. Also, in Windows implementations, because message headers are parsed by PHP and not the mail agent, the headers must be kept as simple as possible to avoid parsing errors. For example, the PHP manual recommends against the use of* `To:` *and* `From:` *headers in the form* `"User Name <address@domain.com>"`*, as such headers are likely to cause errors.*

For a detailed description of these and other issues, visit the PHP manual at `http://www.php.net/mail`*.*

11.10 Generating and Sending MIME E-mail

Problem

You want to generate and send a multipart MIME e-mail message, such as one containing both plain text and inline HTML.

Solution

Use PEAR's Mail_Mime class:

```php
<?php
// include class
include("Mail.php");
include("Mail/mime.php");

// set message parameters
$to = "Joe Doe <joe.doe@some.domain.com>";
$from = "Paul Froe <paul@dummy>";
$subject = "Warning message";
$text = "Danger! System unstable";
$html = "<html><head></head><body><font color='red'><h2>Danger!</h2>⏎
System unstable!</font></body></html>";
```

```
// create MIME object
// add parts to it
$mime = new Mail_mime();
$mime->setTXTBody($text);
$mime->setHTMLBody($html);

// get composite MIME message body
// send it
$body = $mime->get();
$hdrs = $mime->headers(array('From' => $from, 'Subject' => $subject));
$mail = &Mail::factory('mail');
if (!is_a($mail, 'PEAR_Error')) {
    if ($mail->send($to, $hdrs, $body)) {
        echo "Message successfully delivered to mail agent";
    } else {
        echo "Message could not be delivered to mail agent";
    }
} else {
    die("ERROR: Could not create mail object");
}
?>
```

Comments

The simplest way to generate multipart mail messages is with PEAR's Mail_Mime class, freely available from `http://pear.php.net/package/Mail_Mime`. The previous listing illustrates the process by solving the common problem of building an e-mail message containing both plain text and inline HTML code.

Here, a `Mail_Mime()` message object is created with two parts: a plain-text component and an inline HTML component, attached with the `setTXTBody()` and `setHTMLBody()` methods, respectively. As per the MIME specification, these two parts are then concatenated into a single message (separated by appropriate boundary lines). The composite message body is retrieved with the `get()` method, and the corresponding headers are retrieved with the `headers()` method. The message is then transmitted using PEAR's Mail class (required, and freely available from `http://pear.php.net/package/Mail`).

If you'd like to add inline images to the message body, it's fairly easy to do that as well—simply reference the images in your HTML body, and then add them to the message as attachments with the `addHTMLImage()` method. Here's how:

```php
<?php
// include class
include("Mail.php");
include("Mail/mime.php");

// set message parameters
$to = "Joe Doe <joe.doe@some.domain.com>";
$from = "Paul Froe <paul@dummy>";
$subject = "Warning message";
$text = "Danger! System unstable";
$html = "<html><head></head><body><font color='red'><h2>Danger!</h2>↵
System unstable!</font><p align='center'>↵
<img src='skull.jpg'></p></body></html>";
$file = "skull.jpg";

// create MIME object
// add parts to it
$mime = new Mail_mime();
$mime->setTXTBody($text);
$mime->setHTMLBody($html);
$mime->addHTMLImage($file);

// get composite MIME message body
// send it
$body = $mime->get();
$hdrs = $mime->headers(array('From' => $from, 'Subject' => $subject));
$mail = &Mail::factory('mail');
if (!is_a($mail, 'PEAR_Error')) {
    if ($mail->send($to, $hdrs, $body)) {
        echo "Message successfully delivered to mail agent";
    } else {
        echo "Message could not be delivered to mail agent";
    }
} else {
    die("ERROR: Could not create mail object");
}
?>
```

11.11 Generating and Sending E-mail with Attachments

Problem

You want to generate and send an e-mail message with one or more file attachments.

Solution

Use PEAR's Mail_Mime class:

```php
<?php
// include classes
include("Mail.php");
include("Mail/mime.php");

// set message parameters
$to = "Joe Doe <joe.doe@some.domain.com>";
$from = "Paul Froe <paul@dummy>";
$subject = "Knock knock";
$text = "Hey, here's that file you wanted.";
$file = "knock.zip";

// create MIME object
// add parts to it
$mime = new Mail_mime();
$mime->setTXTBody($text);
$mime->addAttachment($file);

// get composite MIME message body/headers
// send it
$body = $mime->get();
$hdrs = $mime->headers(array('From' => $from, 'Subject' => $subject));
$mail = &Mail::factory('mail');
if (!is_a($mail, 'PEAR_Error')) {
    if ($mail->send($to, $hdrs, $body)) {
        echo "Message successfully delivered to mail agent";
    } else {
        echo "Message could not be delivered to mail agent";
    }
} else {
    die("ERROR: Could not create mail object");
}
?>
```

Comments

When you're generating multipart messages, it's a good idea to use PEAR's Mail_ Mime class, freely available from `http://pear.php.net/package/Mail_ Mime`. This class significantly simplifies the creation of complex messages, including messages containing one or more attachments.

The previous listing illustrates the process. First, a `Mail_Mime()` message object is created, and the plain-text body is added to it with the `setTXTBody()` method. Next, a file is attached with the `addAttachment()` method; you can call this method again to add more files. The composite MIME message body and headers are then generated with calls to the `get()` and `headers()` methods, and PEAR's Mail class (required, and freely available from `http://pear.php.net/package/Mail`) is then used to transmit the composite message to the mail agent or SMTP host.

11.12 Parsing Comma-Separated Files

Problem

You want to extract the individual elements of a file containing comma-separated data.

Solution

Use PHP's `fgetcsv()` function:

```php
<?php
// set CSV file
$file = "data.csv";

// open file
$fp = fopen($file, "rb") or die("Cannot open file");

// iterate through file
// retrieve and print each field
while (!feof($fp)) {
    $line = fgetcsv($fp, 1024, ',', '"');
    echo "Author: " . $line[1] . " " . $line[0] . "\n";
    echo "Title: " . $line[2] . "\n";
    echo "Price: $" . $line[3]. "\n\n";
}
```

```
// close file
fclose($fp) or die("Cannot close file");
?>
```

Comments

Just as the `fgets()` function returns a single line from a file, so too does PHP's `fgetcsv()` function parse and return a single record from a comma-separated (CSV) file. The `fgetcsv()` function accepts three arguments: the file pointer, the amount of data to read, and (optionally) the field delimiter and enclosure. Using this information, it reads and parses a line from the file, storing the fields as array elements. Placed in a loop, this process continues until all the records in the file have been read.

The previous listing assumes a data file containing multiple records (rows), each with four fields (columns), separated by commas and enclosed in double quotes, like this:

```
"King","Stephen","Insomnia","7.99"
"Lehane","Dennis","Darkness, Take My Hand","6.99"
"Patterson", "Richard North", "Conviction", "14.99"
"Parker", "Robert B.", "Cold Service", "16.99"
```

After parsing the file with `fgetcsv()`, the result looks like this:

```
Author: Stephen King
Title: Insomnia
Price: $7.99

Author: Dennis Lehane
Title: Darkness, Take My Hand
Price: $6.99

Author: Richard North Patterson
Title: Conviction
Price: $14.99

Author: Robert B. Parker
Title: Cold Service
Price: $16.99
```

11.13 Converting Between ASCII File Formats

Problem

You want to convert an ASCII file for use on a UNIX, MS-DOS, or Macintosh system.

Solution

Write a function to alter the file's line ending character, thereby making it readable on the target platform:

```php
<?php
// function to convert file type
// by altering the line endings
function convertFile($file, $from, $to) {
        // define line endings for each platform
        $ends = array("UNIX" => "\n", "MSDOS" => "\r\n", "MAC" => "\r");

        // check to avoid unknown formats
        if (!array_key_exists($from, $ends) || !array_key_exists($to,⏎
$ends)) {
                die ("Cannot recognize file format");
        }

        // read file contents into string
        $str = file_get_contents($file) or die ("Cannot read from file");

        // alter line endings
        $str = preg_replace("/" . $ends[$from] . "/", $ends[$to], $str);

        // rewrite contents to file
        file_put_contents($file, $str) or die("Cannot write to file");
}

// convert file from UNIX to MS-DOS format
convertFile("data.asc", "UNIX", "MSDOS");
?>
```

Comments

You've probably noticed that text files created on UNIX appear on a single line when viewed in Windows-only text editors. This problem arises because UNIX and Windows use a different sequence of characters to mark the end of a line—UNIX uses the \n character, while Windows uses the \r\n sequence. Macintosh systems add another dimension to the puzzle—they use \r as the line ending character.

To solve the problem, all that's really needed is to alter the line ending character so that it is compatible with the target platform. That's what the convertFile() function in the previous listing does—it reads the named file into a string with the file_get_contents() function, uses preg_replace() to find and replace all occurrences of the current line ending character with a more suitable one, and writes the result back to the file with the file_put_contents() function. The original and desired file formats are passed to the function by means of the $from and $to input arguments.

11.14 Creating PDF Files

Problem

You want to dynamically generate a PDF file.

Solution

Use PHP's PDF extension:

```php
<?php
// create PDF document object
$pdf = pdf_new();

// open PDF file
pdf_open_file($pdf, "screenplay.pdf");

// begin page
pdf_begin_page($pdf, 595, 842);

// get and use a font
$courier = pdf_load_font($pdf, "Courier", "host", "");
pdf_setfont($pdf, $courier, 10);
```

```
// write text
pdf_show_xy($pdf, "No one can tell you what the Matrix is, Neo.", ↵
50, 750);
pdf_show_xy($pdf, "You must see it for yourself.", 50, 730);

// add an image
$image = pdf_load_image($pdf, "jpeg", "matrix.jpg", "");
pdf_place_image($pdf, $image, 50, 650, 0.25);

// end page
pdf_end_page($pdf);

// close and save file
pdf_close($pdf);
?>
```

Comments

PHP's PDF extension makes it possible to dynamically generate PDF files on the fly. The previous listing illustrates the process, beginning by creating a PDF object with a call to `pdf_new()`. Once an object has been initialized, a file name is set with `pdf_open_file()`, and a new document page is generated with `pdf_begin_page()`. A font object is selected and prepared for use with `pdf_findfont()` and `pdf_setfont()`; an image is retrieved from a disk location and written to the page with `pdf_open_image_file()` and `pdf_place_image()`; and a text string is written to a particular (x, y) page coordinate with `pdf_show_xy()`. The `pdf_end_page()` function marks the end of the page, while the `pdf_close()` function saves the file to disk and destroys the PDF object.

It's also possible to dynamically generate the PDF file and have it appear in the user's browser, assuming a correctly configured PDF reader on the client. In this variant, `pdf_open_file()` is called with a null file name, and the PDF buffer is dumped to the client via a call to `pdf_get_buffer()`, with appropriate headers to trigger the client's PDF reader. The following listing illustrates this:

```
<?php
// create PDF document object
$pdf = pdf_new();

// open PDF file
pdf_open_file($pdf, "");

// begin page
pdf_begin_page($pdf, 595, 842);
```

```
// get and use a font
$courier = pdf_load_font($pdf, "Courier", "host", "");
pdf_setfont($pdf, $courier, 10);

// write text
pdf_show_xy($pdf, "No one can tell you what the Matrix is, Neo.", ↵
50, 750);
pdf_show_xy($pdf, "You must see it for yourself.", 50, 730);

// add an image
$image = pdf_load_image($pdf, "jpeg", "matrix.jpg", "");
pdf_place_image($pdf, $image, 50, 650, 0.25);

// end page
pdf_end_page($pdf);

// close and save file
pdf_close($pdf);

// get PDF buffer
$buffer = pdf_get_buffer($pdf);

// output to browser
header("Content-type: application/pdf");
header("Content-Length: " . strlen($buffer));
header("Content-Disposition: inline; filename=screenplay.pdf");
print $buffer;
?>
```

NOTE

In order for this listing to work, PHP must be compiled with support for ext/pdf *(you can obtain instructions from the PHP manual at* http://www.php.net/pdf*).*

TIP

On Windows, you must use absolute paths in order for the listings in this section to work correctly.

11.15 Creating ZIP Archives

Problem

You want to dynamically create a ZIP archive.

Solution

Use PHP's `ext/zip` extension:

```php
<?php
// create object
$zip = new ZipArchive();

// open output file for writing
if ($zip->open("/tmp/www.zip", ZIPARCHIVE::CREATE) !== TRUE) {
    die ("Could not create archive");
}

// add all .php files in directory to archive
foreach (glob ('*.php') as $f) {
    $zip->addFile(realpath($f)) or die ("Could not add file: $f");
}

// close and save archive
$zip->close();
echo "Archive created successfully.";
?>
```

Comments

PHP 5.1 and later includes `ext/zip`, an extension that supports reading and writing compressed ZIP archives using native PHP function calls. The previous listing illustrates how it may be used to create a ZIP archive. After initializing a new instance of the ZipArchive class, the instance's `open()` method is used to create a new archive, and the `addFile()` method is then used to add files to the archive. Once all the files have been added, the instance's `close()` method takes care of compressing and writing the archive to disk.

NOTE

In order for this listing to work, PHP must be compiled with support for `ext/zip` (you can obtain instructions from the PHP manual at `http://www.php.net/zip`).

Users with older versions of PHP will need to use PEAR's Archive_Zip package, freely available from `http://pear.php.net/package/Archive_Zip`, which lets you create new ZIP archives, add or remove files to existing archives, and extract and list archive contents. The following listing illustrates the process of creating a new ZIP archive, first initializing an instance of the Archive_Zip class and then populating an array with the names of files to be added to it. The instance's create() method is then used to actually compress the files into a ZIP archive and save it to disk.

```php
<?php
// include class
include "Archive/Zip.php";

// create object
// specify filename for output file
$zip = new Archive_Zip("www.zip");

// recursively process directories
// add to file array
$iterator = new RecursiveIteratorIterator(⌐
new RecursiveDirectoryIterator("files/"));
foreach ($iterator as $key->$value) {
    $files[] = $iterator->getPathname();
}

// build archive
$zip->create($files) or die("Could not create archive!");
echo "Archive created successfully.";
?>
```

The Archive_Zip class also exposes extract(), listContent(), add(), delete(), and merge() methods—no prizes for guessing what these do!

11.16 Creating TAR Archives

Problem

You want to dynamically create a TAR archive.

Solution

Use PEAR's Archive_Tar class:

```php
<?php
// include class
include "Archive/Tar.php";

// create object
// specify filename for output file
$tar = new Archive_Tar("www.tar");

// recursively process directories
// add to file array
$iterator = new RecursiveIteratorIterator(new ↵
RecursiveDirectoryIterator("files/"));
foreach ($iterator as $key=>$value) {
    $files[] = $iterator->getPathname();
}

// build archive
$tar->create($files) or die("Could not create archive!");
echo "Archive created successfully.";
?>
```

Comments

PEAR's Archive_Tar package, freely available from `http://pear.php.net/`
`package/Archive_Tar`, is particularly helpful for creating files in the Tar (Tape
Archive) format. To use this package, first create an instance of the Archive_Tar class
(passing the name of the output TAR file to the object constructor) and then invoke
the instance's `create()` method with an array containing a file list. The object will
then create a single archive containing all the listed files and save it to disk.

You can extract files from the archive by calling the object's `extract()` method,
or view the contents of an existing archive with the object's `listContent()`
method.

TIP

*If you'd like to create a compressed archive, Archive_Tar supports that option too, allowing you
to apply GZIP or BZIP compression to the TAR archive. To do this, simply add the value `"gz"` or
`"bz2"` as a second argument to the Archive_Tar object constructor when instantiating it. Note
that your PHP build must include support for the `zlib` and `bzip2` compression libraries for
this to work.*

TIP

Read a detailed tutorial on Archive_Tar at `http://www.melonfire.com/`
`community/columns/trog/article.php?id=273.`

11.17 Resizing Images

Problem

You want to dynamically resize and render an image, such as a digital photo in
a Web-based image gallery.

Solution

Use PHP's `imagecopyresampled()` function:

```php
<?php
// define image to resize
$file = "img1154.jpg";

// create object from original image
$imOrig = imagecreatefromjpeg($file);

// get image dimensions
list($width, $height) = getimagesize($file);

// create object for new image
$imNew = imagecreatetruecolor($width * 1.5, $height * 1.5);

// resample and resize old image
imagecopyresampled($imNew, $imOrig, 0, 0, 0, 0, $width * 1.5,
$height * 1.5, $width, $height);

// output resized image
header("Content-type: image/jpeg");
imagejpeg($imNew);
imagedestroy($im);
?>
```

Comments

PHP's image manipulation toolkit contains the `imagecopyresampled()` function, which can be used to alter an image's dimensions and resample it for the new size. This ability to dynamically resize images is particularly handy for Web-based photo galleries, which often need to display photos of varying sizes in a uniform format.

   The previous listing illustrates the process. First, an object representing the original image is created from the image file with the `imagecreatefromjpeg()` function, and its dimensions are calculated. Next, a second object is created to represent the new resized image, and set to 150 percent of the original image size. The `imagecopyresampled()` function then takes care of copying the original (large) image to the new (larger) image, resampling it along the way to maintain fidelity to the original version. The resampled and resized image can now be transmitted to the browser with the `imagejpeg()` function for display.

11.18 Working with Image Metadata

Problem

You want to extract the descriptive information embedded in an image, such as the metadata or thumbnails placed in digital photos.

Solution

Use PHP's Exchangeable Image File Format (EXIF) functions:

```php
<?php
// define directory path
$dir = "canon";

// scan directory for matching files
// extract EXIF information from each
// and display
$fileList = glob("$dir/*.jpg");
if (sizeof($fileList) > 0) {
    foreach ($fileList as $file) {
        $exif = exif_read_data($file, 0, true);
        echo "File: $file\n";
```

```
        foreach ($exif as $section => $data) {
            foreach ($data as $key => $value) {
                echo "$section -> $key = $value\n";
            }
        }
        echo "\n";
    }
}
?>
```

Comments

EXIF is a standard for storing descriptive metadata in image files, particularly JPEG and TIFF files. The format is commonly used by digital camera vendors to embed descriptive information in the headers of digital photos. PHP's exif_read_data() function can read these headers and extract the information stored within them. The previous listing illustrates the process.

A common application of PHP's EXIF support involves extracting an image thumbnail from the EXIF metadata in a digital photo, and using this thumbnail in a Web-based image gallery to preview the actual image. This can be easily accomplished with the exif_thumbnail() function, illustrated here:

```php
<?php
// define directory path
$dir = "canon";

// if file name is provided
// read image thumbnail from file
// send to browser for display
if ($_GET['file']) {
    $file = $_GET['file'];
    $image = exif_thumbnail("$dir/$file");
    if ($image !== false) {
        header("Content-type: image/jpeg");
        echo $image;
    }
// if no file name is provided
// scan directory and list all matching files
// with thumbnails
} else {
    $fileList = glob("$dir/*.jpg");
    if (sizeof($fileList) > 0) {
```

```
    echo "<html> <head></head> <body>\n";
        foreach ($fileList as $file) {
            echo "<img src='" . $_SERVER['PHP_SELF']⏎ .
"?file=" . basename($file) . "'>\n";
            echo "<br />" . basename($file) . "<p />\n";
        }
    echo "</body></html>";
    }
}
?>
```

Here the script checks the named directory for JPEG files and, if available, displays them in a list. Accompanying each file name is a thumbnail of the image, generated by the same script from the EXIF headers. The thumbnail is extracted from the image with the `exif_thumbnail()` function, and sent to the browser with an appropriate content header for display.

> **NOTE**
>
> In order for this listing to work, PHP must be compiled with support for `ext/exif` and `ext/mbstring`. (You can obtain instructions from the PHP manual at `http://www.php.net/exif`.)

11.19 Monitoring Web Pages

Problem

You want to monitor a Web page for changes.

Solution

Periodically calculate a checksum for the page and send notification in the event of a change:

```php
<?php
// set database name (SQLite)
$db = "webmon.db";

// set notification e-mail address
$email = "user@localhost";
```

```
// open database file
$handle = sqlite_open($db) or die ("ERROR: Cannot open database");

// create and execute SELECT query
$sql = "SELECT url, md5 FROM urls";
$result = sqlite_query($handle, $sql)↵
or die ("ERROR: " . sqlite_error_string(sqlite_last_error($handle)) ↵
. " (query was $sql)");

// check for records
if (sqlite_num_rows($result) > 0) {
    while(list($url, $oldMD5) = sqlite_fetch_array($result)) {
        // read URL contents
        // generate new checksum and compare with old
        $contents = join ('', file($url));
        $newMD5 = md5($contents);
        if ($oldMD5 != $newMD5)      {
            // send notification e-mail for changes
            mail($email, "URL Change Notification", "The URL \"$url\ ↵
" has changed since it was last checked.", "From: Web Monitor ↵
<null@localhost>") or die ("ERROR: Cannot send mail");

            // update database with new MD5
            $sql = "UPDATE urls SET md5='$newMD5' WHERE url='$url'";
            sqlite_query($handle, $sql) ↵
or die ("ERROR: " . sqlite_error_string(sqlite_last_error($handle)) ↵
. " (query was $sql)");
        }
    }
} else {
    echo "No records found";
}

// close database file
sqlite_close($handle);
?>
```

Comments

To find out if a particular Web page has changed, calculate a checksum for its contents on a periodic basis and test it against the checksum you created previously. A difference between the two is a clear indication that the Web page has changed since it was last checked.

The previous listing puts this in practice, using a SQLite database to store a list of URLs and their associated checksums (the code to create the SQLite database used in this listing can be obtained from this book's Web site at http://www.php-programming-solutions.com). The previous script queries the database for the list of URLs, reads them in with file(), and calculates a checksum with the md5() function. This MD5 value is then checked against the stored MD5 value for the URL. If there is a difference, it means the content at the URL has changed since it was last checked; this triggers an e-mail alert, and the new MD5 value is saved back to the database in preparation for the next run.

TIP

For automated Web page monitoring, set this script to run daily from your system's cron *table or task scheduler.*

Working with Exceptions and Other Miscellanea

IN THIS CHAPTER:

P HP comes with a full-featured exception handling API, allowing you to wrap your code in try-catch blocks that neatly and efficiently catch and resolve errors. This exception model, new since PHP 5.0, also enables you replace PHP's default exception handling mechanisms with your own custom-crafted alternatives.

This chapter, the last in the book, is broadly classified into two parts. The first discusses common problems related to the aforementioned exception handling and error processing mechanism, while the second serves as a grab bag of solutions for problems that didn't fit in any other chapter. Thus, in addition to finding out how to control the display of error messages and write your own exception handler, you'll also learn how to profile and benchmark your PHP scripts; execute external programs from within PHP; alter the PHP configuration at run time; create compiled PHP bytecode; and create localized PHP applications.

12.1 Handling Exceptions

Problem

You want to recover from exceptions generated by a code block.

Solution

Enclose the code in a `try-catch` block:

```php
<?php
// turn off error messages
error_reporting(E_NONE);

// try this code
try {
    // open file
    if (!$fh = fopen("somefile.txt", "r")) {
        throw new Exception("Could not open file!", 12);
    }

    // read file contents
    if (!$data = fread($fh, filesize("somefile.txt"))) {
        throw new Exception("Could not read file!", 9);
    }
```

```
    // close file
    fclose($fh);

    // print file contents
    echo $data;

// catch errors if any
} catch (Exception $e) {
    echo "Exception! \n";
    echo "Error message: " . $e->getMessage() . " \n";
    echo "Error code: " . $e->getCode() . " \n";
    echo "File and line: " . $e->getFile() . ⏎
"(" . $e->getLine() . ") \n";
    echo "Trace: " . $e->getTraceAsString() . " \n";
}
?>
```

Comments

To use PHP's exception handling model, it is necessary to wrap your program code in Java-style `try-catch` blocks. Here's what a typical `try-catch` block looks like:

```
try {
      execute this block
} catch (exception type 1) {
      execute this block to resolve exception type 1
} catch (exception type 2) {
      execute this block to resolve exception type 2
}     ... and so on ...
```

When PHP encounters code enclosed in such a `try-catch` block, it first attempts to execute the code within the `try` block. If this code is processed without any exceptions being generated, control transfers to the lines following the `try-catch` block. However, if an exception is generated while running the code within the `try` block, PHP stops execution of the block at that point and begins checking each `catch` block to see if there is a handler for the exception. If a handler is found, the code within the appropriate `catch` block is executed; if not, a fatal error is generated.

This approach is illustrated in the previous listing, where exceptions are generated at two stages: first if the file in question cannot be opened, and second if the file's contents cannot be read. In either case, an exception will be generated, and control will pass to the following `catch` block, which will generate an error message. To avoid multiple error messages, PHP's `error_reporting()` function is used to ensure that internal error messages, including fatal errors, are hidden from view; this ensures that the user only sees what the exception handler generates.

The exceptions themselves are generated via PHP's throw statement. The throw statement needs to be passed the exception type, a descriptive message, and an optional error code. When the exception is raised, this description and code will be made available to the exception handler. This is illustrated in the previous listing, where the Exception's getMessage(), getCode(), getFile(), getLine(), and getTraceAsString() methods are used to generate useful information on what went wrong.

12.2 Defining Custom Exceptions

Problem

You want to define your own exceptions, and have each handled in a different way.

Solution

Define new exception types by subclassing the base Exception object, and use multiple catch blocks to customize how each is handled:

```php
<?php
// turn off error messages
error_reporting(E_NONE);

// subclass the Exception class
class LenException extends Exception {}
class NameException extends Exception {}
class UniqueException extends Exception {}

// function to test a password
function changePassword($str) {
    // password too short
    // trigger an exception
    if(strlen($str) < 8)  {
        throw new LenException($str);
    }

    // password contains user name
    // trigger an exception
    if (isset($_SESSION['uname'])) {
        if (ereg($_SESSION['uname'], $str)) {
            throw new NameException($str);
        }
    }
```

```
        // password contains insufficient unique characters
        // trigger an exception
        if(strlen(count_chars($str, 3)) < 6) {
            throw new UniqueException($str);
        }

        echo "Your password was successfully changed ($str).";
    }

// try this code
try {
    changePassword("h3llo");        // too short
    changePassword("g5gg3gh3");     // not enough uniques
    changePassword("h46wkd3g8");    // acceptable
    // catch errors if any
} catch (LenException $e) {
    print "The password supplied is too short (" . $e->getMessage() .↵
"). Please provide a password containing at least 8 characters.";
} catch (NameException $e) {
    print "The password supplied is based on your username. (" .↵
$e->getMessage() . "). Please provide a different password.";
} catch (UniqueException $e) {
    print "The password supplied does not contain a sufficient number ↵
of unique characters (" . $e->getMessage() . "). Please provide a ↵
password containing at least 6 unique characters";
} catch (Exception $e) {
    echo "Exception! \n";
    echo "Error message: " . $e->getMessage() . " \n";
    echo "Error code: " . $e->getCode() . " \n";
    echo "File and line: " . $e->getFile() . "(" . $e->getLine() . ↵
") \n";
    echo "Trace: " . $e->getTraceAsString() . " \n";
}
?>
```

Comments

Different exceptions may need to be handled in different ways—for example, a file access error should be treated differently than an error in an SQL query. PHP enables you to customize how exceptions are handled, by subclassing the generic Exception object and using multiple `catch` blocks, one for each subclass, to handle each one in a different way.

The previous listing illustrates this, by extending the base Exception object to create three new exception classes: `LenException()`, `NameException()`, and `UniqueException()`. Multiple `catch` blocks define a different error message for each exception; depending on which of these exceptions is generated, the appropriate `catch` block is activated and the corresponding error message printed.

NOTE

In the previous listing, once an exception is generated, control will pass to the following `catch` *block. Thus, in order to see the various exception types in action in this example, you will need to manually comment out the first call to* `changePassword()` *before the next one will be executed.*

TIP

A `catch` *block will be triggered by the first matching exception, so you should always arrange your* `catch` *blocks with the most specific ones first. That's why the previous listing has the* `catch` *block for the generic Exception object listed last.*

12.3 Using a Custom Exception Handler

Problem

You want to handle exceptions yourself, rather than having them handled by PHP.

Solution

Write a user-defined function to handle exceptions, and then tell PHP about it with the `set_exception_handler()` function:

```php
<?php
// custom exception handler
function exh($e) {
    // when an exception is caught
    // erase all previously-generated output
    ob_end_clean() or die("Cannot erase output buffer");

    // construct the error string
    $timestamp = date("d-m-Y H:i:s", mktime());
    $errorStr  = "$timestamp ". get_class($e) . ": ";
```

```php
    $errorStr .= $e->getMessage() . " in ";
    $errorStr .= $e->getFile() . "(line " . $e->getLine() . ")\n";

    // log the error to a file
    error_log($errorStr, 3, "error_log") or↵
die("Cannot write to error log");

    // display error message as output
    echo "This is the custom exception handler. Something went wrong,↵
which is why you're meeting me. Give the webmaster a call and ask↵
him to check the error log for [$timestamp]";
}

// turn off error reporting
error_reporting(E_NONE);

// start output buffering
ob_start();

// set a custom handler for all exceptions
set_exception_handler("exh");

// sub-class exception
class LoadException extends Exception { }
class DBException extends Exception { }

// load SQLite extenstion
if (!extension_loaded("sqlite")) {
    if(!dl("php_sqlite.dll")) {
        throw new LoadException("Cannot load extension ↵
file: php_sqlite.dll");
    }
}

// open connection
if (!$handle = sqlite_open('products.db')) {
    throw new DBException("Cannot connect to SQLite database");
}

// create and execute INSERT query
$sql = "INSERT INTO products (id, name) VALUES ('5', 'pears')";
if (!sqlite_query($handle, $sql)) {
    throw new DBException("Cannot execute SQL query [$sql] " ↵
```

```
    . sqlite_error_string(sqlite_last_error($handle)));
}

// close connection
sqlite_close($handle);
echo "SQLite transaction successfully completed";
?>
```

Comments

PHP enables you to divert all exceptions to a custom function that you define instead of sending them to the default exception handler. You must set this custom function up to accept an Exception object as input; you can then process this object whatever way you choose.

The previous listing illustrates how this might work. First, PHP error display is turned off, and output buffering is turned on. Two new exception types are defined by subclassing the base Exception object, and the set_exception_handler() function is used to notify PHP that all exceptions are to be sent to the user-defined function exh().

Next, an attempt is made to load the SQLite extension, connect to an SQLite database, add a new record, and exit. Any exceptions thrown during this process will be handled not by PHP, but by the user-defined function exh(). When this function is invoked, it first clears the output buffer (to ensure that no stray output is sent to the browser or console), and then uses PHP's error_log() function to save details about the exception (including the exception name, message, script name, and line number) to a log file. Given that the output buffer is now empty and it's generally considered a Bad Thing to leave the user staring at an empty screen, the handler also prints a brief error message to the output device before exiting.

Of course, this is just one example—you could just as easily write a custom exception handler that (a) saved exception information to a database; (b) e-mailed it to an administrator; (c) wrote it to the system logger; or (d) or did all of the above. Using the set_exception_handler() function to divert exceptions to your own handler gives you complete flexibility in how exceptions in your applications are handled, and it is very useful in building a professional application.

TIP

Make sure that the definition of the custom exception handler precedes the call to set_exception_handler()*.*

12.4 Suppressing Error Display

Problem

You want to prevent PHP from displaying error messages.

Solution

Use the @ error-suppression operator before a function call:

```php
<?php
// call a function that returns a warning
// suppress warning with @
echo @file_get_contents("non-existent-file.txt");
?>
```

Or, set PHP's error reporting level to E_NONE:

```php
<?php
// suppress all error messages (except fatal errors)
error_reporting(E_ERROR);

// call a function without required arguments
echo strrev();
?>
```

Comments

Prefixing the @ operator to a function invocation suppresses any error messages that function might generate. However, this @ operator should only be used as a last resort in production code, as it can create a great deal of confusion when you're trying to track down bugs at a later date.

A more general approach to error display might be to set PHP's global error reporting level to E_ERROR, which turns off the display of all non-fatal errors. However, parse errors, which occur due to syntactical errors in PHP code, cannot be controlled via this setting, and will continue to display regardless of the error reporting level.

You can turn off the display of all errors (including fatal errors) by setting the error reporting level to E_NONE, as in the following example:

```php
<?php
// suppress all error messages (except parse errors)
error_reporting(E_NONE);
```

```
// call a non-existent function
// returns a fatal error and stops script processing
// error message is suppressed
echo file_mangle("non-existent-file.txt");
?>
```

Although the previous script will not display a visible error message, script execution will still stop at the point of error and statements subsequent to that point will not be executed (possibly leaving the user facing a blank screen). All error_reporting() does is permit control over which errors are displayed; it doesn't prevent them from being generated in the first place.

It must also be noted that suppressing the display of fatal errors, as with E_NONE in the previous listing, is a Bad Thing. It is poor programming practice to hide and ignore errors in this manner; it is far better—and more professional—to anticipate the likely errors ahead of time, and write defensive code that watches for them and handles them appropriately.

TIP

During your development process, go to the other extreme and set PHP's global error reporting level to E_ALL—the highest error reporting level—as this is useful for debugging your code.

12.5 Customizing Error Display

Problem

You want to control the manner in which errors are displayed.

Solution

Divert errors to a user-defined function, set with the set_error_handler() function:

```php
<?php
// custom error handler
function eh ($type, $msg, $file, $line) {
    // construct the error string
    $errorStr = "Date: " . date("d-m-Y H:i:s", mktime()) . "\n";
    $errorStr .= "Error type: $type\n";
```

```
        $errorStr .= "Error message: $msg\n";
        $errorStr .= "Script: $file($line)\n";
        $errorStr .= "Host: " . $_SERVER['HTTP_HOST'] . "\n";
        $errorStr .= "Client: " . $_SERVER['HTTP_USER_AGENT'] . "\n";
        $errorStr .= "Client IP: " . $_SERVER['REMOTE_ADDR'] . "\n";
        $errorStr .= "Request URI: " . $_SERVER['REQUEST_URI'] . "\n\n";

        // display error message
        echo nl2br("Due to an internal error, this script has been ↵
terminated. The following lines display more information on the error: ↵
\n\n $errorStr");

        // end the script
        exit();
}

// define a custom handler for errors
set_error_handler("eh");

// generate a warning
echo file_get_contents("non-existent-file.txt");
?>
```

Comments

PHP's set_error_handler() function can be used to define a custom function, to which all notices and warning messages are automatically sent. This function must be capable of accepting a minimum of two mandatory arguments (the error type and corresponding descriptive message) and up to three additional arguments (the file name and line number where the error occurred and a dump of the variable space at the time of error).

In the previous listing, this user-defined function is named eh(), and when it receives an error, it constructs a simple error message containing information on the time, type, and location of error. This information is then combined with various server environment variables (the client type and IP address, the URL being requested) and displayed to the user.

TIP

Make sure that the definition of the custom error handler precedes the call to set_error_
handler()*.*

It's worth noting, however, that the technique outlined above is only suitable for catching notices and warnings; it cannot be used for fatal errors or parse errors. While parse errors cannot be intercepted due to their very nature, it's possible to use PHP's output buffering functions to catch fatal errors.

The technique essentially consists of initializing an output buffer to hold page content and examining this buffer for error strings before sending it to the client. If no error strings are present, the page may safely be sent as is; if error strings *are* present, the contents of the output buffer can be replaced with a customized error message. The following listing illustrates the code for this technique:

```php
<?php
// custom output buffer handler
function oh($buf) {
    // if buffer contains "fatal error" string
    // construct the error string and display it
    if (preg_match("/Fatal error<\/b>: (.+)/", $buf)) {
        return "This script generated a fatal error and has been ⏎
terminated with extreme prejudice.";
    } else {
        return $buf;
    }
}

// define a custom output handler
ob_start("oh");

// generate a fatal error
abc();
?>
```

Here, a user-defined output handling function, oh(), is called before the contents of the output buffer are sent to the client. This function scans the buffer for "Fatal error" strings and, if found, replaces the buffer with a customized error message. If no such strings are found, the buffer is returned as is to the client.

12.6 Logging Errors

Problem

You want to log error messages or events to a file.

Solution

Use PHP's `error_log()` function:

```php
<?php
$arr = array("chocolate", "strawberry", "peach");
if (!in_array('fish', $arr)) {
    // log error to file
    error_log("No fish available", 3, "error_log");

    // log error to system logger
    error_log("No fish available", 0);

    // log error to e-mail address
    error_log("No fish available", 1, "my.address@my.domain",↵
"From: root@localhost");
    exit();
}
?>
```

Comments

PHP's `error_log()` function is designed to send log messages to different destinations, including a log file, an e-mail address, or the system logger. The function accepts two mandatory arguments—the log message and an integer indicating the destination—and one or more optional arguments, depending on the destination. An integer value of 0 indicates that the message should be sent to the system logging device; a value of 1 indicates that the message should be sent to an e-mail address, with the address and extra headers specified as third and fourth arguments, respectively; a value of 2 indicates that the message should be sent to a remote debugger; and a value of 3 sends the message to a file, with the file location specified as the third parameter.

An alternative to the `error_log()` function is PEAR's Log package, freely available from `http://pear.php.net/package/Log`. This package supports the sending of log messages to even more destinations: a file, an e-mail address, an SQL database, the system logger, and the PHP console. Here's an example of it in action:

```php
<?php
// include class
include "Log.php";

// create Log object
$l = &Log::singleton("file", "my.log");
```

```
// log to file
$arr = array("chocolate", "strawberry", "peach");
if (!in_array("fish", $arr)) {
    $l->log("No fish available", PEAR_LOG_ERR);
}

$conn = @mysql_connect("localhost", "joe", "pass");
if (!$conn){
        $l->log("Could not connect to database in " .↵
$_SERVER["PHP_SELF"], PEAR_LOG_CRIT);
        exit();
}
?>
```

TIP

Notice that the PEAR Log package enables you to specify an optional log level as the second argument to its `log()` *method. This log level may be used to distinguish between critical and non-critical messages, and may be used to filter out high-priority messages from general notices or debug messages. Five different log levels are supported, ranging from notification to critical.*

12.7 Checking Version Information

Problem

You want to find out which version of PHP (or a PHP extension) is in use, perhaps prior to installing your PHP application.

Solution

Use the phpversion() or zend_version() functions to retrieve version information for PHP or the Zend engine:

```
<?php
echo "PHP version: " . phpversion() . " \n";
echo "Zend version: " . zend_version() . " \n";
?>
```

Or, call phpversion() with the extension name as argument to retrieve version information for that extension:

```php
<?php
echo "PHP MySQL library version: " . phpversion('mysql') . " \n";
echo "PHP EXIF library version: " . phpversion('exif') . " \n";
?>
```

Comments

The `phpversion()` function is your one-stop shop to retrieve version information on PHP itself, or any of its extensions. Simply call `phpversion()` to get the current PHP version number, and add an optional extension name argument to get the version number of the corresponding extension.

This function is often used in combination with the `version_compare()` function to check for a minimum PHP version prior to application installation or before calling a relatively new function, as in the next listing:

```php
<?php
// check version
if (!version_compare(phpversion(), '5.2.0', '>=')) {
    die ("You need PHP 5.2.0 or better to run this script. Exiting...");
}
?>
```

> **TIP**
>
> For detailed information on your current PHP build, call `phpinfo()`, as shown here:
> ```php
> <?php
> phpinfo();
> ?>
> ```
> You can also pass `phpinfo()` an additional parameter to customize the output further, grabbing (for example) information on only environment variables, loaded modules, or EGPCS (Environment, Get, Post, Cookies, Server) variables.

12.8 Altering PHP's Run-Time Configuration

Problem

You want to retrieve or alter the value of a PHP configuration variable at run time.

Solution

Use the `ini_get()` function to retrieve the value of a PHP configuration variable:

```php
<?php
// get the value of a PHP configuration variable
echo "The current include path is: " . ini_get('include_path');
?>
```

Use the `ini_set()` function to set or alter the value of a PHP configuration variable at run time:

```php
<?php
// alter the value of a PHP configuration variable
ini_set('max_execution_time', 600);
?>
```

Comments

PHP's `ini_set()` and `ini_get()` functions are commonly used to retrieve or alter the value of PHP variables, such as the script execution timeout or the maximum file upload size, on a per-script basis at run time. The `ini_get()` function accepts the name of a PHP variable and returns its value to the caller; the `ini_set()` function accepts a variable name and value, and sets the variable to that value. The previous listings illustrate how they may be used.

Note that settings changed via `ini_set()` are only valid for the duration of the script in which they are made; once the script terminates, the global value of the variable, as set in the *php.ini* configuration file, again takes precedence.

12.9 Checking Loaded Extensions

Problem

You want to check if a particular PHP extension is loaded before using it in a script.

Solution

Use PHP's `extension_loaded()` function:

```php
<?php
// check if extension is loaded
if (!extension_loaded("mysqli")) {
```

```
        die ("MySQLi extension not loaded, terminating...");
}

// if loaded, attempt connection
$conn = @mysqli_connect("localhost", "user", "pass", "db1")↵
or die("Unable to connect");
unset($conn);
?>
```

Comments

To avoid nasty error messages about undefined functions, it's always a good idea to check for the presence of a particular extension before using it in your scripts. PHP's `extension_loaded()` function accepts the name of an extension, and returns a Boolean value indicating whether or not it is available for use. The previous listing illustrates an example of how it may be used to check for the presence of `ext/mysqli`, terminating the script if the extension is not loaded.

> **NOTE**
>
> The `extension_loaded()` function must be supplied with the internal PHP name for an extension, rather than its file name (the two are often different, especially on Windows systems). You can obtain this list of names by calling the PHP binary with the `-m` option.

12.10 Using Strict Standards

Problem

You want to verify if a PHP script is written for maximum interoperability and forward compatibility.

Solution

Set PHP's error reporting level to `E_STRICT`:

```
<?php
// turn on strict standards
error_reporting(E_STRICT);

// execute some code
echo date("Y-m-d", mktime());
?>
```

Comments

When set to E_STRICT, PHP inspects your code at run time and automatically generates recommendations about how it may be improved. Using E_STRICT can often provide a heads-up on functions that will break in a future version of PHP, and, as such, using it is recommended to improve the long-term maintainability of your code.

The previous listing illustrates this clearly. When the script is executed, PHP will generate a notice about the inappropriate use of mktime(), and instead suggest using the time() function. Try it for yourself and see—you'll be surprised by how much your code can be improved!

12.11 Profiling PHP Scripts

Problem

You want to analyze the performance of a script to identify bottlenecks and areas for optimization.

Solution

Use PHP's Xdebug extension.

Comments

PHP's Xdebug extension, available for both Windows and *NIX flavors of PHP from http://www.xdebug.org/, can be used to profile a PHP script and generate useful data for performance analysis. The profiler can be enabled via a *php.ini* configuration setting (see the following Note, which describes the process in greater detail), and it generates detailed statistics on the amount of time spent per function call in a script and the total time spent on script compilation, processing, and execution. These statistics make it possible to see which function calls are responsible for the maximum processing overhead, and thus identify areas for potential optimization.

Xdebug's profiling information is formatted as a so-called *cachegrind* file, which may be viewed with either WinCacheGrind (http://sourceforge.net/projects/wincachegrind/) on Windows or KCachegrind (http://kcachegrind.sourceforge.net/) on *NIX. Profiles are stored in the output directory specified in the xdebug.profiler_output_dir variable in PHP's *php.ini* configuration file. Figure 12-1 illustrates what such a profile might look like:

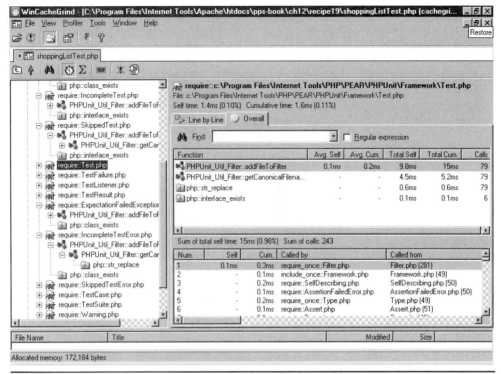

Figure 12-1 *Xdebug profile of a PHP script, as viewed in WinCacheGrind*

NOTE

PHP's Xdebug extension is installed in the usual way, in PHP's ext/ directory, and activated by adding the `zend_extension_ts = /path/to/xdebug/ext` *directive to the* `php.ini` *configuration file. You must also specify the* `xdebug.profiler_enable,` `xdebug.profiler_output_dir,` *and* `xdebug.trace_output_dir` *variables in the configuration file. Profiling will then take place automatically for every script executed through PHP (although this may be disabled on a per-script basis if needed). For detailed installation instructions, visit* `http://xdebug.org/install.php.`

NOTE

The Xdebug extension overrides PHP's default exception handling routines, providing more detailed debugging output and stack traces for both fatal and non-fatal errors. Figure 12-2 has an example.

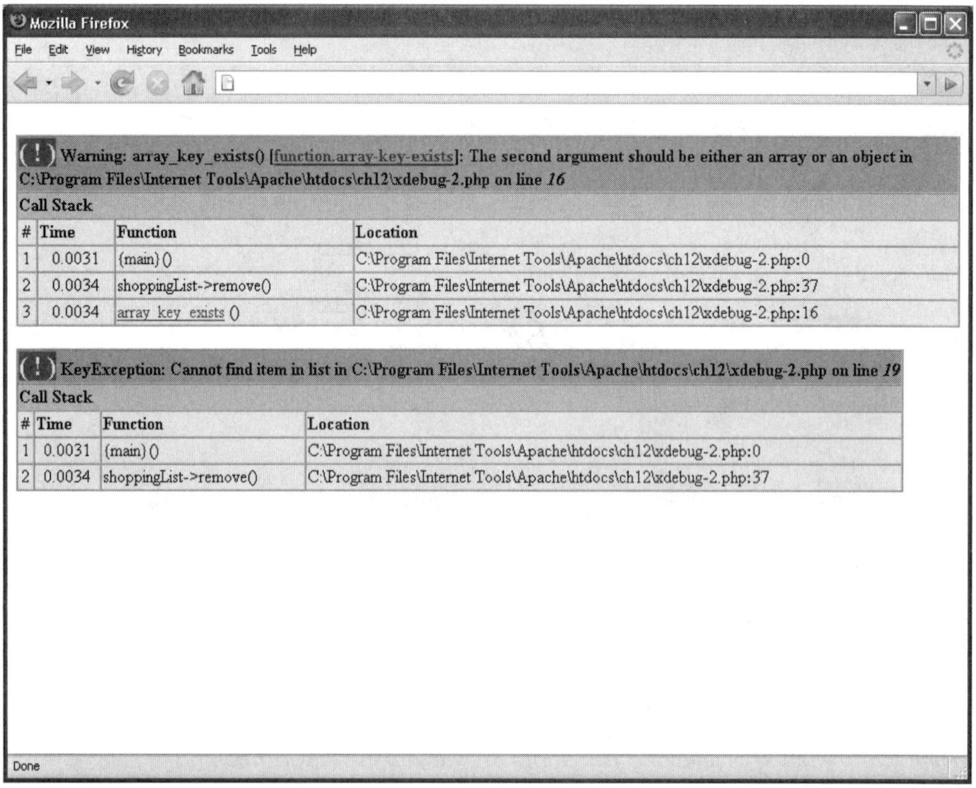

Figure 12-2 *Xdebug stack trace*

An alternative is to use PEAR's Benchmark class, available from `http://pear` `.php.net/package/Benchmark`, to profile your PHP code. Here, the profiler is activated with a call to its `start()` method, and deactivated with a call to `stop()`; these calls typically appear at the beginning and end of a script, although they may also be used to activate the profiler only for specific subsections of code (for example, a particular function or class only). Within these two calls, it's a good idea to set user-defined section "markers" to identify specific activities or transactions the script is undertaking; because these markers are included in the final report, they can help identify which transactions are responsible for what percentage of overhead.

The next listing illustrates this class in action:

```php
<?php
// include class
include "Benchmark/Profiler.php";
```

```
// initialize profiler
$profiler = new Benchmark_Profiler();

// start profiler
$profiler->start();

// open database file
$profiler->enterSection("Connection");  // section start marker
$handle = sqlite_open("products.db") or ↵
die ("ERROR: Cannot open database");
$profiler->leaveSection("Connection");  // section end marker

// create and execute SELECT query
$profiler->enterSection("Query");
$sql = "SELECT id, name FROM products";
$result = sqlite_query($handle, $sql)↵
or die ("ERROR: " . sqlite_error_string(sqlite_last_error($handle)) .↵
" (query was $sql)");

// check for returned rows
// print if available
if (sqlite_num_rows($result) > 0) {
    while($row = sqlite_fetch_array($result)) {
        echo $row[0] . " = " . $row[1] . "\n";
    }
}
$profiler->leaveSection("Query");

// close database file
$profiler->enterSection("Connection");
sqlite_close($handle);
$profiler->leaveSection("Connection");

// stop profiler
$profiler->stop();
$profiler->display();
?>
```

Figure 12-3 illustrates a sample report generated by the profiler.

TIP

You can also use the Benchmark package to obtain detailed timing information on a script. See the listing in "12.13: Benchmarking PHP Scripts" for more.

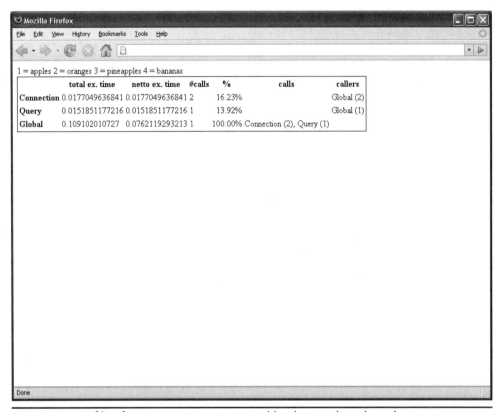

Figure 12-3 *Profile of a PHP script, as generated by the Benchmark package*

12.12 Debugging PHP Scripts

Problem

You want to trace a script's execution or keep a watch on specific variables over the duration of a script.

Solution

Use the PHP_Debug class:

```php
<?php
// include class
include "Debug.php";
include "Debug/Renderer/HTML_Table_Config.php";
```

```php
// create object
$debug = new Debug();
$debug->add("Entering script...");  // set debug message
?>
<html>
<head>
<?php
// generate stylesheet for debug output formatting
$debug->add("Generating CSS...");  // set debug message
$html = Debug_Renderer_HTML_Table_Config::singleton()->getConfig();
print($html['HTML_TABLE_stylesheet']);
?>
</head>
<body>
<?php
// function to get an arbitrary number of bytes
// from a file
function getBytes($file, $startByte, $endByte) {
    // import debugger object
    global $debug;

    $debug->add("Entering getBytes()...");  // set debug message
    $debug->dump($file, "file");             // dump variable
    $debug->dump($startByte, "start byte"); // dump variable
    $debug->dump($endByte, "end byte");      // dump variable

    // check for valid range endpoints
    if ($endByte < $startByte) {
        die("Ending byte number must be greater than or equal to ↵
starting byte number!");
    }

    // open the file for reading
    $fp = fopen($file, "rb") or die("Cannot open file");

    // seek to starting byte
    // retrieve data by character
    // until ending byte
    fseek ($fp, $startByte, SEEK_SET);
    while (!(ftell($fp) > $endByte)) {
        $debug->add("Entering ftell() loop..."); // set debug message
        $data .= fgetc($fp);
        $debug->dump($data, "data string"); // dump variable
    }
```

```
    // close the file
    fclose($fp) or die ("Cannot close file");

    $debug->dump($data, "getBytes retval"); // dump variable
    $debug->add("Exiting getBytes()..."); // set debug message

    // return data to caller
    return $data;
}

// return first 10 bytes of file
echo getBytes("fortunes.txt", 0, 9);

// display debug information
$debug->add("Exiting script...");
$debug->display();
?>
</body>
</html>
```

Comments

The PHP_Debug class, freely available from http://www.php-debug.com/, provides a PEAR-compliant framework for tracing script execution, watching and dumping variables, calculating execution times, and other common debugging tasks. The previous listing illustrates some of these functions in the context of a user-defined function to extract specific byte ranges from a text file.

After initializing an instance of the PHP_Debug class, the instance's add() method can be used to trace script execution by generating messages at user-defined points in the script—for example, when entering a function or a loop. At any stage, the dump() method may be used to view the output of a particular variable, while a watch() method can be used to monitor one or more script variables and send notifications to the debug console when their value changes. At any time, the display() method can be used to send the debugging output to the output device.

Figure 12-4 illustrates the debugging output of the previous listing.

> **NOTE**
>
> The PHP_Debug class overrides PHP's default error handler for warnings and notices, incorporating them in the output of display().

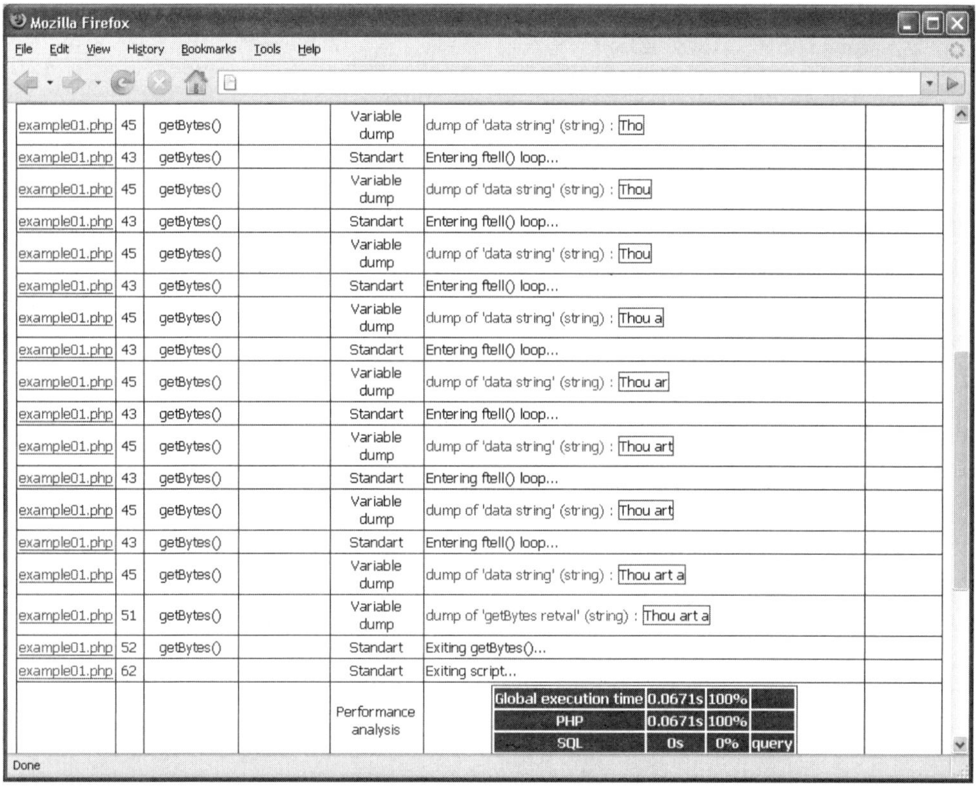

Figure 12-4 *Debugging a PHP script*

12.13 Benchmarking PHP Scripts

Problem

You want to run a script or code block repeatedly to evaluate its performance under load.

Solution

Use PEAR's Benchmark class:

```
<?php
// function to connect to an SQLite database
// execute a query and process the results
```

```
function getData() {
    // connect to database
    $handle = sqlite_open("products.db")↵
or die ("ERROR: Cannot open database");

    // create and execute SELECT query
    $sql = "SELECT id, name FROM products";
    $result = sqlite_query($handle, $sql) or die ("ERROR: " .↵
 sqlite_error_string(sqlite_last_error($handle)) . ↵
" (query was $sql)");

    // check for returned rows
    // print if available
    if (sqlite_num_rows($result) > 0) {
        while($row = sqlite_fetch_array($result)) {
            echo $row[0] . " = " . $row[1] . "\n";
        }
    }

    // close database file
    sqlite_close($handle);
}

// include class
include "Benchmark/Iterate.php";

// initialize iterator
$bench = new Benchmark_Iterate();

// execute function 100 times
// print results
$bench->run(100, 'getData');
$bench->display();
?>
```

Comments

PEAR's Benchmark class, available from `http://pear.php.net/package/Benchmark`, includes an Iterator designed specifically to run a piece of code repeatedly, calculate the time taken for each execution, and generate total and average time statistics. The previous listing illustrates it in action, using it to

pineapples 4 = bananas 1 = apples 2 = oranges 3 = pineapples 4 = bananas

	time index	ex time	%
start_1	1165907963.97420200	-	0.00%
end_1	1165907963.97766800	0.003466	0.00%
start_2	1165907963.97797000	0.000302	0.00%
end_2	1165907963.98086000	0.002890	0.00%
start_3	1165907963.98115800	0.000298	0.00%
end_3	1165907963.98645600	0.005298	0.00%
start_4	1165907963.98675200	0.000296	0.00%
end_4	1165907963.98964600	0.002894	0.00%
start_5	1165907963.98993100	0.000285	0.00%
end_5	1165907963.99284500	0.002914	0.00%
start_6	1165907963.99330600	0.000461	0.00%
end_6	1165907963.99639700	0.003091	0.00%
start_7	1165907963.99668200	0.000285	0.00%
end_7	1165907963.99966800	0.002986	0.00%
start_8	1165907963.99995400	0.000286	0.00%
end_8	1165907964.00282800	0.002874	0.00%
start_9	1165907964.00363000	0.000802	0.00%
end_9	1165907964.00661500	0.002985	0.00%
start_10	1165907964.00690200	0.000287	0.00%
end_10	1165907964.00978000	0.002878	0.00%

Figure 12-5   *Results of repeatedly executing a code block with the Benchmark package*

repeatedly execute a user-defined function that connects to a SQLite database, executes a query, and processes the result. The class' `run()` method specifies the number of iterations as well as the name of the function to run, while the `display()` method generates a report (see Figure 12-5) on the results.

12.14 Creating PHP Bytecode

Problem

You want to encrypt your PHP code so that it cannot be viewed by others.

Solution

Convert your PHP scripts into bytecode with PHP's `ext/bcompiler` extension:

```php
<?php
// define source file
$source = "sqlite-view-records.php";
if (!file_exists($source)) {
    die("Cannot find source file.");
}

// open file handle for writing
$target = basename($source, ".php") . "-bin.php";
$fh = fopen($target, "w") or die("Cannot open file.");

// write header, content and footer
bcompiler_write_header($fh) or die("Cannot write header.");
bcompiler_write_file($fh, $source) or die("Cannot write contents.");
bcompiler_write_footer($fh) or die("Cannot write footer.");

// close file
fclose($fh);

// print success message
echo "Binary file [$target] successfully created";
?>
```

Comments

PHP `ext/bcompiler` extension lets you turn your PHP scripts into binary code, making it impossible for them to be reverse-engineered. The process is fairly simple: create a new file, then use the `bcompiler_write_header()` and `bcompiler_write_footer()` functions to write the appropriate binary header and footer to the file. Sandwiched between these two function calls is `bcompiler_write_file()`, which does the heavy lifting of actually reading the original PHP script, converting it to bytecode and writing it to the new file.

> ### NOTE
> *Although it's not possible to re-create the original ASCII source from a bytecoded file, it may still be possible to view some of the original ASCII strings within it with a hex editor. For this reason, ensure that your scripts don't contain sensitive information (such as MySQL access codes).*

Once created, this bytecode will function in exactly the same manner as the original PHP script—you can access it through a browser as before or execute it at the console through the PHP command-line interface—but if you attempt to view it in an ASCII text editor, you'll see binary strings instead of readable PHP code blocks. This makes this technique particularly suitable for distributing PHP applications in a proprietary format, or to protect particular classes or functions by encoding them.

TIP

According to the PHP manual, encoding your PHP scripts in this manner can improve performance by up to 30 percent; however, the size of the bytecode file will be significantly larger than that of the original script.

NOTE

In order for this listing to work, PHP must be compiled with support for the `bcompiler` *extension (you can obtain instructions from the PHP manual at* `http://www.php.net/bcompiler`*).*

12.15 Creating Standalone PHP Executables

Problem

You want to create a standalone PHP executable that can be run at the console without requiring the presence of the PHP interpreter.

Solution

Create your PHP script in the usual way:

```
File: print-primes.php
<?php
// list all primes between 2 and some integer
// using the Sieve of Erastothenes
function listPrimes($end) {
    // generate an array of all possible integers
    // between the first prime and the supplied limit
    $sieve = range(2, $end);
```

```
    // retrieve the size of the array
    $size = sizeof($sieve);

    // reset internal array pointer to beginning of array
    reset($sieve);

    // iterate over the array
    while (list($key, $val) = each($sieve)) {
        // for each element
        // check if subsequent elements are divisible by it
        // remove them from the array if so
        for ($x=$key+1; $x<$size; $x++) {
            if ($sieve[$x] % $val == 0) {
                unset($sieve[$x]);
            }
        }
    }

    // at the end, elements left in array are primes
    return $sieve;
}

// list all the primes between 2 and 100
// result: "2 3 5 7...83 89 97"
echo implode(" ", listPrimes(100));
?>
```

Then use the Bambalam PHP EXE Compiler/Embedder (Windows) to turn it into an executable:

```
shell> bamcompile.exe print-primes.php
Bambalam PHP EXE Compiler/Embedder 1.21

Mainfile: print-primes.php
Outfile: print-primes.exe

Encoding and embedding print-primes.php
get-php-version.exe created successfully!

shell> print-primes.exe
2 3 5 7 11 13 17 19 23 29 31 37 41 43 47 53 59 61 67 71 73 79 83 89 97
```

Comments

The Bambalam PHP EXE Compiler/Embedder, freely available from `http://www.bambalam.se/bamcompile/`, is a command-line tool to convert one or more PHP scripts into standalone Windows executables. This makes it possible to create independent PHP applications that will work on any Windows system, while also preventing easy access to the application's source code. If a script uses one or more extensions, the compiler supports adding these extensions to the standalone executable to eliminate external dependencies. The previous listing illustrates the process of turning a PHP script into an executable.

Note that the Bambalam PHP compiler doesn't create machine code, but instead simply embeds the target PHP script(s) inside a launcher executable. This launcher, which is similar to the PHP interpreter, creates a PHP environment for the target PHP script(s) to execute.

> ### NOTE
> *The Bambalam PHP compiler is an open-source tool, released without any warranties. As such, its behavior may not always be consistent and the final standalone executable may not always work as advertised, a problem most noticeable with the embedding of external extensions. Further, the compiler uses a PHP 4.x launcher, and doesn't support PHP 5.x or PHP 6.x as of this writing. Extensive testing is recommended if you plan to use this tool for production use.*

12.16 Localizing Strings

Problem

You want your application to display in the local language.

Solution

Select a locale, and then wrap the strings you wish to translate in calls to `gettext()` such that PHP knows to replace them with local translations:

```php
<?php
// set language to French
putenv("LANGUAGE=fr_FR");
setlocale(LC_ALL, "fr_FR");

// set path to translation table
bindtextdomain("messages", "locale/");
```

```
// attach to domain
textdomain("messages");

// perform translation
// result: "Comment allez-vous?"
echo gettext("How are you?");
?>
```

Comments

PHP's `gettext()` function provides a framework to internationalize your application by replacing its input arguments with a locale-specific translation. The previous listing illustrates the process. First, the locale must be specified, both by setting the `$LANGUAGE` environment variable and setting the PHP locale with `setlocale()`. Next, the `bindtextdomain()` function sets the disk path to the binary translation files and binds it to a "domain," and the `textdomain()` function attaches the application to the domain.

With these preliminaries out of the way, the `gettext()` function is called on every string that requires translation. In the previous listing, the language is set to French, and so `gettext()` will look up the disk location `locale/fr_FR/LC_MESSAGES/messages.mo` for the binary translation file, find the string, and replace it with its translated equivalent.

Creating Translation Files

In order for this solution to work, your PHP build must include support for the `ext/gettext` extension. Additionally, you will need to create compressed binary translation files (`.mo` files) for the languages you plan to support. Very briefly, the process to create `.mo` files for a language is as follows:

1. Install the gettext-runtime, gettext-tools, and libiconv packages.
2. Extract all translatable strings from your application scripts with the xgettext utility.
3. Edit the resulting `.po` file and enter translations for each string.
4. Turn the `.po` file into a compressed binary `.mo` file with the msgfmt utility.
5. Place the `.mo` file in your PHP application's locale/ directory.

You can obtain the tools required for this process (on both *NIX and Windows) from `http://www.gnu.org/software/gettext/`, while you can obtain instructions on the process from `http://en.wikipedia.org/wiki/Gettext` and the discussion thread at `http://www.aota.net/forums/showthread.php?threadid=10615`.

12.17 Executing External Programs

Problem

You want to execute an external program from within a PHP script, and capture its output in a PHP variable.

Solution

Use PHP's `exec()` function:

```php
<?php
// get uptime
echo "Current server uptime is: " . exec(escapeshellcmd("/bin/uptime"));
?>
```

Comments

PHP's `exec()` function accepts a single argument, representing the command to be executed, runs it, and returns the last line of output. In case the command generates more than a single line of output, this output may be captured in a PHP array, specified as the second argument to `exec()`. Here's an example:

```php
<?php
// get process listing
exec(escapeshellcmd("/bin/ps ax"), $out);
echo "<xmp>" . join("\n", $out) . "</xmp>";
?>
```

An alternative to `exec()` is the `passthru()` function, which returns the raw output from a command and is good for sending binary data from a command-line call to a requesting client. Here's an example of how you might use it:

```
<?php
// display image
header("Content-type: image/jpeg");
passthru(escapeshellcmd("/bin/cat logo.jpg"));
?>
```

NOTE

Using user-supplied input in an `exec()` call is always a risky proposition, because there's always a possibility that a hacker might use special characters in the input to open a back door into the system. For this reason, you must always "sanitize" command strings and arguments by escaping special characters within them with quotes and backslashes. PHP provides the `escapeshellcmd()` and `escapeshellarg()` functions for this purpose.

12.18 Using an Interactive Shell

Problem

You want to enter PHP commands interactively, at a shell prompt.

Solution

Use PHP with the `-a` command-line argument:

```
shell> php -a
Interactive mode enabled

<?php
echo "hello world";
hello world
print strlen("99 bottles of beer");
18
echo ini_get('error_reporting');
2039
?>
```

Comments

Other scripting languages, such as Perl and Ruby, come with an interactive shell that enables developers to enter commands and view the response immediately. PHP too has such a built-in capability, which is activated by calling the php binary with the -a command-line option. The previous listing illustrates it in action.

It's also possible to emulate this interactive shell with PEAR's PHP_Shell package, available from http://pear.php.net/package/PHP_Shell. Once the package is installed, activate it by executing the *examples/php_shell_cmd.php* program from the package distribution. This will launch the shell, and enable you to interactively use PHP by typing in commands at the shell prompt and receiving an immediate response. For example:

```
shell> php -q php-shell-cmd.php
PHP-Barebone-Shell - Version 0.3.0
(c) 2006, Jan Kneschke <jan@kneschke.de>

>> use '?' to open the inline help

>> echo "hello world";
hello world
>> print strlen("mary had a little lamb");
22
>> ini_get('post_max_size');
'8M'
>>
```

12.19 Using Unit Tests

Problem

You want to apply test-driven development (TDD) techniques for a PHP application, class, or function.

Solution

First, use the PHPUnit testing framework to define unit tests for your application:

File: shoppingListTest.php

```
<?php
// include testing framework
include_once "PHPUnit/Framework.php";
```

```php
// include class to be tested
include "shoppingList.php";

// test class
class shoppingListTest extends PHPUnit_Framework_TestCase {
    // initialization
    public function setUp() {
        $this->groceries = new shoppingList;
    }

    // deinitialization
 public function tearDown() {
        unset($this->groceries);
    }

    // test the add() method
    public function testAddingItem() {
        $this->groceries->add("milk", 2);
        $actual = $this->qroceries->get();
        $expected = array("milk" => 2);
        $this->assertEquals($expected, $actual);
    }

    // test the remove() method with a valid item
    public function testRemovingItem() {
        $this->groceries->add("milk", 2);
        $this->groceries->add("eggs", 6);
        $this->groceries->remove("milk");
        $actual = $this->groceries->get();
        $expected = array("eggs" => 6);
        $this->assertEquals($expected, $actual);
    }

    // test the add() and remove() method in combination
    public function testAddingRemovingItem() {
        $this->groceries->add("milk", 2);
        $this->groceries->add("soap", 3);
        $this->groceries->add("spoons", 24);
        $this->groceries->add("eggs", 7);
        $this->groceries->remove("spoons");
        $actual = $this->groceries->get();
        $expected = array("eggs" => 7, "milk" => 2, "soap" => 3);
        $this->assertEquals($expected, $actual);
    }
```

```php
    // test the pretty() method
    public function testPretty() {
        $this->groceries->add("milk", 2);
        $this->groceries->add("soap", 3);
        $this->groceries->add("spoons", 24);
        $actual = $this->groceries->pretty();
        $expected = "milk(2) soap(3) spoons(24) ";
        $this->assertEquals($expected, $actual);
    }

    // test the remove() method with an invalid item
    public function testException() {
        try {
            $this->groceries->add("milk", 2);
            $this->groceries->add("eggs", 6);
            $this->groceries->remove("sugar");
        } catch (KeyException $expected) {
            return;
        }
        $this->fail("A KeyException was not thrown");
    }
}
?>
```

File: shoppingList.php

```php
<?php
// example class
class shoppingList {
    // constructor
    public function __construct() {
        $stack = array();
    }

    // add item to list with quantity
    public function add($item, $quantity) {
        $this->stack[$item] = $quantity;
    }

    // remove item from list
    public function remove($item) {
        if (array_key_exists($item, $this->stack)) {
            unset($this->stack[$item]);
```

```
            } else {
                throw new KeyException("Cannot find item in list");
            }
        }

        // get list
        public function get() {
            return $this->stack;
        }

        // pretty-print list
        public function pretty() {
            foreach ($this->stack as $k=>$v) {
                $str .= "$k($v) ";
            }
            return $str;
        }
    }

// define custom exception for use
// in example class
class KeyException extends Exception { }
?>
```

Then execute these tests by running the test fixture through PHPUnit's command-line test runner:

```
shell> ./phpunit.php shoppingListTest shoppingListTest.php
PHPUnit 3.0.0 by Sebastian Bergmann.
.....
Time: 00:00
OK (5 tests)
```

Comments

PHPUnit, available from http://phpunit.sourceforge.net/, is an open-source framework for automated unit testing in PHP. You may use it to write test cases for a PHP application or class, and exposes common test assertion methods such as assertEquals(), assertTrue(), assertFalse(), assertSame(), assertContains(), and assertType(), as well as custom methods to test exceptions and printed output.

The previous listing assumes that testing is required for a user-defined class, shoppingList(), which implements a PHP associative array to hold item names and quantities. This class should expose four methods in its first iteration: add(), which adds a new item to the list with its associated quantity; remove(), which removes an existing item from the list, throwing a custom KeyException if the item does not exist; get(), which returns the list to the caller; and pretty(), which prints the current contents of the list in a human-readable format. The PHP code for this class can be seen in the file *shoppingList.php*, included in the previous listing.

To implement unit tests for this class, it is necessary to first include the PHPUnit testing framework, as well as the class definition. Tests are themselves defined within a class, which extends the PHPUnit_Framework_TestCase class and is named like the class to be tested with an additional "Test" suffix; thus, tests for the shoppingList() class are defined in a new shoppingListTest() class. Two public methods, setUp() and tearDown(), work as the equivalent of class constructors and destructors, with the former initializing all the objects needed for the test and the latter de-initializing them.

The tests themselves are defined as public methods of the class, and use various test assertion methods to verify if the class does in fact work as advertised. Thus, for example, the testRemove() method tests the shoppingList() class' remove() method by first adding various items to the shopping list, and then removing one of them and checking what the list actually contains ($actual) against what it should contain ($expected). This check is performed via a call to the assertEquals() test assertion method, which essentially checks that the two arguments passed to it are, in fact, equal and returns a test failure notice if they are not.

Once the test fixture is defined, it may be run through PHPUnit's command-line test runner. This test runner accepts, as command-line arguments, the name of the test class and the location of the file containing its definition; it then runs the various test cases defined within it, and returns a message indicating the number of successful and failed tests. The previous listing illustrates the output of a successful test run; the following one illustrates what happens when one or more tests fail:

```
shell> ./phpunit.php shoppingListTest shoppingListTest.php
PHPUnit 3.0.0 by Sebastian Bergmann.
.FF..
Time: 00:00
There were 2 failures:

1) testRemovingItem(shoppingListTest)
Failed asserting that
Array
```

```
(
    [milk] => 2
    [eggs] => 6
)
 is equal to
Array
(
    [eggs] => 6
)

2) testAddingRemovingItem(shoppingListTest)
Failed asserting that
Array
(
    [milk] => 2
    [soap] => 3
    [spoons] => 24
    [eggs] => 7
)
 is equal to
Array
(
    [eggs] => 7
    [milk] => 2
    [soap] => 3
)

FAILURES!
Tests: 5, Failures: 2.
```

As this output illustrates, test failures are marked with an "F" in the immediate output returned by the test runner, and PHPUnit also generates detailed information on which assertion failed, providing ready clues as to which of the original class' methods are broken (in this case, the remove() method).

> ### TIP
>
> *PHPUnit also supports various test extensions, such as testing for returned exceptions or output generated by echo and print. This listing illustrates one such extension in the testException() method, which checks to see if a custom KeyException is generated when an attempt is made to remove a nonexistent item from the shopping list.*

You can obtain detailed information on these test extensions, and PHPUnit in general, from the PHPUnit Pocket Guide, a free book written by the author of the PHPUnit framework, Sebastian Bergmann. Read it online at `http://www` `.phpunit.de/pocket_guide/`.

NOTE

TDD is a development technique from so-called "extreme programming" methodology. It consists of first defining a test case for a new software feature and then implementing the feature by only writing the code necessary to pass the test. Proponents claim that this approach results in higher software quality and less code bloat.

Index